# PERSONAL NARRATIVE

## OF A

# PILGRIMAGE TO EL-MEDINAH AND MECCAH.

# PERSONAL NARRATIVE

OF A

# PILGRIMAGE TO EL-MEDINAH AND MECCAH.

RICHARD F. BURTON

WITH INTRODUCTION BY BAYARD TAYLOR.

GYAN

*Published by*

Gyan Publishing House
5, Ansari Road
Daryaganj, New Delhi-110002
Phone: 011-47034999, 9811692060
E-mail: books@gyanbooks.com

*Distribution Network*
gyanbooks.com
India, USA, Canada, UK, Australia, France



ISBN : 978-81-212-9458-4 (PB)
First Published, 1856

2nd Impression 2023

*Printed at:* Gyan Press, Delhi.



**PERSONAL NARRATIVE OF A PILGRIMAGE TO EL-MEDINAH AND MECCAH**

Author: RICHARD F. BURTON

LITH. OF SARONY & C° NEW YORK.

SKETCH OF EL MEDINAH, BY A NATIVE ARTIST

New York G. P. Putnam & C°

LITH of SARONY & Co NEW YORK

PILGRIMS COSTUME

# PERSONAL NARRATIVE

OF A

# PILGRIMAGE TO EL-MEDINAH AND MECCAH.

BY RICHARD F. BURTON,

LIEUT. BOMBAY ARMY.

WITH INTRODUCTION BY BAYARD TAYLOR.

"Our notions of Meccah must be drawn from the Arabians; as no unbeliever is permitted to enter the city, our travellers are silent."—*Gibbon*, chap. 50.

With Map, and Two Illustrations.

FIRST AMERICAN EDITION.

NEW YORK:
G. P. PUTNAM & CO., 321 BROADWAY.

1856.

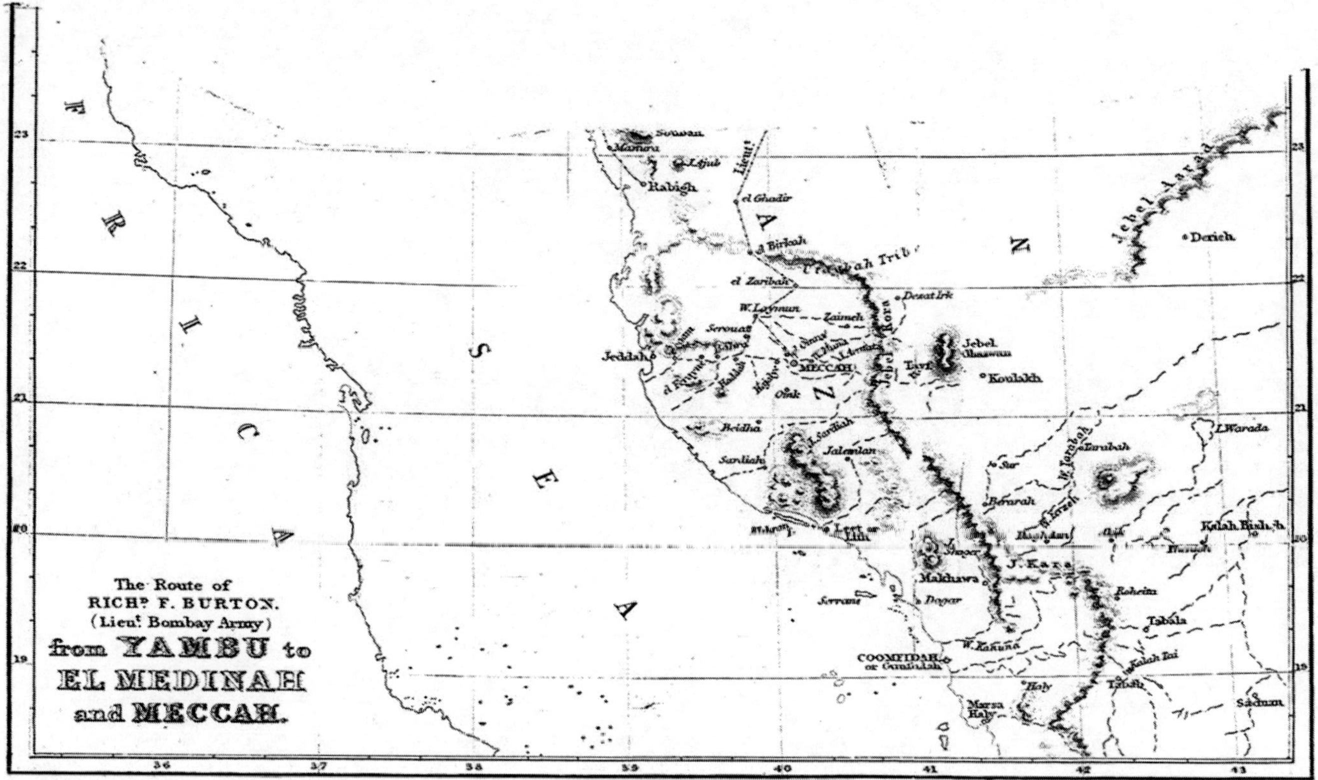


London, Longman & Co.

Drawn & Engraved by E. Weller, Duke Str. Bloomsbury.

## PUBLISHERS' PREFACE.

The English Edition of "Burton's Pilgrimage to El Medinah and Meccah" was originally published in three volumes, large octavo. In order to meet the requirements of the American public, both as regards the size and expense of the work, it has been deemed expedient to abridge and condense some chapters. The portions omitted, however, do not affect the narrative or the incidents of the visit to the Holy Places, but chiefly relate to Lieut. Burton's preliminary residence in Egypt, and to historical and ethnological considerations. An Appendix, containing a *resumé* of former explorations, is also omitted, but its place is supplied by the introductory essay by Bayard Taylor.

We believe that the readers of the narrative of Lieut. Burton's singular and dangerous journey will sustain us in the assertion, that no volume of modern travel possesses greater intrinsic interest or originality, while for graphic description it compares favorably with the "Eōthen" of Kinglake, or the "Crescent and the Cross" of Warburton.

G. P. PUTNAM & CO.

321 Broadway, N. Y.

# EDITOR'S PREFACE

## TO THE ENGLISH EDITION.

The interest just now felt in everything that relates to the East would alone be sufficient to ensure to the author of "El Medinah and Meccah" the favorable consideration of the Reading Public. But when it is borne in mind that since the days of William Pitts of Exeter (A.D. 1678–1688) no European travellers, with the exception of Burckhardt* and Lieut. Burton,† have been able to send us back an account of their travels there, it cannot be doubted but that the present work will be hailed as a welcome addition to our knowledge of these hitherto mysterious *penetralia* of Mahommedan superstition. In fact, El Medinah may be considered almost a virgin theme; for as Burckhardt was prostrated by sickness throughout the period of his stay in the Northern Hejaz, he was not able to describe it as satisfactorily or minutely as he did the southern country,—he could not send a plan of the mosque, or correct the popular but erroneous ideas which prevail concerning it and the surrounding city.

* In 1811.

† Captain Sadlier is not mentioned, as his Frankish dress prevented his entering the city.

The reader may question the propriety of introducing, in a work of description, anecdotes which may appear open to the charge of triviality. The author's object, however, seems to be to illustrate the peculiarities of the people,—to dramatize, as it were, the dry journal of a journey,—and to preserve the tone of the adventures, together with that local coloring in which mainly consists "*l'education d'un voyage.*"

It was during a residence of many years in India that Mr. Burton had fitted himself for his late undertaking, by acquiring, through his peculiar aptitude for such studies, a thorough acquaintance with various dialects of Arabia and Persia; and, indeed, his Eastern cast of features seemed to point him out as the very person of all others best suited for an expedition like that described in the following pages.

It will be observed that in writing Arabic, Hindoostannee, Persian, or Turkish words, the author has generally adopted the system proposed by Sir William Jones and modified by later Orientalists. But when a word (like Fát-háh for Fatihah) has been "stamped" by general popular use, the conversational form has been preferred; and the same, too, may be said of the common corruptions, Cairo, Kadi, &c., which, in any other form, would appear to us pedantic and ridiculous. Still, in the absence of the author, it must be expected that some trifling errors and inaccuracies will have here and there crept in.

# CONTENTS.

# INTRODUCTORY NOTICE.

BY BAYARD TAYLOR.

The present century is already remarkable beyond the last, for the extent and richness of its contributions to geographical knowledge; but the generation in which we live will be especially noted hereafter as that which has preeminently invaded the few lingering haunts of fable, and brought their cherished mysteries under the microscopic lenses of modern eyes. Within ten years the courageous M. Huc has penetrated through the vast interior realms of China and Tartary, to the sacred city of Lha-Ssa, of which he has given the first satisfactory description; Lieutenant Lynch has exploded the superstitious terrors with which the Dead Sea was regarded; Dr. Barth has returned safely to Europe, after a residence of seven months at Timbuctoo; Dr. Krapf has looked upon the snowy pinnacles of the long lost Mountains of the Moon; and now, Lieutenant Burton, having penetrated to Medina and Mecca, and entered the holiest sanctuaries of the Moslem faith, presents us with the picturesque story of his pilgrimage.

The extreme reverence in which these cities are held,

and that jealousy which prevents all acknowledged followers of other religions from visiting, or even approaching them, undoubtedly grew out of the fierce and fanatical character of Mohammedanism in its earlier days. The violence of that fanaticism is now over. Except in Arabia, the cradle and stronghold of Islam, the Frank Christians mingle freely with the followers of the Prophet, not only without indignity, but in many places as their friends and protectors. The rapid spread of intercourse between the East and the West, and, more than all, the recent alliance of Christian and Moslem powers in the war against Russia, has greatly weakened, and, in the course of time, may wholly obliterate, the bitterness of that religious prejudice which has hitherto been the characteristic of such intercourse. Its effect is already seen, in the facility with which travellers now obtain access to the sacred mosques of Constantinople and Cairo. Even the Mosque of Omar, at Jerusalem, where, five years ago, Christians were stoned for attempting to enter—whose gates would not open to a Frank for a firman of the Sultan himself—has alike become accessible to profane feet. The same change will eventually overtake the more bigoted population of the Hedjaz, and future travellers, perhaps, in green veils and spectacles, may languidly scrutinize the mosques of Mecca. The success of such men as Burckhardt and Burton should not be ascribed, however, to this circumstance. It is entirely due to their courage, prudence, and perseverance, and to their intimate acquaintance with eastern life, and the ceremonials of the Moslem faith.

The design of visiting Mecca has been a favorite one with travellers for centuries past, but the difficulties in the way of its prosecution have been so great, that the number of those who succeeded may be reckoned upon the fingers of one's hand. Lieutenant Burton, in an Appendix to the English edition of his work, gives extracts from the descriptions of his predecessors, which differ from his own and Burckhardt's in some trifling particulars, but correspond much more nearly than might have been expected from travellers of such different epochs. Gibbon, at the time of writing his "Decline and Fall of the Roman Empire," was not aware any Christian had reached Mecca up to that time. It appears, however, from Mr. Burton's investigations, that two persons had accomplished the journey—Lodovico Bartema, a gentleman of Rome, in the year 1603; and Joseph Pitts, of Exon, England, in 1680. To these may be added, in later years, Giovanni Finati, an Italian renegade, and Burckhardt, both in 1814, and Burton, in 1853. The French apostates in the service of Mohammed Ali, some of whom made the usual pilgrimage, as good Mussulmans, need not be reckoned. Some of them have published accounts of their experiences, it is true; but, as new converts to the faith, they were regarded with distrust, and thereby prevented from making measurements or observations. Their accounts are therefore very inaccurate, and contribute nothing to our knowledge of the holy cities.

The first traveller on the list, Lodovico Bartema, visited Damascus in his wanderings through the East, and there won the friendship of a Mameluke captain, who was a renegade Christian. Disguising himself as a Mameluke, he accompanied the latter on a pilgrimage to Mecca, apparently conducting himself as a devout Mussulman, for his real character was not suspected, although he was afterwards imprisoned for a time in Yemen, on acknowledging himself a Christian. His narrative has all the quaint simplicity and picturesque character of those of the early travellers, with no more credulity than is necessary to give piquancy to his story. Lieutenant Burton, who of course is thoroughly competent to judge on this point, places him in the foremost rank of the old oriental travellers, for correctness of observation and readiness of wit.

Joseph Pitts was an English boy, who, for love of adventure going to sea in his fifteenth or sixteenth year, was captured by Algerine pirates and sold as a slave. His master, who had been a great sinner, determined to convert him, as an atonement for his own impiety, and achieved his object by means of the bastinado. Pitts submitted to this violent conversion, and performed all the external forms and ceremonies required of him; but hated the new faith in his heart, with a vehemence which was not in the least abated by fifteen years of Moslem life. He was taken to Mecca and El Medinah by his master, remained some months in the former city, and returned to Cairo. Having received his freedom, he determined to make his escape, in which, after various adventures, he succeeded, and returned safely to England. His descriptions of the Beit Allah (house of God) at Mecca, the ceremonies on Mount Arafat, the stoning of the devil, and other features of the pilgrimage, are very circumstantial and correct, considering that they were written from memory, after a lapse of many years. Lieutenant Burton finds little fault with Pitts, except his hatred and bigotry, which the manner of his conversion may well explain.

Finati was an ignorant and unprincipled Italian renegade, who made the campaign against the Wahabees for the recovery of Mecca and Medina, in the army of Mohammed Ali. Mr. Bankes, the English traveller, afterwards took him into his service, and translated the narrative of his adventures, which was dictated in Italian, as he was unable to write. The particulars he gives concerning the holy places of Mecca are very imperfect and unsatisfactory. Burckhardt, who made his visit to Mecca and Medina in the same year as Finati, may be considered as the first enlightened and experienced traveller who describes those places. He ventured on the undertaking only after years of preparation in the East, and a familiarity with the language and the faith so complete, that, under his assumed name of Shekh Ibrahim, his real character was unsuspected. Once only, when visiting Mohammed Ali, at Tayf, was he subjected to a rigid examination on points of Mohammedan doctrine, by two learned *shekhs ul-Islam*, at the instance of the pasha, who had heard suspicions whispered against him in Cairo. Burckhardt passed the test triumphantly, the shekhs declaring, that he was not only a genuine Mussulman, but one of unusual learning and piety. After performing all the ceremonies of the pilgrimage, he returned to Mecca, where he remained three months, before visiting Medina. At the latter place he was too ill to make many observations, and his descriptions are more meagre than usual. His accounts of the holy edifices of Mecca, and the pilgrim ceremonies, however, are very complete, and Burton pays the highest tribute to his correctness, by copying entire his description of the Kaaba.

The present author, therefore, traverses a partly beaten track, but a track wherein the last success reflects as much honor as the first. His experiment, in fact, was even more daring than that of Burckhardt, whose assumed character was already recognised throughout the Orient, and who, after his examination at Tayf, was placed beyond the reach of suspicion. Burton, on the other hand, was a novice in this special field, and was obliged to disguise himself under a totally different character. He took his part with admirable boldness and skill, and when once suspected by the young Meccan rogue, Mohammed, whose travels had made his vision precociously keen, was zealously defended by the remainder of the party, who completely silenced his accuser. Burton's narrative is especially valuable for his full and accurate particulars of the religious observances of the pilgrimage, and the various formulas of salutation and prayer. In this respect there is no other work of the kind equal to it. His descriptions of the holy edifices are scrupulously technical and careful; and he gives us, for the first time, sketches of the sacred cities which impress us with their fidelity to nature. We could have desired more ample pictures of the scenery through which he passed, and the spirited account of the voyage from Suez to Yambu shows that he is not deficient in descriptive power. But much allowance must be made for the night travels of the pilgrim caravan, and the consequent fatigue of the traveller. He has the advantage over Burckhardt of writing in his mother-tongue, and his narrative is much richer in those characteristic personal incidents and adventures which are the vital spirit of books of travel.

It is to be hoped that so prudent, daring, and intelligent a traveller will be permitted to carry out his original scheme of exploring the interior of the Arabian peninsula—one of the richest and most interesting fields of research now remaining. Certainly no one is better qualified for the undertaking.

B. T.

New York, *July* 1*st*, 1856.

# A PILGRIMAGE

TO

# EL MEDINAH AND MECCAH.

## CHAPTER I.

### TO ALEXANDRIA.

#### A FEW WORDS CONCERNING WHAT INDUCED ME TO A PILGRIMAGE.

In the autumn of 1852, through the medium of General Monteith, I offered my services to the Royal Geographical Society of London, for the purpose of removing that opprobrium to modern adventure, the huge white blot which in our maps still notes the eastern and the central regions of Arabia. A deputation from that distinguished body, with their usual zeal for discovery and readiness to encourage the discoverer, honored me by warmly supporting, in a personal interview with the Chairman of the Court of Directors to the East India Company, my application for three years' leave of absence on special duty from India to Muscat. But they were unable to prevail upon Sir James Hogg, who, remembering the fatalities which of late years have befallen sundry soldier-travellers in the East, refused his sanction, alleging as a reason that the contemplated journey was of too dangerous a nature. In compensation, however, for the disappointment, I was graciously allowed the additional furlough of a year, in order to pursue my Arabic studies in lands where the language is best learned.

What remained for me but to prove, by trial, that what might be perilous to other travellers is safe to me. The "experimentum crucis" was a visit to El Hejaz, at once the most difficult and the most dangerous point by which a European can enter Arabia. I had intended, had the period of leave originally applied for been granted, to land at Muscat—a favorable starting-place—and there to apply myself, slowly and surely, to the task of spanning the deserts. But now I was to hurry, in the midst of summer, after a four years' sojourn in Europe, during which many things Oriental had fallen away from my memory, and—after passing through the ordeal of Egypt, a country where the police is curious as in Rome or Milan—to begin with the Moslem's Holy Land, the jealously guarded and exclusive Haram. However, being liberally supplied with the means of travel by the Royal Geographical Society; thoroughly tired of "progress" and of "civilization;" curious to see with my eyes what others are content to "hear with ears," namely, Moslem's inner life in a really Mohammedan country; and longing, if truth be told, to set foot on that mysterious spot which no tourist had yet described, measured, sketched and daguerreotyped, I resolved to resume an old character of a Persian wanderer,* and to make the attempt.

The principal object with which I started was this:—To cross the unknown Arabian Peninsula, in a direct line from either El Medinah to Muscat, or diagonally from Meccah to

* The vagrant, the merchant, and the philosopher, amongst Orientals, are frequently united in the same person.

Makallah on the Indian Ocean. By what circumstances my plans were defeated, the reader will discover in the course of this volume. The secondary objects were numerous. I was desirous to find out if any market for horses could be opened between Central Arabia and India, where the studs are beginning to excite general dissatisfaction; to obtain information concerning the Great Eastern wilderness, the vast expanse marked Ruba el Khali (the empty abode) in our maps; to inquire into the hydrography of the Hejaz, its water-shed, the disputed slope of the country, and the existence or non-existence of perennial streams; and finally, to try, by actual observation, the truth of a theory proposed by the learned Orientalist, Col. Sykes, namely, that if history speak truth, in the population of the vast Peninsula there must exist certain physiological differences sufficient to warrant our questioning the common origin of the Arab family. As regards the horses, I am satisfied that from the Eastern coast something might be done,—nothing on the Western, where the animals, though "thorough-bred," are mere "weeds," of a foolish price, and procurable only by chance. Of the Ruba el Khali I have heard enough, from credible relators, to conclude that its horrid depths swarm with a large and half-starving population; that it abounds in wadys, valleys, gullies, and ravines, partially fertilized by intermittent torrents; and therefore, that the land is open only to the adventurous traveller. Moreover, I am satisfied, that in spite of all geographers, from Ptolemy to Jormard, Arabia, which abounds in *fiumaras*,*

* In a communication made to the Royal Geographical Society, and published in the 24th vol. of the Journal, I have given my reasons for naturalising this word. It will be used in the following pages to express a "hill water-course, which rolls a torrent after rain, and is either partially or wholly dry during the drought season." It is, in fact, the Indian "Nullah."

possesses not a single perennial stream worthy the name of river; and the testimony of the natives induces me to think, with Wallin, contrary to Ritter and others, that the Peninsula falls instead of rising towards the south. Finally, I have found proof, to be produced in a future part of this publication, for believing in three distinct races. 1. The aborigines of the country, driven, like the Bheels and other autochthonic Indians, into the eastern and south-eastern wilds bordering upon the ocean. 2. A Syrian or Mesopotamian stock, typified by Shem and Joktan, that drove the indigenæ from the choicest tracts of country; these invaders still enjoy their conquests, representing the great Arabian people. And 3. An impure Egypto-Arab clan—we personify it by Ishmael, his son Nebajoth and Edom (Esau, the son of Isaac)—that populated and still populates the Sinaitic Peninsula. And in most places, even in the heart of Meccah, I met with debris of heathenry, proscribed by Mohammed, yet still popular, though the ignorant observers of the old customs assign to them a modern and a rationalistic origin.

I have entitled this account of my summer's tour through El Hejaz, a personal narrative, and I have labored to make its nature correspond with its name, simply because "it is the personal that interests mankind." Many may not follow my example;* but some, perchance, will be curious to see what measures I adopted, in order to appear

* The only European I have met with who visited Meccah without apostatising, is M. Bertolucci, Swedish Consul at Cairo. This gentleman persuaded the Bedouin camel men who were accompanying him to Taif, to introduce him in disguise; he naïvely owns that his terror of discovery prevented his making any observations. Dr. Wallin, of Finland, performed the Haj in 1845; but his "somewhat perilous position, and the filthy company of Persians," were effectual obstacles to his taking notes.

suddenly as an Eastern upon the stage of Oriental life; and as the recital may be found useful by future adventurers, I make no apology for the egotistical semblance of the narrative. Those who have felt the want of some "silent friend" to aid them with advice, when it must not be asked, will appreciate what may appear to the uninterested critic mere outpourings of a mind full of self.

In April, 1853, I left London for Southampton. By the advice of a brother officer—little thought at that time the adviser or the advised how valuable was the suggestion—my Eastern dress was called into requisition before leaving town, and all my "impedimenta" were taught to look exceedingly Oriental. Early the next day a "Persian Prince" embarked on board the Peninsular and Oriental Company's screw steamer "Bengal."

A fortnight was profitably spent in getting into the train of Oriental manners. For what polite Chesterfield says of the difference between a gentleman and his reverse—namely, that both perform the same offices of life, but each in a several and widely different way—is notably as applicable to the manners of the Eastern as of the Western men. Look, for instance, at an Indian Moslem drinking a glass of water. With us the operation is simple enough, but his performance includes no less than five novelties. In the first place, he clutches his tumbler as though it were the throat of a foe; secondly, he ejaculates, "In the name of Allah the Compassionate, the Merciful!" before wetting his lips; thirdly, he imbibes the contents, swallowing them, not drinking, and ending with a satisfied grunt; fourthly, before setting down the cup, he sighs forth, "Praise be to Allah!"—of which you will understand the full meaning in the Desert; and, fifthly, he replies, "May Allah make it pleasant to thee!" in answer to his friend's polite "Pleasurably and health!" Also he is careful to avoid the irreligious action of drinking the pure element in a standing position, mindful, however, of the three recognised exceptions, the fluid of the Holy Well, Zem-zem, water distributed in charity, and that which remains after Wuzu, the lesser ablution. Moreover, in Europe one forgets the use of the right hand, the manipulation of the rosary, the abuse of the chair,—your genuine Oriental looks almost as comfortable in one as a sailor upon the back of a high-trotting horse—the rolling gait with the toes straight to the front, the grave look and the habit of pious ejaculations.

Our voyage over the "summer sea" was an eventless one.

The ship was in every way comfortable; the cook, strange to say, was good, and the voyage lasted long enough, and not too long. On the evening of the thirteenth day after our start, the big-trowsered pilot, so lovely in his deformities to western eyes, made his appearance, and the good screw "Bengal" found herself at anchor off the Headland of Figs.

Having been invited to start from the house of a kind friend, I disembarked with him, and rejoiced to see that by dint of a beard and a shaven head I had succeeded in misleading the inquisitive spirit of the populace. The mingled herd of spectators before whom we passed in review on the landing-place, hearing an audible "Alhamdulillah,"* whispered "Moslem!" The infant population spared me the compliments usually addressed to hatted heads; and when a little boy, presuming that the occasion might possibly open the hand of generosity, looked in my face and

* "Praise be to Allah, Lord of the (three) worlds!" a pious ejaculation, which leaves the lips of the True Believer on all occasions of concluding actions.

exclaimed, "Bakhshish,"* he obtained in reply "Mafish;"† which convinced the bystanders that the sheep-skin contained a real sheep. We then mounted a carriage, fought our way through the donkeys, and in half an hour found ourselves, chibouque in mouth and coffee-cup in hand, seated on divans in my friend's hospitable house.

Wonderful was the contrast between the steamer and that villa on the Mahmudiyah canal! Startling the sudden change from presto to adagio life! In thirteen days we had passed from the clammy grey fog, that atmosphere of industry which kept us at an anchor off the Isle of Wight, through the liveliest air of the inland sea, whose sparkling blue and purple haze spread charms even on Africa's beldame features, and now we were sitting silent and still, listening to the monotonous melody of the East—the soft night-breeze wandering through starlight skies and tufted trees, with a voice of melancholy meaning.

And this is the Arab's *Kaif*. The savoring of animal existence; the passive enjoyment of mere sense; the pleasant languor, the dreamy tranquillity, the airy castle-building, which in Asia stand in lieu of the vigorous, intensive, passionate life of Europe. It is the result of a lively, impressible, excitable nature, and exquisite sensibility of nerve,—a facility for voluptuousness unknown to northern regions; where happiness is placed in the exertion of men-

* "*Bakhshish*," says a modern writer, "is a fee or present which the Arabs (he here means the Egyptians, who got the word from the Persians through the Turks) claim on all occasions for services you render them, as well as for services they have rendered you. This bakhshish, in fact, is a sort of alms or tribute, which the poor Arab believes himself entitled to claim from every respectable-looking person."

† Mafish, "There is none," equivalent to, "I have left my purse at home." Nothing takes the Oriental mind so much as a retort alliterative or jingling.

tal and physical powers; where niggard earth commands ceaseless sweat of brow, and damp chill air demands perpetual excitement, exercise, or change, or adventure, or dissipation, for want of something better. In the East, man requires but rest and shade: upon the banks of a bubbling stream, or under the cool shelter of a perfumed tree, he is perfectly happy, smoking a pipe, or sipping a cup of coffee, or drinking a glass of sherbet, but, above all things, deranging body and mind as little as possible; the trouble of conversations, the displeasures of memory, and the vanity of thought being the most unpleasant interruptions to his *Kaif.* No wonder that Kaif is a word untranslatable in our mother-tongue!*

The better to blind the inquisitive eyes of servants and visitors, my friend lodged me in an outhouse, where I could revel in the utmost freedom of life and manners. And although some Armenian Dragoman, a restless spy like all his race, occasionally remarked that "voilà un Persan diablement degagé," none, except those who were entrusted with the secret, had any idea of the part I was playing. The domestics, devout Moslems, pronounced me to be an Ajemi,* a kind of Mohammedan, not a good one like themselves, but still, better than nothing. I lost no time in securing the assistance of a Shaykh,† and plunged once more into the intricacies of the Faith, revived my recollections of religious ablution, read the Koran, and again became an adept in the art of prostration. My leisure hours were employed in visiting the baths and coffee-houses, in attend-

* In a coarser sense "kaif" is applied to all manner of intoxication. Sonnini is not wrong when he says, "the Arabs give the name of Kaif to the voluptuous relaxation, the delicious stupor, produced by the smoking of hemp."

† A Persian opposed to an Arab.

‡ A priest, elder, chieftain, language-master, &c. &c.

ing the bazaars, and in shopping,—an operation which hereabouts consists of sitting upon a chapman's counter, smoking, sipping coffee, and telling your beads the while, to show that you are not of the slaves for whom time is made; in fact, in pitting your patience against that of your adversary the shopman.

Careful of graver matters, I also attended the mosque, and visited the venerable localities in which modern Alexandria abounds.

It is not to be supposed that the people of Alexandria could look upon my phials and pill-boxes, without a yearning for their contents. An Indian doctor, too, was a novelty to them; Franks they despised, but a man who had come so far from the West! Then there was something infinitely seducing in the character of a magician, doctor, and fakir, each admirable of itself, thus combined to make "great medicine." Men, women, and children besieged my door, by which means I could see the people face to face, and especially the fair sex, of which Europeans, generally speaking, know only the worst specimens. Even respectable natives, after witnessing a performance of "Mandal" and the Magic mirror,* opined that the stranger was a holy man, gifted with supernatural powers, and knowing everything. One old person sent to offer me his daughter in marriage; he said nothing about dowry, but on this occasion I thought proper to decline the honor. And a middle-aged lady proffered me the sum of 100 piastres, nearly one pound

* Form of Oriental divination which owes its present celebrity in Europe to Mr. Lane. Both it and the magic mirror are hackneyed subjects, but I have been tempted to a few words concerning them in another part of this volume. Meanwhile I request the reader not to set me down as a mere charlatan; medicine in the East is so essentially united with superstitious practices, that he who would pass for an expert practitioner, must necessarily represent himself an "adept."

sterling, if I would stay at Alexandria, and superintend the restoration of her blind eye.

But the reader must not be led to suppose that I acted "Carabin," or "Sangrado," without any knowledge of my trade. From youth I have always been a dabbler in medical and mystical study. Moreover, the practice of physic is comparatively easy amongst dwellers in warm latitudes, uncivilised people, where there is not that complication of maladies which troubles more polished nations. And further, what simplifies extremely the treatment of the sick in these parts is, the undoubted periodicity of disease, reducing almost all to one type—ague.* Many of the complaints of tropical climates, as medical men well know, display palpably intermittent symptoms unknown to colder countries; and speaking from individual experience, I may safely assert that in all cases of suffering, from a wound to ophthalmia, this phenomenon has forced itself into my notice. So much by way of excuse. I therefore considered myself as well qualified for the work as if I had taken out a *buono per l'estero* diploma at Padua.

After a month's hard work at Alexandria, I prepared to assume the character of a wandering Dervish, after reforming my title from "Mirsa" † to "Shaykh" Abdullah.‡ A

* Hence the origin, I believe, of the chronothermal practice, a discovery which physic owes to Dr. Dickson.

† The Persian "Mister." In future chapters the reader will see the uncomfortable consequences of my having appeared in Egypt as a Persian. Although I found out the mistake, and worked hard to correct it, the bad name stuck to me; bazaar reports fly quicker and hit harder than newspaper paragraphs.

‡ Arab Christians sometimes take the name of "Abdullah," servant of God—"which," as a modern traveller observes, "all sects and religions might be equally proud to adopt." The Moslem Prophet said, "the names most approved of God are, Abdullah, Abd-el-rahman (slave of the compassionate), and such like."

reverend man, whose name I do not care to quote, some time ago initiated me into his order, the Kadiriyah, under the high-sounding name of Bismillah-Shah: * and, after a due period of probation, he graciously elevated me to the proud position of a Murshid § in the mystic craft. I was therefore sufficiently well acquainted with the tenets and practices of these Oriental Freemasons. No character in the Moslem world is so proper for disguise as that of the Dervish. It is assumed by all ranks, ages, and creeds; by the nobleman who has been disgraced at court, and by the peasant who is too idle to till the ground; by Dives, who is weary of life, and by Lazarus, who begs bread from door to door. Further, the Dervish is allowed to ignore ceremony and politeness, as one who ceases to appear upon the stage of life; he may pray or not, marry or remain single as he pleases, be respectable in cloth of frieze as in cloth of gold, and no one asks him—the chartered vagabond—Why he comes here? or Wherefore he goes there? He may wend his way on foot alone, or ride his Arab steed followed by a dozen servants; he is equally feared without weapons, as swaggering through the streets armed to the teeth. The more haughty and offensive he is to the people, the more they respect him; a decided advantage to the traveller of choleric temperament. In the hour of imminent danger, he has only to become a maniac, and he is safe; a madman in the East, like a notable eccentric character in the West, is allowed to say or do whatever the spirit directs. Add to this character a little knowledge of medicine, a "moderate

* "King-in-the-name-of-Allah," a kind of Oriental "Praise-God-Barebones." When a man appears as a Fakir or Dervish, he casts off, in process of regeneration, together with other worldly sloughs, his laical name for some brilliant coat of nomenclature rich in religious promise.

† A Murshid is one allowed to admit Murids or apprentices into the order.

skill in magic and a reputation for caring for nothing but study and books," together with capital sufficient to save you from the chance of starving, and you appear in the East to peculiar advantage. The only danger of the "Path"* is, that the Dervish's ragged coat not unfrequently covers the cut-throat, and, if seized in the society of such a "brother," you may reluctantly become his companion, under the stick or on the stake. For be it known, Dervishes are of two orders, the Sharai, or those who conform to religion, and the Be-Sharai, or Luti, whose practices are hinted at by their own tradition that "he we daurna name" once joined them for a week, but at the end of that time left them in dismay, and returned to whence he came.

* The Tarikat or path, which leads, or is supposed to lead, to Heaven.

## CHAPTER II.

### I LEAVE ALEXANDRIA.

THE thorough-bred wanderer's idiosyncrasy I presume to be a composition of what phrenologists call "inhabitiveness" and "locality" equally and largely developed. After a long and toilsome march, weary of the way, he drops into the nearest place of rest to become the most domestic of men. For a while he smokes the "pipe of permanence"* with an infinite zest; he delights in various siestas during the day, relishing withal a long sleep at night; he enjoys dining at a fixed dinner hour, and wonders at the demoralisation of the mind which cannot find means of excitement in chit-chat or small talk, in a novel or a newspaper. But soon the passive fit has passed away; again a paroxysm of ennui coming on by slow degrees, Viator loses appetite, he walks about his room all night, he yawns at conversations, and a book acts upon him as a narcotic. The man wants to wander, and he must do so or he shall die.

After about a month most pleasantly spent at Alexandria, I perceived the approach of the enemy, and as nothing ham-

* The long pipe which at home takes the place of the shorter chibouque used on the road.

pered my incomings and outgoings, I surrendered. The world was "all before me," and there was pleasant excitement in plunging single-handed into its chilling depths. My Alexandrian Shaykh, whose heart fell victim to a new "jubbeh," which I had given in exchange for his tattered zaabut,* offered me, in consideration of a certain monthly stipend, the affections of a brother and religious refreshment, proposing to send his wife back to her papa, and to accompany me, in the capacity of private chaplain, to the other side of Kaf.† I politely accepted the "Bruderschaft," but many reasons induced me to decline his society and services. In the first place, he spoke the detestable Egyptian jargon. Secondly, it was but prudent to lose the "spoor" between Alexandria and Suez. And, thirdly, my "brother" had shifting eyes (symptoms of fickleness), close together (indices of cunning); a flat-crowned head, and large ill-fitting lips; signs which led me to think lightly of his honesty, firmness, and courage. Phrenology and physiognomy, be it observed, disappoint you often amongst civilised people, the proper action of whose brains and features is impeded by the external pressure of education, accident, example, habit, necessity, and what not. But they are tolerably safe guides when groping your way through the mind of man in his natural state, a being of impulse in that chrysalis stage of mental development which is rather instinct than reason. But before my departure there was much to be done.

* The jubbeh is a long outer garment, generally of cloth, worn by learned and respectable men. The zaabut is a large bag-sleeved black or brown colored robe, made of home-spun woollen, the garb of the peasant, the hedge-priest, and the dervish.

† The mountain which encircles the globe, according to the sacred geography of the Moslems. To "go to Kaf" is equivalent to our "go to Jericho," or—somewhere else.

The land of the Pharaohs is becoming civilised, and unpleasantly so; nothing can be more uncomfortable than its present middle state, between barbarism and the reverse. The prohibition against carrying arms is rigid as in Italy; all "violence" is violently denounced, and beheading being deemed cruel, the most atrocious crimes, as well as those small political offences, which in the days of the Mamelukes would have led to a beyship or a bow-string, receive fourfold punishment by deportation to Faizoghli, the local Cayenne. If you order your peasant to be flogged, his friends gather in threatening hundreds at your gates; when you curse your boatman, he complains to your consul; the dragomans afflict you with strange wild notions about honesty; a government order prevents you from using vituperative language to the "natives" in general; and the very donkey boys are becoming cognisant of the right of man to remain unbastinadoed. Still the old leaven remains behind: here, as elsewhere in "morning-land," you cannot hold your own without employing your fists. The passport system, now dying out of Europe, has sprung up, or rather revived in Egypt, with peculiar vigor. Its good effects claim for it our respect; still we cannot but lament its inconvenience. *We*, I mean real Easterns. As strangers—even those whose beards have whitened in the land—know absolutely nothing of what unfortunate natives must endure, I am tempted to subjoin a short sketch of my adventures in search of a Tezkireh at Alexandria.*

Through ignorance which might have cost me dear but for my friend's weight with the local authorities, I had neglected to provide myself with a passport in England, and it was not without difficulty, involving much unclean dressing and an unlimited expenditure of broken English,

* A passport in this country is called a Tezkireh.

that I obtained from the consul at Alexandria, a certificate, declaring me to be an Indo-British subject named Abdullah, by profession a doctor, aged thirty, and not distinguished —at least so the frequent blanks seemed to denote—by any remarkable conformation of eyes, nose, or cheek. For this I disbursed a dollar.

My new passport would not carry me without the Zabit or Police Magistrate's counter-signature, said the consul. Next day I went to the Zabit, who referred me to the Muhafiz (Governor) of Alexandria, at whose gate I had the honor of squatting at least three hours, till a more compassionate clerk vouchsafed the information that the proper place to apply to was the Diwan Kharijiyeh (the Foreign Office). Thus a second day was utterly lost. On the morning of the third I started, as directed, for the palace, which crowns the Headland of Figs. It is a huge and couthless shell of building in parallelogrammic form, containing all kinds of public offices in glorious confusion, looking with their glaring white-washed faces upon a central court, where a few leafless wind-wrung trees seem struggling for the breath of life in an eternal atmosphere of clay, dust, and sun-blaze.

The first person I addressed was a Kawwas or police officer, who, coiled comfortably up in a bit of shade fitting his person like a robe, was in full enjoyment of the Asiatic "Kaif." Having presented the consular certificate and briefly stated the nature of my business, I ventured to inquire what was the right course to pursue for a visá.

They have little respect for Dervishes, it appears, at Alexandria!

M'adri—"Don't know," growled the man of authority, without moving any thing but the quantity of tongue necessary for articulation.

Now there are three ways of treating Asiatic officials,—

by bribe, by bullying, or by bothering them with a dogged perseverance into attending to you and your concerns. The latter is the peculiar province of the poor; moreover, this time I resolved, for other reasons, to be patient. I repeated my question in almost the same words. Ruh! "Be off," was what I obtained for all reply. But this time the questioned went so far as to open his eyes. Still I stood twirling the paper in my hands, and looking very humble and very persevering, till a loud Ruh ya Kalb! "Go O dog!" converted into a responsive curse the little speech I was preparing about the brotherhood of El-Islam and the mutual duties obligatory on true believers. I then turned away slowly and fiercely, for the next thing might have been a cut with the Kurbaj,* and, by the hammer of Thor! British flesh and blood could never have stood that.

After which satisfactory scene,—for satisfactory it was in one sense, proving the complete fitness of the Dervish's dress,—I tried a dozen other promiscuous sources of information,—policemen, grooms, scribes, donkey boys, and idlers in general. At length, wearied of patience, I offered a soldier some pinches of tobacco, and promised him an oriental sixpence if he would manage the business for me. The man was interested by the tobacco and the pence; he took my hand, and inquiring the while he went along, led me from place to place, till, mounting a grand staircase, I stood in the presence of Abbas Effendi, the governor's Naib or deputy.

It was a little, whey-faced, black-bearded Turk, coiled up in the usual conglomerate posture upon a calico-covered divan, at the end of a long bare large-windowed room. Without deigning even to nod the head, which hung over

* A whip of dried and twisted hippopotamus hide, the ferule, horsewhip, and "cat' o' nine tails" of Egypt.

his shoulder with transcendent listlessness and affectation of pride, in answer to my salams and benedictions, he eyed me with wicked eyes, and faintly ejaculated "Min ent?" * Then hearing that I was a Dervish and doctor—he must be an Osmanli Voltairian, that little Turk—the official snorted a contemptuous snort. He condescendingly added, however, that the proper source to seek was "Taht," which meaning simply "below," conveyed rather imperfect information in a topographical point of view to a stranger.

At length, however, my soldier guide found out that a room in the custom-house bore the honorable appellation of "Foreign Office." Accordingly I went there, and, after sitting at least a couple of hours at the bolted door in the noon-day sun, was told, with a fury which made me think I had sinned, that the officer in whose charge the department was, had been presented with an olive branch in the morning, and consequently that business was not to be done that day. The angry-faced official communicated the intelligence to a large group of Anadolian, Caramanian, Boshniac, and Roumelian Turks,—sturdy, undersized, broad-shouldered, bare-legged, splay-footed, horny-fisted, dark-browed, honest-looking mountaineers, who were lounging about with long pistols and yataghans stuck in their broad sashes, head-gear composed of immense tarbooshes with proportionate turbans coiled round them, and two or three suits of substantial clothes, even at this season of the year, upon their shoulders.

Like myself they had waited some hours, but they were not patient under disappointment: they bluntly told the angry official that he and his master were a pair of idlers, and the curses that rumbled and gurgled in their hairy

* For "man anta?" who art thou?

throats as they strode towards the door, sounded like the growling of wild beasts.

Thus was another day truly orientally lost. On the morrow, however, I obtained permission, in the character of Dr. Abdullah, to visit any part of Egypt I pleased, and to retain possession of my dagger and pistols.

And now I must explain what induced me to take so much trouble about a passport. The home reader naturally inquires, why not travel under your English name?

For this reason. In the generality of barbarous countries you must either proceed, like Bruce, preserving the "dignity of manhood," and carrying matters with a high hand, or you must worm your way by timidity and subservience; in fact, by becoming an animal too contemptible for man to let or injure. But to pass through the Holy Land, you must either be a born believer, or have become one; in the former case you may demean yourself as you please, in the latter a path is ready prepared for you. My spirit could not bend to own myself a renegade—to be pointed at and shunned and catechised, an object of suspicion to the many and of contempt to all. Moreover, it would have obstructed the aim of my wanderings. The convert is always watched with Argus eyes, and men do not willingly give information to a "new Moslem," especially a Frank: they suspect his conversion to be a feigned or forced one, look upon him as a spy, and let him see as little of life as possible. Firmly as was my heart set upon travelling in Arabia, by Heaven! I would have given up the dear project rather than purchase a doubtful and partial success at such a price. Consequently, I had no choice but to appear as a born believer, and part of my birthright in that respectable character was toil and trouble in obtaining a tezkirah.

Then I had to provide myself with certain necessaries

for the way. These were not numerous. The silver-mounted dressing-case is here supplied by a rag containing a miswak,* a bit of soap and a comb (wooden), for bone and tortoiseshell are not, religiously speaking, correct. Equally simple was my wardrobe; a change or two of clothing.† The only article of canteen description was a zemzemiyah, a goat-skin water-bag, which communicates to its contents, especially when new, a ferruginous aspect and a wholesome, though hardly an attractive flavor of tanno-gelatine. This was a necessary; to drink out of a tumbler, possibly fresh from pig-eating lips, would have entailed a certain loss of reputation. For bedding and furniture I had a coarse Persian rug—which, besides being couch, acts as chair, table, and oratory—a cotton stuffed chintz-covered pillow, a blanket in case of cold, and a sheet, which does duty for tent and mosquito curtains in nights of heat.‡ As shade is a convenience not always procurable, another necessary was a huge cotton umbrella of Eastern make, brightly yellow, suggesting the idea of an overgrown marigold. I had also a substantial housewife, the gift of a kind friend; it was a roll of canvas, carefully soiled, and garnished with

* A stick of soft wood chewed at one end. It is generally used throughout the East, where brushes should be avoided, as the natives always suspect hogs' bristles.

† It is a great mistake to carry too few clothes, and those who travel as Orientals should always have at least one very grand suit for use on critical occasions. Throughout the East a badly dressed man is a pauper, and a pauper—unless he belongs to an order having a right to be poor—is a scoundrel.

‡ Almost all Easterns sleep under a sheet, which becomes a kind of respirator, defending them from the dews and mosquitoes by night and the flies by day. The "rough and ready" traveller will learn to follow the example, remembering that "nature is founder of customs in savage countries;" whereas, amongst the *soi-disant* civilized, nature has no deadlier enemy than custom.

needles and thread, cobblers'-wax, buttons, and other such articles. These things were most useful in lands where tailors abound not; besides which, the sight of a man darning his coat or patching his slippers teems with pleasing ideas of humility. A dagger, a brass inkstand, and penholder stuck in my belt, and a mighty rosary, which on occasion might have been converted into a weapon of offence, completed my equipment. I must not omit to mention the proper method of carrying money, which in these lands should never be entrusted to box or bag. A common cotton purse secured in a breast pocket (for Egypt now abounds in that civilized animal the pickpocket), contained silver pieces and small change. My gold, of which I carried twenty-five sovereigns, and papers, were committed to a substantial leathern belt of Maghrabi manufacture, made to be strapped round the waist under the dress. This is the Asiatic method of concealing valuables, and a more civilized one than ours in the last century, when Roderic Random and his companion "sewed their money between the lining and the waistband of their breeches, except some loose silver for immediate expense on the road." The great inconvenience of the belt is its weight, especially where dollars must be carried, as in Arabia, causing chafes and inconvenience at night. Moreover, it can scarcely be called safe. In dangerous countries wary travellers will adopt surer precautions.*

A pair of common native khurjin or saddle-bags contained my wardrobe, the "bed," readily rolled up into a bundle,

* Some prefer a long chain of pure gold divided into links and covered with leather, so as to resemble the twisted girdle which the Arab fastens round his waist. It is a precaution well known to the wandering knights of old. Others, again, in very critical situations, open with a lancet the shoulder, or any other fleshy part of the body, and insert a precious stone, which does not show in its novel purse.

and for a medicine chest* I bought a pea-green box with red and yellow flowers, capable of standing falls from a camel twice a day.

The next step was to find out when the local steamer would start for Cairo, and accordingly I betook myself to the Transit Office. No vessel was advertised; I was directed to call every evening till satisfied. At last the fortunate event took place. A "weekly departure," which, by the by, occurred once every fortnight or so, was in order for the next day. I hurried to the office, but did not reach it till past noon—the hour of idleness. A little, dark gentleman, so formed and dressed as exactly to resemble a liver-and-tan bull-terrier, who, with his heels on the table, was dozing, cigar in mouth, over the last "Galignani," positively refused, after a time—for at first he would not speak at all—to let me take my passage till three in the

* Any "Companion to the Medicine Chest" will give, to those that require such information, the names of drugs and instruments necessary for a journey: but it must be borne in mind that hot countries require double quantities of tonics, and half the allowance of cathartics, necessary in cold climates. Sonnini, however, is right when he says of the Egyptian fellahs, that their stomachs, accustomed to digest bread badly baked, acrid and raw vegetables, and other green and unwholesome nourishment, require doses fit only for horses.

Advisable precautions are, in the first place, to avoid, if travelling as a native, any signs of European manufacture in knives, scissors, weights, scales, and other such articles. Secondly, glass bottles are useless; the drugs should be stowed away in tin or wooden boxes, such as the natives of the country use, and when a phial is required it must be fitted into an *etui* of some kind. By this means, ground glass stoppers, and plentiful cotton stuffing, the most volatile essences may be carried about without great waste. After six months of the driest heat in Egypt and Arabia, not more than about one-fourth of my Prussic acid and chloroform had evaporated. And, thirdly, if you travel in the East, a few bottles of tincture of cantharides—highly useful as a rubefacient, excitant, et cetera—must never be omitted.

afternoon. I inquired when the boat started, upon which he referred me, as I had spoken bad Italian, to the advertisement. I pleaded inability to read or write, whereupon he testily cried, "Alle nove! alle nove!"—at nine! at nine! Still appearing uncertain, I drove him out of his chair, when he rose with a curse, and read 8 A. M. An unhappy Eastern, depending upon what he said, would have been precisely one hour too late.

Thus were we lapsing into the real good old Indian style of doing business. Thus Indicus orders his first clerk to execute some commission; the senior, having "work" upon his hands, sends a junior; the junior finds the sun hot, and passes on the word to a "peon;" the "peon" charges a porter with the errand, and the porter quietly sits or dozes in his place, trusting that fate will bring him out of the scrape, but firmly resolved, though the shattered globe fall, not to stir an inch.

The reader, I must again express a hope, will pardon the egotism of these descriptions—my object is to show him how business is carried on in these hot countries, business generally. For had I, instead of being Abdullah the Dervish, been a rich native merchant, it would have been the same. How many complaints of similar treatment have I heard in different parts of the Eastern world! and how little can one realise them without having actually experienced the evil! For the future, I shall never see a "nigger" squatting away half a dozen mortal hours in a broiling sun, patiently waiting for something or for some one, without a lively remembrance of my own cooling of the *calces* at the custom-house of Alexandria.

At length, about the end of May, all was ready. Not without a feeling of regret I left my little room among the white myrtle blossoms and the oleander flowers. I kissed, with humble ostentation, my kind host's hand, in presence of his servants, bade adieu to my patients, who now amounted to about fifty, shaking hands with all meekly and with religious equality of attention, and, mounted in a "trap" which looked like a cross between a wheelbarrow and a dog-cart, drawn by a kicking, jibbing, and biting mule, I set out for the steamer.

## CHAPTER III.

### THE NILE STEAMBOAT.

In the days of the Pitts we have invariably a "Relation" of Egyptian travellers who embark for a place called "Roseet," on the "River Nilus." Wanderers of the Brucian age were wont to record their impressions of voyage upon land subjects observed between Alexandria and Cairo. A little later we find every one inditing rhapsodies about, and descriptions of, his or her dahabiyeh (barge) on the canal. After this came the steamer. And after the steamer will come the railroad, which may disappoint the author tourist, but will be delightful to that sensible class of men who wish to get over the greatest extent of ground with the least inconvenience to themselves and others. Then shall the Mahmudiyah—ugliest and most wearisome of canals—be given up to cotton boats and grain barges, and then will note-books and the headings of chapters ignore its existence.

I saw the canal at its worst, when the water was low, and have not one syllable to say in its favor. Instead of thirty hours, we took three mortal days and nights to reach Cairo, and we grounded with painful regularity four or five times between sunrise and sunset. In the scenery on the banks sketchers and describers have left you nought to see. The Pyramids of Cheops and Cephren, "rearing their majestic heads above the margin of the desert," only suggest the remark that they have been remarkably well-sketched; and thus you proceed till with a real feeling of satisfaction you moor alongside of the tumble-down old suburb Bulak.

I had taken a third-class or deck passage, whereby the evils of the journey were exasperated. A roasting sun pierced the canvas awning like hot water through a gauze veil, and by night the cold dews fell raw and thick as a Scotch mist. The cooking was abominable, and the dignity of Dervish-hood did not allow me to sit at meat with infidels, or to eat the food they had polluted. So the Dervish squatted apart, smoking perpetually, with occasional interruptions to say his prayers and to tell his beads upon the mighty rosary, and he drank the muddy water of the canal out of a leathern bucket, and he munched his bread and garlic* with a desperate sanctimoniousness.

* Those skilled in simples, Eastern as well as Western, praise garlic highly, declaring that it "strengthens the body, prepares the constitution for fatigue, brightens the sight, and, by increasing the digestive power, obviates the ill effects arising from sudden change of air and water." The old Egyptians highly esteemed this vegetable, which, with onions and leeks, enters into the list of articles so much regretted by the Hebrews (Numbers, xi. 5; Koran, Chap. 2). The modern people of the Nile, like the Spaniards, delight in onions, which, as they contain between 25 and 30 per cent. of gluten, are highly nutritive. In Arabia, however, the stranger must use this vegetable sparingly. The city people despise it as the food of a fellah—a boor. The Wahhabis have a prejudice against onions, leeks, and garlic, because the Prophet disliked their strong smell, and all strict Moslems refuse to eat them immediately before visiting the mosque or meeting for public prayer

The "Little Asthmatic," as the steamer is called, was crowded, and discipline not daring to mark out particular places, the scene on board of her was a motley one. There were two Indian officers, who naturally spoke to none but each other, drank bad tea, and smoked their cigars like Britons. A troop of the Kurd Kawwas, escorting treasure, was surrounded by a group of noisy Greeks; these men's gross practical jokes sounding anything but pleasant to the solemn Moslems, whose saddle-bags and furniture were at every moment in danger of being defiled by abominable drinks and the ejected juices of tobacco. There was one pretty woman on board, a Spanish girl, who looked strangely misplaced—a rose in a field of thistles. Some silent Italians, with noisy interpreters, sat staidly upon the benches. It was soon found out, through the communicative dragoman, that their business was to buy horses for H. M. of Sardinia: they were exposed to a volley of questions delivered by a party of French tradesmen returning to Cairo, but they shielded themselves and fought shy with Machiavellian dexterity. Besides these was a German—a "beer-bottle in the morning and a bottle of beer in the evening," to borrow a simile from his own nation—a Syrian merchant, the richest and ugliest of Alexandria, and a few French house-painters going to decorate the Pacha's palace at Shoobra. These last were the happiest of our voyagers,—veritable children of Paris, Montagnards, Voltairiens, and thorough-bred Sans-Soucis. All day they sat upon deck chattering as only their lively nation can chatter, indulging in ultra-gallic maxims, then singing, then dancing, then sleeping and rising to play, to drink, talk, dance, and sing again. They being new comers, free from the western *morgue* so soon caught by Oriental Europeans, were particularly civil to me, even wishing to mix me a strong draught; but I was not so fortunate with all on board. A large shopkeeper threatened to "*briser*" my "figure" for putting my pipe near his "pantaloons; but seeing me finger my dagger curiously, though I did not shift my pipe, he forgot to remember his threat. I had taken charge of a parcel for one M. P——, a student of Coptic, and remitted it to him on board; of this little service the only acknowledgment was a stare and a petulant inquiry why I had not given it to him before. And one of the Englishmen, half publicly, half privily, as though communing with himself, condemned my organs of vision because I happened to touch his elbow. He was a man in my own service; I pardoned him in consideration of the compliment paid to my disguise.

Two fellow-passengers were destined to play an important part in my comedy of Cairo. Just after we had started, a little event afforded us some amusement. On the bank appeared a short, fat, pursy kind of man, whose efforts to board the steamer were notably ridiculous. With attention divided between the vessel and a carpet bag carried by his donkey boy, he ran along the sides of the canal, now stumbling into hollows, then climbing heights, then standing shouting upon the projections with the fierce sun upon his back, till every one thought his breath was completely gone. But no! game to the backbone, he would have perished miserably rather than lose his fare: "perseverance," say the copy-books, "accomplishes great things:" at last he was taken on board, and presently he lay down to sleep. His sooty complexion, lank black hair, features in which appeared *beaucoup de finesse*, that is to say, abundant rascality, an eternal smile and treacherous eyes, his gold* ring, dress of showy colors, fleshy stomach, fat legs, round back, and a peculiar manner of frowning and fawning simultaneously,

* The stricter sort of Moslems, such as the Arabs, will not wear gold ornaments, which are forbidden by their law.

marked him an Indian. When he awoke he introduced himself to me as Miyan Khudabakhsh Namdar, a native of Lahore: he carried on the trade of a shawl merchant in London and Paris, where he lived two years, and after a pilgrimage intended to purge away the sins of civilized lands, had settled at Cairo.

My second friend, Haji Wali, I will introduce to the reader in a future chapter.

Long conversations in Persian and Hindostani, abridged the tediousness of the voyage, and when we arrived at Bulak, the polite Khudabakhsh insisted on my making his house my home. I was unwilling to accept the man's civility, disliking his looks, but he advanced cogent reasons for changing my mind. His servants cleared my luggage through the custom-house, and a few minutes after our arrival I found myself in his abode near the Ezbekiyah Gardens, sitting in a cool mashrabiyah * that gracefully projected over a garden, and sipping the favorite glass of pomegranate syrup.

As the wakálahs or caravanserais were at that time full of pilgrims, I remained with Khudabakhsh ten days or a fortnight. But at the end of that time, my patience was thoroughly exhausted. My host had become a civilized man, who sat on chairs, ate with a fork, talked European politics, and had learned to admire, if not to understand liberty—liberal ideas! and was I not flying from such things? Besides which, we English have a peculiar national quality, which the Indians, with their characteristic acuteness, soon perceived, and described by an opprobrious name. Observing our solitary habits, that we could not and would not,

* The projecting latticed window, made of wood richly carved, for which Cairo was once so famous. But they are growing out of fashion with young Egypt, disappearing before glass and unsightly green blinds.

sit and talk and sip sherbet and smoke with them, they called us "Jungli"—wild men, fresh caught in the jungle and sent to rule over the land of Hind.* Certainly nothing suits us less than perpetual society, an utter want of solitude, when one cannot retire into oneself an instant without being asked some puerile question by a friend, or look into a book without a servant peering over one's shoulder; when from the hour you rise to the time you rest, you must ever be talking or listening, you must converse yourself to sleep in a public dormitory, and give ear to your companions' snores and mutterings at midnight.†

The very essence of Oriental hospitality, however, is this family style of reception, which costs your host neither coin nor trouble. You make one more at his eating tray, and an additional mattress appears in the sleeping room. When you depart, you leave if you like a little present, merely for a memorial, with your entertainer; he would be offended if you offered it him openly as a remuneration,‡ and you give some trifling sums to the servants. Thus you will be welcome wherever you go. If perchance you are

* Caste in India arises from the peculiarly sociable nature of the native mind, for which reason "it is found existing among sects whose creeds are as different and as opposite as those of the Hindoo and the Christian." Hence, nothing can be more terrible to a man than expulsion from caste; the excommunication of our feudal times was not a more dreadful form of living death.

† With us, every man's house is his castle. But caste divides a people into huge families, each member of which has a right to know every thing about his "caste-brother," because a whole body might be polluted and degraded by the act of an individual. Hence there is no such thing as domestic privacy, and no system of espionage devised by rulers could be so complete as that self-imposed by the Hindoos.

‡ I speak of the rare tracts in which the old barbarous hospitality still lingers.

detained perforce in such a situation,—which may easily happen to you, medical man,—you have only to make yourself as disagreeable as possible, by calling for all manner of impossible things. Shame is a passion with Eastern nations. Your host would blush to point out to you the indecorum of your conduct; and the laws of hospitality oblige him to supply the every want of a guest, even though he be a *détênu*.

## CHAPTER IV.

### LIFE IN THE WAKÁLAH.

The "wakálah," as the caravanserai or khan is called in Egypt, combines the offices of hotel, lodging house, and store. It is at Cairo, as at Constantinople, a massive pile of buildings surrounding a quadrangular "hosh" or court-yard. On the ground-floor are rooms like caverns for merchandise, and shops of different kinds—tailors, cobblers, bakers, tobacconists, fruiterers, and others. A roofless gallery or a covered verandah, into which all the apartments open, runs round the first and sometimes the second story: the latter, however, is usually exposed to the sun and wind. The accommodations consist of sets of two or three rooms, generally an inner one and an outer; this contains a hearth for cooking, a bathing place, and similar necessaries. The staircases are high, narrow, and exceedingly dirty, dark at night and often in bad repair; a goat or donkey is tethered upon the different landings; here and there a fresh skin is stretched in process of tanning, and the smell reminds the veteran traveller of those closets in the old French inns where cats used to be prepared for playing the part of jugged hare. The interior is unfurnished; even the pegs upon which clothes are hung have been pulled down for firewood: the walls are bare but for stains, thick cobwebs depend in festoons from the blackened rafters of the ceiling, and the stone floor would disgrace a civilised prison: the windows are huge apertures carefully barred with wood or iron, and in rare places show remains of glass or paper pasted over the frameworks. In the court-yard the poorer sort of travellers consort with tethered beasts of burden, beggars howl, and the slaves lie basking and scratching themselves upon mountainous heaps of cotton bales and other merchandise.

This is not a tempting picture, yet is the wakálah a most amusing place, presenting a succession of scenes which would delight lovers of the Dutch school—a rich exemplification of the grotesque, and what is called by our artists the "dirty picturesque."

I could find no room in the Wakálah Khan Khalil, (the Long's, or Meurice's, of native Cairo.) I was therefore obliged to put up with the Jemaliyah, the Greek quarter, a place swarming with drunken Christians, and therefore not altogether fashionable. Even for this I had to wait a week. The pilgrims were flocking to Cairo, and to none other would the prudent hotel keepers open their doors, for the following sufficient reasons. When you enter a wakálah the first thing you have to do is to pay a small sum, varying from two to five shillings, for the miftah (the key). This is generally equivalent to a month's rent, so the sooner you leave the house the better for it. I was obliged to call myself a Turkish pilgrim in order to get possession of two most comfortless rooms, which I afterwards learned were celebrated for making travellers ill, and I had to pay eighteen piastres for the key and eighteen ditto per mensem for rent, besides five piastres to the man who swept and washed the place. So that for this month my house hire amounted to nearly four pence a day.

But I was fortunate enough in choosing the Jemaliyah Wakálah, for I found a friend there. On board the steamer a fellow voyager, seeing me sitting alone and therefore as he conceived in discomfort, placed himself by my side and opened a hot fire of kind inquiries. He was a man about forty-five, of middle size, with a large round head closely shaven, a bull-neck, limbs sturdy as a Saxon's, a thin red beard, and handsome features beaming with benevolence. A curious dry humor he had, delighting in "quizzing," but in so quiet, solemn, and quaint a way that before you knew him you could scarcely divine his drift.

"Thank Allah we carry a doctor!" said my friend more than once, with apparent fervor of gratitude, after he had discovered my profession. I was fairly taken by the pious ejaculation, and some days elapsed before the drift of his remark became apparent.

"You doctors," he explained, when we were more intimate, "what do you do? a man goes to you for ophthalmia. It is a purge, a blister, and a drop on the eye! Is it for fever? well! a purge and kinakina (quinine). For dysentery? a purge and extract of opium. Wallah! I am as good a physician as the best of you," he would add, with a broad grin, "if I only knew a few break-jaw Arabic names of diseases."

Haji Wali therefore emphatically advised me to make bread by honestly teaching languages. "We are doctor-ridden," said he, and I found it was the case.

When we lived under the same roof, the Haji and I became fast friends. During the day we called on each other frequently, we dined together, and passed the evening in a mosque, or some other place of public pastime. Coyly at first, but less guardedly as we grew bolder, we smoked the forbidden weed "hashish,"* conversing lengthily the while about that world of which I had seen so much. Originally from Russia he also had been a traveller, and in his wanderings had cast off most of the prejudices of his people. "I believe in Allah and his Prophet, and in nothing else," was his sturdy creed; he rejected alchemy, genii, and magicians, and truly he had a most unoriental distaste for tales of wonder. When I entered the wakálah, he constituted himself my cicerone, and especially guarded me against the cheating of tradesmen. By his advice I laid aside the dervish's gown, the large blue pantaloons, and the short shirt, in fact all connexion with Persia and the Persians. "If you persist in being an Ajemi," said the Haji, "you will get yourself into trouble; in Egypt you will be cursed, in Arabia you will be beaten because you are a heretic, you will pay the treble of what other travellers do, and if you fall sick you may die by the roadside." After long deliberation about the choice of nations I became a Pathan.† Born in India,

* By the Indians called Bhang, the Persians Bang, and the natives of Barbary, I believe, Fasukh. The Hottentots use it, and even the Siberians, we are told, intoxicate themselves by the vapor of this seed thrown upon red-hot stones. Egypt surpasses all other nations in the variety of compounds into which this fascinating drug enters, and will one day probably supply the Western world with "Indian hemp," when its solid merits are duly appreciated. At present in Europe it is chiefly confined, as cognac and opium used to be, to the apothecary's shelves. Some adventurous individuals at Paris, after the perusal of "Monte Christo," attempted an "orgie" in one of the cafés, but with poor success.

† The Indian name of an Afghan, supposed to be a corruption of the Arabic Fathan (a conqueror), or a derivation from the Hindostani *paithna,* to penetrate (into the hostile ranks). It is an honorable term in Arabia, where "Khurasani" (a native of Khorassan) leads men to suspect a Persian, and the other generic appellation of the Afghan tribes.

of Afghan parents, who had settled in the country, educated at Rangoon, and sent out to wander, as men of that race frequently are from early youth, I was well guarded against the danger of detection by a fellow countryman. To support the character requires a knowledge of Persian, Hindostani, and Arabic, all of which I knew sufficiently well to pass muster; any trifling inaccuracy was charged upon my long residence at Rangoon. This was an important step. The first question at the shop, on the camel, and in the mosque is, "What is thy name?" the second, "Whence comest thou?" This is not generally impertinent, or intended to be annoying; if, however, you see any evil intention in the questioner, you may rather roughly ask him, "What may be his maternal parent's name"—equivalent to inquiring, *Anglicè*, in what church his mother was married—and escape your difficulties under cover of a storm. But this is rarely necessary. I assumed the polite and pliant manners of an Indian physician, and the dress of a small Effendi,* still, however, representing myself to be a Dervish, and frequenting the places where Dervishes congregate. "What business," asked the Haji, "have those reverend men with politics or statistics, or any of the information which you are collecting? Call yourself a religious wanderer if you like, and let those who ask the object of your peregrinations know that you are under a vow to visit all the holy places in Islam. Thus you will persuade them that you are a man of rank under a cloud, and you will receive much more civility than perhaps you deserve," concluded my friend, with a dry laugh. The remark proved his sagacity, and, after ample experience, I had not to repent having been guided by his advice.

After lodging myself in the Wakálah, my first object

* Gentleman.

was to make a certain stir in the world. In Europe, your travelling doctor advertises the loss of a diamond ring, the gift of a Russian autocrat, or he monopolises a whole column in a newspaper, feeing perhaps a title for the use of a signature; the large brass plate, the gold-headed cane, the rattling chariot, and the summons from the sermon, complete the work. Here there is no such royal road to medical fame. You must begin by sitting with the porter, who is sure to have blear eyes, into which you drop a little nitrate of silver, whilst you instil into his ear the pleasing intelligence that you never take a fee from the poor. He recovers; his report of you spreads far and wide, crowding your doors with paupers. They come to you as though you were their servant, and when cured turn their backs upon you for ever. Hence it is that European doctors generally complain of ingratitude on the part of their Oriental patients. It is true that if you save a man's life he naturally asks you for the means of preserving it. Moreover, in none of the Eastern languages with which I am acquainted, is there a single term conveying the meaning of our "gratitude," and none but the Germans have ideas unexplainable by words. But you must not condemn this absence of a virtue without considering the cause. An Oriental deems that he has a right to your surplus. "Daily bread is divided" (by heaven) he asserts, and eating yours he considers it his own. Thus it is with other things. He is thankful to Allah for the gifts of the Creator, but he has a claim to the good offices of a fellow creature. In rendering him a service you have but done your duty, and he would not pay you so poor a compliment as to praise you for the act. He leaves you, his benefactor, with a short prayer for the length of your days. "Thank you," being expressed by "Allah increase thy weal!" or the selfish wish that your shadow (with which you protect him and his fellows) may never be less. And this is probably the last you hear of him.

There is a discomfort in such proceedings, a reasonable, a metaphysical coldness, uglily contrasting in theory with the genial warmth which a little more heart would infuse into them. In theory, I say, not in practice. What can be more troublesome than, when you have obliged a man, to run the gauntlet of his and his family's thanksgivings. "To find yourself become a master from being a friend," a great man where you were an equal; not to be contradicted, where shortly before every one gave his opinion freely. You must be unamiable if these considerations deter you from benefiting your friend, yet, I humbly opine, you still may fear his gratefulness.

To resume. When the mob has raised you to fame, patients of a better class will slowly appear on the scene. After some coquetting about "etiquette," whether you are to visit them or they are to call upon you, they make up their minds to see you, and to judge with their eyes whether you are to be trusted or not; whilst you, on your side, set out with the determination that they shall at once cross the Rubicon,—in less classical phrase, swallow your drug. If you visit the house, you insist on the patient's servants attending you; he must also provide and pay for an ass for your conveyance, no matter if it be only to the other side of the street. Your confidential man accompanies you, primed for replies to the "fifty searching questions" of the "servants' hall." You are lifted off the saddle tenderly, as nurses dismount their charges, when you arrive at the gate, and you waddle up stairs with dignity. Arrived at the sick room, you salute those present with a general "peace be upon you!" to which they respond, "and upon you be the peace and the mercy of Allah, and his blessing!" To the invalid you say, "There is nothing the matter, please Allah, except the health;" to which the proper answer—for here every sign of ceremony has its countersign—is, "may Allah give thee health!" You then sit down and acknowledge the presence of the company by raising your right hand to your lips and forehead, bowing the while circularly; each individual returns the civility by a similar gesture. Then inquiry about the state of your health ensues. Then you are asked what refreshment you will take: you studiously mention something not likely to be in the house, but at last you rough it with a pipe and a cup of coffee. Then you proceed to the patient, who extends his wrist, and asks you what his complaint is. Then you examine his tongue, you feel his pulse, you look learned, and—he is talking all the time—after hearing a detailed list of all his ailments, you gravely discover them, taking for the same as much praise to yourself as does the practising phrenologist, for a similar simple exercise of the reasoning faculties. The disease to be respectable must invariably be connected with one of the four temperaments, or the four elements, or the "humors of Hippocrates." Cure is easy, but it will take time, and you, the doctor, require attention; any little rudeness it is in your power to punish by an alteration in the pill, or the powder, and, so unknown is professional honor, that none will brave your displeasure. If you would pass for a native practitioner, you must then proceed to a most uncomfortable part of your visit, bargaining for fees. Nothing more effectually arouses suspicion than disinterestedness in a doctor. I once cured a rich Hazramaut merchant of rheumatism, and neglected to make him pay for treatment; he carried off one of my coffee cups, and was unceasingly wondering where I came from. So I made him produce five piastres, a shilling, which he threw upon the carpet, cursing Indian avarice. "You will bring on another illness," said my friend the Haji, when he heard of it. Properly speaking the fee for a visit to a respectable man is 20 piastres, but with the rich patient you begin by making a bargain. He complains, for instance, of dysentery and sciatica. You demand 10*l.* for the dysentery, and 20*l.* for the sciatica. But you will rarely get it, The Eastern pays a doctor's bill as an Irishman does his "rint," making a grievance of it. Your patient will show indisputable signs of convalescence: he will laugh and jest half the day; but the moment you appear, groans and a lengthened visage, and pretended compaints welcome you. Then your way is to throw out some such hint as

"The world is a carcass, and they who seek it are dogs."

And you refuse to treat the second disorder, which conduct may bring the refractory one to his senses. "Dat Galenus opes," however, is a Western apothegm: the utmost "Jalinus" can do for you here is to provide you with the necessaries and the comforts of life. Whatever you prescribe must be solid and material, and if you accompany it with something painful, such as rubbing unto scarification with a horse brush, so much the better. Easterns, as our peasants in Europe, like the doctor to "give them the value of their money." Besides which, rough measures act beneficially upon their imagination. So the Hakim of the King of Persia cured fevers by the bastinado; patients are beneficially baked in a bread-oven at Bagdad; and an Egyptian at Alexandria, whose quartan resisted the strongest appliances of European physic, was effectually healed by the actual cautery, which a certain Arab Shaykh applied to the crown of his head. When you administer with your own hand the remedy—half-a-dozen huge bread pills, dipped in a solution of aloes or cinnamon water, flavored with assafœtida, which in the case of the dyspeptic rich often suffice, if they will but diet themselves—you are careful to say,

"In the name of Allah, the compassionate, the merciful." And after the patient has been dosed, "Praise be to Allah, the curer, the healer;" you then call for pen, ink, and paper, and write some such prescription as this:—

"A *

"In the name of Allah, the compassionate, the merciful, and blessings and peace be upon our Lord the Prophet, and his family, and his companions one and all! But afterwards let him take bees-honey and cinnamon and album græcum, of each half a part, and of ginger a whole part, which let him pound and mix with the honey, and form boluses, each bolus the weight of a miskal, and of it let him use every day a miskal on the saliva.† Verily its effects are wonderful. And let him abstain from flesh, fish, vegetables, sweet-meats, flatulent food, acids of all descriptions, as well as the major ablution, and life in perfect quiet. So shall he be cured by the help of the King the Healer.‡ And the peace."§

The diet, I need scarcely say, should be rigorous; nothing has tended more to bring the European system of medicine into contempt among orientals than our inattention to this branch of the therapeutic art. When an Indian takes cathartic medicine, he prepares himself for it by diet and rest two or three days before its adhibition, and as gradually after the dose, he relapses into his usual habits; if he break through the regime it is concluded that fatal results must ensue. The ancient Egyptians we learn from Herodotus devoted a certain number of days in each month

* A monogram generally placed at the head of writings. It is the initial letter of "Allah," and the first of the alphabet, used from time immemorial to denote the origin of creation. "I am Alpha and Omega, the first and the last."

† "Al' ar-rik," that is to say, fasting—the first thing in the morning.

‡ The Almighty.

§ Was'-salam, *i. e.* adieu.

to the use of alteratives, and the period was consecutive, doubtless in order to graduate the strength of the medicine. The Persians, when under salivation, shut themselves up in a warm room, never undress, and so carefully guard against cold that they even drink tepid water. When the Afghan princes find it necessary to employ Chob-Chini, (the Jin-seng, or China root so celebrated as a purifier, tonic, and aphrodisiac) they choose the spring season; they remove to a garden, where flowers and trees and bubbling streams soothe their senses; they carefully avoid fatigue and trouble of all kinds, and will not even hear a letter read, lest it should contain bad news.

When the prescription is written out, you affix an impression of your ring seal to the beginning and the end of it, that no one may be able to add to or to take from its contents. And when you send medicine to a patient of rank, who is sure to have enemies, you adopt some similar precaution against the box or the bottle being opened. One of the Pashas whom I attended—a brave soldier, who had been a favorite with Mohammed Ali, and therefore was degraded by his successor—kept an impression of my ring in wax, to compare with that upon the phials. Men have not forgotten how frequently, in former times, those who became obnoxious to the state were seized with sudden and fatal cramps in the stomach. In the case of the doctor it is common prudence to adopt these precautions, as all evil consequences would be charged upon him, and he would be exposed to the family's revenge.

Cairo, though abounding in medical practitioners, can still support more; but they must be Indians, or Chinese, or Maghrabis to thrive. The Egyptians are thoroughly disgusted with European treatment, which is here about as efficacious as in India—that is to say, not at all. But they are ignorant of the medicine of Hind, and therefore great is its name; deservedly perhaps, for skill in simples and dietetics. Besides which the Indian may deal in charms and spells—things to which the latitude gives such force that even Europeans learn to put faith in them. The traveller who, on the banks of the Seine, scoffs at Sights and Sounds, Table-turning and Spirit-rapping, in the wilds of Tartary and Thibet sees a something supernatural and diabolical in the bungling *Sie-fa* of the *Bokte*.* Some sensible men, who pass for philosophers among their friends, have been caught by the incantations of the turbaned and bearded Cairo magician. In our West African colonies the phrase "growing black," was applied to colonists, who, after a term of residence, became thoroughly imbued with the superstitions of the land. And there are not wanting old English Indians, intelligent men, that place firm trust in tales and tenets too puerile even for the Hindus to believe. As "Hindi" I could use animal magnetism, taking care, however, to give the science a specious supernatural appearance. Haji Wali, who, professing positive scepticism, showed the greatest interest in the subject, as a curiosity, advised me not to practise pure mesmerism; otherwise, that I should infallibly become a "Companion of Devils." "You must call this an Indian secret," said my friend, "for it is clear that you are no Mashaikh,† and

* Certain Lamas who, we learn from M. Huc, perform famous Sie-fa, or supernaturalisms, such as cutting open the abdomen, licking red-hot irons, making incisions in various parts of the body, which an instant afterwards leave no trace behind, &c., &c. The devil may "have a great deal to do with the matter," in Tartary, for all I know; but I can assure M. Huc, that the Rufia Dervishes in India and the Saadiyah at Cairo perform exactly the same feats. Their jugglery, seen through the smoke of incense, and amidst the enthusiasm of a crowd, is tolerably dexterous, and no more.

† A holy man.

people will ask where are your drugs, and what business have you with charms?" It is useless to say that I followed his counsel; yet patients would consider themselves my Murids, and delighted in kissing the hand of the minor saint.

The Haji repaid me for my docility by vaunting me everywhere as the very phœnix of physicians. My first successes were in the Wakálah. Opposite to me there lived an Arab slave dealer, whose Abyssinians constantly fell sick. A tender race, they suffer when first transported to Egypt from many complaints, especially consumption, dysentery, and varicose veins. I succeeded in curing one girl. As she was worth at least fifteen pounds, the gratitude of her owner was great, and I had to dose half a dozen others, in order to cure them of the pernicious and price-lowering habit of snoring. Living in rooms opposite these slave girls, and seeing them at all hours of the day and night, I had frequent opportunities of studying them. They were average specimens of the steatopygous Abyssinian breed, broad-shouldered, thin-flanked, fine-limbed, and with haunches of a prodigious size. None of them had handsome features, but the short curly hair that stands on end being concealed under a kerchief, there was something pretty in the brow, eyes, and upper part of the nose, coarse and sensual in the pendent lips, large jowl, and projecting mouth, whilst the whole had a combination of piquancy with sweetness. Their style of flirtation was peculiar.

"How beautiful thou art, O Maryam!—what eyes!—what—"

"Then why," would respond the lady, "don't you buy me?"

"We are of one faith—of one creed—formed to form each other's happiness."

"Then why don't you buy me?"

"Conceive, O Maryam, the blessing of two hearts—"

"Then why don't you buy me?"

And so on. Most effectual gag to Cupid's eloquence! Yet was not the plain-spoken Maryam's reply without its moral. How often is it our fate in the West, as in the East, to see in bright eyes, and to hear from rosy lips, an implied, if not an expressed, "Why don't you buy me?" or, worse still, "Why can't you buy me?"

All I required in return for my services from the slave-dealer, whose brutal countenance and manners were truly repugnant, was to take me about the town, and explain to me certain mysteries in his craft, which knowledge might be useful in time to come. Little did he suspect who his interrogator was, and freely in his unsuspiciousness he entered upon the subject of slave hunting in the Somali country and Zanzibar, of all things the most interesting to me. I have nothing new to report concerning the present state of bondsmen in Egypt. England has already learned that slaves are not necessarily the most wretched and degraded of men. Some have been bold enough to tell the British public, that, in the generality of Oriental countries,* the serf fares far better than the servant, or indeed than the poorer orders of freemen. "The laws of Mahomet enjoin his followers to treat slaves with the greatest mildness, and the Moslems are in general scrupu-

* In the generality, not in all. Nothing, for instance, can be more disgraceful to human nature than the state of prœdial slavery, or serfs attached to the glebe, when Malabar was under the dominion of the "mild Hindu." And as a rule in the East, it is only the domestic slaves who taste the sweets of slavery. Yet there is truth in Sonnini's terrible remark: "The severe treatment under which the slaves languish in the West Indies is the shameful prerogative of civilization, and is unknown to those nations among whom barbarism is reported to hold sway."

lous observers of the Prophet's recommendation. Slaves are considered members of the family, and in houses where free servants are kept besides, they seldom do any other work than filling the pipes, presenting the coffee, accompanying their master when going out, rubbing his feet when he takes his nap in the afternoon, and driving away the flies from him. When a slave is not satisfied he can legally compel his master to sell him. He has no care for food, lodging, clothes, and washing, and has no taxes to pay; he is exempt from military service and soccage, and in spite of his bondage is freer than the freest Fellah in Egypt."* This is, I believe, a true statement, but of course it in nowise affects the question of slavery in the abstract.

A certain amount of reputation was the consequence of curing the Abyssinian girls: my friend Haji Wali carefully told the news to all the town, and before fifteen days were over I found myself obliged to decline extending a practice which threatened me with fame.

Servants are most troublesome things to all Englishmen in Egypt, but especially to one travelling as a respectable native, and therefore expected to have slaves. After much deliberation I resolved to take a Berberi and accordingly summoned a Shaykh—there is a Shaykh for every thing down to thieves in Asia—and made known my want. The list of *sine qua nons* was necessarily rather an extensive one,—good health and a readiness to travel anywhere, a little skill in cooking, sewing and washing, willingness to fight, and a

* The author has forgotten to mention one of the principal advantages of slaves, namely, the prospect of arriving at the highest rank of the empire. The Pacha of the Syrian caravan with which I travelled to Damascus had been the slave of a slave, and he is but a solitary instance of cases perpetually occurring in all Moslem lands. "*C'est un homme de bonne famille,*" said a Turkish officer in Egypt, "*il a été acheté.*"

habit of regular prayers. After a day's delay the Shaykh brought me a specimen of his choosing, a broad-shouldered, bandy-legged fellow, with the usual bull-dog expression of the Berberis, in his case rendered still more expressive by the drooping of an eyelid—an accident brought about with acrid juice in order to avoid conscription. He responded sturdily to all my questions. Some Egyptian donkey boys and men were making a noise in the room at the time, and the calm ferocity with which he ejected them commanded my approval. When a needle, thread, and an unhemmed napkin were handed to him, he sat down, held the edge of the cloth between his big toe and its neighbor, and finished the work in quite a superior style. Walking out he armed himself with a Kurbaj, which he used, now lightly, then heavily, upon all laden animals, biped and quadruped, that came in the way. His conduct proving equally satisfactory in the kitchen, after getting security from him, and having his name registered by the Shaykh, I closed with him for eighty piastres a month. But Ali the Berberi and I were destined to part. Before a fortnight he stabbed his fellow servant—a Surat lad, who wishing to return home forced his services upon me, and for this trick he received with his dismissal, 400 blows on the feet by order of the Zabit, or police magistrate. After this I tried a number of servants, Egyptians, Saidi, and clean and unclean eating Berberis. Recommended by different Shaykhs all had some fatal defect—one cheated recklessly, another robbed me, a third drank, a fourth was always in scrapes for infringing the Julian edict, and the last, a long-legged Nubian, after remaining two days in the house, dismissed me for expressing a determination to travel by sea from Suez to Yambu. I kept one man; he complained that he was worked to death: two—they did nothing but fight; and three—they left me, as Mr. Elwes said of old, to serve myself. At last thoroughly tired of Egyptian domestics, and one servant being really sufficient for comfort, as well as suitable to my assumed rank, I determined to keep only the Indian boy. He had all the defects of his nation; a brave at Cairo, he was an arrant coward at el Medinah: the Bedouins despised him heartily for his effeminacy in making his camel kneel to dismount, and he could not keep his hands from picking and stealing. But the choice had its advantages: his swarthy skin and chubby features made the Arabs always call him an Abyssinian slave, which, as it favored my disguise, I did not care to contradict; he served well, was amenable to discipline, and, being completely dependent upon me, was therefore less likely to watch and especially to prate about my proceedings. As master and man we performed the pilgrimage together; but, on my return to Egypt after the pilgrimage, Shaykh Nur, finding me to be a Sahib,* changed for the worse. He would not work, and reserved all his energy for the purpose of pilfering, which he practised so audaciously upon my friends, as well as upon myself, that he could not be kept in the house.

Perhaps the reader may be curious to see the necessary expenses of a bachelor residing at Cairo. He must observe, however, in the following list that I was not a strict economist, and, besides that, I was a stranger in the country: inhabitants and old settlers would live as well for little more than two-thirds the sum.

| | Piastres. | Foddthah. |
|---|---|---|
| House rent at 18 piastres per mensem . | 0 | 24 |
| Servant at 80 piastres per do. . | 2 | 26 |

* The generic name given by Indians to English officials.

| | | Piastres. | Foddthah. |
|---|---|---|---|
| Breakfast for self and servant. | 10 eggs | 0 | 5 |
| | Coffee | 0 | 10 |
| | Water melon | 1 | 0 |
| | Two rolls of bread | 0 | 10 |
| Dinner. | 2 lbs. of meat | 2 | 20 |
| | Two rolls of bread | 0 | 10 |
| | Vegetables | 0 | 20 |
| | Rice | 0 | 5 |
| | Oil and clarified butter | 1 | 0 |
| Sundries. | A skin of Nile water | 0 | 0 |
| | Tobacco* | 1 | 0 |
| | Hommam, (hot bath) | 3 | 20 |
| | Total | 13 | 30 |

Equal to about two shillings and ninepence.

* There are four kinds of tobacco smoked in Egypt.

The first and best is the well-known Latakia, generally called "Jebeli," either from a small seaport town about three hours' journey south of Latakia, or more probably because grown on the hills near the ancient Laodicea. Pure, it is known by its blackish color, fine shredding, absence of stalk, and an undescribable odor, to me resembling that of creosote; the leaf, too, is small, so that when made into cigars it must be covered over with a slip of the yellow Turkish tobacco called Bafrah. Except at the highest houses unadulterated Latakia is not to be had in Cairo. Yet, mixed as it is, no other growth exceeds it in flavor and fragrance. Miss Martineau smoked it, we are told, without inconvenience, and it differs from our Shag, Bird's-eye, and Returns in degree, as does Chateau Margaux from a bottle of cheap strong Spanish wine. To bring out its flavor, the connoisseur smokes it in long pipes of cherry, jasmine, maple, or rosewood, and these require a servant skilled in the arts of cleaning and filling them. The best Jebeli at Cairo costs about seven piastres the pound; after which a small sum must be paid to the Farram, or chopper, who prepares it for use.

2nd. Suri (Syrian), or Shami, or Suryani, grown in Syria, an inferior growth, of a lighter color than Latakia, and with a greenish tinge; when cut, its value is about three piastres per pound. Some smokers mix this leaf with Jebeli, which, to my taste, spoils the flavor of the

In these days who at Cairo without a Shaykh? I thought it right to conform to popular custom, and accordingly, after having secured a servant, my efforts were directed to finding a teacher—the pretext being that as an Indian doctor I wanted to read Arabic works on medicine, as well as to perfect myself in divinity and pronunciation.†

latter without improving the former. The strongest kind, called Korani or Jebayl, is generally used for cigarettes; it costs, when of first rate quality, about five piastres per pound.

3rd. Tumbak, or Persian tobacco, called Hejazi, because imported from the Hejaz, where everybody smokes it, and supposed to come from Shiraz, Kazerun, and other celebrated places in Persia. It is all but impossible to buy this article unadulterated, except from the caravans returning after the pilgrimage. The Egyptians mix it with native growths, which ruins its flavor, and gives it an acridity that "catches the throat," whereas good tumbak never yet made a man cough. Yet the taste of this tobacco, even when second-rate, is so fascinating to some smokers that they will use no other. To be used it should be wetted and squeezed, and it is invariably inhaled through water into the lungs: almost every town has its favorite description of pipe, and these are of all kinds, from the pauper's rough cocoa-nut mounted with two reeds, to the prince's golden bowl set with the finest stones. Tumbak is cheap, costing about four piastres a pound, but large quantities of it are used.

4th. Hummi, as the word signifies, a "hot" variety of the tumbak grown in Yemen and other countries. It is placed in the tile on the Buri or cocoa-nut pipe, unwetted, and has a very acrid flavor. Being supposed to produce intoxication, or rather a swimming in the head, hummi gives its votaries a bad name: respectable men would answer "no" with rage if asked whether they are smoking it, and when a fellow tells you that he has seen better days, but that now he smokes hummi in a Buri, you understand him that his misfortunes have affected either his brain or his morality. Hence it is that this tobacco is never put into pipes intended for smoking the other kinds. The price of hummi is about five piastres per pound.

† A study essential to the learned, as in some particular portions of the Koran, a mispronunciation becomes a sin.

My theological studies were in the Shafei school for two reasons: in the first place, it is the least rigorous one of the four orthodox, and secondly, it most resembles the Shiah heresy, with which long intercourse with Persians had made me familiar. My choice of doctrine, however, confirmed those around me in their conviction that I was a rank heretic, for the Ajemi, taught by his religion to conceal offensive tenets, in lands where the open profession would be dangerous, always represents himself to be a Shafei. This, together with the original mistake of appearing publicly at Alexandria as a Mirza in a Persian dress, caused me infinite small anuoyance at Cairo, in spite of all precautions and contrivances. And throughout my journey, even in Arabia, though I drew my knife every time an offensive hint was thrown out, the ill-fame clung to me like the shirt of Nessus.

It was not long before I happened to hit upon a proper teacher, in the person of Shaykh Mohammed el Attar, or the druggist. He had known prosperity, having once been a Khatib (preacher) in one of Mohammed Ali's mosques. But his Highness the late Pasha had dismissed him, which disastrous event, with its subsequent train of misfortunes, he dates from the melancholy day when he took to himself a wife. He talks of her abroad as a stern and rigid master dealing with a naughty slave, though, by the look that accompanies his rhodomontade, I am convinced that at home he is the very model of "managed men." His dismissal was the reason that compelled him to fall back upon the trade of a druggist, the refuge for the once wealthy, though now destitute, sages of Egypt.

His little shop in the Jemeliyah Quarter is a perfect gem of Nilotic queerness. A hole pierced in the wall of some house, about five feet long and six deep, it is divided into two compartments separated by a thin partition of wood, and communicating by a kind of arch cut in the boards. The inner box, germ of a back parlor, acts store-house, as the pile of empty old baskets tossed in dusty confusion upon the dirty floor shows. In the front is displayed the stock in trade, a matting full of Persian tobacco and pipe bowls of red clay, a palm-leaf bag containing vile coffee and large lumps of coarse whity-brown sugar, wrapped up in browner paper. On the shelves and ledges are rows of well-thumbed wooden boxes, labelled with the greatest carelessness, pepper for rhubarb, arsenic for tafl, or wash-clay, and sulphate of iron where sal ammoniac should be. There is also a square case containing under lock and key, small change, and some choice articles of commerce, damaged perfumes, bad antimony for the eyes, and pernicious rouge. And dangling close above it is a rusty pair of scales, ill poised enough for Egyptian justice herself to use. To hooks over the shop-front are suspended reeds for pipes, tallow candles, dirty wax tapers, and cigarette paper; instead of plate-glass windows and brass-handled doors, a ragged net keeps away the flies when the master is in, and the thieves when he goes out to recite in the Hasanayn mosque his daily "Ya Sin."* A wooden shutter which closes down at night-time, and by day two palm-stick stools intensely dirty and full of fleas, occupying the place of the Mastabah,† which accommodated the purchasers, complete the furniture of my preceptor's establishment.

* One of the most esteemed chapters of the Koran, frequently recited as a Wazifah or daily task by religious Moslems in Egypt.

† The Mastabah here is a long earthen bench plastered over with clay, and raised about two feet from the ground, so as to bring the purchaser's head to a level with the shop. Mahommed Ali ordered the people to remove them, as they narrowed the streets: their place is now supplied by "Kafas," cages or stools of wicker-work.

There he sits or rather lies (for verily, I believe he sleeps through three-fourths of the day), a thin old man about fifty-eight, with features once handsome and regular, a sallow face, shaven head, deeply wrinkled cheeks, eyes hopelessly bleared, and a rough grey beard ignorant of oil and comb. His turban, though large, is brown with wear, his coat and small-clothes display many a hole, and though his face and hands must be frequently washed preparatory to devotion, still they have the quality of always looking unclean. It is wonderful how fierce and gruff he is to little boys and girls who flock to him grasping farthings for pepper and sugar. On such occasions I sit admiring to see him, when forced to exertion, wheel about on his place, making a pivot of that portion of our organization which mainly distinguishes our species from the other families of the Simiadæ, to reach some distant drawer, or to pull down a case from its accustomed shelf. How does he manage to say his prayers, to kneel and prostrate himself upon that two feet of ragged rug, scarcely sufficient for a British infant to lie upon? He hopelessly owns that he knows nothing of his craft, and the seats before his shop are seldom occupied. His great pleasure appears to be when the Haji and I sit by him a few minutes in the evening, bringing with us pipes, which he assists us to smoke, and ordering coffee, which he insists upon sweetening with a lump of sugar from his little store. There we make him talk and laugh, and occasionally quote a few lines strongly savoring of the jovial: we provoke him to long stories about the love borne him in his student days by the great and holy Shaykh Abdul Rahman, and the antipathy with which he was regarded by the equally great and holy Shaykh Nasr el Din, his memorable single imprisonment for contumacy, and the temperate but effective lecture, beginning with "O almost entirely destitute of shame!" delivered on that occasion in presence of other under-graduates by the Right Reverend principal of his college. Then we consult him upon matters of doctrine, and quiz him tenderly about his powers of dormition, and flatter him, or rather his age, with such phrases as, "the water from thy hand is of the waters of Zemzem," "we have sought you to deserve the blessings of the wise upon our undertakings." Sometimes, with interested motives it must be owned, we induce him to accompany us to the Hammam,* where he insists upon paying the smallest sum, quarrelling with every thing and every body, and giving the greatest trouble. We are generally his only visitors; acquaintances he appears to have few, and no friends; he must have had them once for he was rich, not so now, so they have fallen away from the poor old man.

When the Shaykh Mohammed sits with me or I climb up into his little shop for the purpose of receiving a lesson from him, he is quite at his ease, reading when he likes, or making me read, and generally beginning each lecture with some such preamble as this:—

"*Aywa! aywa! aywa!*"† even so, even so, even so! "we take refuge with Allah from the stoned fiend! In the name of Allah, the compassionate, the merciful, and the blessings of Allah upon our lord Mahommed, and his

* The Hammam, or hot bath, being a kind of religious establishment, is one of the class of things—so uncomfortably numerous in Eastern countries—left *ala jud'ak,* "to thy generosity." Consequently you are pretty sure to have something disagreeable there, which you would vainly attempt to avoid by liberality. The best way to deal with all such extortioners, with the Lawingi (undresser) of a Cairo Hammam, or the "jarvey" of a London Hansom, is to find out the fare, and never to go beyond it—never to be generous.

† This word is often used to signify simply "yes." It is corrupted from A' w'allah, "yes, by Allah." In pure Arabic "ay" or "I" is synonymous with our "yes" or "ay;" and "Allah" in these countries enters somehow into every other phrase.

family, and his companions one and all! Thus saith the author, may Almighty Allah have mercy upon him! 'Section I, of chapter two, upon the orders of prayer,'" &c.

He becomes fiercely sarcastic when I differ with him in opinion, especially upon a point of the grammar, or the theology over which his beard has grown grey.

"Subhan Allah! Allah be glorified!* What words are these? If thou be right, enlarge thy turban,† and throw away thy drugs, for verily it is better to quicken men's souls than to destroy their bodies, O Abdullah!"

Oriental like, he revels in giving good counsel.

"Thou art always writing, O my brave!" (this is said on the few occasions when I venture to make a note in my book), "what evil habit is this? Surely thou hast learned it in the lands of the Frank. Repent!"

He loathes my giving medical advice gratis.

"Thou hast two servants to feed, O my son! The doctors of Egypt never write A, B, without a reward. Wherefore art thou ashamed? Better go and sit upon the mountains at once, and say thy prayers day and night!"

And finally he is prodigal of preaching upon the subject of household expenses.

"Thy servant did write down 2 lbs. of flesh yesterday! What words are those, O he? Dost thou never say, 'Guard us, Allah, from the sin of extravagance?'"

He delights also in abruptly interrupting a serious subject when it begins to weigh upon his spirits. For instance,

* This is, of course, ironical: "Allah be praised for creating such a prodigy of learning as thou art!"

† The larger the turban, the greater are the individual's pretensions to religious knowledge and respectability of demeanor. This is the custom in Egypt, Turkey, Persia, and many other parts of the Moslem world.

"Now, the waters of ablution being of seven different kinds, it results that——hast thou a wife? No? Then, verily, thou must buy thee a female slave, O youth! This conduct is not right, and men will say of thee——Repentance · I take refuge with Allah*——'of a truth his mouth watereth for the spouses of other Moslems.'"

But sometimes he nods over a difficult passage under my very eyes, or he reads it over a dozen times in the wantonness of idleness, or he takes what school-boys call a long "shot" most shamelessly at the signification. When this happens I lose my temper, and raise my voice, and shout, "Verily there is no power nor might save in Allah, the High, the Great!" Then he looks at me, and with passing meekness whispers—

"Fear Allah, O man!"

* Religious formula used when compelled to mention anything abominable or polluting to the lips of a pious man.

## CHAPTER V.

### THE MOSQUE.

THE Arab mosque is an unconscious revival of the forms used from the earliest ages to denote by symbolism the worship of the generative and the creative gods. The reader will excuse me if I only glance at a subject of which the investigation would require a volume, and which, discussed at greater length, would be out of place in such a narrative as this.

The first mosque in El-Islam was erected by Mohammed Kuba at El Medinah; shortly afterwards, when he entered Meccah as a conqueror, he destroyed the idols of the Arab pantheon, and purified that venerable building of its abominations. He had probably observed in Syria the two forms appropriated by the Christians to their places of worship, the cross and the Basilica; he therefore preferred a square to a parallelogram, some authors say with, others, without a cloister, for the prayers of the "saving faith." At length in the reign of El Walid (about A. H. 90) the cupola, the niche, and the minaret made their appearance, and what is called the Saracenic style became the order of the Moslem world.

From time immemorial, in hot and rainy lands, a hypæthral court surrounded by a covered portico, either circular or square, was used for the double purpose of church and mart,—a place where God and Mammon were worshipped turn by turn. In some places we find rings of stones, like the Persian Pyrœtheia, in others, round concave buildings representing the vault of heaven, where fire, the divine symbol, was worshipped, and in Arabia, columnal aisles, which, surmounted by the splendid blue vault, resemble the palm-grove. The Greeks adopted this area in the fanes of Creator Bacchus; and at Puzzuoli, near Naples, it may be seen in the building vulgarly called the Temple of Serapis. It was equally well known to the Celts; in some places the Temenos was circular, in others a quadrangle. And such to the present day is the mosque of El-Islam.

Even the Riwak or porches surrounding the area in the mosque, are a revival of older forms. "The range of square building which enclose the temple of Serapis are not, properly speaking, parts of the fane, but apartments of the priests, places for victims, and sacred utensils, and chapels dedicated to subordinate deities, introduced by a more complicated and corrupt worship, and probably unknown to the founders of the original edifice." The cloisters in the mosque became cells, used as lecture rooms, and libraries for books bequeathed to the college. They are unequal, because some are required to be of larger, others to be of smaller dimensions. The same reason causes difference of size when the distribution of the building is into four hyposteles which open upon the area; that in the direction of the Kaabah, where worshippers mostly congregate, demanding greater depth than the other three. The wings were not unfrequently made unequal, either from want of building materials, or because the same extent of accommodation was not required in both. The columns were of different substances; some of handsome marble, others of rough stone meanly plastered over with dissimilar capitals, vulgarly cut shafts of various sizes, here with a pediment, there without—now turned upside down, now joined together by halves in the centre, and almost invariably nescient of intercolumnar rule. This is the result of Byzantine syncretism, carelessly and ignorantly grafted upon Arab ideas of the natural and the sublime. Loving and admiring the great, or rather the huge in plan, they care little for the execution of mere details, and they have not the acumen to discern the effect which clumsy workmanship, crooked lines, and visible joints—parts apparently insignificant—exercise upon the whole of an edifice. Their use of colors was a false taste, commonly displayed by mankind in their religious houses, and statues of the gods. The Hindus paint their pagodas inside and outside, and rub vermilion, in token of honor, over their deities. The Persian Colossi of Kaiomars and his consort on the Balkh road, and the Sphynx of Egypt, as well as the temples of the Nile, still show traces of artificial complexion. The fanes in classic Greece, where we might expect a purer taste, have been dyed. In the Forum Romanum, one of the finest buildings still bears stains of the Tyrian purple. And to mention no other instances in the churches and belfries of Modern Italy, we see alternate bands of white and black material so disposed as to give them the appearance of giant zebras. The origin of "Arabesque" must be referred to one of the principles of El-Islam. The Moslem, forbidden by his law to decorate his mosque with statuary and pictures,* supplied their

* That is to say, imitations of the human form. All the doctors of El-Islam, however, differ on this head; some absolutely forbidding any delineation of what has life, under the pain of being cast into hell; others permitting pictures even of the bodies, though not of the faces

place with quotations from the Koran, and inscriptions, "plastic metaphysics," of marvellous perplexity. His alphabet lent itself to the purpose, and hence probably arose that almost inconceivable variety of lacelike fretwork of incrustations, arabesques, and geometric flowers, in which his eye delights to lose itself.

The Meccan mosque became a model to the world of El-Islam, and the nations that embraced the new faith copied the consecrated building, as religiously as Christendom produced imitations of the Holy Sepulchre.* The mosque of Omar at Jerusalem, of Amr at Babylon on the Nile, and Taylun at Cairo, were erected with some trifling improvements, such as the arched cloisters and inscribed cornices, upon the plan of the Kaabah. From Egypt and Palestine the ichnography spread far and wide. It was modified, as might be expected, by national taste. What in Arabia was simple and elegant, became highly ornate in Spain, florid in Turkey, and effeminate in India. Still divergence of detail had not, even after the lapse of twelve centuries, materially altered the fundamental form.

Perhaps no Eastern city affords more numerous or more accessible specimens of mosque architecture than Cairo. Between 300 and 400 places of worship, some stately piles, others ruinous hovels, many new, more decaying and earthquake shaken, with minarets that rival in obliquity the

of men. Other nations are comparatively lax. The Alhambra abounds in paintings and frescoes. The Persians never object to depict in books and on walls the battles of Rustam, and the Turks preserve in the Seraglio treasury of Constantinople portraits, by Greek and other artists, of their Sultans in regular succession.

* At Bruges, Bologna (St. Stefano), and Nuremberg, there are imitations of the Holy Sepulchre. The Nuremberg church was built by a merchant, who travelled three times to Palestine in order to ensure correctness, and totally failed.

Pisan monster, are open to the traveller's inspection. And Europeans by following the advice of their hotel-keeper, have penetrated, and can penetrate into any one they please.*

The Jama Taylun is simple and massive, yet elegant, and in some of its details peculiar. One of the four colonnades still remains to show the original magnificence of the building; the other porches are walled in, and inhabited by paupers.

In the centre of a quadrangle about one hundred paces square is a domed building springing from a square which occupies the proper place of the Kaabah. This "Jama †" is interesting as a point of comparison. If it be an exact copy of the Meccan temple, as it stood in A. D. 879, it shows that the latter has greatly altered in this our modern days.

Next in date to the Taylun Mosque is that of the Sultan El Hakim, third Caliph of the Fatimites. The minarets are remarkable in shape, as well as size: they are unprovided with the usual outer gallery, are based upon a cube of masonry, and pierced above with apertures apparently meaningless. A learned Cairene informed me that these spires were devised by the eccentric monarch to disperse, like large censers, fragrant smoke over the city during the hours of prayer. The Azhar and Hasanayn Mosques are celebrated for sanctity, but remarkable for nothing save ugliness. Few buildings, however, give a nobler idea of both founder and architect than that which bears Sultan

* In Niebuhr's time, a Christian passing one of the very holy buildings on foot, was liable to be seized and circumcised. All mosques may now be entered with certain precautions.

† A "jama" is a place where people assemble to pray—a house of public worship. "A masjid" is any place of prayer, private or public. From "masjid" we derive our "mosque."

Hasan's name. The stranger stands almost awe-struck before walls high towering without a single break, a hypæthral court, severe in masculine beauty, a gateway that might suit the palace of the Titans, and the massive grandeur of its lofty minaret. This mosque, with its fortress aspect, owns no more relationship to the efforts of a later age than does Canterbury Cathedral to an Anglo-Indian "Gothic." For dignified elegance and refined taste, the mosque and tomb of Kaid Bey and the other Mameluke kings are admirable. Even in their present state beauty presides over decay, and the traveller has seldom seen aught more striking than the rich light of the stained glass pouring through the first shades of evening upon the marble floor.

We will now enter the El Azhar mosque. At the dwarf wooden railings we take off our slippers, hold them in the left hand, sole to sole, that no dirt may fall from them, and cross the threshold with the right foot, ejaculating Bismillah, &c. Next we repair to the Meyzaah, or large tank, for ablution, without which it is scarcely lawful to appear in the house of Allah. We then seek some proper place for devotion, place our slippers on some other object in front of us to warn the lounger, and perform a prayer of two prostrations in honor of the mosque. This done, we may wander about, and consider the several objects of curiosity.

The moon shines splendidly upon a vast hypæthral court, paved with stones which are polished like glass by the feet of the Faithful. There is darkness in the body of the building, a large parallelogrammic hall, at least twice too long for its height, supported by a forest of pillars, thin, poor-looking crooked marble columns, planted avenue-like, and lined with torn and dirty matting. A few oil lamps shed doubtful light upon scanty groups, who are debating some point of grammar, or listening to the words of wisdom that fall from the mouth of a Waiz.* Presently they will leave the hypostyle, and throw themselves upon the flags of the quadrangle, where they may enjoy the open air, and avoid some fleas. It is now "long vacation:" so the holy building has become a kind of caravanserai for travellers; perhaps a score of nations meet in it; there is a confusion of tongues, and the din at times is deafening. Around the court runs a tolerably well-built colonnade, whose entablature is garnished with crimson arabesques, and in the inner wall are pierced apartments, now closed with plank doors. Of the Riwaks, as they are called, the Azhar contains twenty-four, one for each recognised nation in El-Islam, and of these, fifteen are still open to students. Inside them we find nothing but matting, and a pile of large dingy wooden boxes, which once contained the college library, but are now, generally speaking, empty.†

The Azhar is the grand collegiate mosque of this city,— once celebrated throughout the world of El-Islam. It was built, I was told, originally in poor style by one Jauhar, the slave of a Moorish merchant, in consequence of a dream

* An "adviser," or "lecturer,"—any learned man who delivers a discourse upon the principles of El-Islam.

† Cairo was once celebrated for its magnificent collections of books. Besides private libraries, each large mosque had its bibliotheca. But Cairo has now for years supplied other countries with books, and the decay of religious zeal has encouraged the unprincipled to steal and sell MSS. Cairo has still some large libraries, but most of them are private property, and the proprietors will not readily lend or give access to their treasures. The principal opportunity of buying books is during the month Ramazan, when they are publicly sold in the Azhar mosque. The Orientalist will, however, meet with many disappointments; besides the difficulty of discovering good works, he will find in the booksellers, scribes, *et hoc genus omne*, a finished race of scoundrels.

that ordered him to "erect a place whence the light of science should shine upon El-Islam."

It gradually increased by "Wakf"* of lands, money, and books. Of late years it has considerably declined, the result of sequestrations, and of the diminished esteem in which the purely religious sciences are now held in the land of Egypt. Yet it is calculated that between 2000 and 3000 students of all nations and ages receive instruction here gratis. Each one is provided with bread, in a quantity varying with the amount of endowment in the Riwak set apart for his nation, with some article of clothing on festival days, and a few piastres once a year. The professors, who are about 150 in number, may not take fees from their pupils; some lecture on account of the religious merit of the action, others to gain the high title of "Teacher in El Azhar."

The following is the course of study in the Azhar. The school-boy of four or five years' standing has been taught, by a liberal application of the maxim, "the green rod is of the trees of Paradise," to chaunt the Koran without understanding it, the elementary rules of arithmetic, and, if he is destined to be a learned man, the art of writing. He then registers his name in El Azhar, and applies himself to the branches of study most cultivated in El-Islam, namely Nahw (syntax), Fikh (divinity), Hadis (the traditions of the Prophet), and Tafsir, or exposition of the Koran.

The young Egyptian reads at the same time the Sarf, or the Grammar of the Verb, and El Nahw, or the Grammar and Syntax of the Noun. But as Arabic is his mother-tongue, he is not required to study the former so deeply as are the Turks, the Persians, and the Indians. If he desire,

* An "entailed bequest."

however, to be a proficient, he must carefully peruse five books in El Sarf*, and six in El Nahw.†

Master of grammar, our student now applies himself to its proper end and purpose, Divinity. Of the four schools, those of Abu Hanifah and El Shafei are most common in Cairo; the followers of Ibn Malik abound only in Southern Egypt and the Berberah country, and the Hanbali is almost unknown. The theologian begins with what is called a Matn or text, a short, dry, and often obscure treatise, a mere string of precepts; in fact, the skeleton of the subject. This he learns by repeated perusal, till he can quote almost every passage literally. He then passes to its "Sharh," or commentary, generally the work of some other savant, who explains the difficulty of the text, amplifies its Laconicisms, enters into exceptional cases, and deals with principles and reasons, as well as with mere precept.

In order to become a Fakih, or divine of distinguished fame, the follower of Abu Hanifah must peruse about ten

* The popular volumes are, 1. El Amsilah, showing the simple conjugation of the triliteral verb; 2. Bisia, the work of some unknown author, explaining the formation of the verb into increased infinities, the quadrilateral verb, &c.; 3. The Maksua, a well-known book written by the great Imam Abu' Hanifah; 4. The "Izzi," an explanatory treatise, the work of a Turk, "Izzah Effendi." And lastly, the Marah of Ahmed el Saudi. These five tracts are bound together in a little volume, printed at the government establishment.

El Amsilah is explained in Turkish, to teach boys the art of "parsing:" Egyptians generally confine themselves in El Sarf to the Izzi, and the Lamiyat el Afal of the grammarian Ibn Malik.

† First, the well-known "Ajrumiyah" (printed by M. Vaucelle), and its commentary, El Kafrawi. Thirdly, the Alfiyyah (Thousand Distichs) of Ibn Malik, written in verse for mnemonic purposes, but thereby rendered so difficult as to require the lengthy commentary of El Ashmumi. The fifth is the well-known work called the Katr el Nidu (the Dew Drop), celebrated from Cairo to Cabul; and last of all the "Azhari."

volumes, some of huge size, written in a diffuse style: the Shafei's reading is not quite so extensive. Theology is much studied, because it leads directly to the gaining of daily bread, as priest or tutor; and other scientific pursuits are neglected for the opposite reason.

The theologian in Egypt, as in other parts of El Islam, must have a superficial knowledge of the Prophet's traditions. Of these there are eight well known collections, but the three first only are those generally read.

School-boys are instructed, almost when in their infancy, to intone the Koran; at the university they are taught a more exact system of chaunting. The style called "Hafs" is most common in Egypt, as it is indeed throughout the Moslem world. And after learning to read the holy volume, some savans are ambitious enough to wish to understand it: under these circumstances they must dive into the exposition of the Koran.

Our student is now a perfect Fakih or Mulla. But the poor fellow has no scholarship or fellowship—no easy tutorship—no fat living to look forward to. After wasting seven years, or twice seven years, over his studies, and reading till his brain is dizzy, his digestion gone, and his eyes half blind, he must either starve upon college alms, or squat, like my old Shaykh Mohammed, in a druggist's shop, or become pedagogue and curate in some country place, on the pay of 8*l.* per annum. With such prospects it is wonderful how the Azhar can present any attractions; but the southern man is essentially an idler, and many become Olema, like Capuchins, in order to do nothing. A favored few rise to the degree of Mudarris (professors), and thence become Kazis and Muftis. This is another inducement to matriculate; every undergraduate having an eye upon the Wazi-ship, with as much chance of obtaining it as the country *paroco* has to become a cardinal. Others again devote themselves to laical pursuits, degenerate into Wakils (lawyers), or seek their fortunes as Katibs—public or private accountants.*

To conclude this part of the subject, I cannot agree with Dr. Bowring when he harshly says, upon the subject of Moslem education: "The instruction given by the Doctors of the law in the religious schools, for the formation of the Mohammedan priesthood, is of the most worthless character." His opinion is equally open to objection with that of those who depreciate the law itself because it deals rather in precepts than in principle, in ceremonies and ordinances, rather than in ethics and æsthetics. Both are what Eastern faiths and Eastern training have ever been,—both are eminently adapted for the child-like state of the Oriental mind. When the people learn to appreciate ethics, and to understand psychics and æsthetics, the demand will create a supply. Meanwhile they leave transcendentalism to their poets, and busy themselves with preparing for heaven by practising the only part of their faith now intelligible to them—the material.

It is not to be supposed that a people in this stage of civilization could be so fervently devout as the Egyptians are without the bad leaven of bigotry. The same tongue which is employed in blessing the Almighty, is, it is conceived, doing its work equally well in cursing his enemies.

* As a specimen of the state of periodical literature in Egypt, I may quote the history of the "Bulak Independent," as Europeans facetiously call it. When Mohammed Ali, determining to have an "organ," directed an officer to be editor of a weekly paper, the officer replied, that no one would read it, and consequently that no one would pay for it. The Pacha remedied this by an order that a subscription should be struck off from the pay of all employees, European and Egyptian, whose salary amounted to a certain sum. Upon which the editor accepted the task, but being paid before his work was published, he of course never supplied his subscribers with their copies.

Wherefore the Kafir is denounced by every sex, age, class, and condition, by the man of the world, as by the boy at the school, out of, as well as in, the mosque. If you ask your friend who is the person with a black turban, he replies,

"A Christian. Allah make his countenance cold!"

If you inquire of your servant, who are the people singing in the next house, it is ten to one that his answer will be,

"A Jew. May his lot be Jehannum!"

It appears unintelligible, still it is not less true, that Egyptians who have lived as servants under European roofs for years, retain the liveliest loathing for the manners and customs of their masters. Few Franks, save those who have mixed with the Egyptians in Oriental disguise, are aware of their repugnance to, and contempt for, Europeans—so well is the feeling veiled under the garb of innate politeness, and so great is their reserve, when conversing with those of strange religions. I had a good opportunity of ascertaining the truth when the first rumor of a Russian war arose. Almost every able-bodied man spoke of hastening to the Jihan,* and the only thing that looked like apprehension was the too eager depreciation of their foes. All seemed delighted at the idea of French co-operation, for, somehow or other, the Frenchman is everywhere popular. When speaking of England, they were not equally easy: heads were rolled, pious sentences were ejaculated, and finally out came the old Eastern cry, "Of a truth they are Shaitans, those English." The Austrians are despised, because the East knows nothing of them since the days of Osmanlee hosts threatened the gates of Vienna. The Greeks are hated as clever scoundrels,

* A crusade, a holy war.

ever ready to do El-Islam a mischief. The Maltese, the greatest of cowards off their own ground, are regarded with a profound contempt: these are the protégés which bring the British nation into disrepute at Cairo. And Italians are known only as "*istruttori*" and "*distruttori*"—doctors, druggists, and pedagogues.

Yet Egyptian human nature is, like human nature everywhere, contradictory. Hating and despising Europeans, they still long for European rule. This people admire an iron-handed and lion-hearted despotism; they hate a timid and grinding tyranny.

## CHAPTER VI.

### PREPARATIONS TO QUIT CAIRO.

Besides patients I had made some pleasant acquaintances at Cairo. Anton Zananire, a young Syrian of considerable attainments as a linguist, paid me the compliment of permitting me to see the fair face of his "Hareem." Mr. Hatchadoor Noory, an Armenian gentleman, well known in Bombay, amongst other acts of kindness, introduced me to one of his compatriots, Khwayah Yusuf, whose advice, as an old traveller, was most useful to me. He had wandered far and wide, picking up everywhere some scrap of strange knowledge, and his history was a romance. Expelled for a youthful peccadillo from Cairo, he started upon his travels, qualified himself for sanctity at Meccah and El Medinah, became a religious beggar at Bagdad, studied French at Paris, and finally settled down as a professor of languages, under an amnesty, at Cairo. In his house I saw an Armenian marriage. The occasion was a memorable one: after the gloom and sameness of Moslem society, nothing could be more gladdening than the unveiled face of a pretty woman. Some of the guests were undeniably charming brunettes, with the blackest possible locks, and the brightest conceivable eyes; only one pretty girl wore the national costume;* yet they all smoked chibouques and sat upon the divans, and as they entered the room, with a sweet simplicity, kissed the hands of the priest, and of the other old gentlemen present.

Among the number of my acquaintances was a Meccan boy, Mohammed El Basyuni, from whom I bought the pilgrim-garb called "El-ihram" and the Kafan or shroud, with which the Moslem usually starts upon such a journey as mine was. He, being on his way homewards after a visit to Constantinople, was most anxious to accompany me in the character of a "companion." But he had travelled too much to suit me; he had visited India, seen Englishmen, and lived with the "Nawwab Baloo" of Surat. Moreover, he showed signs of over-wisdom. He had been a regular visitor, till I cured one of his friends of an ophthalmia, after which he gave me his address at Meccah, and was seen no more. Haji Wali described him and his party to be "Nas jarrár" (extractors) and certainly he had not misjudged them. But the sequel will prove how Providence disposes of what man proposes, and as the boy, Mohammed, eventually did become my companion throughout the pilgrimage, I will place him before the reader as summarily as possible.

He is a beardless youth, of about eighteen, chocolate brown, with high features, and a bold profile; his bony and decided Meccan cast of face is lit up by the peculiar Egyptian eye, which seems to descend from generation to

* It has been too frequently treated of, to leave room for a fresh description. Though pretty and picturesque, it is open to the reproach of Moslem dressing, namely, that the in-door toilette admits of a display of bust, and is generally so scanty and flimsy that it is unfit to meet the eye of a stranger. This, probably the effect of secluding women, has now become a cause for concealing them.

generation. His figure was short and broad, with a tendency to be obese, the result of a strong stomach and the power of sleeping at discretion. He could read a little, write his name, and was uncommonly clever at a bargain. Meccah had taught him to speak excellent Arabic, to understand the literary dialect, to be eloquent in abuse, and to be profound at prayer and pilgrimage. Constantinople had given him a taste for Anacreontic singing, and female society of the questionable kind, a love of strong waters,—the hypocrite looked positively scandalised when I first suggested the subject,—and an off-hand latitudinarian mode of dealing with serious subjects in general. I found him to be the youngest son of a widow, whose doting fondness had moulded his disposition; he was selfish and affectionate, as spoiled children usually are, volatile, easily offended, and as easily pacified (the Oriental), coveting other men's goods, and profuse of his own (the Arab), with a matchless intrepidity of countenance (the traveller), brazen lunged, not more than half brave, exceedingly astute, with an acute sense of honor, especially where his relations were concerned (the individual). I have seen him in a fit of fury because some one cursed his father; and he and I nearly parted because on one occasion I applied to him an epithet which, etymologically considered, might be exceedingly insulting to a high-minded brother, but which in popular *parlance* signifies nothing. This "*point d'honneur*" was the boy Mohammed's strong point.

During my residence in Cairo I laid in my stores for the journey. These consisted of tea, coffee, rice, loaf-sugar, dates, oil, vinegar, tobacco, lanterns, and cooking utensils, a small bell-shaped tent, costing twelve shillings, and three water skins for the desert. The provisions were placed in a "Kafas" or hamper artistically made of palm sticks, and in a huge Sahharah, or wooden box, about three feet each way, covered with leather or skin, and provided with a small lid fitting into the top. The former, together with my green box containing medicines, and saddle-bags full of clothes, hung on one side of the camel, a counterpoise to the big Sahharah on the other flank, Bedouins always requiring a tolerably equal balance of weight. On the top of the load transversely was placed a Shibriyah or cot, in which Shaykh Nur squatted like a large crow. This worthy had strutted out into the streets armed with a pair of horse-pistols and a sword almost as long as himself. No sooner did the mischievous boys of Cairo—they are as bad as the *gamins* of Paris and London—catch sight of him than they began to scream with laughter at the sight of the "Hindi (Indian) in arms," till like a vagrant owl pursued by a flight of larks he ran back into the caravanserai.

Having spent all my ready money at Cairo I was obliged to renew the supply. My native friends advised me to take at least eighty pounds, and considering the expense of outfit for desert travelling, the sum did not appear excessive. I should have found some difficulty in raising the money had it not been for the kindness of a friend at Alexandria and a compatriot at Cairo. My Indians scrutinised the diminutive square paper*—my letter of credit—as a raven

* At my final interview with the committee of the Royal Geographical Society, one member advised an order to be made out on the Society's bankers; another, kindly offered to give me one on his own, Coutts, &c.; but I, having more experience in Oriental travelling, begged only to be furnished with a most diminutive piece of paper permitting me to draw upon the Society, which was at once given by Dr. Shaw, the Secretary, and which proved of so much use eventually.

It was purposely made as small as possible, in order to fit into a talisman case. But the traveller must bear in mind, that if his letters of credit be addressed to Orientals, the sheet of paper should always be large, and grand-looking. These people have no faith in notes,—commercial, epistolary, or diplomatic.

may sometimes be seen peering, with head askance, into the interior of a suspected marrow-bone. "Can this be a *bonâ fide* draft?" they mentally inquired. And finally they offered, most politely, to write to England for me to draw the money, and to forward it in a sealed bag directed "El Medinah." I need scarcely say that such a style of transmission would, in the case of precious metals, have left no possible chance of its safe arrival. When the difficulty was overcome, I bought fifty pounds worth of German dollars, and invested the rest in English and Turkish sovereigns. The gold I myself carried; part of the silver I sewed up in Shaykh Nur's leather waistbelt, and part was packed in the boxes, for this reason,—when Bedouins begin plundering a respectable man, if they find a certain amount of ready money in his baggage, they do not search his person. If they find none they proceed to a personal inspection, and if his waist-belt be empty they are rather disposed to rip open his stomach, in the belief that he must have discovered some peculiarly ingenious way of secreting valuables. Having got through this difficulty I immediately fell into another. My hardly-earned Alexandrian passport required a double viza, one at the Zabit's office, the other at the consul's. After returning to Egypt I found it was the practice of travellers who required any civility from the English official at Cairo to enter the presence furnished with an order from the Foreign Office.

I had neglected the precaution, and had ample reason to regret having done so. Failing at the British consulate, and unwilling to leave Cairo without being "*en règle*,"—the Egyptians warned me that Suez was a place of obstacles to pilgrims—I was obliged to look elsewhere for protection. My friend Haji Wali was the first consulted: after a long discussion he offered to take me to his consul, the Persian, and to find out for what sum I could become a temporary subject of the Shah. We went to the sign of the "Lion and the Sun," and found the dragoman, a subtle Syrian Christian, who, after a rigid inquiry into the state of my purse (my country was no consideration at all), introduced me to the Great Man. I have described this personage once already, and truly he merits not a second notice. The interview was a ludicrous one. He treated us with exceeding *hauteur*, motioned me to sit almost out of hearing, and after rolling his head in profound silence for nearly a quarter of an hour, vouchsafed the information that though my father *might* be a Shirazi, and my mother an Afghan, he had not the honor of my acquaintance. His companion, a large old Persian with Polyphemean eyebrows and a mulberry beard, put some gruff and discouraging questions. So I quoted the verses

> "He is a man who benefits his fellow men,
> Not he who says 'why,' and 'wherefore,' and 'how much?'"

upon which an imperious wave of the arm directed me to return to the dragoman, who had the effrontery to ask me four pounds sterling for a Persian passport. I offered one. He derided my offer, and I went away perplexed. On my return to Cairo some months afterwards, he sent to say that had he known me as an Englishman, I should have had the document gratis,—a civility for which he was duly thanked.

At last my Shaykh Mohammed hit upon *the* plan. "Thou art," said he, "an Afghan, I will fetch hither the principal of the Afghan college at the Azahar, and he, if thou make it worth his while" (this in a whisper) "will be thy friend." The case was looking desperate; my preceptor was urged to lose no time.

Presently Shaykh Mohammed returned in company with the principal, a little, thin, ragged-bearded, one-eyed, hare-lipped divine, dressed in very dirty clothes, of nondescript cut. Born at Muscat of Afghan parents, and brought up at Meccah, he was a kind of cosmopolite, speaking five languages fluently, and full of reminiscences of toil and travel. He refused pipes and coffee, professing to be ascetically disposed: but he ate more than half my dinner, to reassure me I presume, should I have been fearful that abstinence might injure his health. We then chatted in sundry tongues. I offered certain presents of books, which were rejected (such articles being valueless), and the Shaykh Abd el Wahhab having expressed his satisfaction at my account of myself, told me to call for him at the Azhar mosque next morning.

Accordingly at six A.M. Shaykh Mohammed and Abdullah Khan,*—the latter equipped in a gigantic sprigged-muslin turban, so as to pass for a student of theology—repaired to El Azhar. Passing through the open quadrangle we entered the large hall which forms the body of the mosque. In the northern wall was a dwarf door, leading by breakneck stairs to a pigeon-hole, the study of the learned Afghan Shaykh. We found him ensconced behind piles of musty and greasy manuscripts, surrounded by scholars and scribes, with whom he was cheapening books. He had not much business to transact; but long before he was ready, the stifling atmosphere drove us out of the study, and we repaired to the hall. Presently the Shaykh joined us, and we all rode on away to the citadel, and waited in a mosque till the office hour struck. When the doors were opened we went into the "divan," and sat patiently till the Shaykh found an opportunity of putting in a word. The officials were two in number; one an old invalid, very thin and sickly-looking,

* Khan is a title assumed in India and other countries by all Afghans, and Pathans, their descendants, simple as well as gentle.

dressed in the Turco-European style, whose hand was being severely kissed by a troop of religious beggars, to whom he had done some small favors; the other was a stout young clerk, whose duty it was to engross, and not to have his hand kissed.

My name and other essentials were required, and no objections were offered, for who holier than the Shaykh Abd el Wahhab ibn Yunus el Sulaymani? The clerk filled up a paper in the Turkish language, apparently borrowed from the European method for spoiling the traveller, certified me, upon the Shaykh's security, to be one Abdullah, the son of Yusuf (Joseph), originally from Cabool, described my person, and in exchange for five piastres handed me the document. I received it with joy, and still keep it as a trophy.

With bows, and benedictions, and many wishes that Allah might make it the officials' fate to become pilgrims, we left the office, and returned towards El Azhar. When we had nearly reached the mosque, Shaykh Mohammed lagged behind, and made the sign. I drew near the Afghan, and asked for his hand. He took the hint, and muttering "it is no matter!"—"it is not necessary—"by Allah it is not required!" extended his fingers, and brought the musculus "*guineorum*" to bear upon three dollars.

Poor man! I believe it was his necessity that consented to be paid for the doing a common act of Moslem charity; he had a wife and children, and the calling of an Alim * is no longer worth much in Egypt.

I wasted but little time in taking leave of my friends, telling them by way of precaution, that my destination was Meccah *viâ* Jeddah, and firmly determining, if possible, to make El Medinah *via* Yambu. "Conceal," says the Arabic proverb, "thy tenets, thy treasure, and thy travelling."

* A theologian, a learned man.

## CHAPTER VII.

### FROM CAIRO TO SUEZ.

SHAYKH Nassar, a Bedouin of Tur (Mount Sinai), being on his way homewards, agreed to let me have two dromedaries for the sum of 50 piastres, or about ten shillings each. Being desirous to start with a certain display of respectability, I accepted these terms: a man of humble pretensions would have travelled with a single animal, and a camel-man running behind him. But, besides ostentation, I wanted my attendant to be mounted, that we might make a forced march in order to ascertain how much a four years' life of European effeminacy had impaired my powers of endurance. The reader may believe the assertion that there are few better tests than an eighty-four mile ride in midsummer, on a bad wooden saddle, borne by a worse dromedary, across a desert.

I started my Indian boy and heavy luggage for Suez two days before the end of the Eed,—laden camels generally taking fifty-five or sixty hours to do the journey, and I spent the intermediate time with Haji Wali. He advised me to mount about 3 P. M., so that I might arrive at Suez on the evening of the next day, and assisted me in making due preparations of water, provisions, tobacco, and a bed for the road. Early on the morning of departure the Afghan Shaykh came to the caravanserai, and breakfasted with us, "because Allah willed it." After a copious meal he bestowed upon me a stately benediction, and would have embraced me, but I humbly kissed his hand: sad to relate, immediately that his back was turned, Haji Wali raised his forefinger to a right angle with the palm, and burst into a shout of irreverent laughter. At 3 o'clock Nassar, the Bedouin, came to announce that the dromedaries were saddled. I dressed myself, sticking a pistol in my belt, and passing the crimson silk cord of the hamail or pocket Koran over my shoulder, in token of being a pilgrim—distributing a few trifling presents to friends and servants, and accompanied by the Shaykh Mohammed, and Haji Wali, descended the stairs with an important gait. In the court-yard sat the camels, (dromedaries they could not be called,) and I found that a second driver was going to accompany us. I objected to this, as the extra Bedouin would, of course, expect to be fed by me; but Nassar swore the man was his brother, and, as you rarely gain by small disputes with these people, he was allowed to have his own way.

Then came the preparatory leave-takings. Haji Wali embraced me heartily, and so did my poor old Shaykh, who, despite his decrepitude and my objections, insisted upon accompanying me to the city gate. I mounted the camel, crossed my legs before the pommel—stirrups are not used in Egypt—and, preceding my friend, descended the street leading towards the dessert. As we emerged from the huge gateway of the caravanserai all the bystanders exclaimed, "Allah bless thee, Y'al Hajj,* and restore thee to

* "O pilgrim!"

thy country and thy friends!" And passing through the Bab el Nasr, where I addressed the salutation of peace to the sentry, and to the officer commanding the guard, both gave me God-speed with great cordiality—the pilgrim's blessing in Asia, like the old woman's in Europe, being supposed to possess peculiar efficacy. Outside the gate my friends took a final leave of me, and I will not deny having felt a tightening of heart as their honest faces and forms faded in the distance.

But Shaykh Nassar switches his camel's shoulder, and appears inclined to take the lead. This is a trial of manliness. There is no time for emotion. Not a moment can be spared, even for a retrospect. I kick my dromedary, who steps out into a jog-trot. The Bedouins with a loud ringing laugh attempt to give me the go-by. I resist, and we continue like children till the camels are at their speed, though we have eighty-four miles before us, and above an atmosphere like a furnace blast. The road is deserted at this hour, otherwise grave Moslem travellers would have believed the police to be nearer than convenient to us.

Presently we drew rein, and exchanged our pace for one more seasonable, whilst the sun began to tell on man and beast. High raised as we were above the ground, the reflected heat struck us sensibly, and the glare of a macadamized road added a few extra degrees of caloric.* The

* It is Prince Puckler Muskau, if I recollect rightly, who mentions that in his case a pair of dark spectacles produced a marked difference of apparent temperature, whilst travelling over the sultry sand of the desert. I have often remarked the same phenomenon. The Arabs, doubtless for some reason of the kind, always draw their head-kerchiefs, like hoods, far over their brows, and cover up their mouths, even when the sun and wind are behind them. Inhabitants of the desert are to be recognised by the net-work of wrinkles traced in the skin round the

Bedouins, to refresh themselves, prepare to smoke. They fill my chibouque, light it with a flint and steel, and cotton dipped in a solution of gunpowder, and pass it over to me.* After a few puffs I return it to them, and they smoke it turn by turn. Then they begin to while away the tedium of the road by asking questions, which *passe-temps* is not easily exhausted; for they are never satisfied till they know as much of you as you do of yourself. They next resort to talking about victuals, for with this hungry race of Bedouins, food, as a topic of conversation, takes the place of money in more civilised lands. And lastly, even this engrossing subject being exhausted for the moment, they take refuge in singing; and, monotonous and droning as it is, their song has yet an artless plaintiveness, which admirably suits the singer and the scenery. If you listen to the words, you will surely hear allusions to bright verdure, cool shades, bubbling rills, or something which hereabouts man hath not, and yet which his soul desires.

And now, while Nassar and his brother are chanting a duet, the refrain being,

> "W'al arzu mablul bi matar,"
> "And the earth was wet with rain,"

I must crave leave to say a few words, despite the trite-

orbits, the result of half-closing their eyelids; but this is done to temper the intensity of the light.

* Their own pipe-tubes were of coarse wood, in shape somewhat resembling the German pipe. The bowl was of soft stone, apparently steatite, which, when fresh, is easily fashioned with a knife. In Arabia the Bedouins, and even the towns-people, use on journeys an earthen tube from five to six inches shorter than the English "clay," thicker in the tube, with a large bowl, and colored yellowish-red. It contains a handful of tobacco, and the smoker emits puffs like a chimney. In some of these articles the bowl forms a rectangle with the tube; in others, the whole is an unbroken curve, like the old Turkish Meerschaum.

ness of the subject, about the modern Sinaitic race of Arabs.

A wonderful change has taken place in the Bedouin tribes. Niebuhr notes the trouble they gave him, and their perpetual hankering for both murder and pillage. Even in the late Mohammed Ali's early reign, no governor of Suez dared to flog, or to lay hands upon a Turi, whatever offence he might have committed within the walls of the town. Now the wild man's sword is taken from him before he is allowed to enter the gates, and my old acquaintance, Giaffar Bey, would think no more of belaboring a Bedouin than of flogging a Fellah.* Such is the result of Mohammed Ali's rigorous policy.

The most good-humored and sociable of men, they delight in a jest, and may readily be managed by kindness and courtesy. Yet they are passionate, nice upon points of honor, revengeful, and easily offended, where their peculiar prejudices are misunderstood. Those travellers who complain of their insolence and extortion may have been

* In the mouth of a Turk, no epithet is more contemptuous than that of "Fellah ibn Fellah"—"boor, son of a boor!" The Osmanlis have, as usual, a semi-religious tradition to account for the superiority of their nation over the Egyptians. When the learned doctor, Abu Abdullah Mohammed ben Idris el Shafei, returned from Mecca to the banks of the Nile, he mounted, it is said, a donkey belonging to one of the *Asinarii* of Bulak. Arriving at the caravanserai, he gave the man ample fare, whereupon the Egyptian putting forth his hand, and saying "haat," called for more. The doctor doubled the fee; still the double was demanded. At last the divine's purse was exhausted, and the proprietor of the donkey waxed insolent. A wandering Turk seeing this, took all the money from the Egyptian, paid him his due, solemnly kicked him, and returned the rest to El Shafei, who asked him his name—"Osman"—and his nation—the "Osmanli"—blessed him, and prophesied to his countrymen supremacy over the Fellahs and donkey boys of Egypt.

either ignorant of their language, or offensive to them by assumption of superiority—in the Desert man meets man—or physically unfitted to acquire their esteem.

We journeyed on till near sunset through the wilderness without ennui. It is strange how the mind can be amused amid scenery that presents so few objects to occupy it. But in such a country every slight modification of form or color rivets observation: the senses are sharpened, and perceptive faculties, prone to sleep over a confused shifting of scenery, act vigorously when excited by the capability of embracing each detail. Moreover, desert views are eminently suggestive; they appeal to the future, not to the past; they arouse because they are by no means memorial. To the solitary wayfarer there is an interest in the wilderness unknown to Cape seas and Alpine glaciers, and even to the rolling prairie—the effect of continued excitement on the mind, stimulating its powers to their pitch. Above, through a sky terrible in its stainless beauty, and the splendors of a pitiless blinding glare, the Simoom caresses you like a lion with flaming breath. Around lie drifted sand heaps, upon which each puff of wind leaves its own trace in solid waves, flayed rocks, the very skeletons of mountains, and hard unbroken plains, over which he who rides is spurred by the idea, that the bursting of a water skin, or the pricking of a camel's hoof, would be a certain death of torture—a haggard land, infested with wild beasts, and wilder men—a region whose very fountains murmur the warning words, "Drink and away!" What can be more exciting? what more sublime? Man's heart bounds in his breast at the thought of measuring his puny force with nature's might, and of emerging triumphant from the trial. This explains the Arab's proverb, "Voyaging is a victory." In the desert even more than upon the ocean, there is present death:

hardship is there, and piracies, and shipwreck—solitary, not in crowds, where, as the Persians say, "Death is a festival"—and this sense of danger, never absent, invests the scene of travel with an interest not its own.

Let the traveller who suspects exaggeration leave the Suez road for an hour or two, and gallop northwards over the sands: in the drear silence, the solitude, and the fantastic desolation of the place, he will feel what the Desert may be.

And then the Oases,* and little lines of fertility—how soft and how beautiful!—even though the Wady El Ward (the Vale of Flowers) be the name of some stern flat upon which a handful of wild shrubs blossom while struggling through a cold season's ephemeral existence. In such circumstances the mind is influenced through the body. Though your mouth glows, and your skin is parched, yet you feel no languor, the effect of humid heat; your lungs

* Nothing can be more incorrect than the vulgar idea of an Arabian Oasis, except it be the popular conception of an Arabian desert. One reads of "isles of the sandy sea," but never sees them. The real "wady" is, generally speaking, a rocky valley, bisected by the bed of a mountain torrent, dry during the hot season. In such places the Bedouins love to encamp, because they find food and drink—water being always procurable by digging.

When the supply is perennial, the wady becomes the site of a village. The Desert is as unaptly compared to a "sandy sea." Most of the wilds of Arabia resemble the tract between Suez and Cairo; only the former are of primitive formation, whereas the others are of a later date. Sand heaps are found in every desert, but sand plains are merely a local feature, not the general face of the country. The wilderness east of the Nile is generally a hard dry earth, which requires only a monsoon to become highly productive: even where silicious sand covers the plain, the waters of a torrent, depositing *humus* or vegetable mould, bind the particles together, and fit it for the reception of seed.

are lightened, your sight brightens, your memory recovers its tone, and your spirits become exuberant; your fancy and imagination are powerfully aroused, and the wildness and sublimity of the scenes around you stir up all the energies of your soul—whether for exertion, danger, or strife. Your *morale* improves: you become frank and cordial, hospitable and single-minded: the hypocritical politeness and the slavery of civilization are left behind you in the city. Your senses are quickened: they require no stimulants but air and exercise. In the Desert, spirituous liquors excite only disgust. There is a keen enjoyment in a mere animal existence. The sharp appetite disposes of the most indigestible food, the sand is softer than a bed of down, and the purity of the air suddenly puts to flight a dire cohort of diseases. Hence it is that both sexes, and every age, the most material as well as the most imaginative of minds, the tamest citizen, the most peaceful student, the spoiled child of civilization, all feel their hearts dilate, and their pulses beat strong as they look down from their dromedaries upon the "glorious Desert." Where do we hear of a "traveller" being disappointed by it? It is another illustration of the ancient truth, that nature returns to man, however unworthily he has treated her. And believe me, gentle reader, that when once your tastes have conformed to the tranquillity of such travel, you will suffer real pain in returning to the turmoil of civilization. You will anticipate the bustle and the confusion of artificial life, its luxury and its false pleasures, with repugnance. Depressed in spirits, you will for a time after your return feel incapable of mental or bodily exertion. The air of cities will suffocate you, and the care-worn and cadaverous countenances of citizens will haunt you like a vision of judgment.

As the black shadow mounted in the East,* I turned off the road, and was suddenly saluted by a figure rising from a little hollow with an "As' Salamo Alaykum" of truly Arab sound.† I looked at the speaker for a moment without recognising him. He then advanced with voluble expressions of joy, invited me to sup, seized my camel's halter without waiting for an answer, "nakh'd‡" him, led me hurriedly to a carpet spread in a sandy hollow, pulled off my slippers, gave me cold water for ablution, told me that he had mistaken me at a distance for a "Sherif" of the Arabs, but was delighted to find himself in error, and urged me to hurry over ablution, otherwise that night would come on before we could say our prayers. It was Mohammed El Basyuni, the Meccan boy of whom I had bought my pilgrim-garb at Cairo. After prayer he lighted a pipe, and immediately placed the snake-like tube in my hand; this is an argument which the tired traveller can rarely resist. He then began to rummage my saddle-bags; drew forth stores of provisions, rolls, water-melons, boiled eggs, and dates, and whilst lighting the fire and boiling coffee, managed to distribute his own stock, which was neither plentiful nor first-rate, to the camel-men. Shaykh Nassar and his brother looked aghast at this movement, but the boy was inexorable. They tried a few rough hints, which he noticed by singing a Hindostani couplet that asserts the impropriety of anointing rats' heads with jasmine

* This, as a general rule in El-Islam, is a sign that the Maghrib or evening prayer must not be delayed.

† This salutation of peace is so differently pronounced by every eastern nation that the observing traveller will easily make of it a shibboleth.

‡ To "nakh," in Arabic, is to gurgle "Ikh! ikh!" in the bottom of one's throat till the camel kneels down. We have no English word for this proceeding.

oil. They suspected abuse, and waxed cross; he acknowledged this by deriding them. And I urged him on, wanting to see how the city Arab treats the countryman. He then took my tobacco pouch from the angry Bedouins, and in a stage whisper reproved me for entrusting it to such thieves, insisting at the same time upon drinking all the coffee, so that the poor guides had to prepare for themselves. He improved every opportunity of making mischief.

After an hour most amusingly spent in this way, I arose and insisted upon mounting. Shaykh Nassar and his brother had reckoned upon living gratis, for at least three days, judging it improbable that a soft Effendi would hurry himself. When they saw the fair vision dissolved, they began to finesse; they induced the camel man, who ran by the side of Mohammed's dromedary, to precede the animal, a favorite manœuvre to prevent overspeed. Ordered to fall back, the man pleaded fatigue and inability to walk. The boy Mohammed immediately asked if I had any objection to dismount one of my guides, and to let his weary attendant ride for an hour or so. I at once assented, and the Bedouins obeyed me with ominous grumblings. When we resumed our march, the melancholy Arabs had no song left in them, whereas Mohammed chanted vociferously, and quoted bad Hindostani and worse Persian till silence was forcibly imposed upon him. The camel men lagged behind, in order to prevent my dromedary advancing too fast, and the boy's guide, after dismounting, would stride along in front of us, under pretext of showing the way. And so we jogged on, now walking, then trotting, till the dromedaries began to grunt with fatigue, and the Arabs clamored for a halt.

At midnight we reached the centre station, and lay down under its walls to take a little rest. The dews fell heavily, wetting the sheets that covered us; but who cares for such trifles in the Desert? The moon shone bright;* the breeze blew coolly, and the jackal sang a lullaby which lost no time in producing the soundest sleep. As the wolf's tail† appeared in the heavens we arose, mounted our camels, and resumed the march in real earnest. The dawn passed away in its delicious coolness, and sultry morning came on. Then day arose in its fierceness, and the noontide sun made the plain glow with terrible heat. Still we pressed onwards.

At 3 P. M. we turned off the road into a dry water-course. The sand was dotted with the dried-up leaves of the Datura, and strongly perfumed by a kind of Absinthe, the sweetest herb of the Desert. A Mimosa was there, and although its shade at this season is little better than a cocoa tree's‡ the Bedouins would not neglect it. We lay down upon the sand to rest among a party of Maghrabi pilgrims travelling to Suez. It was impossible to help pitying their state, nor could I eat, seeing them hungry, thirsty, and way-worn. So Nassar served out about a pint of water and a little bread to each man. Then they asked for more. None was to be had, so they cried out that money would do as well. I had determined upon being generous to the extent of a few pence. Custom, as well as inclination, was in favor of the act; but when the alms became a demand, and the demand was backed by fierce looks and a derisive sneer, and a kind

* "The sun shall not smite thee by day, nor the moon by night." (Psalm cxxi. 6.) Easterns still believe firmly in the evil effects of moonlight on the human frame. From Sindh to Abyssinia, the traveller will hear tales of wonder concerning it.

† The wolf's tail is the Persian name for the first brushes of grey light which appear as forerunners of dawn.

‡ We are told in verse of "a cocoa's feathery shade." But to realise the prose picture, let the home reader, choosing some sultry August day, fasten a large fan to a long pole, and enjoy himself under it.

of reference to their knives, gentle charity took the alarm and fled. My pistols kept them at bay, for they were only making an attempt to intimidate, and though I took the precaution of sitting apart from them, there was no real danger. Of the Maghrabis I shall have more to say when relating my voyage in the Pilgrim Ship: they were the only travellers from whom we experienced the least annoyance. Numerous parties of Turks, Arabs, and Afghans, and a few Indians, were on the same errand as ourselves. All, as we passed them, welcomed us with the friendly salutation that so becomes men engaged in a labor of religion.

Suez was now near. In the blue distance rose the castellated peaks and the wide sand-tracts over which lies the land route to El Hejaz. Before us the sight ever dear to English eyes,—a strip of sea gloriously azure, with a gallant steamer walking the waters. On the right-hand side lay the broad slopes of Jebel Mukuttum, a range of hills which flanks the road all the way from Cairo. It was at this hour a spectacle not easily to be forgotten. We drew up at a small building called Bir Suways (well of Suez), and under pretext of watering the cattle, I sat for half an hour admiring the charms of the Desert. The eye never tires of loveliness of hue, and the memory of the hideousness of this range, when a sun in front exposed each barren and deformed feature, supplied the evening view with another element of attraction.

It was already night when we passed through the tumbling gateway of Suez; and there still remained the task of finding my servant and effects. After wandering in and out of every Wakâlat in the village, we accidentally heard that an Indian had taken lodgings at a hostelry bearing the name of Jirjis. On arriving there our satisfaction was diminished by the intelligence that the same Indian, after locking the door, had gone out with his friends to a ship in the harbor; in fact, that he had made all preparations for running away. I dismounted, and tried to persuade the porter to break open the wooden bolt, but he absolutely refused, and threatened the police. Meanwhile Mohammed had found a party of friends, men of El Medinah, returning to the pilgrimage after a begging tour through Egypt and Turkey. The meeting was characterised by vociferous inquiries, loud guffaws, and warm embraces. I was invited to share their supper, and their dormitory,—an uncovered platform projecting from the gallery over the square court below, but I had neither appetite nor spirits to be sociable. The porter, after persuasion, showed me an empty room, in which I spread my carpet. That night was a sad one. My eighty-four mile ride had made every bone ache; I had lost much epidermis, and the sun had seared every portion of skin exposed to it. So, lamenting my degeneracy and the ill effects of four years' domicile in Europe, and equally disquieted in mind about the fate of my goods and chattels, I fell into an uncomfortable sleep.

## CHAPTER VIII.

### SUEZ.

Early on the morning after my arrival, I arose, and consulted my new acquaintances about what steps should be taken towards recovering the missing property. They unanimously advised a visit to the governor, whom, however, they described to be a "Kelb ibn Kelb," (dog, son of a dog,) who never returned Moslems' salutations, and thought all men dirt to be trodden under foot by the Turks. The boy Mohammed showed his *savoir faire* by extracting from his huge box a fine embroidered cap, and a grand peach-colored coat, with which I was instantly invested; he dressed himself with similar magnificence, and we then set out to the "palace."

Giaffar Bey,—he has since been deposed,—then occupied the position of judge, officer commanding, collector of customs, and magistrate of Suez. The large old Turk received me most superciliously, disdained all return of salaam, and fixing upon me two little eyes like gimlets demanded my business. I stated that one Shaykh Nur, my Indian servant, had played me false; therefore I required permission to break into the room supposed to contain my effects. He asked my profession. I replied the medical. This led him to inquire if I had any medicine for the eyes, and being answered in the affirmative, he sent a messenger with me to enforce obedience on the part of the porter. The obnoxious measure was, however, unnecessary. As we entered the caravanserai there appeared at the door the black face of Shaykh Nur, looking, though accompanied by sundry fellow countrymen, uncommonly as if he merited and expected the bamboo. He had, by his own account, been seduced into the festivities of a coal hulk manned by Indian Lascars, and the vehemence of his self-accusation saved him from the chastisement which I had determined to administer.

I must now briefly describe the party into which fate threw me: the names of these men will so frequently appear in the following pages, that a few words about their natures will not be misplaced.

First of all comes Omar Effendi,—so called in honor,—a Daghistani or Circassian, the grandson of a Hanafi Mufti at El Medinah, and the son of a Shayk Rakl, an officer whose duty it is to lead dromedary-caravans. He sits upon his cot, a small, short, plump body, of yellow complexion and bilious temperament, grey-eyed, soft-featured, and utterly beardless,—which affects his feelings,—he looks fifteen, and owns to twenty-eight. His manners are those of a student; he dresses respectably, prays regularly, hates the fair sex, like an Arab, whose affections and aversions are always in extremes, is serious, has a mild demeanor, an humble gait, and a soft slow voice. When roused he becomes furious as a Bengal tiger. His parents have urged him to marry, and he, like Camaralzaman, has informed his father that he is a person of great age, but little sense. Urged moreover by a melancholy turn of mind, and the want of leisure for study at El Medinah, he fled the paternal domicile, and entered himself a pauper (student) in the Azhar mosque. His disconsolate friends and afflicted relations sent a confidential man to fetch him home by force, should it be necessary; he has yielded, and is now awaiting the first opportunity of travelling, if possible, gratis to El Medinah.

That confidential man is a negro-servant, called Saad, notorious in his native city as El Jinni, the devil. Born and bred a slave in Omar Effendi's family, he obtained manumission, became a soldier in El-Hejaz, was dissatisfied with pay perpetually in arrears, turned merchant, and wandered far and wide, to Russia, to Gibraltar, and to Baghdad. He is the pure African, noisily merry at one moment, at another silently sulky, affectionate and abusive, brave and boastful, reckless and crafty, exceedingly quarrelsome, and unscrupulous to the last degree. The bright side of his character is his love for, and respect to, the young master Omar Effendi; yet even him he will scold in a paroxysm of fury, and steal from him whatever he can lay his hands on. He is generous with his goods, but is ever borrowing and never paying money; he dresses like a beggar, with the dirtiest tarboosh upon his tufty poll, and only a cotton shirt over his sooty skin, whilst his two boxes are full of handsome apparel for himself and the three ladies his wives at El Medinah. He knows no fear but for those boxes. Frequently during our search for a vessel he forced himself into Giaffar Bey's presence, and demeaned himself so impudently, that we expected to see him lamed by the bastinado; his forwardness, however, only amused the dignitary. He wanders all day about the bazaar, talking about freight and passage, for he has resolved, cost what it will, to travel gratis, and with doggedness like his, he must succeed.

Shaykh Hamid el Lamman derives his cognomen, the "clarified butter-seller," from a celebrated saint and Sufi of the Kadiriyah order, who left a long line of holy descendants at El Medinah. This Shaykh squats upon a box full of presents for the daughter of his paternal uncle,* a perfect specimen of the town Arab. His head is crowned with a rough Shushah or tuft of hair on the poll;† his face is of a dirty brown, his little goat's beard untrimmed; his feet are bare, and his only garment is an exceedingly unclean, ochre-colored blouse, tucked at the waist into a leathern girdle beneath it. He will not pray, because he is unwilling to take pure clothes out of his box; but he smokes when he can get other people's tobacco, and groans between the whiffs, conjugating the verb all day, for he is of active mind. He can pick out his letters, and he keeps in his bosom a little dog's-eared MS. full of serious romances and silly prayers, old and exceedingly ill written: this he will draw forth at times, peep into for a moment, devoutly kiss, and restore to its proper place with all the veneration of the vulgar for a book. He can sing all manner of songs, slaughter a sheep with dexterity, deliver a grand call to prayer, shave, cook, fight, and he excels in the science of vituperation: like Saad, he never performs his devotions, except when necessary to "keep up appearances." His brow crumples at the word wine, but there is quite another expression about the region of the mouth; and Stamboul, where he has lived some months, without learning ten words of Turkish, is a notable place for displaying prejudice.

* His wife.

† When travelling, the Shushah is allowed to spread over the greatest portion of the scalp, to act as a protection against the sun; and the hair being shaved off about two inches all round the head, leaves a large circular patch. Nothing can be uglier than such tonsure, and it is contrary to the strict law of the Prophet. The Arab, however, knows by experience, that habitual exposure of the scalp to a burning sun seldom fails to damage its precious contents. He, therefore, wears a Shushah during his wanderings, and removes it on his return home.

Stretched on a carpet, smoking a Persian Kalioon all day, lies Salih Shakkar, a Turk, born at El Medinah. We were intimate enough on the road, when he borrowed from me a little money. But at El Medinah he cut me pitilessly, as a "town man" does a country acquaintance accidentally met, and of course he tried, though in vain, to evade repaying his debt. He had a tincture of letters, and appeared to have studied critically the subject of "largesse." "The generous is Allah's friend, aye, though he be a sinner, and the miser is Allah's foe, aye, though he be a saint," was a venerable saying always in his mouth. He also informed me that Pharaoh, although the quintessence of impiety, is mentioned by name in the Koran, by reason of his liberality, whereas, Nimrod, another monster of iniquity, is only alluded to, because he was a stingy tyrant. It is almost needless to declare that Salih Shakkar was, as the Indians say, a very "fly-sucker."* There were two other men of El Medinah in the Wakàlat Gírgis; but I omit description, as we left them, they being penniless, at Suez. One of them, Mahommed Shiklibha, I afterwards met at Meccah, and seldom have I seen a more honest and warm-hearted fellow. When we were embarking at Suez, he fell upon Hamid's bosom, and both of them wept at the prospect of parting even for a few days.

All the individuals above mentioned lost no time in opening the question of a loan. It was a lesson in oriental metaphysics to see their condition. They had a twelve days' voyage, and a four days' journey, before them; boxes to carry, custom-houses to face, and stomachs to fill; yet the whole party could scarcely, I believe, muster two dollars of ready money. Their boxes were full of valuables, arms, clothes, pipes, slippers, sweetmeats, and other "notions,"

* "Makhi-chus," equivalent to our "skin-flint."

but nothing short of starvation would have induced them to pledge the smallest article.

I foresaw that their company would be an advantage, and therefore I hearkened favorably to the honeyed request for a few crowns. The boy Mohammed obtained six dollars; Hamid about five pounds,—I intended to make his house at El Medinah my home; Umar Effendi three dollars; Saad the Devil, two—I gave the money to him at Yambu,—and Salih Shakkar fifty piastres. But since in these lands, as a rule, no one ever lends coins, or borrowing ever returns them, I took care to exact service from the first, to take two rich coats from the second, a handsome pipe from the third, a "bala" or yataghan from the fourth, and from the fifth an imitation Cashmere shawl. After which, we sat down and drew out the agreement. It was favorable to me: I lent them Egyptian money, and bargained for repayment in the currency of El Hejaz, thereby gaining the exchange, which is sometimes 16 per cent. My companions having received these small sums, became affectionate and eloquent in my praise: they asked me to make one of their number for the future at their meals, overwhelmed me with questions, insisted upon a present of sweetmeats, detected in me a great man under a cloud,—perhaps my claims to being a Dervish assisted them to this discovery,—and declared that I should perforce be their guest at Meccah and El Medinah. This sudden elevation led me into an imprudence which might have cost me dear. It aroused the only suspicion about me ever expressed during the summer's trip. My friends had looked at my clothes, overhauled my medicine chest, and criticised my pistols; they sneered at my copper-cased watch,* and remembered having seen a

* This being an indispensable instrument for measuring distances, I had it divested of gold case, and provided with a facing carefully stained

compass at Constantinople. Therefore I imagined they would think little about a sextant. This was a mistake. The boy Mohammed I afterwards learned, waited only my leaving the room to declare that the would-be Haji was one of the infidels from India, and a council sat to discuss the case. Fortunately for me Umar Effendi had looked over a letter which I had written to Haji Wali that morning, and he had at various times received categorical replies to certain questions in high theology. He felt himself justified in declaring, *ex cathedrâ*, the boy Mohammed's position perfectly untenable. And Shaykh Hamid, who looked forward to being my host, guide, and debtor in general, and probably cared scantily for catechism or creed, swore that the light of El Islam was upon my countenance, and consequently that the boy Mohammed was a pauper, a "fakir," an owl, a cut-off one, a stranger, and a Wahhabi, for daring to impugn the faith of a brother believer. The scene ended with a general abuse of the acute youth, who was told on all sides that he had no shame and was directed to fear Allah. I was struck with the expression of my friends' countenances when they saw the sextant, and, determining with a sigh to leave it behind, I prayed five times a day for nearly a week.

We all agreed not to lose an hour in securing places on board some vessel bound to Yambu, and my companions, hearing that my passport as a British Indian was scarcely "en régle," earnestly advised me to have it signed by the

and figured with Arabic numerals. In countries where few can judge of a watch by its works, it is as well to secure its safety by making the exterior look as mean as possible. The watches worn by respectable people in El Hejaz are almost always old silver pieces, of the turnip shape, with hunting cases and an outer *etui* of thick leather. Mostly they are of Swiss or German manufacture, and they find their way into Arabia *viâ* Constantinople and Cairo.

governor without delay, whilst they occupied themselves about the harbor. They warned me that if I displayed the Turkish Tezkireh given to me at the citadel of Cairo, I should infallibly be ordered to await the caravan, and lose their society and friendship. Pilgrims arriving at Alexandria, be it known to the reader, are divided into bodies, and distributed by means of Tezkirehs to the three great roads, namely, Suez, Cosseir, and the Haj route by land round the Gulf of Akabah. After the division has once been made, government turns a deaf ear to the representations of individuals. The Bey of Suez has an order to obstruct pilgrims as much as possible till the end of the season, when they are hurried down that way, lest they should arrive at Meccah too late. As most of the Egyptian high officials have boats, which sail up the Nile laden with pilgrims and return freighted with corn, the government naturally does its utmost to force the delays and discomforts of this line upon strangers. Knowing these facts, I felt that a difficulty was at hand. The first thing was to take Shaykh Nur's passport, which was "en régle," and my own which was not, to the Bey for signature. He turned the papers over and over, as if unable to read them, and raised false hopes high by referring me to his clerk. The under official at once saw the irregularity of the document, asked me why it had not been visé at Cairo, swore that under such circumstances nothing would induce the Bey to let me proceed, and when I tried persuasion, waxed insolent. My last hope at Suez was to obtain assistance from Mr. George West, H. B. M. sub-vice-consul. I therefore took the boy Mohammed with me, choosing him on purpose, and excusing the step to my companions by concocting an artful fable about my having been, in some part of Afghanistan, a benefactor to the British nation. We proceeded to the consulate. Mr. West, who had been told by an imprudent friend to expect me, saw through the disguise, despite the jargon assumed to satisfy official scruples, and nothing could be kinder than the part he took. His clerk was directed to place himself in communication with the Bey's factotum, and when objections to signing the Alexandrian Tezkireh were offered, the vice-consul said that he would, at his own risk, give me a fresh passport as a British subject from Suez to Arabia. His firmness prevailed, and on the second day, the documents were returned to me in a satisfactory state.

Nothing more comfortless than our days and nights in the "George" Inn. The ragged walls of our rooms were clammy with dirt, the smoky rafters foul with cobwebs, and the floor, bestrewed with kit, in terrible confusion, was black with hosts of ants and flies. Pigeons nestled on the shelf, cooing amatory ditties the live-long day, and cats, like tigers, crawled through a hole in the door, making night hideous with their cat-a-waulings. Now a curious goat, then an inquisitive jackass, would walk stealthily into the room, remark that it was tenanted, and retreat with dignified demeanor, and the mosquitoes sang Io Pæans over our prostrate forms throughout the twenty-four hours. I spare the reader the enumeration of the other Egyptian plagues that infested the place. After the first day's trial, we determined to spend the hours of light in the passages, lying upon our boxes or rugs, smoking, wrangling, and inspecting one another's chests: the latter occupation was a fertile source of disputes, for nothing was more common than for a friend to seize an article belonging to another, and to swear by the Prophet's beard that be admired it, and therefore would not return it. The boy Mohammed and Shaykh Nur, who had been intimates the first day, differed in opinion on the second, and on the third came to pushing each other against the wall. Sometimes we went into the Bazar, a shady street flanked with poor little shops, or we sat in the coffee-house,* drinking hot salt water tinged with burnt bean, or we prayed in one of the three tumble-down old mosques, or we squatted upon the pier, lamenting the want of Hammams, and bathing in the tepid sea. The only society we found —excepting an occasional visitor—was that of a party of Egyptian women, who with their husbands and families occupied some rooms adjoining ours. At first they were fierce, and used bad language, when the boy Mohammed and I, whilst Omar Effendi was engaged in prayer, and the rest were wandering about the town, ventured to linger in the cool passage, where they congregated, or to address a facetious phrase to them. But hearing that I was a Hakim-bashi—for fame had promoted me to the rank of a "Physician General" at Suez—all had some ailments; they began prudently with requesting me to display the effects of my drugs by dosing myself, but they ended submissively by swallowing nauseous compounds in a body. To this succeeded a primitive form of flirtation, which mainly consisted of the demand direct. The most charming of the party was one Fattûmah, a plump-personed dame fast verging upon her thirtieth year, fond of a little flattery, and possessed, like all her people, of a most voluble tongue. Sometimes the entrance of the male Fellahs† interrupted

* We were still at Suez, where we could do as we pleased. But respectable Arabs in their own country, unlike Egyptians, are seldom to be seen in the places of public resort. "Go to the coffee-house, and sing there!" is a reproach sometimes addressed to those who have a habit of humming in decent society.

† The palmy days of the Egyptian husband, when he might use the stick, the sword, or the sack with impunity, are, in civilized places at least, now gone by. The wife has only to complain to the Cadi, or to the governor, and she is certain of redress. This is right in the ab-

these little discussions, but people of our respectability and nation were not to be imposed upon by such husbands. In their presence we only varied the style of conversation—inquiring the amount of "Mahr," or marriage settlement, deriding the cheapness of womanhood in Egypt, and requiring to be furnished on the spot with brides at the rate of ten shillings a head.* More often the amiable Fattúmah—the fair sex in this country, though passing frail, have the best tempers in the world—would laugh at our impertinences. Sometimes, vexed by our imitating her Egyptian accent, mimicking her gestures, and depreciating her countrywomen, she would wax wroth, and order us to be gone, and stretch out her forefinger—a sign that she wished to put out our eyes, or adjure Allah to cut the heart out of our bosoms. Then the "Marry me, O Fattúmah, O daughter, O female pilgrim!" would give way to "Y'al-ago-o-oz!" (O old woman and decrepit!) "O daughter of sixty sires, and only fit to carry wood to market!"—whereupon would burst a storm of wrath, at the tail of which all of us, like children, starting upon our feet, rushed out of one another's way. This was the amusement of the day. At night we, men, assembling upon the little terrace, drank tea, recited stories, read books, talked of our travels, and indulged in various pleasantries.

The population of Suez now numbers about 4,800. As usual in Mohammedan countries no census is taken here. Some therefore estimate the population at 6,000. Sixteen years ago it was supposed to be under 3,000. After that

stract, but in practice it acts badly. The fair sex is so unruly in this country, that strong measures are necessary to coerce it, and in the arts of deceit men have little or no chance against women.

* The amount of settlement being, among Moslems as among Christians, the test of a bride's value—moral and physical, it will readily be understood that our demand was more facetious than complimentary.

time it rapidly increased till 1850, when a fatal attack of cholera reduced it to about half its previous number. The average mortality is about twelve a month.*

The people of Suez are a finer and a fairer race than the Cairenes. The former have more the appearance of Arabs: their dress is more picturesque, their eyes are carefully darkened with Kohl, and they wear sandals not slippers. They are, according to all accounts, a turbulent and somewhat fanatic set, fond of quarrels, and slightly addicted to "pronunciamentos." The general programme of one of these latter diversions is said to be as follows. The boys will first be sent by their fathers about the town in a disorderly mob, and ordered to cry out "Long live the Sultan!" with its usual sequel, "Death to the infidels!" The infidels, Christians or others, must hear and may happen to resent this; or possibly the governor, foreseeing a disturbance, orders an ingenuous youth or two to be imprisoned, or to be caned by the police. Whereupon some person, rendered influential by wealth or religious reputation, publicly complains that the Christians are all in all, and that in these evil days El Islam is going to destruction. On this occasion the speaker conducts himself with such insolence, that the governor must perforce consign him to confinement, which exasperates the populace still more. Secret meetings are now convened, and in them the chiefs of corporations assume a prominent position. If the disturbance be intended by its main spring to subside quietly, the conspirators are allowed to take their own way; they will drink copiously, become lions about midnight, and recover their hare-hearts before noon next day. But if mischief be intended, a case of bloodshed is brought about, and then nothing can arrest

* This may appear a large mortality; but at Alexandria it is said the population is renewed every fourteen years.

the torrent of popular rage. The Egyptian, with all his good humor, merriment, and nonchalance, is notorious for doggedness, when, as the popular phrase is, his "blood is up." And this, indeed, is his chief merit as a soldier. He has a certain mechanical dexterity in the use of arms, and an Egyptian regiment will fire a volley as correctly as an English battalion. But when the head, and not the hands, is required, he notably fails, as all Orientals do. The reason of their superiority in the field is their peculiar stubbornness, and this, together with their powers of digestion and of enduring hardship on the line of march, is the quality that made them terrible to their old conquerors, the Turks.

## CHAPTER IX.

### THE PILGRIM SHIP.

IMMENSE was the confusion on the eventful day of our departure. Suppose us standing upon the beach, on the morning of a fiery July day, carefully watching our hurriedly-packed goods and chattels, surrounded by a mob of idlers, who are not too proud to pick up waifs and strays, whilst pilgrims rush about apparently mad, and friends are weeping, acquaintances vociferating adieux, boatmen demanding fees, shopmen claiming debts, women shrieking and talking with inconceivable power, children crying—in short, for an hour or so we were in the thick of a human storm. To confound confusion, the boatmen have moored their skiff half a dozen yards away from the shore, lest the porters should be unable to make more than double their fare from the Hajis. Again the Turkish women raise a hideous howl, as they are carried off struggling vainly in brawny arms; the children howl because their mothers howl; and the men scold and swear, because in such scenes none may be silent.

From the beach we poled to the little pier, where sat the Bey in person to perform a final examination of our passports. Several were detected without the necessary document. Some were bastinadoed, others peremptorily ordered back to Cairo, and the rest were allowed to proceed. At about 10 A. M. we hoisted sail, and ran down the channel leading to the roadstead.

Our Pilgrim Ship, the "Golden Wire," was a Sambuk, of about fifty tons, with narrow wedge-like bows, a clean water line, a sharp keel, undecked, except upon the poop, which was high enough to act as a sail in a gale of wind. She carried two masts, imminently raking forward, the main considerably larger than the mizen; the former was provided with a huge triangular latine, very deep in the tack, but the second sail was unaccountably wanting. She had no means of reefing, no compass, no log, no sounding lines, nor even the suspicion of a chart. Such probably were the craft which carried old Sesostris across the Red Sea to Dire; such the cruisers which once every three years left Ezion-Geber for Tarshish; such the transports of which one hundred and thirty were required to convey Ælius Gallus, with his ten thousand men; and—the East moves slowly—such most probably in A. D. 1900 will be the "Golden Wire," which snall convey future pilgrims from Suez to El-Hejaz. "Bakhshish" was the last as well as the first odious sound I heard in Egypt. The owner of the shore-boat would not allow us to climb the sides of our vessel before paying him his fare, and when we did so he asked for Bakhshish. If Easterns would only imitate the example of Europeans—I never yet saw an Englishman give Bakhshish to a soul—the nuisance would soon be done away with. But on this occasion all my companions complied with the request, and at times it is unpleasant to be singular. The first look at the interior of our vessel showed a hopeless sight; for Ali Murad, the greedy owner, had promised to take sixty passengers in the hold, but had stretched the number to ninety-seven. Piles of boxes and luggage in every shape and form filled the ship from stem to stern, and a torrent of Hajis were pouring over the sides like ants into the Indian sugar-basin. The poop, too, where we had taken our places, was covered with goods, and a number of pilgrims had established themselves there by might, not by right.

Presently, to our satisfaction, appeared Saad the Devil, equipped as an able seaman, and looking most unlike the proprietor of two large boxes full of valuable merchandise. This energetic individual instantly prepared for action. With our little party to back him, he speedily cleared the poop of intruders and their stuff by the simple process of pushing or rather throwing them off it into the hold below. We then settled down as comfortably as we could; three Syrians, a married Turk with his wife and family, the rais or captain of the vessel, with a portion of his crew, and our seven selves, composing a total of eighteen human beings, upon a space certainly not exceeding ten feet by eight. The cabin—a miserable box about the size of the poop, and three feet high—was stuffed, like the hold of a slave ship, with fifteen wretches, children and women, and the other ninety-seven were disposed upon the luggage, or squatted on the bulwarks. Having some experience in such matters, and being favored by fortune, I found a spare bedframe slung to the ship's side; and giving a dollar to its owner, a sailor—who flattered himself that, because it was his, he would sleep upon it—I instantly appropriated it, preferring any hardship outside to the condition of a packed herring inside the place of torment.

Our Maghrabis were sturdy young fellows, round-headed, broad-shouldered, tall, and large-limbed, with frowning eyes, and voices in a habit of perpetual roar. Their manners were rude, and their faces full of fierce contempt or insolent familiarity. A few old men were there, with countenances expressive of intense ferocity; women as savage and full of fight as men; and handsome boys with shrill voices, and hands always upon their daggers. The women were mere bundles of dirty white rags. The males were clad in Burnooses—brown or striped woollen cloaks with hoods; they had neither turban nor tarboosh, trusting to their thick curly hair, or to the prodigious hardness of their scalps, as a defence against the sun; and there was not a slipper nor a shoe amongst the party. Of course all were armed; but, fortunately for us, none had anything more formidable than a cut-and-thrust dagger about ten inches long. These Maghrabis travel in hordes under a leader who obtains the temporary title of "Maula" —the master. He has generally performed a pilgrimage or two, and has collected a stock of superficial information, which secures for him the respect of his followers, and the profound contempt of the heaven-made Ciceroni of Meccah and El Medinah. No people endure greater hardships when upon the pilgrimage than these Africans, who trust almost entirely to alms and to other such dispensations of Providence. It is not therefore to be wondered at that they rob whenever an opportunity presents itself. Several cases of theft occurred on board the "Golden Wire;" and as a plunderer seldom allows himself to be baulked by insufficient defence, they are perhaps deservedly accused of having committed some revolting murders.

The first thing to be done after gaining standing-room was to fight for greater comfort. A few Turks, ragged old men, were mixed up with the Maghrabis, and the former began the war by contemptuously elbowing and scolding their wild neighbors. The Maghrabis, under their leader, "Maula Ali," a burly savage, in whom I detected a ridiculous resemblance to an old and well-remembered schoolmaster, retorted so willingly that in a few minutes nothing was to be seen but a confused mass of humanity, each item indiscriminately punching and pulling, scratching and biting, butting and trampling, whatever was obnoxious to such operations, with cries of rage, and all the accompaniments of a proper fray. One of our party on the poop, a Syrian, somewhat incautiously, leapt down to aid his countrymen by restoring order. He sank immediately below the living mass; and when we fished him out his forehead was cut open, half his beard had disappeared, and a fine sharp set of teeth belonging to some Maghrabi had left their mark in the calf of his leg. The enemy showed no love of fair play, and never appeared contented unless five or six of them were setting upon a single man. This made matters worse. The weaker of course drew their daggers, and a few bad wounds were soon given and received. In a few minutes five men were completely disabled, and the victors began to dread the consequences of their victory.

Then the fighting stopped, and as many could not find places, it was agreed that a deputation should wait upon Ali Murad, the owner, to inform him of the crowded state of the vessel. After keeping us in expectation at least three hours, he appeared in a row-boat, and, preserving a respectful distance, informed us that any one who pleased might leave the ship, and take back his fare. This left the case exactly as it was before; none would abandon his party to go on shore: so Ali Murad was rowed off towards Suez, giving us a parting injunction to be good, and not fight; to trust in Allah, and that Allah would make all things easy to us. His departure was the signal for a second fray, which in its accidents differed a little from the first. During the previous disturbance we kept our places with weapons in our hands. This time we were summoned by the Maghrabis to relieve their difficulties, by taking about half a dozen of them on the poop. Saad the Devil at once rose with an oath, and threw amongst us a bundle of "Nebut"—goodly ashen staves, six feet long, thick as a man's wrist, well greased, and tried in many a rough bout. He shouted to us, "Defend yourselves, if you don't wish to be the meat of the Maghrabis!" and to the enemy, "Dogs and sons of dogs! now shall you see what the children of the Arab are"—"I am Omar of Daghistan!" "I am Abdullah, the son of Joseph!" "I am Saad, the Devil!" we exclaimed, "renowning it" by this display of name and patronymic. To do the enemy justice they showed no sign of flinching; they swarmed towards the poop like angry hornets, and encouraged each other with loud cries of "Allah akbar!" But we had a vantage ground about four feet above them, and their palm sticks and short daggers could do nothing against our terrible quarter-staves. In vain the "Jacquerie" tried to scale the poop and to overpower us by numbers; their courage only secured them more broken heads.

At first I began to lay on with *main morte*, really fearing to kill some one with such a weapon; but it soon became evident that the Maghrabis' heads and shoulders could bear and did require the utmost exertion of strength. Presently a thought struck me. A large earthen jar full of drinking water,*—in its heavy frame of wood the weight might have been 100lbs,—stood upon the edge of the poop, and the thick of the fray took place beneath. Seeing an opportunity I crept up to the jar, and, without attracting attention, by

* In these vessels each traveller, unless a previous bargain be made, is expected to provide his own water and fire-wood. The best way, however, is, when the old wooden box called a tank is sound, to pay the captain for providing water, and to keep the key.

a smart push with the shoulder rolled it down upon the swarm of assailants. The fall caused a shriller shriek to rise above the ordinary din, for heads, limbs, and bodies were sorely bruised by the weight, scratched by the broken potsherds, and wetted by the sudden discharge. A fear that something worse might be forthcoming made the Maghrabis shrink off towards the end of the vessel. After a few minutes, we, sitting in grave silence, received a deputation of individuals in whity-brown Burnooses, spotted and striped with what Mephistopheles calls a "curious juice." They solicited peace, which we granted upon the condition that they would bind themselves to keep it. Our heads, shoulders, and hands were penitentially kissed, and presently the fellows returned to bind up their hurts in dirty rags. We owed this victory entirely to our own exertions, and the meek Omar was by far the fiercest of the party.

At length, about 3 P.M. on the 6th of July, 1854, we shook out the sail, and, as it bellied in the favorable wind, we recited the Fat-hah * with up-raised hands which we afterwards drew down our faces. As the "Golden Wire" started from her place, I could not help casting one wistful look upon the British flag floating over the Consulate. But the momentary regret was stifled by the heart-bounding which prospects of an adventure excite, and by the real pleasure of leaving Egypt. I had lived there a stranger in the land, and a hapless life it had been: in the streets every man's face was the face of a foe as he looked upon the Persian. Whenever I came in contact with the native officials insolence marked the event; and the circumstance of living within hail of my fellow countrymen, and yet an impossibility of enjoying their society, still throws a gloom over the memory of my first sojourn in Egypt.

* The first chapter of the Koran.

The ships of the Red Sea—infamous region of rocks, reefs, and shoals—cruise along the coast by day, and for the night lay to in the first cove they can find; they do not sail when it blows hard, and as in winter time the weather is often stormy and the light of day does not last long, the voyage is intolerably slow. At sunset we stayed our adventurous course, and were still within sight of Suez, comfortably anchored. The Eastern shore was dotted with the little grove of palm trees which clusters around the Uyun Musa, or Moses' Wells; and on the west, between two towering ridges, lay the mouth of the valley down which the Israelites fled to the Sea of Sedge. The view was by no means deficient in a sort of barbarous splendor. Verdure there was literally none, but under the violet and orange tints of the sky the chalky rocks became heaps of topazes, and the black ridges masses of amethyst. The rising mists, here silvery white, there deeply rosy, and the bright blue of the waves,* lining long strips of golden sand, compensated for the want of softness by a semblance of savage gorgeousness.

Next morning, before the cerulean hue had vanished from the hills, we set sail. It was not long before we came to a proper sense of our position. The box containing my store of provisions, and, worse still, my opium, was at the bottom of the hold, perfectly unapproachable; we had, therefore, the pleasure of breaking our fast on "mare's skin,"† and a species of biscuit, hard as a stone and quite as

* Most travellers remark that they have never seen a brighter blue than that of the Red Sea. It was the observation of an early age that "the Rede Sea is not more rede than any other sea, but in some place thereof is the gravelle rede, and therefore men clepen it the Rede Sea."

† Jild el Farasa, composition of apricot paste, dried, spread out, and folded into sheets, exactly resembling the article after which it is named. Turks and Arabs use it when travelling; they dissolve it in water, and eat it as a relish with bread or biscuit.

tasteless. During the day, whilst unsufferable splendor reigned above, a dashing of the waters below kept my nest in a state of perpetual drench. At night rose a cold bright moon, with dews falling so thick and clammy that the skin felt as though it would never be dry again.

The gale was light that day, and the sunbeams were fire; our crew preferred crouching in the shade of the sail to take advantage of what wind there was. In spite of our impatience we made but little way, and near sunset we anchored on a tongue of sand.

That evening we enjoyed ourselves upon clean sand, whose surface, drifted by the wind into small yellow waves, by a little digging and heaping up, was easily converted into the coolest and most comfortable of couches. Indeed, after the canescent heat of the day, and the tossing of our ill-conditioned vessel, we should have been contented with lodgings far less luxurious. Fuel was readily collected, and while some bathed the others erected a hearth—three large stones and a hole open to leeward—lit the fire, and put the pot on to boil. Shaykh Nur had fortunately brought a line with him; we had been successful in fishing; a little rice also had been bought; with this boiled and rock cod broiled upon the charcoal, we made a dinner that caused every one to forget the breakfast of mare's skin and hard biscuit. Presently the rais joined our party, and the usual story-telling began. The old man knew the name of each hill, and had a legend for every nook and corner in sight. He dwelt at length upon the life of Abu Zulaymah, the patron saint of these seas, whose little tomb stands at no great distance from our bivouac place, and told us how he sits watching over the safety of pious mariners in a cave among the neighboring rocks, and sipping his coffee, which is brought in a raw state from Meccah by green birds, and prepared in the usual way by the hands of ministering angels. He showed us the spot where the terrible king of Egypt, when close upon the heels of the children of Israel, was whelmed in the "hill of waters*," and he warned us that next day our way would be through breakers, and reefs, and dangerous currents, over whose troubled depths, since that awful day, the Ifrit of the storm has never ceased to flap his sable wing. The wincing of the hearers proved that the shaft of the old man's words was sharp; but as night was advancing, we unrolled our rugs, and fell asleep upon the sand, all of us happy, for we had eaten and drunk, and—since man is a hopeful animal—expecting on the morrow that the Ifrit would be merciful, and allow us to eat fresh dates at the harbor of Tur.

Fair visions of dates doomed to the Limbo of things which should have been! The grey dawn looked down upon us in difficulties. The water is deep near this coast; we had anchored at high tide close to the shore, and the ebb had left us high and dry. When this fact became apparent, a storm was upon the point of breaking. The Maghrabis, but for our interference, would have bastinadoed the rais, who, they said with some reason, ought to have known better. When this phase of feeling passed away, they applied themselves to physical efforts. Physical force, however, failed, upon which they changed their tactics. At the suggestion of their "Maula," they prepared to burn incense in honor of the Shaykh Abu Zulaymah. The material not being forthcoming, they used coffee, which perhaps accounts for the short-comings of that holy man. After this the rais remembered that their previous exertions

* Burckhardt mentions the Arab legend that the spirits of the drowned Egyptians may be seen moving at the bottom of the sea, and Finati adds that they are ever busy recruiting their numbers with shipwrecked mariners.

had not begun under the auspices of the Fát-hah. Therefore they prayed, and then re-applied themselves to work. Still they failed. Finally, each man called aloud upon his own particular saint or spiritual guide, and rushed forward as if he alone sufficed for the exploit. Shaykh Hamid unwisely quoted the name, and begged the assistance of his great ancestor, the "clarified-butter-seller;" the obdurate "Golden Wire" was not moved, and Hamid retired in momentary confusion.

It was now about nine A. M., and the water had risen considerably. My morning had been passed in watching the influx of the tide, and the grotesque efforts of the Maghrabis. When the vessel showed some symptoms of unsteadiness, I arose, walked gravely up to her, ranged the pilgrims around her with their shoulders to the sides, and told them to heave with might when they should hear me invoke the revered name of the Indian saint. I raised my hands and voice; "Ya Pirau Pir!" Ya Abd el Kader Jilani * was the signal. Each Maghrabi worked like an Atlas, the "Golden Wire" canted half over, and, sliding heavily through the sand, once more floated off into deep water. This was generally voted a minor miracle, and the Effendi was greatly respected—for a day or two.

The wind was fair, but we had all to re-embark, an operation which went on till noon. After starting, I remarked the natural cause which gives this Birkat Faraún—"Pharaoh's Bay,"—a bad name. Here the gulf narrows, and the winds which rush down the clefts and valleys of the lofty mountains on the Eastern and Western shores, meeting tides and counter-currents, cause a perpetual commotion. In the evening, or rather late in the afternoon, we anchored,

* A celebrated Sufi or mystic, whom many Indians reverence as the Arabs do their Prophet.

to our infinite disgust, under a ridge of rocks, behind which lies the plain of Tur. The rais deterred all from going on shore by terrible stories about the Bedouins that haunt the place, besides which there was no sand to sleep upon. We remained, therefore, on board, that night, and, making sail early the next morning, threaded through reefs and sand-banks into the intricate and dangerous entrance of Tur about noon.

Nothing can be meaner than the present appearance of the old Phœnician colony, although its position as a harbor, and its plentiful supply of fruit and fresh water, make it one of the most frequented places on the coast. The only remains of any antiquity—except the wells—are the fortifications which the Portuguese erected to keep out the Bedouins. The town is inhabited principally by Greek and other Christians, who live by selling water and provisions to ships. A fleecy cloud hung lightly over the majestic head of Jebel Tur, about eventide, and the outlines of the giant hills stood "picked out" from the clear blue sky. Our rais, weather-wise man, warned us that these were indications of a gale, and that, in case of rough weather, he did not intend to leave Tur. I was not sorry to hear this. We had passed a pleasant day, drinking sweet water, and eating the dates, grapes, and pomegranates, which the people of the place carry down to the beach for the benefit of hungry pilgrims. Besides which, there were various sights to see, and with these we might profitably spend the morrow. We therefore pitched the tent upon the sand, and busied ourselves with extricating a box of provisions—a labor rendered lighter by the absence of the Maghrabis, some of whom were wandering about the beach, whilst others had gone off to fill their bags with fresh water. We found their surliness insufferable; even when we were passing from poop to forecastle, landing or boarding, they grumbled forth their dissatisfaction.

Our rais was not mistaken in his prediction. When morning broke, we found the wind strong, and the sea white with foam. Most of us thought lightly of these terrors, but our valorous captain swore that he dared not for his life cross the mouth of ill-omened Akabah in such a storm. We breakfasted, therefore, and afterwards set out to visit Moses' hot baths, mounted on wretched donkeys with pack-saddles, ignorant of stirrups, and without tails, whilst we ourselves suffered generally from boils, which, as usual upon a journey, make their appearance in localities the most inconvenient. After a ride of two or three miles, we entered the gardens, and came suddenly upon the Hamman. It is a prim little bungalow, built by the present Pasha of Egypt for his own accommodation, glaringly whitewashed, and garnished with divans and calico curtains of a gorgeous hue. The guardian had been warned of our visit, and was present to supply us with bathing-cloths and other necessaries. One by one, we entered the cistern, which is now in an inner room. The water is about four feet deep, warm in winter, cool in summer, of a saltish and bitter taste, but celebrated for its invigorating qualities, when applied externally. On one side of the calcareous rock, near the ground, is the hole opened for the spring by Moses' rod, and near it are the marks of Moses' nails—deep indentations in the stone, which were probably left there by some extinct Saurian. Our cicerone informed us that formerly the finger marks existed, and that they were long enough for a man to lie in. The same functionary attributed the sanitary properties of the spring to the blessings of the Prophet, and when asked why Moses had not made sweet water to flow, informed us that the great law-giver had intended the spring for bathing in, not for drinking. We sat with him, eating the small yellow dates of Tur, which are delicious, melting like honey in the mouth, and leaving a surpassing *arrière goût.* After finishing sundry pipes and cups of coffee, we gave the man a few piastres, and, mounting our donkeys, started eastward for the Bir Musa, or well of Moses, which we reached in half an hour. It is a fine old well, built round and domed over with roughly squared stones. The sides of the pit were so rugged that a man could climb down them, and at the bottom was a pool of water, sweet and abundant.

In the even, when we returned to our tent, a Syrian, one of our party on the poop, came out to meet us with the information that several large vessels had arrived from Suez, comparatively speaking empty, and that the captain of one of them would land us at Yambu for three dollars a head. The proposal was a tempting one. But presently it became apparent that my companions were unwilling to shift their precious boxes, and moreover, that I should have to pay for those who could not, or would not pay for themselves,—that is to say, for the whole party. As such a display of wealth would have been unadvisable, I dismissed the idea with a sigh. Amongst the large vessels was one freighted with Persian pilgrims, a most disagreeable race of men on a journey or a voyage. They would not land at first, because they feared the Bedouins. They would not take water from the town people, because some of these were Christians. Moreover, they insisted upon making their own call to prayer, which heretical proceeding—it admits five extra words—our party, orthodox Moslems, would rather have died than permitted. When their crier, a small wizen-faced man, began the Azan, we received it with a shout of derision, and some, hastily snatching up their weapons, offered him an opportunity of martyrdom. The Maghrabis, too, hearing that the Persians were Rafaz (heretics), crowded fiercely round to do a little fighting for the faith. The long-bearded men took the alarm. They were twice the number of our small party, and therefore had been in the habit of strutting about with nonchalance, and looking at us fixedly, and otherwise demeaning themselves in an indecorous way. But when it came to the point, they showed the white feather. These Persians accompanied us to the end of our voyage. As they approached the Holy Land, visions of the "nebut" caused a change for the better in their manners. At Mahar they meekly endured a variety of insults, and at Yambu they cringed to us like dogs.

## CHAPTER X.

### TO YAMBU.

On the 11th July, about dawn, we left Tur, with the unpleasant certainty of not touching ground for thirty-six hours. I passed the time in steadfast contemplation of the webs of my umbrella, and in making the following meteorological remarks.

*Morning.* The air is mild and balmy as that of an Italian spring; thick mists roll down the valleys along the sea, and a haze like mother-o'-pearl crowns the headlands. The distant rocks show Titanic walls, lofty donjons, huge projecting bastions, and moats full of deep shade. At their base runs a sea of amethyst, and as earth receives the first touches of light, their summits, almost transparent, mingle with the jasper tints of the sky. Nothing can be more delicious than this hour. But morning soon fades. The sun bursts up from behind the main, a fierce enemy, a foe that will compel every one to crouch before him. He dyes the sky orange, and the sea "incarnadine," where its violet surface is stained by his rays, and mercilessly puts to flight the mists and haze and the little agate-colored masses of cloud that were before floating in the firmament: the atmosphere is so clear that now and then a planet is visible. For the two hours following sunrise the rays are endurable; after that they become a fiery ordeal. The morning beams oppress you with a feeling of sickness; their steady glow, reflected by the glaring waters, blinds your eyes, blisters your skin, and parches your mouth: you now become a monomaniac; you do nothing but count the slow hours that must "minute by" before you can be relieved.

*Noon.* The wind, reverberated by the glowing hills, is like the blast of a lime-kiln. All color melts away with the canescence from above. The sky is a dead milk-white, and the mirror-like sea so reflects the tint that you can scarcely distinguish the line of the horizon. After noon the wind sleeps upon the reeking shore; there is a deep stillness; the only sound heard is the melancholy flapping of the sail. Men are not so much sleeping as half senseless; they feel as if a few more degrees of heat would be death.

*Sunset.* The enemy sinks behind the deep cerulean sea, under a canopy of gigantic rainbow which covers half the face of heaven. Nearest to the horizon is an arch of tawny orange; above it another of the brightest gold, and based upon these a semicircle of tender sea green blends with a score of delicate gradations into the sapphire sky. Across the rainbow the sun throws its rays in the form of spokes tinged with a beautiful pink. The Eastern sky is mantled with a purple flush that picks out the forms of the hazy desert and the sharp-cut hills. Language is a thing too cold, too poor, to express the harmony and the majesty of this hour, which is evanescent, however, as it is lovely. Night falls rapidly, when suddenly the appearance of the zodiacal light restores the scene to what it was. Again the grey hills and the grim rocks become rosy or golden, the palms green, the sands saffron, and the sea wears a lilac surface of dimpling waves. But after a quarter of an hour all fades once more;

the cliffs are naked and ghastly under the moon, whose light falling upon this wilderness of white crags and pinnacles is most strange—most mysterious.

*Night.* The horizon is all of darkness, and the sea reflects the white visage of the moon as in a mirror of steel. In the air we see giant columns of pallid light, distinct, based upon the indigo-colored waves, and standing with their heads lost in endless space. The stars glitter with exceeding brilliance. You feel the "sweet influence of the Pleiades." You are bound by the "bond of Orion." Hesperus bears with him a thousand things. In communion with them your hours pass swiftly by, till the heavy dews warn you to cover up your face and sleep. And with one look at a certain little star in the north, under which lies all that makes life worth living through—you fall into oblivion.

Those thirty-six hours were a trial even to the hard-headed Bedouins. The Syrian and his two friends were ill. Omar Effendi, it is true, had the courage to say his sunset prayers, but the exertion so altered him that he looked another man. Salih Shakkar in despair ate dates till threatened with dysentery. Saad the Devil had rigged out for himself a cot three feet long, which, arched with bent bamboo and covered with cloaks, he had slung on the larboard side; but the loud grumbling which proceeded from his nest proved that his precaution had not been a remedy. Even the boy Mohammed forgot to chatter, to scold, to smoke, and to make himself generally disagreeable. The Turkish lady appeared dying, and was not strong enough to wail. How the poor mother stood her trials so well, made every one wonder. The most pleasant trait in my companions' characters was the consideration they showed to her, and their attention to her children. Whenever one of the party drew forth a little delicacy—a few dates or a pomegranate

—they gave away a share of it to the children, and most of them took their turns to nurse the baby. This was genuine politeness—kindness of heart. It would be well for those who sweepingly accuse Easterns of want of gallantry to contrast this trait of character with the savage scenes of civilization that take place among the "Overlands" at Cairo and Suez. No foreigner could be present for the first time without bearing away the lasting impression that the sons of Great Britain are model barbarians. On board the "Golden Wire" Salih Shakkar was the sole base exception to the general gallantry of my companions.

As the sun starts towards the west, falling harmlessly upon our heads, we arise, still faint and dizzy, calling for water, which before we had not the strength to drink, and pipes, and coffee, and similar luxuries. Our primitive kitchen is a square wooden box, lined with clay, and filled with sand, upon which three or four large stones are placed to form a hearth. Preparations are now made for the evening meal, which is of the simplest description. A little rice, a few dates, or an onion, will keep a man alive in our position; a single "good dinner" would justify long odds against his seeing the next evening. Moreover, it is impossible in such cases to have an appetite, fortunately, as our store of provisions is a scanty one. Arabs consider it desirable on a journey to eat hot food once in twenty-four hours; so we determine to cook, despite all difficulties. The operation, however, is by no means satisfactory; twenty expectants surround the single fire, and there is sure to be a quarrel amongst them every five minutes.

As the breeze, cooled by the dew, begins to fan our parched faces, we recover our spirits amazingly. Songs are sung, and stories are told, and rough jests are bandied about, till not unfrequently Oriental sensitiveness is sorely touched. Or, if we see the prospect of storm or calm, we draw forth, and piously peruse, a "Hizlr el Bahr."* And lastly, we lie down upon our cribs, wrapped up in thickly padded cotton coverlets, and forget the troubles of the past day, and the discomforts of that to come.

Late on the evening of the 11th July we passed in sight of the narrow mouth of Akabah, whose *famosi rupes* are a terror to the voyagers of these latitudes. After passing Akabah, we saw nothing but sea and sky, and we spent a weary night and day tossing upon the waters,—our only exercise: every face brightened as, about sunset, on the 12th, we suddenly glided into the mooring-place.

"Damghah Anchorage"—is scarcely visible from the sea. An islet of limestone rock defends the entrance, leaving a narrow passage on each side. It is not before he enters that the mariner discovers the extent and the depth of this creek, which indents far into the land, and offers 20 feet of fine clear anchorage which no swell can reach. Inside it looks more like a lake, and at night its color is gloriously blue even as Geneva itself.

The Rais, as usual, attempted to deter us from landing, by romancing about the "Bedoynes and Ascopards," representing them to be "folke ryghte felonouse and foule and of cursed kynde." To which we replied by shouldering our Nebuts and scrambling into the cock-boat. On shore we found a few wretched looking beings, seated upon heaps of dried wood, which they sold to travellers, and three boat loads of Syrian pilgrims who had preceded us. We often envied them their small swift craft, with their double latine sails disposed in "hare-ears,"—which, about evening time in the far distance, looked like white gulls alighting on the purple wave; and they justified our envy by arriving at Yambu

* The peculiar fitness of these devotional exercises, is derived from the supposition that it makes all safe upon the ocean wave.

two days before us. The pilgrims had bivouacked upon the beach, and were engaged in drinking their after dinner coffee. They received us with all the rites of hospitality, as natives of the Medinah should everywhere be received; we sat an hour with them, ate a little fruit, satisfied our thirst, smoked their pipes, and when taking leave blessed them. Then returning to the vessel, we fed, and lost no time in falling asleep.

The dawn of the next day saw our sail flapping in the idle air. And it was not without difficulty that in the course of the forenoon we entered Wijh Harbor, distant from Damghah but very few miles. Wijh is also a natural anchorage, in no way differing from that where we passed the night, except in being smaller and shallower. The town is a collection of huts meanly built of round stones, and clustering upon a piece of elevated rock on the northern side of the creek. It is distant about five miles from the inland fort of the same name, which receives the Egyptian caravan, and thrives like its port, by selling water and provisions to pilgrims.

With reeling limbs we landed at Wijh, and finding a large coffee-house above and over the beach, we installed ourselves there. But the Persians who had preceded us had occupied all the shady places outside; we were forced to content ourselves with the interior. It was a building of artless construction, consisting of little but a roof supported by wooden posts, roughly hewn from date trees, and round the tamped earthen floor ran a raised bench of unbaked brick forming a divan for mats and sleeping rugs. In the centre a huge square Mastabah, or platform, answered a similar purpose. Here and there appeared attempts at long and side walls, but these superfluities had been allowed to admit daylight through large gaps. In one corner stood an altar-like elevation, also of earthen work, containing a hole for a charcoal fire, upon which were three huge coffee pots dirtily tinned. Near it were ranged the Shishas, or Egyptian hookahs, old, exceedingly unclean, and worn by age and hard work. A wooden framework, pierced with circular apertures, supported a number of porous earthenware *gúllehs*, full of cold sweet water; the charge for these was, as usual in El Hejaz, five paras apiece. Such was the furniture of the café, and the only relief to the barrenness of the view was a fine mellowing atmosphere composed of smoke, steam, flies, and gnats in about equal proportions. I have been diffuse in my description of this coffee-house, as it was a type of its class: from Alexandria to Aden the traveller will everywhere meet with buildings of the same kind.

My character that day was severely tried. Besides the Persian pilgrims, a number of nondescripts who came in the same vessel were hanging about the coffee-house, lying down, smoking, drinking water, bathing and correcting their teeth with their daggers. One inquisitive man was always at my side. He called himself a Pathan (Afghan settled in India); he could speak five or six languages, knew a number of people everywhere, and had travelled far and wide over Central Asia. These men are always good detectors of an incognito. I avoided answering his question about my native place, and after telling him that I had no longer name or nation, being a Dervish, asked him, when he insisted upon my having been born somewhere, to guess for himself. To my joy he claimed me for a brother Pathan, and in course of conversation he declared himself to be the nephew of an Afghan merchant, a gallant old man who had been civil to me at Cairo. We then sat smoking together with "effusion." Becoming confidential, he complained that he, a Sunni or orthodox Moslem, had been abused, maltreated, and beaten by his fellow travellers, the heretical pilgrims. I naturally offered to arm my party, to take up our cudgels, and to revenge my compatriot. This thoroughly Afghan style of doing business could not fail to make him him sure of his man. He declined, however, wisely remembering that he had nearly a fortnight of the Persians' society still to endure. But he promised himself the gratification, when he reached Meccah, of sheathing his knife in the chief offender's heart.

At 8 A.M. next morning we left Wijh, after passing a night tolerably comfortable, by contrast, in the coffee-house. We took with us the stores necessary, for though our Rais had promised to anchor under Jeber Hasan that evening no one believed him. We sailed among ledges of rock, golden sands, green weeds, and in some places through yellow lines of what appeared to me at a distance foam after a storm. All day a sailor sat upon the mast-head, looking at the water, which was transparent as blue glass, and shouting out the direction. This precaution was somewhat stultified by the roar of voices, which never failed to mingle with the warning, but we wore every half hour, and did not run aground.

Near sunset the wind came on to blow freshly, and we cast anchor together with the Persian pilgrims upon a rock. This was one of the celebrated coral reefs of the Red Sea, and the sight justified Forskal's emphatic description of it—*luxus lususque naturæ.* It was a huge ledge or platform rising but little above the level of the deep; the water-side was perpendicular as the wall of a fort, and whilst a frigate might have floated within a yard of it, every ripple dashed over the reef, replenishing the little basins and hollows in the surface. The color of the waves near it was a vivid amethyst. In the distance the eye rested upon what appeared to be meadows of brilliant flowers resembling those of earth, only brighter far and more lovely. Nor was this land of the sea wholly desolate. Gulls and terns here swam the tide, there, seated upon the coral, devoured their prey. In the air, troops of birds contended noisily for a dead flying-fish, and in the deep water they chased a shoal, which, in their fright and hurry to escape the pursuers, veiled the surface with spray and foam. And as night came on the scene shifted, displaying fresh beauties. Shadows clothed the background, whose features, dimly revealed, allowed full scope to the imagination. In the fore part of the picture lay the sea, shining under the rays of the moon with a metallic lustre, while its border, where the wavelets dashed upon the reef, was lit by what the Arabs call the "jewels of the deep"—brilliant flashes of phosphoric light giving an idea of splendor which art would strive in vain to imitate. Altogether it was a bit of fairy land, a spot for nymphs and sea-gods to disport upon; you might have heard, without astonishment, old Proteus calling his flocks with the wreathed horn; and Aphrodite seated in her conch would have been only a fit and proper climax of its loveliness.

At dawn next day we started; we made Jebel Hasan* about noon, and an hour or so before sunset we glided into Marsa Maliar.

Wading on shore, we cut our feet with the sharp rocks. I remember to have felt the acute pain of something running into my toe, but after looking at the place and extracting what appeared to be a bit of thorn, I dismissed the subject, little guessing the trouble it was to give me. Having scaled the rocky side of the cove, we found some half naked Arabs lying in the shade; they were unarmed, and had nothing about them except their villanous countenances wherewith to terrify the most timid. These men

* The word Jebel will frequently occur in these pages. It is applied by the Arabs to any rising ground or heap of rocks, and, therefore, must not always be translated "mountain."

still live in caves, like the Shamud tribe of tradition; they are still Ichthyophagi, existing without any other subsistence but what the sea affords. They were unable to provide us with dates or milk, but they sold us a kind of fish called Bui, which, boiled upon the embers, proved delicious.

Our next day was a silent and a weary one, for we were all heartily sick of being on board-ship. We should have made Yambu in the evening but for the laziness of the Rais. Having duly beaten him, we anchored on the open coast, insufficiently protected by a reef, and almost in sight of our destination.

We slept upon the sands and rose before dawn, determined to make the Rais start in time that day. A slip of land separated us from our haven, but the wind was foul, and by reason of rocks and shoals, we had to make a considerable *detour*.

It was about noon on the 12th day after our departure from Suez, when, after slowly beating up the narrow creek leading to Yambu harbor, we sprang into a shore boat and felt new life, when bidding an eternal adieu to the "Golden Wire."

I might have escaped much of this hardship and suffering by hiring a vessel to myself. There would then have been a cabin to retire into at night, and shade from the sun; moreover the voyage would have lasted five, not twelve days. But I wished to witness the scenes on board a pilgrim ship,—scenes so much talked of by the Moslem palmer home returned. Moreover, the hire was exorbitant, ranging from 40*l.* to 50*l.*, and it would have led to a greater expenditure, as the man who can afford to take a boat must pay in proportion during his land journey. In these countries you perforce go on as you begin: to "break one's expenditure," that is to say, to retrench one's expenses, is considered all but impossible; the prudent traveller, therefore, will begin as he intends to go on.

# CHAPTER XI.

## THE HALT AT YAMBU.

YANBU EL BAHR is a place of considerable importance, and shares with others the title of "Gate of the Holy City." It is the third quarter of the caravan road from Cairo to Meccah; and here, as well as at El Bedr, pilgrims frequently leave behind them in hired warehouses goods too heavy to be transported in haste, or too valuable to risk in dangerous times. Yambu being the port of El Medinah, as Jeddah is of Meccah, is supported by a considerable transport trade and extensive imports from the harbor on the western coasts of the Red Sea. Here the Sultan's dominion is supposed to begin, whilst the authority of the Pacha of Egypt ceases; there is no Nizám, however, in the town,* and the governor is a Sheríf or Arab chief.

The town itself is in no wise remarkable. The customhouse fronts the landing-place upon the harbor; it is managed by Turkish officials,—men dressed in tarbooshes, who repose the live-long day upon the divans near the windows. In the case of us travellers they had a very simple

* The Nizám, as Europeans now know, is the regular Turkish infantry.

way of doing business, charging each person of the party three piastres for each large box, but by no means troubling themselves to meddle with the contents.

The population of Yambu—one of the most bigoted and quarrelsome races in El Hejaz—strikes the eye after arriving from Egypt, as decidedly a new feature. The Shaykh, or gentleman of Yambu, is over-armed and over-dressed as Fashion, the tyrant of the desert as well as of the court, dictates to a person of his consequence. The civilized traveller from El Medinah sticks in his waist-shawl a loaded pistol,* garnished with crimson silk cord, but he partially conceals the butt-end under the flap of his jacket. The irregular soldier struts down the street a small armory of weapons: one look at the man's countenance suffices to tell you what he is. Here and there stalk grim Bedouins, wild as their native wastes, and in all the dignity and pride of dirt; they also are armed to the teeth, and even the presence of the policeman's quarter-staff cannot keep their swords in their scabbards: what we should call the peaceful part of the population never leave the house without a "nebût" (staff) over the right shoulder, and the larger, the longer, and the heavier the weapon is, the more gallantry does the bearer claim. The people of Yambu practise the use of this implement diligently; they become expert in delivering a head blow so violently as to break through any guard, and with it they always decide their trivial quarrels. The dress of the women differs but little from that of the Egyptians, except in the face veil, which is generally white. There is an independent bearing about

* Civilians usually stick one pistol in the belt; soldiers or fighting men two, or more, with all the necessary concomitants of pouches, turnscrews, and long iron ramrods, which, opening with a screw, disclose a long thin pair of pincers, wherewith fire is put upon the chibouque.

the people strange in the East; they are proud without insolence, and look manly without blustering. Their walk partakes somewhat of the nature of a strut, owing, perhaps, to the shape of the sandals, not a little assisted by the self-esteem of the wearer, but there is nothing offensive in it; moreover, the population has a healthy appearance, and, fresh from Egypt, I could not help noticing their freedom from ophthalmic disease.

On the afternoon of the day of our arrival we sent for a *Mukharrij*,* and began to treat for camels. We agreed to pay three dollars for each camel, half in ready money, the other half after reaching our destination, and to start on the evening of the next day with a grain-caravan, guarded by an escort of irregular cavalry. I hired two animals, one for my luggage and servant, the other for the boy Mohammed and myself, expressly stipulating that we were to ride the better, and that if it broke down on the road, its place should be supplied by another as good. My friends could not dissemble their uneasiness, when informed by the *Mukharrij* that the Hazimi tribe was "out," and that travellers had to fight every day. The Daghistanis also contributed to their alarm. "We met," said they, "between two hundred and three hundred devils on a Razzia near El Medinah; we gave them the Salam, but they would not reply, although we were all on dromedaries. Then they asked us if we were men of El Medinah, and we replied, 'Yes,' and lastly, they wanted to know the end of our journey; so we said Bir

* The Shaykh, or agent of the camels, without whose assistance it would be difficult to hire beasts. He brings the Bedouins with him, talks them over to fair terms, sees the "arbún," or earnest money, delivered to them, and is answerable for their not failing in their engagement.

Abbas."* The Bedouins who had accompanied the Daghistanis belonged to some tribe unconnected with the Hazimi: the spokesman rolled his head, as much as to say, "Allah has preserved us!" "Sir," said Shaykh Nur to me, "we must wait till all this is over." I told him to hold his tongue, and sharply reproved the boy Mohammed, upon whose manner the effect of finding himself suddenly in a fresh country had wrought a change for the worse. "Why ye were lions at Cairo—and here, at Yambu, you are cats—hens!" It was not long, however, before the youth's impudence returned upon him with increased violence.

We sat through the afternoon in the little room on the terrace, whose reflected heat, together with the fiery winds from the wilderness, seemed to incommode even my companions. After sunset we dined in the open air, a body of twenty: master, servants, children, and strangers. All the procurable rugs and pillows had been seized to make a divan, and we all squatted round a large cauldron of boiled rice, containing square masses of mutton, the whole covered with clarified butter. Saad the Devil was now in his glory. With what anecdotes the occasion supplied him!—his tongue seemed to wag with a perpetual motion—for each man he had a boisterous greeting, and to judge

* The not returning "Salam" was a sign on the part of the Bedouins that they were out to fight, and not to make friends; and the dromedary riders, who generally travel without much to rob, thought this behavior a declaration of desperate designs. The Bedouins asked if they were El Medinah men; because the former do not like, unless when absolutely necessary, to plunder the people of the Holy City. And the Daghistanis said their destination was Bir Abbas, a neighboring, instead of Yambu, a distant port, because those who travel on a long journey, being supposed to have more funds with them, are more likely to be molested.

from his whisperings he must have been in every one's privacy and confidence. Conversation over, pipes and coffee was prolonged to 10 P. M.—a late hour in these lands; then we prayed the Ishah,* and, spreading our mats upon the terrace, slept in the open air.

The forenoon of the next day was occupied in making sundry small purchases. We laid in seven days' provision for the journey, repacked our boxes, polished and loaded our arms, and attired ourselves appropriately for the road. I bought for my own conveyance a *shugduf* or litter, for which I paid two dollars. It is a vehicle appropriated to women and children, fathers of families, married men, "Shelebis,"† and generally to those who are too effeminate to ride. My reason for choosing it was, that notes are more easily taken in it than on a dromedary's back; the excuse of lameness prevented it detracting from my manhood, and I was careful when entering any populous place to borrow or hire a saddled beast.

Our party dined early that day, for the camels had been sitting at the gate since noon. We had the usual trouble in loading them; the owners of the animals vociferating about the unconscionable weight, the owners of the goods swearing that such weight a child could carry, while the beasts, taking part with their proprietors, moaned piteously, roared, made vicious attempts to bite, and started up with an agility that threw the half secured boxes or sacks headlong to the ground. About 3 P. M. all was ready—the camels formed into Indian file, and were placed standing in the streets—but, as usual with Oriental travellers, all the men dispersed about the town, so we did not mount before it was late in the afternoon.

I must now take the liberty of presenting to the reader

* The night prayer. † "Exquisites."

an Arab Shaykh, fully equipped for travelling. Nothing can be more picturesque than the costume, and it is with regret that we see it exchanged in the towns and more civilized parts for any other: The long locks or the shaven scalps are surmounted by a white cotton skull-cap, over which is a kufiyah—a large square kerchief of silk and cotton mixed, and generally of a dull red color, with a bright yellow border, from which depend crimson silk twist, ending in little tassels that reach the wearer's waist. Doubled into a triangle, and bound with a fillet of rope, a skein of yarn, or a twist of wool, the kerchief fits the head closely behind; it projects over the forehead, shading the eyes, and thus gives a fierce look to the countenance. On certain occasions one end is brought round the lower part of the face, and is fastened behind the head, leaving only the eyes visible. This veiling the features is technically called *Lisam*—the chiefs generally fight so, and it is the usual disguise when a man fears the avenger of blood, or a woman starts to take her *Sar*.* In hot weather it is supposed to keep the Simoom, in cold weather the catarrh, from the lungs.

The body dress is simply a *Kamís* or cotton shirt; tight sleeved, opening in front, and adorned round the waist and collar, and down the breast, with embroidery like net-work, it extends from neck to foot. Some wear wide trousers, but the Bedouins consider such things effeminate, and they have not yet fallen into the folly of socks and stockings. Over the Kamís is thrown a long skirted and short-sleeved cloak of camel's hair, called an Aba. It is made in many patterns, and of all materials from pure silk to coarse sheep's wool; some prefer it brown, others white, others striped: in El Hejaz the favorite Aba is a white one,

* "The "blood revenge."

embroidered with gold, tinsel, or yellow thread in two large triangles, capped with broad bands and other figures running down the shoulders and sides of the back. It is lined inside the shoulders and breast with handsome stuffs of silk and cotton mixed, and is tied in front by elaborate strings, and tassels or acorns of silk and gold. A sash confines the Kamís at the waist, and supports the silver-hilted dagger or crooked dagger, and the picturesque Arab sandal completes the costume. Finally, the Shaykh's arms are a matchlock slung behind his back, and a sword; in his right hand he carries a light crooked stick about two feet and a half long, called a *Mas-hab*, used for guiding camels, or a short javelin.

The poorer class of Arabs twist round their waist, next to the skin, a long plait of greasy leather, to support the back, and they gird the shirt at the middle merely with a cord, or with a coarse sash. The dagger is stuck in the sash, and a bandoleer slung over the shoulders carries their cartridge-case, powder-flask, flint and steel, priming-horn, and other necessaries. With the traveller, the waist is an elaborate affair. Below all is worn the money pouch, concealed by the Kamís; the latter is girt with a waist shawl, over which is strapped a leathern belt for carrying arms. The latter article should always be well garnished with a pair of long-barrelled and silver-mounted flint pistols, a large and a small dagger, and an iron ramrod with pincers inside; a little leathern pouch fastened to the waist strap on the right side contains cartridge, wadding, and a flask of priming powder. The sword hangs over the shoulder with crimson silk cords and huge tassels; well dressed men apply the same showy ornaments to their pistols. In the hand may be carried a bell-mouthed blunderbuss, or, better still, a long single-barrel gun with an ounce bore. All these weapons must shine like silver, if you wish to be respected; for attention to arms is here a sign of manliness.

Pilgrims, especially those from Turkey, carry a "Hamail," to denote their holy errand. This is a pocket Koran, in a handsome gold embroidered crimson velvet or red morocco case, slung by red silk cords over the left shoulder. It must hang down by the right side, and should never for respect depend below the waist-belt. For this I substituted a most useful article. To all appearance a "Hamail," it had inside three compartments, one for my watch and compass, the second for ready money, and the third contained penknife, pencils, and slips of paper, which I could hold concealed in the hollow of my hand. These were for writing and drawing: opportunities of making a "fair copy" into the diary-book,* are never wanting to the acute traveller. He must, however, beware of sketching before the Bedouins, who would certainly proceed to extreme measures, suspecting him to be a spy or a sorcerer.† Nothing

* My diary-book was made up for me by a Cairene: it was a long thin volume fitting into a breast-pocket, where it could be carried without being seen. I began by writing notes in the Arabic character, but as no risk appeared, my journal was afterwards kept in English. More than once, by way of experiment, I showed the writing on a loose slip of paper to my companions, and astonished them with the strange character derived from Solomon and Alexander, the Lord of the two Horns, which we Afghans still use.

† An accident of this kind happened not long ago to a German traveller in the Hadramaut, who shall be nameless. He had the mortification to see his sketch-book, the labor of months, summarily appropriated and destroyed by the Arabs. I was told by a Hadramaut man at Cairo, and by several at Aden, that the gentleman had at the time a narrow escape with his life; the Bedouins wished to put him to death as a spy, sent by the Frank to *ensorceler* their country, but the Shaykhs forbade bloodshed, and merely deported the offender. Travellers caught sketching are not often treated with such forbearance.

so effectually puzzles these people as our habit of putting everything on paper; their imaginations are set at work, and then the worst may be expected from them. The only safe way of writing in presence of a Bedouin would be when drawing out a horoscope or preparing a charm; he also objects not, if you can warm his heart upon the subject, to seeing you take notes in a book of genealogies. You might begin with, "And you, men of Harb, on which origin do you pride yourselves?" And while the listeners become fluent upon the, to them, all interesting theme, you could put down whatever you please upon the margin. The towns-people are more liberal, and years ago the holy shrines have been drawn, and even lithographed, by Eastern artists: still, if you wish to avoid all suspicion, you must rarely be seen with pen or with pencil in hand.

At 6 P. M. descending the stairs of our Wakálat, we found the camels standing loaded in the street and shifting their ground in token of impatience.* My shugduf, perched upon the back of a tall strong animal, nodded and swayed about with his every motion, impressing me with the idea that the first step would throw it over the shoulders or the crupper. The camel-men told me I must climb up the animal's neck, and so creep into the vehicle. But my foot disabling me from such exertion, I insisted on their bringing the beast to squat, which they did grumblingly. We took leave of Omar Effendi's brothers and their dependents, who insisted on paying us the compliment of accompanying us to the gate. Then we mounted and started, which was a signal for all our party to disperse once more. Some heard the report of a vessel having arrived from Suez, with Ma-

* All Arabs assert that it pains the loaded camel's feet to stand still, and certainly the "fidgetiness" of the animal to start, looks as if he had some reason to prefer walking.

hammed Shiklibah and other friends on board; these hurried down to the harbor for a parting word. Others, declaring they had forgotten some necessaries for the way, ran off to the bazaar to spend one last hour in gossiping at the coffee-house. Then the sun set, and prayers must be said. The brief twilight had almost faded away before all had mounted. With loud cries, we threaded our way through long, dusty, narrow streets, flanked with white-washed habitations at considerable intervals, and large heaps of rubbish, sometimes higher than the houses. We were stopped at the gate to ascertain if we were strangers, in which case the guard would have done his best to extract a few piastres before allowing our luggage to pass; but he soon perceived by my companions' accent, that they were sons of the Holy City—consequently, that the case was hopeless. The moon rose fair and clear, dazzling us with light as we emerged from the shadowy streets, and when we launched into the Desert the sweet air delightfully contrasted with the close offensive atmosphere of the town. My companions, as Arabs will do on such occasions, began to sing.

## CHAPTER XII.

### FROM YAMBU TO BIR ABBAS.

On the 18th July, about 7 P. M., we passed through the gate of Yambu, and took a due easterly course. Our route lay over the plain between the mountains of Radhawh on the left and the sea on the right hand; the land was desert, that is to say, a hard level plain, strewed with rounded lumps of granite and greenstone schist, with here and there a dwarf acacia, and a tuft of rank camel grass. By the light of a glorious moon nearly at its full I was able to see the country tolerably well.

Our little party consisted of twelve camels, and we travelled in Indian file, head tied to tail, with but one outrider, Omar Effendi, whose rank required him to mount a dromedary with showy trappings. All the party, except Omar Effendi, in token of poverty, were dressed in the coarsest and dirtiest of clothes,—the general suit consisting of a shirt torn in divers places and a bit of rag wrapped round the head. They carried short chibouques without mouth-pieces, and tobacco-pouches of greasy leather. Though the country hereabouts is perfectly safe, all had their arms in readiness, and the unusual silence that succeeded to the singing, (even Saad the Devil held his tongue,) was sufficient to show how much they feared for themselves and their property. After a slow march of two hours facing the moon, we turned somewhat towards the N. E., and began to pass over undulating ground, in which a steady rise was perceptible. We arrived at the halting-place at three in the morning after a short march of about eight hours, during which we could not have passed over more than sixteen miles. The camels were *nakh'd;* the boxes were taken off and piled together as a precaution against invisible robbers; my little tent, the only one in the party, was pitched; we then spread our rugs upon the ground and lay down to sleep.

We arose at about 9 A. M., and after congratulating one another upon being once more in the "dear Desert," we proceeded in exhilarated mood to light the fire for pipes and breakfast. The meal was soon dispatched, after which I proceeded to inspect our position.

About a mile to the westward lay the little village of Musahlah,* a group of miserable clay hovels. On the south was a strip of bright blue sea, and all around, an iron plain producing naught but stones and grass-hoppers, bounded northward by a grisly wall of blackish rock. Here and there a shrub fit only for fuel, or a tuft of coarse grass, crisp with heat, met the eye. All was sun-parched; the furious heat from above was drying up the sap and juice of the land, as the shivering and quivering atmosphere showed; moreover the heavy dews of these regions, forming in large drops upon the plants and stones, concentrate the morning rays

* The reader must be warned that these little villages in Arabia, as in Sindh and Belochistan, are continually changing their names, whilst the larger settlements always retain the same. The traveller, too, must beware of writing down the first answer he receives; in one of our maps a village on the Euphrates is gravely named "M'adri," ("Don't know.")

upon them like a system of burning glasses. After making these few observations I followed the example of my companions, and went to sleep.

At 2 P.M. we were roused to a dinner as simple as the breakfast had been. Our potations began before dinner with a vile-tasted but wholesome drink called Akit; * at the meal we drank leather-flavored water, and ended with a large cupful of scalding tea. Enormous quantities of liquid were consumed, for the sun seemed to have got into our throats, and the perspiration trickled from us as after a shower of rain. Whilst we were eating, a Bedouin woman passed close by the tent, leading a flock of sheep and goats, seeing which I expressed a desire to drink milk. My companions sent by one of the camel-men a bit of bread, and asked in exchange for a cupful of "laban." † Thus I learned that the Arabs, even in this corrupt region, still adhere to the meaningless custom of their ancestors, who chose to make the term "labbán" (milk-seller) an opprobrium and a disgrace. Possibly the origin of the prejudice might be the recognising of a traveller's guest-right to call for milk gratis. However this may be, no one will in the present day sell this article of consumption, even at civilized Meccah, except Egyptians, a people supposed to be utterly without honor. As a general rule in the Hejaz, milk abounds in the spring, but at all other times of the year it is difficult to be procured. The Bedouin woman managed, however, to send me back a cupful.

At 3 P.M. we were ready to start, and all saw, with un-

* The Arabs make it by evaporating the serous part of the milk; the remainder is then formed into cakes or lumps with the hand, and spread upon hair cloth to dry. They eat it with clarified butter, and drink it melted in water. It is considered a cooling and refreshing beverage, but boasts few attractions to the stranger.

† In Arabic and Hebrew milk.

speakable gratification, a huge black nimbus rise and range itself, like a good genius, between us and our terrible foe, the sun. We hoped that it contained rain, but presently a blast of hot wind, like the breath of a volcano, blew over the plain, and the air was filled with particles of sand. When we had loaded and mounted, my coachmen, two in number, came up to the shugduf and demanded "bakhshish," which, it appears, they are now in the habit of doing each time the traveller starts. I was at first surprised to find the word here, but after a few days of Bedouin society, my wonder diminished. The men were Beni-Harb of the great Hejazi tribe, which has kept its blood pure for the last thirteen centuries, how much more we know not—but they had been corrupted by intercourse with pilgrims, retaining none of their ancestral qualities but greed of gain, revengefulness, pugnacity, and a frantic kind of bravery, displayed on rare occasions. I taunted them severely with their resemblance to the Fellahs of Egypt. They would have resented this with asperity, had it proceeded from their own people, but the Turkish pilgrim—the character in which they knew me, despite my Arab dress—is a privileged person. Their outer man was contemptible; small chocolate-colored beings, stunted and thin, with mops of coarse bushy hair burned brown by the sun, straggling beards, vicious eyes, frowning brows, screaming voices, and well-made, but attenuated, limbs. On their heads were (kerchiefs) in the last stage of wear; a tattered shirt, indigo-dyed, and girt with a bit of common rope, composed their brief clothing; and their feet were protected from the stones by soles of thick leather, kept in place by narrow thongs tied to the ancle. Both were armed, one with a matchlock, and a *Shintiyan* * in a leathern scabbard, slung over the

* The Shintiyan is the common sword-blade of the Bedouins. Excellent weapons abound in this country, the reason being, that there is a

shoulder, the other with a *nebút*, and both showed at the waist the Arab's invariable companion, the dagger.

Our party was now a strong one. We had about 200 camels carrying grain, attended by their proprietors, truculent looking as the contrabandists of the Pyrenees. The escort was composed of seven Irregular Turkish cavalry, tolerably mounted, and supplied each with an armory in epitome. They were privily derided by our party, who, being Arabs, had a sneaking fondness for the Bedouins, however loath they might be to see them amongst the boxes.

For three hours we travelled in a south-easterly direction upon a hard plain and a sandy flat, on which several waters from the highlands find a passage to the sea westward. Gradually we were siding towards the mountains, and at sunset I observed that we had sensibly neared them. We dismounted for a short halt, and, strangers being present, my companions said their prayers before sitting down to smoke—a pious exercise in which they did not engage for three days afterwards, when they met certain acquaintances at El Hamra. As evening came on, we emerged from a scent of acacias and tamarisk and turned due east, traversing an open country with a perceptible rise. Scarcely was it dark before the cry of "Harámi" (thieves) rose loud in the rear. All the camel-men brandished their huge staves, and rushed back vociferating in the direction of the robbers. They were followed by all the horsemen, and truly, had the thieves possessed the usual acuteness of the profession, they might have driven off the camels in our van with safety and convenience. But these contemptible beings

perpetual demand for them, and when once purchased, they become heir-looms in the family. I have heard that when the Beni Bu Ali tribe, near Ras el Khaymah, was defeated with slaughter by Sir Lionel Smith's expedition, the victors found many valuable old European blades in the hands of the slain.

were only half a dozen in number, and they had lighted their matchlocks, which drew a bullet or two in their direction, whereupon they ran away. This incident aroused no inconsiderable excitement, for it seemed ominous of worse things about to happen to us when entangled in the hills, and the faces of my companions, perfect barometers of fair and foul tidings, fell to zero. For nine hours we journeyed through a brilliant moonlight, and as the first grey streak appeared in the Eastern sky we entered a scanty "*misyal*,"* or *fiumara*, strewed with pebbles and rounded stones, about half a mile in breadth, and flanked by almost perpendicular hills of primitive formation. I began by asking the names of peaks and other remarkable spots, when I found that a folio volume would not contain a three months' collection; every hill and dale, flat, valley, and water-course here has its proper name or rather names. The ingenuity shown by the Bedouins in distinguishing between localities the most similar, is the result of a high organization of the perceptive faculties, perfected by the practice of observing a recurrence of landscape features few in number and varying but little amongst themselves. After travelling two hours up this torrent bed, winding in an easterly direction, and crossing some "*Harrah*," or ridges of rock, and "*Ria*," steep descents, we found ourselves at 8 A.M., after a march of about thirty-four miles, at Bir Said (Said's well), our destination.

I had been led to expect a pastoral scene, wild flowers, flocks, and flowing waters at the "well;" so I looked with a jaundiced eye upon a deep hole full of slightly brackish water dug in a tamped hollow—a kind of punch-bowl with granite walls, upon whose grim surface a few thorns, of passing hardihood, braved the sun for a season. Not a

* The dry channel of a hill water-course.

house was in sight—it was as barren and desolate a spot as the sun ever "viewed in his wide career." But this is what the Arabian traveller must expect. He is to traverse, for instance, the Wady El Ward—the vale of flowers; he indulges in sweet recollections of Indian lakes beautiful with the lotus, and Persian plains upon which narcissus is the meanest of grasses; he sees a plain like tamp-work, where knobs of granite act daisies, and at every fifty yards some hapless bud or blossom dying of inanition among the stones.

The sun scorched our feet as we planted the tent, and, after drinking our breakfast, we passed the usual day of perspiration and semi-lethargy. In discomfort man naturally hails a change, even though it be one from bad to worse. When our enemy began slanting towards the west, we felt ready enough to proceed on our journey. The camels were laden shortly after 3 P. M., and we started with water jars in our hands through a storm of simoom.

We travelled five hours in a north-easterly course up a diagonal valley, through a country fantastic in its desolation—a mass of huge hills, barren plains, and desert vales. Even the sturdy acacias here failed, and in some places the camel grass could not find earth enough to take root in. The road wound among mountains, rocks, and hills of granite, over broken ground, flanked by huge blocks and boulders, piled up as if man's art had aided nature to disfigure herself. Vast clefts seamed like scars the hideous face of earth; here they widened into dark caves, there they were choked up with glistening drift sand. Not a bird or a beast was to be seen or heard; their presence would have argued the vicinity of water, and though my companions opined that Bedouins were lurking among the rocks, I decided that these Bedouins were the creatures of their fears. Above, a sky like polished blue steel, with a tremendous blaze of yellow light, glared upon us without the thinnest veil of mist cloud. The distant prospect, indeed, was more attractive than the near view, because it borrowed a bright azure tinge from the intervening atmosphere; but the jagged peaks and the perpendicular streaks of shadow down the flanks of the mountainous background showed that no change for the better was yet in store for us.

Between 10 and 11 P. M. we reached human habitations —a phenomenon unseen since we left Musahhal—in the long straggling village called El Hamra, from the redness of the sands near which it is built, or El Wasitah, the "half-way" village, because it is the middle station between Yambu and El Medinah. It is therefore considerably out of place in Burckhardt's map, and those who copy from it make it about half-way nearer the seaport than it really is. We wandered about nearly an hour in search of an encamping place, for the surly villagers ordered us off every flatter bit of ground, without however deigning to show us where our jaded beasts might rest. At last, after much wrangling, we found the usual spot; the camels were unloaded, the boxes and baggage were disposed in a circle for greater security against the petty pilferers in which this part of the road abounds, and my companions spread their rugs so as to sleep upon their valuables. I placed a drawn sword by my side,* and a cocked pistol under my pillow; the saddle-bag, a carpet spread upon the cool loose sand, formed by no means an uncomfortable couch, and upon it I enjoyed a sound sleep till daybreak.

Rising at dawn, I proceeded to visit the village. It is

* This act, by the by, I afterwards learned to be a great act of imprudence. Nothing renders the Arab thief so active as the chance of stealing a good weapon.

built upon a narrow shelf at the top of a precipitous hill to the North, and on the South runs a sandy Fiumara, about half a mile broad. On all sides are rocks and mountains, rough and stony; so you find yourself in another of those punch-bowls which the Arabs seem to consider choice sites for settlements. Water of good quality is readily found in it by digging a few feet below the surface at the angles where the stream as it runs forms the deepest hollows, and in some places the stony sides give out bubbling springs.*

El Hamra itself is a collection of stunted houses, or rather hovels, made of unbaked brick and mud, roofed over with palm leaves, and pierced with air holes, which occasionally boast a bit of plank for a shutter. It appears thickly populated in the parts where the walls are standing, but it abounds in ruins. It is well supplied with provisions, which are here cheaper than at El Medinah. In the village are a few shops where grain, huge plantains, ready-made bread, rice, clarified butter, and other edibles, are to be purchased. Palm orchards of considerable extent supply it with dates. The bazaar is, like the generality of such places in Eastern villages, a long lane, here covered with matting, there open to the sun, and the streets—if they may be so called—though narrow, are full of dust and glare. Near the encamping ground of caravans is a fort for the officer commanding a troop of Albanian cavalry, whose duty it is to defend the village, to hold the country, and to escort merchant travellers. Around the El Hamra fort are clusters of palm-leaf huts, where the soldiery lounge and smoke, and near it the usual coffee-house, a

* Near El Hamra, at the base of the southern hills, within fire of the forts, there is a fine spring of sweet water. All such fountains are much prized by the people, who call them "rock-water," and attribute to them tonic and digestive virtues.

shed kept by an Albanian. These places are frequented probably on account of the intense heat inside the fort.

We passed a comfortless day at the "Red village." Large flocks of sheep and goats were being driven in and out of the place, but their surly shepherds would give no milk, even in exchange for bread and meat. Before breakfast I bought a moderately sized sheep for a dollar. Shaykh Hamid killed it, according to rule, and my companions soon prepared a feast of boiled mutton. But our day was especially soured by a report, that Saad, the great robber-chief, and his brother, were in the field; consequently that our march would be delayed for some time: every half-hour some fresh tattle from the camp or the coffee-house added fuel to the fire of our impatience.

Saad, the old man of the mountains, was described to me as a little brown Bedouin, contemptible in appearance, but remarkable for courage and ready wit. He has a keen scent for treachery and requires to keep it in exercise. A blood feud with Abdul Muttaleb, the present sherif of Meccah, who slew his nephew, and the hostility of several Sultans, has rendered his life an eventful one. He lost all his teeth by poison, which would have killed him, had he not in mistake, after swallowing the potion, corrected it by drinking off a large pot of clarified butter. Since that time he has lived entirely upon fruits which he gathers for himself, and coffee which he prepares with his own hand. In Sultan Mohammed's time he received from Constantinople a gorgeous purse, which he was told to open himself, as it contained something for his private inspection. Suspecting treachery he gave it for this purpose to a slave, bidding him carry it to some distance; the bearer was shot by a pistol cunningly fixed, like Rob Roy's, in the folds of the bag. But whether this well-known story be "true or only well found," it is certain that Shaykh Saad now fears the Turks, even "when they bring gifts." The Sultan sends or is supposed to send him presents of fine horses, robes of honor, and a large quantity of grain. But the Shaykh, trusting to his hills rather than to steeds, sells them; he gives away the dresses to his slaves, and distributes the grain amongst his clansmen. Of his character men tell two tales; some praise his charity, and call him the friend of the poor, as certainly as he is a foe to the rich. Others on the contrary describe him as cruel, cold-blooded, and notably, even among Arabs, revengeful and avaricious. The truth probably lies between these two extremes, but I observed that those of my companions who spoke most highly of the robber chief when at a distance seemed to be in the *sudori freddi* whilst under the shadow of his hills.

El Hamra is the third station from El Medinah, in the Darb Sultani—"Sultan's" or "High Road," the westerly line leading to Meccah along the sea-coast. When the robbers permit, the pilgrims prefer this route to all others on account of its superior climate, the facility of procuring water and supplies, the vicinity of the sea, and the circumstance of its passing through "Bedr," the scene of the Prophet's principal military exploits. After mid-day, (on the 21st July,) when we had made up our minds that fate had determined we should halt at El Hamra, a caravan arrived from Meccah, and the new travellers had interest to procure an escort and permission to proceed towards El Medinah without delay. The good news filled us with joy. A little after 4 P. M. we urged our panting camels over the fiery sands to join the Meccans, who were standing ready for the march, on the other side of the torrent bed, and at five we started in an easterly direction.

My companions had found friends and relations in the Meccan caravan,—the boy Mohammed's elder brother, about whom more anon, was of the number;—they were full of news and excitement. At sunset they prayed with unction: even Saad and Hamid had not the face to sit their camels during the halt, when all around were washing, sanding themselves, and busy with their devotions. We then ate our suppers, remounted, and started once more. Shortly after night set in, we came to a sudden halt. A dozen different reports arose to account for this circumstance, which was occasioned by a band of Bedouins, who had manned a gorge, and sent forward a "parliamentary" ordering us forthwith to stop. They at first demanded money to let us pass; but at last, hearing that we were sons of the Holy Cities, they granted us transit on the sole condition that the military,—whom they, like Irish peasants, hate and fear,—should return to whence they came. Upon this, our escort, 200 men, wheeled their horses round and galloped back to their barracks. We moved onwards, without, however, seeing any robbers; my camel-man pointed out their haunts, and showed me a small bird hovering over a place where he supposed water trickled from the rock.

Our night's journey had no other incident. We travelled over rising ground with the moon full in our faces, and about midnight passed through another long straggling line of villages, called Jadaydeh. At 4 A. M., having travelled about twenty-four miles due east, we encamped at Bir Abbas.

## CHAPTER XIII.

### FROM BIR ABBAS TO EL MEDINAH.

THE position of Bir Abbas exactly resembles that of El Hamra, except that the bulge of the hill-girt fiumara is at this place about two miles wide. "There are the usual stone forts and palm-leaved hovels for the troopers," stationed here to hold the place and to escort travellers, with a coffee-shed, and a hut or two, called a bazaar, but no village. The encamping ground was a bed of loose sand, with which the violent simoom wind filled the air: not a tree nor a bush was in sight; a species of hardy locust and swarms of flies were the only remnants of animal life. Although we were now some hundred feet, to judge by the water-shed, above the level of the sea, the mid-day sun scorched even through the tent; our frail tenement was more than once blown down, and the heat of the sand made the work of repitching it a painful one. Again my companions, after breakfasting, hurried to the coffee-house, and returned one after the other with dispiriting reports. Before noon a small caravan which followed us came in with two dead bodies,—a trooper shot by the Bedouins, and an Albanian killed by sun-stroke, or the fiery wind. Shortly after mid-day a Cafila, travelling in an opposite direction, passed by us; it was composed chiefly of Indian pilgrims, habited in correct costume, and hurrying towards Meccah in hot haste. They had been allowed to pass unmolested, because probably a pound sterling could not have been collected from a hundred pockets, and Saad the robber sometimes does a cheap good deed. But our party having valuables with them did not seem to gather heart from this event. In the evening we all went out to see some Arab Shaykhs who were travelling to Bir Abbas in order to receive their salaries. Without such *douceurs*, it is popularly said and believed, no stone walls could enable a Turk to hold El Hejaz against the hill men. The party looked well; they were Harbis, dignified old men in the picturesque Arab costume, with erect forms, fierce thin features, and white beards, well armed, and mounted upon high-bred and handsomely equipped dromedaries from El Shark.* Preceded by their half-naked clansmen, carrying spears twelve or thirteen feet long, garnished with single or double tufts of black ostrich feathers, and ponderous matchlocks, which were discharged on approaching the fort, they were not without a kind of barbaric pomp.

Immediately after the reception of these Shaykhs, there was a parade of the Arnaut Irregular horse. About 500 of them rode out to the sound of a *nakús* or little kettle-drum, whose puny notes strikingly contrasted with this really martial sight. The men, it is true, were mounted on lean Arab and Egyptian nags, were ragged looking as their clothes, and each trooper was armed in his own way,

* El Shark, "the East," is the popular name in the Hejaz for the western region as far as Baghdad and Bussora, especially Nijd. The latter province supplies the Holy Land with its choicest horses and camels.

though all had swords, pistols, and matchlocks, or firelocks of some kind. But they rode hard as Galway squireens, and there was a gallant reckless look about the fellows which prepossessed me strongly in their favor. Their animals, too, though notable "screws," were well trained, and their accoutrements were intended for use, not show. I watched their manœuvres with curiosity. They left their cantonments one by one, and, at the sound of the tom-tom, by degrees formed a plump—*column* it could not be called —all huddled together in confusion. Presently the little kettle-drum changed its note and the parade its aspect. All the serried body dispersed as Light Infantry would, continuing their advance, now hanging back, then making a rush, and all the time keeping up a hot fire upon the enemy. At another signal they suddenly put their horses to full speed, and, closing upon the centre, again advanced in a dense mass. After three quarters of an hour parading, sometimes charging singly, often in bodies, now to the right, then to the left, and then straight in front, when requisite halting and occasionally retreating, Parthian-like, the Arnauts turned *en masse* towards their lines. As they neared them, all broke off and galloped in, *ventre à terre*, discharging their shotted guns with much recklessness against objects assumed to denote the enemy. But ball cartridge seemed to be plentiful hereabouts; during the whole of this and the next day, I remarked that bullets were fired away in mere fun.*

* The Albanians, delighting in the noise of musketry, notch the ball in order to make it sing the louder. When fighting, they often adopt the excellent plan—excellent, when rifles are not procurable—of driving a long iron nail through the bullet, and fixing its head into the cartridge. Thus the cartridge is strengthened, the bullet is rifled, and the wound which it inflicts is a fatal one. Round balls are apt to pass into and out of savages without killing them, and many an Afghan,

A distant dropping of fire-arms ushered in the evening of our first melancholy day at Bir Abbas. This, said my companions, was a sign that the troops and the hill-men were fighting at no great distance. They communicated the intelligence, as if it ought to be an effectual check upon my impatience to proceed; it acted, however, in the contrary way. I supposed that the Bedouins, after battling out the night, would be less warlike the next day; the others, however, by no means agreed in opinion with me. At Yambu the whole party had boasted loudly that the people of El Medinah could keep their Bedouins in order, and had twitted the boy Mohammed with their superiority in this respect to his townsmen, the Meccans. But now that a trial was impending, I saw none of the fearlessness so conspicuous when the peril was only possible. The change was charitably to be explained by the presence of their valuables; the "*sahharahs*," like conscience, making cowards of them all. But the young Meccan, who, having sent on his box by sea from Yambu to Jeddah, felt merry, like the empty traveller, would not lose the opportunity to pay off old scores. He taunted the Medinites till they stamped and raved with fury. At last, fearing some violence, and feeling that I was answerable for the boy's safety to his family,—having persuaded him to accompany me on the journey,—seizing him by the nape of the neck and the upper posterior portion of his nether garments, I drove him before me into the tent.

That night I slept within my shugduf, for it would have been mere madness to lie on the open plain in a place so infested by banditti. The being armed is but a poor precaution near this robbers' haunt. If a man be wounded in

after being shot or run through the body, has mortally wounded his English adversary before falling.

the very act of plundering, an exorbitant sum must be paid for blood-money. If you kill him, even to save your life, then adieu to any chance of escaping destruction. I was roused three or four times during the night by jackals and dogs prowling about our little camp, and thus observed that my companions, who had agreed amongst themselves to keep watch by turns, had all fallen into a sound sleep. However, when we awoke in the morning, the usual inspection of goods and chattels showed that nothing was missing.

The next day was a forced halt, a sore stimulant to the traveller's ill-humor; and the sun, the sand, the dust, the furious simoom, and the want of certain small supplies, aggravated our grievance. My sore foot had been inflamed by a dressing of onion skin which the Lady Maryam had insisted upon applying to it. Still I was resolved to push forward by any conveyance that could be procured, and offered ten dollars for a fresh dromedary to take me on to El Medinah. Shaykh Hamid also declared he would leave his box in charge of a friend and accompany me. Saad the Devil flew into a passion at the idea of any member of the party escaping the general evil, and he privily threatened Mohammed to cut off the legs of any camel that ventured into camp. This, the boy,—who, like a boy of the world as he was, never lost an opportunity of making mischief,—instantly communicated to me, and it brought on a furious dispute. Saad was reproved and apologised for by the rest of the party, and presently he himself was pacified, principally, I believe, by the intelligence that no camel was to be hired at Bir Abbas. One of the Arnaut garrison, who had obtained leave to go to El Medinah, came to ask us if we could mount him, as otherwise he should be obliged to walk the whole way. With him we debated the propriety of attempting a passage through the hills by one of the many bye-paths that traverse them; the project was amply discussed, and duly rejected.

We passed the day in the usual manner; all crowded together for shelter under the tent—even Maryam joined us, loudly informing Ali, her son, that his mother was no longer a woman but a man—whilst our party generally, cowering away from the fierce glances of the sun, were either eating or occasionally smoking, or were occupied in cooling and drinking water. About sunset-time came a report that we were to start that night. None could believe that such good was in store for us; before sleeping, however, we placed each camel's pack apart, so as to be ready for loading at a moment's notice, and we took care to watch that our Bedouins did not drive their animals away to any distance. At last about 11 P. M., as the moon began to peep over the eastern wall of rock, was heard the glad sound of the little kettle-drum calling the Albanian troopers to mount and march. In the shortest possible time all made ready, and hurriedly crossing the sandy flat, we found ourselves in company with three or four caravans, forming one large body for better defence against the dreadful Hawamid. By dint of much manœuvring, arms in hand—Shaykh Hamid and the "Devil" took the prominent parts—we, though the last comers, managed to secure places about the middle of the line.

We travelled that night up the fiumara in an easterly direction, and at early dawn found ourselves in an ill-famed gorge called Shuab el Hajj (the "Pilgrim's Pass"). The loudest talkers became silent as we neared it, and their countenances showed apprehension written in legible characters. Presently from the high precipitous cliff on our left thin blue curls of smoke,—somehow or other they caught every eye,—rose in the air, and instantly afterwards rank the loud sharp cracks of the hillmen's matchlocks, echoed by the rocks on the right. A number of Bedouins were to be seen swarming like hornets over the crests of the rocks, boys as well as men carrying huge weapons, and climbing with the agility of cats. They took up comfortable places in the cut-throat eminence, and began firing upon us with perfect convenience to themselves. It was useless to challenge the Bedouins to come down and fight us upon the plain like men; they will do this on the eastern coast of Arabia, but rarely, if ever, in El Hejaz. And it was equally unprofitable for our escort to fire upon a foe ensconced behind stones. Besides which, had a robber been killed, the whole country would have risen to a man; with a force of 3,000 or 4,000, they might have gained courage to overpower a caravan, and in such a case not a soul would have escaped. As it was, the Bedouins directed their fire principally against the unhappy Albanians. Some of these called for assistance to the party of Shaykhs that accompanied us from Bir Abbas, but the dignified old men, dismounting and squatting round their pipes in council, came to the conclusion that, as the robbers would probably turn a deaf ear to their words, they had better spare themselves the trouble of speaking. We had therefore nothing to do but to blaze away as much powder, and to veil ourselves in as much smoke as possible; the result of the affair was that we lost twelve men, besides camels and other beasts of burden.

After another hour's hurried ride through the Wady Sayyalah appeared Shuhada, to which we pushed on,

> "Like nighted swain on lonely road,
> When close behind fierce goblins tread."

Shuhada is a place which derives its name, "The Martyrs," because here are supposed to be buried forty braves that fell in one of Mohammed's many skirmishes. Some authorities consider it the cemetery of the people of Wady Sayyalah. The once populous valley is now barren, and one might easily pass by the consecrated spot without observing a few ruined walls and a cluster of rude graves of the Bedouins, each an oval of rough stones lying beneath the thorn trees on the left of and a little off the road. Another half hour took us to a favorite halting-place, Bir El Hindi,* so callèd from some forgotten Indian who dug a well there. But we left it behind, wishing to put as much space as we could between our tents and the nests of the Hamidah. Then quitting the fiumara, we struck northwards into a well-trodden road running over stony rising ground. The heat became sickening; here, and in the East generally, at no time is the sun more dangerous than between 8 and 9 A. M.: still we hurried on. It was not before 11 A. M. that we reached our destination, a rugged plain covered with stones, coarse gravel, and thorn trees in abundance, and surrounded by inhospitable rocks, pinnacle-shaped, of granite below, and in the upper parts fine limestone. The well was at least two miles distant, and not a hovel was in sight: a few Bedouin children belonging to an outcast tribe fed their starveling goats upon the hills. That night we must have travelled about twenty-two miles; the direction of the road was due east, and the only remarkable feature in the ground was its steady rise.

We pitched the tent under a villanous Mimosa, the

* The Indians sink wells in Arabia for the same reason which impels them to dig tanks at home,—"nam ke waste,"—"for the purpose of name;" thereby denoting, together with a laudable desire for posthumous fame, a notable lack of ingenuity in securing it. For it generally happens that before the third generation has fallen, the well and the tank have either lost their original names, or have exchanged them for newer and better ones.

tree whose shade is compared by poetic Bedouins to the false friend who deserts you in your utmost need. I enlivened the hot dull day by a final dispute with Saad the Devil. His alacrity at Yambu obtained for him the loan of a couple of dollars: he had bought grain at El Hamra, and now we were near El Medinah; still there was not a word about repayment. And knowing that an Oriental debtor discharges his debt as he pays his rent,—namely, with the greatest unwillingness,—and that, on the other hand, an Oriental creditor will devote the labor of a year to recovering a sixpence, I resolved to act as a native of the country, placed in my position, would, and by dint of sheer dunning and demanding pledges try to recover my property. About noon Saad the Devil, after a furious rush, bare-headed, through the burning sun, flung the two dollars down upon my carpet: however, he presently recovered, and, as subsequent events showed, I had chosen the right part. Had he not been forced to repay his debt he would have despised me as a "freshman," and asked for more. As it was, the boy Mohammed bore the brunt of unpopular feeling, my want of liberality being traced to his secret and perfidious admonitions. He supported his burden the more philosophically, because, as he notably calculated, every dollar saved at El Medinah would be spent under his stewardship at Meccah.

At 4 P. M. we left Suwaykah, all of us in the crossest of humors, and travelled in a N. E. direction. So out of temper were my companions, that at sunset, of the whole party, Omar Effendi was the only one who would eat supper. The rest sat upon the ground, pouting, grumbling, and—they had been allowed to exhaust my stock of Latakia—smoking Syrian tobacco as if it were a grievance. Such a game at naughty children, I have seldom seen played even by the Oriental men. The boy Mohammed privily remarked to me that the camel-men's beards were now in his fist,—meaning that we were out of their kinsmen, the Harb's, reach. He soon found an opportunity to quarrel with them; and, because one of his questions was not answered in the shortest possible time, he proceeded to abuse them in language which sent their hands flying in the direction of their swords. Despite, however, this threatening demeanor, the youth, knowing that he now could safely go to any lengths, continued his ill words, and Mansúr's face was so comically furious, that I felt too much amused to interfere. At last the camel-men disappeared, thereby punishing us most effectually for our sport. The road lay up rocky hill and down stony vale; a tripping and stumbling dromedary had been substituted for the usual one: the consequence was that we had either a totter or a tumble once per mile during the whole of that long night. In vain the now fiery Mohammed called for the assistance of the camel-men with the full force of his lungs: "Where be those owls, those oxen of the oxen, those beggars, those cut-off ones, those foreigners, those sons of flight? withered be their hands! palsied be their fingers! the foul mustachioed fellows, basest of the Arabs, that ever hammered tent-peg, sneaking cats, goats of El Akhfash! Truly I will torture them to the torture of oil, the mines of infamy! the cold of countenance!"* The Bedouin brotherhood of the camel-men looked at him wickedly, muttering the while "By Allah! and by Allah! and by Allah! O boy, we will flog thee like a hound when we catch thee in the Desert!" Some days after our arrival at Medinah, Shaykh Hamid warned

* A "cold-of-countenance" is a fool. Arabs use the word "cold" in a peculiar way. "May Allah refrigerate thy countenance!" *i. e.* may it show misery and want. "By Allah, a cold speech!" that is to say, a silly or an abusive tirade.

him seriously never again to go such perilous lengths, as the Beni Harb were celebrated for shooting or poniarding the man who ventured to use even the mild epithet "O jackass!" to them.

The sun had risen before I shook off the lethargic effects of such a night. All around me were hurrying their camels, regardless of rough ground, and not a soul spoke a word to his neighbor. "Are there robbers in sight?" was the natural question. "No!" replied Mohammed; "they are walking with their eyes,* they will presently see their homes!" Rapidly we passed the Wady el Akik, of which a thousand pretty things have been said by the Arab poets. It was as "dry as summer's dust," and its "beautiful trees" appeared in the shape of vegetable mummies. Half an hour after leaving the "blessed valley" we came to a huge flight of steps roughly cut in a long broad line of black scoriaceous basalt. This is called the Mudarraj or flight of steps over the western ridge of the so-called El Harratain. It is holy ground; for the prophet spoke well of it. Arrived at the top we passed through a lane of black scoria, with steep banks on both sides, and after a few minutes a full view of the city suddenly opened upon us.

We halted our beasts as if by word of command. All of us descended, in imitation of the pious of old, and sat down, jaded and hungry as we were, to feast our eyes with a view of the Holy City. "O Allah! this is the Haram (sanctuary) of the Prophet; make it to us a protection from hell fire, and a refuge from eternal punishment! O open the gates of thy mercy, and let us pass through them to the land of joy!" and "O Allah, bless the last of Prophets,

* That is to say, they would use, if necessary, the dearest and noblest parts of their bodies (their eyes) to do the duty of the basest (*i. e.* their feet).

the seal of prophecy, with blessings in number as the stars of heaven, and the waves of the sea, and the sands of the waste—bless him, O Lord of Might and Majesty, as long as the corn field and the date grove continue to feed mankind!'" And again, "Live for ever, O most excellent of Prophets!—live in the shadow of happiness during the hours of night and the times of day, whilst the bird of the tamarisk (the dove) moaneth like the childless mother, whilst the west wind bloweth gently over the hills of Nejd, and the lightning flasheth bright in the firmament of El Hejaz!" Such were the poetical exclamations that rose all around me, showing how deeply tinged with imagination becomes the language of the Arab under the influence of strong passion or religious enthusiasm. I now understood the full value of a phrase in the Moslem ritual, "And when his (the pilgrim's) eyes *fall upon the trees of El Medinah,* let him raise his voice and bless the Prophet with the choicest of blessings." In all the fair view before us, nothing was more striking, after the desolation through which we had passed, than the gardens and orchards about the town. It was impossible not to enter into the spirit of my companions, and truly I believe that for some minutes my enthusiasm rose as high as theirs. But presently, when we remounted, the traveller returned strong upon me: I made a rough sketch of the town, put questions about the principal buildings, and in fact collected materials for the next chapter.

The distance traversed that night was about twenty miles in a direction varying from easterly and north-easterly. We reached El Medinah on the 25th July, thus taking nearly eight days to travel over little more than 130 miles. This journey is performed with camels in four days, and a good dromedary will do it without difficulty in half that time.

## CHAPTER XIV.

### THROUGH THE SUBURB OF EL MEDINAH TO HAMID'S HOUSE.

As we looked eastward the sun arose out of the horizon of low hill, blurred and dotted with small tufted trees, which from the morning mists gained a giant stature, and the earth was stained with gold and purple. Before us lay a spacious plain, bounded in front by the undulating ground of Nejd; on the left was a grim barrier of rocks, the celebrated Mount Ohod, with a clump of verdure and a white dome or two nestling at its base. Rightwards, broad streaks of lilac-colored mists were thick with gathered dew, there pierced and thinned by the morning rays, stretched over the date groves and the gardens of Kuba, which stood out in emerald green from the dull tawny surface of the plain. Below, at the distance of about two miles lay El Medinah; at first sight it appeared a large place, but a closer inspection proved the impression to be an erroneous one. A tortuous road from the Harrah to the city, wound across the plain and led to a tall rectangular gateway, pierced in the ruinous mud wall which surrounds the suburb. This is the "Ambari" entrance. It is flanked on the left (speaking as a sketcher) by the domes and minarets of a pretty Turkish building, a "Takiyah," erected by the late Mohammed Ali for the reception of Dervish travellers; on the right by a long low line of white-washed buildings garnished with ugly square windows, an imitation of civilised barracks. Beginning from the left hand, as we sat upon the ridge, the remarkable features of the town thus presented themselves in succession. Outside, amongst the palm-trees to the north of the city, were the picturesque ruins of a large old *sebil*, or public fountain, and between this and the enceinte, stood a conspicuous building, in the Turkish pavilion style—the governor's palace. On the north-west angle of the town wall is a tall white-washed fort, partly built upon an outcropping mass of rock; its ramparts and embrasures give it a modern and European appearance, which contrasts strangely with its truly Oriental history.* In the suburb "El Munakhah" rise the bran-new domes and minarets of the five mosques, standing brightly out from the dull grey mass of house and ground. And behind is the most easterly part of the city: remarkable from afar, is the gem of El Medinah, the four tall substantial towers, and the flashing green dome under which the Prophet's remains rest. Half concealed by this mass of buildings and by the houses of the town are certain white specks upon a green surface, the tombs that adorn the venerable cemetery of El Bakia. And from that point southwards began the mass of palm groves celebrated in El Islam as the "trees of El Medinah." The foreground was well fitted to set off such a view; fields of black basaltic scoriæ showing clear signs of a volcanic origin, were broken up into huge blocks and boulders, through which a descent, tolerably steep for camels, wound down into the plain.

* In the East, wherever there is a compound of fort and city, that place has certainly been in the habit of being divided against itself.

After a few minutes' rest I remounted, and slowly rode on towards the gate. Even at this early hour the way was crowded with an eager multitude coming out to meet the caravan. My companions preferred walking, apparently for the better convenience of kissing, embracing, and shaking hands with relations and friends. Truly the Arabs show more heart on these occasions than any Oriental people I know; they are of a more affectionate nature than the Persians, and their manners are far more demonstrative than those of the Indians. The respectable Maryam's younger son, a pleasant contrast to her surly elder, was weeping aloud for joy as he ran round his mother's camel, he standing on tiptoe, she bending double in vain attempts to exchange a kiss; and, generally, when near relatives or intimates, or school companions, met, the fountains of their eyes were opened. Friends and comrades greeted each other, regardless of rank or fortune, with affectionate embraces, and an abundance of gestures, which neither party seemed to think of answering. The general mode of embracing was to throw one arm over the shoulder and the other round the side, placing the chin first upon the left and then upon the right collar bone, and rapidly shifting till a "*jam satis*" suggested itself to both parties. Inferiors saluted their superiors by attempting to kiss hands, which were violently snatched away; whilst mere acquaintances gave each other a cordial "*poignée de mains*," and then raising the finger tips to their lips kissed them with apparent relish.

Passing through the Bab Ambari we defiled slowly down a broad dusty street, and traversed the *Harat*, or Quarter of the same name, El Ambariyah, the principal one in the Munakhah suburb. The street was by no means remarkable after Cairo; only it is rather wider and more regular than the traveller is accustomed to in Asiatic cities. I was astonished to see on both sides of the way, in so small a place, so large a number of houses too ruinous to be occupied. Then we crossed a bridge,—a single little round arch of roughly hewn stone, built over the bed of a torrent, which in some parts appeared about fifty feet broad, with banks shrouding a high and deeply indented water-mark.

The Shaykh had preceded us early that morning, in order to prepare an apartment for his guests, and to receive the first loud congratulations and embraces of his mother and the daughter of his uncle.* Apparently he had not concluded this pleasing office when we arrived, for the camels were kneeling at least five minutes at his door, before he came out to offer the usual hospitable salutation. I stared to see the difference of his appearance this morning. The razor had passed over his head and face; the former was now surmounted by a muslin turban of goodly size, wound round a new embroidered cap, and the latter, besides being clean, boasted of neat little mustachios turned up like two commas, and a well-trimmed goat's beard narrowed until it resembled what our grammars call an "exclamation point." (!) The dirty torn shirt, with a bit of rope round the loins, had been exchanged for a *jubbah* or outer cloak of light pink merino, a long-sleeved *caftan* of rich flowered stuff, a fine shirt of *Halaili*† and a grand silk sash, of a plaid pattern, elaborately fringed at both ends, and wound round two thirds of his body for better display. His pantaloons were also of *Halaili* with tasteful edgings like a "panta-

* Arabs, and, indeed, most Orientals, are generally received, after returning from a journey, with shrill cries of joy by all the fair part of the household, and this demonstration they do not like strangers to hear.

† *Halaili* is a cotton stuff, with long stripes of white silk, a favorite material amongst the city Arabs. At Constantinople, where the best is made, the piece, which will cut into two shirts, costs about thirty shillings.

lette's" about the ancles, and his bare and sun-burnt feet had undergone a thorough purification before being encased in new *mizz** and *papooshes* of bright lemon-colored leather of the newest and most fashionable Constantinople cut. In one of his now delicate hands the Shaykh bore a mother-of-pearl rosary, token of piety, in the other a handsome pipe with a jasmine stick, and an expensive amber mouth-piece; his tobacco pouch dangling from his waist, as well as the little purse in the bosom pocket of his coat, was of broad cloth richly embroidered with gold. In course of time I saw that all my companions had metamorphosed themselves in an equally remarkable manner. Like men of sense they appeared in tatters where they were, or when they wished to be, unknown, and in fine linen where the world judged their prosperity by their attire.

The Shaykh, whose manners had changed with his dress, from the vulgar and boisterous to a certain staid courtesy, took my hand, and led me up to the *majlis*,† which was swept and garnished with all due apparatus for the forthcoming reception ceremony. And behind us followed the boy Mohammed, looking more downcast and ashamed of himself than I can possibly describe; he was still in his rags, and he felt keenly that every visitor staring at him would mentally inquire "who may that snob be?" With the deepest dejectedness he squeezed himself into a corner, and Shaykh Nur, who was foully dirty as an Indian *en voyage* always is, would have joined him in his shame, had I not ordered the "slave" to make himself generally useful. It is customary for all relations and friends to call upon the tra-

* The "*Mizz*" (in colloquial Arabic *Misd*) are the tight-fitting inner slippers of soft Cordovan leather, worn as stockings inside the slipper.

† The *majlis* ("the place of sitting") is the drawing or reception room; it is usually in the first story of the house, below the apartments of the women.

veller the day he returns, that is to say, if amity is to endure. The pipes therefore stood ready filled, the divans were duly spread, and the coffee* was being boiled upon a brazier in the passage. Scarcely had I taken my place at the cool window sill,—it was the best in the room,—before the visitors began to pour in, and the Shaykh rose to welcome and embrace them. They sat down, smoked, chatted politics, asked all manner of questions about the other wayfarers and absent friends, drank coffee, and after an hour's visit, rose abruptly, and, exchanging embraces, took leave. The little men entered the assembly, after an *accolade* at the door, noiselessly, squatted upon the worst seats with polite *congées* to the rest of the assembly, smoked, and took their coffee, as it were, under protest, and glided out of the room as quietly as they crept in. The great people, generally busy and consequential individuals, upon whose countenances were written the words "well to do in the world," appeared with a noise that made each person in the room rise reverentially upon his feet, sat down with importance, monopolised the conversation, and, departing in a dignified

* The coffee drank at El Medinah is generally of a good quality. In Egypt that beverage in the common coffee-shops is,—as required to be by the people who frequent those places,—"bitter as death, black as Satan, and hot as Jehannum." To effect this desideratum, therefore, they toast the grain to blackness, boil it to bitterness, and then drink scalding stuff of the consistency of water-gruel. At El Medinah, on the contrary,—as indeed in the houses of the better classes even in Egypt,—the grain is carefully picked, and that the flavor may be preserved, it is never put upon the fire until required. It is toasted too till it becomes yellow, not black; and afterwards is bruised, not pounded to powder. The water into which it is thrown is allowed to boil up three times, after which a cold sprinkling is administered to clear it, and then the fine light-dun infusion is poured off into another pot. The Arabs seldom drink more than one cup of coffee at a time, but with many the time is every half hour of the day.

manner, expected all to be standing on the occasion. The Holy war, as usual, was the grand topic of conversation. The Sultan had ordered the Czar to become a Moslem. The Czar had sued for peace, and offered tribute and fealty. But the Sultan had exclaimed, "No, by Allah! El Islam!" The Czar could not be expected to take such a step without a little hesitation, but "Allah smites the faces of the Infidels!" Abdel Mejid would dispose of the "Moskow"* in a short time; after which he would turn his victorious army against all the idolaters of Feringistan, beginning with the English, the French, and the Aroám or Greeks. Amongst much of this nonsense,—when applied to for my opinion, I was careful to make it popular,—I heard news foreboding no good to my journey towards Muscat. The Bedouins had decided that there was to be an Arab contingent, and had been looking forward to the spoils of Europe; this had caused quarrels, as all the men wanted to go, and not a ten-year-old would be left behind. The consequence was, that this amiable people was fighting in all directions. At least so said the visitors, and I afterwards found out that they were not far wrong.

To the plague of strangers succeeded that of children. No sooner did the *majlis* become, comparatively speaking, vacant, than they rushed in *en masse;* treading upon our toes, making the noise of a nursery of madlings, pulling to pieces everything they could lay their hands upon, and using language that would have alarmed an old man-o'-war's-man.† In fact, no one can conceive the plague but

* The common name for the Russians in Egypt and El Hejaz.

† Parents and full-grown men amuse themselves with grossly abusing children, almost as soon as they can speak, in order to excite their rage, and to judge of their dispositions. This supplies the infant population with a large stock-in-trade of ribaldry. They literally lisp in bad language.

those who have studied the "*enfans terribles*" which India sends home in cargoes. One urchin, scarcely three years old, told me that his father had a sword at home with which he would cut my throat from ear to ear, suiting the action to the word, because I objected to his perching upon my wounded foot. By a few taunts, I made the little wretch almost mad with rage; he shook his infant fist at me, and then opening his enormous round black eyes to their utmost stretch, he looked at me, and licked his knee with portentous meaning. Shaykh Hamid, happening to come in at the moment, stood aghast at the doorway, hand on chin, to see the Effendi subject to such indignity, and it was not without trouble that I saved the offender from summary nursery discipline. Another scamp caught up one of my loaded pistols before I could snatch it out of his hand, and clapped it to his neighbor's head; fortunately, it was on half-cock, and the trigger was a stiff one. Then a serious and majestic boy about six years old, with an ink-stand in his belt, in token of his receiving a literary education, seized my pipe and began to smoke it with huge puffs. I ventured laughingly to institute a comparison between his person and the pipe-stick, when he threw it upon the ground, and stared at me fixedly with flaming eyes and features distorted by anger. The cause of this "boldness" soon appeared. The boys, instead of being well beaten, were scolded with fierce faces, a mode of punishment which only made them laugh. They had their redeeming points, however; they were manly angry boys, who punched one another like Anglo-Saxons in the house, and abroad they are always fighting with sticks and stones. And they examined our weapons,—before deigning to look at anything else,—as if eighteen instead of five had been the general age.

At last I so far broke through the laws of Arab politeness as to inform my host in plain words, that I was hungry, thirsty, and sleepy, and that I wanted to be alone before visiting the Haram. The good-natured Shaykh, who was preparing to go out at once in order to pray at his father's grave, immediately brought me breakfast, lighted a pipe, spread a bed, darkened the room, turned out the children, and left me to the society I most desired—my own. I then overheard him summon his mother, wife, and other female relatives into the store-room, where his treasures had been carefully stored away. During the forenoon, in the presence of the visitors, one of Hamid's uncles had urged him, half jocularly, to bring out the *sahharah*. The Shaykh did not care to do anything of the kind. Every time a new box is opened in this part of the world, the owner's generosity is appealed to by those whom a refusal offends, and he must allow himself to be plundered with the best possible grace. Hamid therefore prudently suffered all to depart before exhibiting his spoils; which, to judge by the exclamations of delight which they elicited from feminine lips, proved a satisfactory collection to those concerned.

After sleeping, we all set out in a body to the Haram, as this is a duty which must not be delayed by the pious. The boy Mohammed was in better spirits,—the effect of having borrowed, amongst other articles of clothing, an exceedingly gaudy embroidered coat from Shaykh Hamid. As for Shaykh Nur, he had brushed up his tarboosh, and, by means of some cast-off dresses of mine, had made himself look like a respectable Abyssinian slave, in a nondescript toilette, half Turkish, half Indian. I propose to reserve the ceremony of *ziyarat*, or visitation, for another chapter, and to conclude this with a short account of our style of living at the Shaykh's hospitable house.

Hamid's abode is a small corner building, open on the north and east to the Barr El Munakhah: the ground floor contains only a kind of vestibule, in which coarse articles, like old *shugdufs*, mats and bits of sacking are stowed away; the rest is devoted to purposes of sewerage. Ascending dark winding steps of ragged stone covered with hard black earth, you come to the first floor, where the men live. It consists of two rooms to the front of the house, one a *majlis* or sitting room, and another converted into a store. Behind them is a dark passage, into which the doors open; and the back part of the first story is a long windowless room, containing a *hanafiyah*,* and other conveniences for purification. The kitchen is on the second floor, which I did not inspect, it being as usual occupied by the Harem. The *majlis* has dwarf windows, or rather apertures in the northern and eastern walls, with rude wooden shutters and reed blinds—the embrasures being garnished with cushions, where you sit, morning and evening, to enjoy the cool air; the ceiling is of date sticks laid across palm rafters stained red, and the walls are of rough scoriæ, burnt bricks, and wood-work cemented with lime. The only signs of furniture in the sitting-room are a diwan † round the sides and a carpet in the centre. A huge wooden box, like a seaman's chest, occupies one of the corners. In the southern wall there is a *suffeh*, or little shelf of common stone, supported by a single arch; upon

* The Hanafiyah is a large vessel of copper, sometimes tinned, with a cock in the lower part, and, generally, an ewer, or a basin, to receive the water.

† The diwan is a line of flat cushions ranged round the room, either placed upon the ground, or on wooden benches, or on a step of masonry, varying in height according to the fashion of the day. Cotton-stuffed pillows, covered with chintz for summer, and silk for winter, are placed against the wall, and can be moved to make a luxurious heap; their covers are generally all of the same color, except those at the end.

this are placed articles in hourly use, perfume-bottles, coffee-cups, a stray book or two, and sometimes a turban, to be out of the children's way. Two hooks on the western wall, placed jealously high up, support a pair of pistols with handsome crimson cords and tassels, and half a dozen cherry-stick pipes.

The passage, like the stairs, is spread over with hard black earth, and regularly watered twice a day during hot weather. The household consisted of Hamid's mother, wife, some nephews and nieces, small children who ran about in a half wild and more than half nude state, and two African slave girls. When the Damascus caravan came in, it was further reinforced by the arrival of his three younger brothers.

The majlis was tolerably cool during the early part of the day; in the afternoon the sun shone fiercely upon it. I have described the establishment at some length as a specimen of how the middle classes of society are lodged at El Medinah. The upper classes affect Turkish and Egyptian luxuries in their homes, as I had an opportunity of seeing at Omar Effendi's house in the "Barr;" and the abodes of the poorer classes are everywhere in these countries very similar.

Our life in Shaykh Hamid's house was quiet, but not disagreeable. I never once set eyes upon the face of woman there, unless the African slave girls be allowed the title. Even these at first attempted to draw their ragged veils over their sable charms, and would not answer the simplest question; by degrees they allowed me to see them, and they ventured their strange voices to reply to me; still they never threw off a certain appearance of shame.* I

* Their voices are strangely soft and delicate, considering the appearance of the organs from which they proceed. Possibly this may be a characteristic of the African races; it is remarkable amongst the Somâli women.

never saw, nor even heard, the youthful mistress of the household, who stayed all day in the upper rooms. The old lady, Hamid's mother, would stand upon the stairs, and converse aloud with her son, and when few people were about the house with me. She never, however, as afterwards happened to an ancient dame at Meccah, came and sat by my side. When lying during mid-day in the gallery, I often saw parties of women mount the stairs to the *Gynæconitis*, and sometimes an individual would stand to shake a muffled hand* with Hamid, to gossip a while, and to put some questions concerning absent friends; but they were most decorously wrapped up, nor did they ever deign to *déroger*, even by exposing an inch of cheek.

At dawn we arose, washed, prayed, and broke our fast upon a crust of stale bread, before smoking a pipe, and drinking a cup of coffee. Then it was time to dress, to mount, and to visit the Haram in one of the holy places outside the city. Returning before the sun became intolerable, we sat together, and with conversation, shishas, and chibouques, coffee and cold water perfumed with mastich-smoke, we whiled away the time till an early dinner which appeared at the primitive hour of 11 A. M. The meal, here called El Ghada, was served in the *majlis* on a large copper tray, sent from the upper apartments. Ejaculating "Bismillah"—the Moslem grace—we all sat round it, and dipped equal hands into the dishes set before us. We had usually unleavened bread, different kinds of meat and vegetable stews, and at the end of the first course plain boiled rice, eaten with spoons; then came the fruits, fresh dates, grapes, and

* After touching the skin of a strange woman, it is not lawful in El Islam to pray without ablution. For this reason, when a fair dame shakes hands with you, she wraps up her fingers in a kerchief, or in the end of her veil.

pomegranates. After dinner I used invariably to find some excuse—such as the habit of a "Kaylúlah" (mid-day siesta)* or the being a "Saudawi"† or person of melancholy temperament, to have a rug spread in the dark passage behind the *majlis*, and there to lie reading, dozing, smoking or writing, *en cachette*, in complete *déshabille* all through the worst part of the day, from noon to sunset. Then came the hour for receiving or paying visits. The evening prayers ensued, either at home or in the Haram, followed by our supper, another substantial meal like the dinner, but more plentiful, of bread, meat, vegetables, plain rice and fruits, concluding with the invariable pipes and coffee. To pass our *soirée*, we occasionally dressed in common clothes, shouldered a nebút,‡ and went to the café; sometimes on

* Kaylúlah is the half hour's siesta about noon. It is a Sunnat, and the Prophet said of it, "Kilu, fa inna 'sh'Shayátína lá Takil,"—"Take the mid-day siesta, for, verily, the devils sleep not at this hour." "Aylulah" is the sleeping after morning prayers, which causes heaviness and inability to work. Ghayulah is the sleeping about 9 A. M., the effect of which is poverty and wretchedness. Kaylúlah (with the guttural kaf) is sleeping before evening prayers, a practice reprobated in every part of the East. And, finally, Faylulah is sleeping immediately after sunset,—also considered highly detrimental.

† The Arabs, who suffer greatly from melancholia, are kind to people afflicted with this complaint; it is supposed to cause a distaste for society, and a longing for solitude, an unsettled habit of mind, and a neglect of worldly affairs. Probably it is the effect of overworking the brain, in a hot dry atmosphere. I have remarked, that in Arabia students are subject to it, and that amongst their philosophers and literary men, there is scarcely an individual who was not spoken of as a "Saudawi."

‡ This habit of going out at night in common clothes, with a nebút upon one's shoulder, is, as far as I could discover, popular at El Medinah, but confined to the lowest classes at Meccah. The boy Mohammed always spoke of it with undisguised disapprobation. During my stay at Meccah, I saw no such cotusme amongst respectable people there; though sometimes, perhaps, there was a suspicion of a disguise.

festive occasions we indulged in a Taatumah (or Itmiyah), a late supper of sweetmeats, pomegranates and dried fruits. Usually we sat upon mattresses spread upon the ground in the open air at the Shaykh's door, receiving evening visits, chatting, telling stories, and making merry, till each, as he felt the approach of the drowsy god, sank down into his proper place, and fell asleep.

Whatever may be the heat of the day, the night at El Medinah, owing, I suppose, to its elevated position, is cool and pleasant. In order to allay the dust, the ground before the Shaykh's door was watered every evening, and the evaporation was almost too great to be safe,—the boy Mohammed suffered from a smart attack of lumbago, which, however, yielded readily to frictions of olive oil in which ginger had been boiled. Our greatest inconvenience at night time was the pugnacity of the animal creation. The horses of the troopers tethered in the Barr were sure to break loose once in twelve hours. Some hobbled old nag, having slipped his head-stall, would advance with kangaroo-leaps towards a neighbor against whom he had a private grudge. Their heads would touch for a moment; then came a snort and a whining, a furious kick, and lastly, a second horse loose and dashing about with head and tail viciously cocked. This was the signal for a general breaking of halters and heel-ropes; after which a "stampedo" scoured the plain, galloping, rearing, kicking, biting, snorting, pawing, and screaming, with the dogs barking sympathetically, and the horse-keepers shouting in hot pursuit. It was a strange sight to see by moon-light, the forms of these "demon steeds" exaggerated by the shadows; and on more than one occasion we had all to start up precipitately from our beds, and yield them to a couple of combatants who were determined to fight out their quarrel *à l'outrance*, wherever the battle-field might be.

The dogs at El Medinah are not less pugnacious than the horses.* They are stronger and braver than those that haunt the streets at Cairo; like the Egyptians, they have amongst themselves a system of police regulations, which brings down all the *posse comitatus* upon the unhappy straggler who ventures into a strange quarter of the town.

There are certain superstitions about the dog resembling ours, only, as usual, more poetical and less grotesque, current in El Hejaz. Most people believe that when the animal howls without apparent cause in the neighborhood of a house, it forebodes death to one of the inmates. For the dog they say can distinguish the awful form of Azrael, the angel of death, hovering over the doomed abode, whereas man's spiritual sight is dull and dim by reason of his sins.

When the Damascus caravan entered El Medinah, our day became a little more amusing. From the windows of Shaykh Hamid's house there was a perpetual succession of strange scenes. A Persian nobleman, also, had pitched his tents so opportunely near the door, that the whole course of his private life became public and patent to the boy Mohammed, who amused his companions by reporting all manner of ludicrous scenes. The Persian's wife was rather a pretty woman, and she excited the youth's fierce indignation, by not veiling her face when he gazed at her,—thereby showing that, as his beard was not grown, she considered him a mere boy. "I will ask her to marry me," said Mohammed, "and thereby rouse her shame!" He did so, but, unhappy youth! the Persian never even ceased fanning herself. The boy Mohammed was for once confounded.

* Burckhardt remarks that El Medinah is the only town in the East from which dogs are excluded. This was probably as much a relic of Wahhabeism (that sect hating even to look at a dog), as arising from apprehension of the mosque being polluted by canine intrusion.

## CHAPTER XV.

### A VISIT TO THE PROPHET'S TOMB.

HAVING performed the greater ablution, and used the tooth-stick as directed, and dressed ourselves in white clothes, which the prophet loved, we were ready to start upon our holy errand. As my foot still gave me great pain, Shaykh Hamid sent for a donkey. A wretched animal appeared, raw-backed, lame of one leg, and wanting an ear, with accoutrements to match, and pack-saddle without stirrups, and a halter instead of a bridle. Such as the brute was, however, I had to mount it, and to ride through the Misri gate, to the wonder of certain Bedouins, who, like the Indians, despise the ass.

> "Honorable is the riding of a horse to the rider,
> But the mule is a dishonor, and the ass a disgrace,"

says their song. The Turkish pilgrims, however, who appear to take a pride in ignoring all Arab points of prejudice, generally mount donkeys when they cannot walk. The Bedouins therefore settled among themselves, audibly enough, that I was an Osmanli, who of course could not understand Arabic, and put the question generally, "by what curse of Allah they had been subjected to ass-riders?"

But Shaykh Hamid is lecturing me upon the subject of the mosque.

The Masjid El Nabawi, or the Prophet's Mosque, is one of the Haramain, or the "two sanctuaries" of El Islam, and is the second of the three* most venerable places of worship in the world; the other two being the Masjid El Haram of Meccah (connected with Abraham) and the Masjid El Aksa of Jerusalem (the peculiar place of Solomon). A *Hadís* or traditional saying of Mohammed asserts, "One prayer in this my mosque is more efficacious than a thousand in other places, save only the Masjid El Haram."† It is therefore the visitor's duty, as long as he stays at El Medinah, to pray the five times per diem there, to pass the day in it reading the Koran, and the night, if possible, in watching and devotion.

A visit to the Masjid El Nabawi, and the holy spots within it, is technically called "Ziyárat" or Visitation. An essential difference is made between this rite and Hajj pilgrimage. The latter is obligatory by Koranic order upon every Moslem once in his life: the former is only a meritorious action. "Tawáf," or circumambulation of the House of Allah at Meccah, must never be performed at the Prophet's tomb. This should not be visited in the *ihram* or pilgrim dress; men should not kiss it, touch it with the hand, or press the bosom against it, as at the Kaabah; or rub the face with dust collected near the sepulchre; and

* Others add a fourth, namely, the Masjid El Takwa, at Kuba.

† The Moslem divines, however, naïvely remind their readers, that they are not to pray once in the El Medinah mosque, and neglect the other 999, as if absolved from the necessity of them.

those who prostrate themselves before it, like certain ignorant Indians, are held to be guilty of deadly sin. On the other hand, to spit upon any part of the mosque, or to treat it with contempt, is held to be the act of an infidel.

Thus learning and the religious have settled, one would have thought, accurately enough the spiritual rank and dignity of the Masjid El Nabawi. But mankind, especially in the East, must always be in extremes. The orthodox school of El Malik holds El Medinah, on account of the sanctity of, and the religious benefits to be derived from Mohammed's tomb, more honorable than Meccah. The Wahhabis, on the other hand, rejecting the intercession of the Prophet on the day of judgment; considering the grave of a mere mortal unworthy of notice; and highly disgusted by the idolatrous respect paid to it by certain foolish Moslems, plundered the sacred building with sacrilegious violence, and forbade visitors from distant countries to enter El Medinah.* The general *consensus* of El Islam admits the superiority of the Bait Allah ("House of God") at Meccah to the whole world, and declares El Medinah to be more venerable than every part of Meccah, and consequently all the earth, except only the Bait Allah.

Passing through the muddy streets,—they had been freshly watered before evening time,—I came suddenly upon the mosque. Like that at Meccah the approach is choked up by ignoble buildings, some actually touching the holy "enceinte," others separated by narrow lanes. There is no outer front, no general aspect of the Prophet's mosque; consequently, as a building, it has neither beauty nor dignity. And entering the Bab el Rahmah—the Gate of Pity,—by a

* In A.D. 1807, they prevented Ali Bey (the Spaniard Badia) from entering El Medinah, and it appears that he had reason to congratulate himself upon escaping without severe punishment.

diminutive flight of steps, I was astonished at the mean and tawdry appearance of a place so universally venerated in the Moslem world. It is not, like the Meccan mosque, grand and simple—the expression of a single sublime idea: the longer I looked at it, the more it suggested the resemblance of a museum of second-rate art, a curiosity-shop, full of ornaments that are not accessories, and decorated with pauper splendor.

The Masjid el Nabi is a parallelogram about 420 feet in length by 340 broad, the direction of the long walls being nearly north and south. As usual in El Islam, it is a hypæthral building with a spacious central area, called El Sahn, El Hosh, El Haswah, or El Ramlah, surrounded by a peristyle with numerous rows of pillars like the colonnades of an Italian monastery. Their arcades or porticoes are flat-ceilinged, domed above with the small half-orange cupola of Spain, and divided into four parts by narrow passages, three or four steps below the level of the pavement. Along the whole inner length of the northern short wall runs the Mejídi Riwak, so called from the reigning sultan. The western long wall is occupied by the Kiwak of the Rahmah Gate; the eastern by that of the Bab el Nisa, the "women's entrance."* Embracing the inner length of the southern short wall, and deeper by nearly treble the amount of columns, than the other porticoes, is the main colonnade, called El Rauzah, the *adytum* containing all that is venerable in the building. These four riwaks, arched externally, are supported internally by pillars of different shape and material, varying from fine porphyry to dirty plaster; the southern one, where the sepulchre or cenotaph stands, is paved with handsome slabs of white marble and marquetry work, here

* This gate derives its peculiar name from its vicinity to the Lady Fatimah's tomb; women, when they do visit the mosque, enter it through all the doors indifferently.

and there covered with coarse matting, and above this by unclean carpets, well worn by faithful feet.*

But this is not the time for Tafarruj, or lionising; Shaykh Hamid warns me with a nudge, that other things are expected of a Zair. He leads me to the Bab el Salam, fighting his way through a troop of beggars, and inquires markedly if I am religiously pure. Then, placing our hands a little below and on the left of the waist, the palm of the right covering the back of the left, in the position of prayer, and beginning with the right feet,‡ we pace slowly forwards down the line called the Muwajihat el Sharifah, or "the Holy Fronting," which, divided off like an aisle, runs parallel with the southern wall of the mosque. On my right hand walked the Shaykh, who recited aloud the following prayer, which I repeated after him.§ It is literally rendered, as, indeed, are all the formulæ, and the reader is requested to excuse the barbarous fidelity of the translation. "In the name of Allah and in the Faith of Allah's Prophet! O Lord cause me to enter the entering of Truth, and cause me to issue forth the issuing of Truth, and permit me to draw near to thee, and make me a Sultan Victorious!"‖ Then

* These carpets are swept by the eunuchs, who let out the office for a certain fee to pilgrims, every morning, immediately after sunrise. Their diligence, however, does by no means prevent the presence of certain little parasites, concerning which politeness is dumb.

† Because if not pure, ablution is performed at the well in the centre of the hypæthra. Zairs are ordered to visit the mosque perfumed and in their best clothes, and the Hanafi school deems it lawful on this occasion only to wear dresses of pure silk.

‡ In this mosque, as in all others, it is proper to enter with the right foot, and retire with the left.

§ I must warn the reader that almost every Muzzawwir has his own litany, which descends from father to son: moreover all the books differ at least as much as do the oral authorities.

‖ That is to say, "over the world, the flesh, and the devil."

followed blessings upon the Prophet, and afterwards; "O Allah! open to me the doors of thy mercy, and grant me entrance into it, and protect me from the Stoned Devil!"

During this preliminary prayer we had passed down two thirds of the Muwajihat el Sharifah. On the left hand is a dwarf wall, about the height of a man, painted with arabesques, and pierced with four small doors which open into the Muwajihat. In this barrier are sundry small erections, the niche called the Mihrab Sulaymani,* the Mambar, or pulpit, and the Mihrab el Nabawi.† The two niches are of beautiful mosaic, richly worked with various colored marbles, and the pulpit is a graceful collection of slender columns, elegant tracery, and inscriptions admirably carved. Arrived at the western small door in the dwarf wall, we entered the celebrated spot called El Rauzah, or the Garden, after a saying of the Prophet's, "between my Tomb and my Pulpit is a Garden of the Gardens of Paradise."‡ On the north and

* This by strangers is called the Masalla Shafei, or the Place of Prayer of the Shafei school. It was sent from Constantinople about 100 years ago, by Sultan Sulayman the Magnificent. He built the Sulaymaniyah minaret, and has immortalised his name at El Medinah, as well as at Meccah, by the number of his donations to the shrine.

† Here is supposed to have been one of the Prophet's favorite stations of prayer. It is commonly called the Musalla Hanafi, because now appropriated by that school.

‡ This tradition, like most others referring to events posterior to the Prophet's death, is differently given, and so important are the variations, that I only admire how all El Islam does not follow Wahhabi example and summarily consign them to oblivion. Some read "between my dwelling-house (in the mosque) and my place of prayer (in the Barr el Munakhah) is a Garden of the Gardens of Paradise. Others again, "between my house and my pulpit is a Garden of the Gardens of Paradise." A third tradition—"Between my tomb and my pulpit is a Garden of the Gardens of Paradise, and verily my pulpit is in my Full Cistern." Tara, or "upon a Full Cistern of the Cisterns of Paradise," has given rise to a new superstition. "Tara," according to some com-

west sides it is not divided from the rest of the portico; on the south lies the dwarf wall, and on the east it is limited by the west end of the lattice-work containing the tomb. Accompanied by my *Muzawwir* I entered the Rauzah, and was placed by him with the Mukabbariyah * behind me, fronting Meccah, with my right shoulder opposite to and about twenty feet distant from the dexter pillar of the Prophet's Pulpit.† There, after saying the afternoon prayers,‡ I performed the usual two prostrations in honor of the temple,§

mentators, alludes especially to the cistern El Kausar; consequently this Rauzah is, like the black stone at Meccah, *bonâ fide*, a bit of Paradise, and on the day of resurrection, it shall return bodily to the place whence it came. Be this as it may, all Moslems are warned that the Rauzah is a most holy spot. None but the Prophet and his son-in-law Ali ever entered it, when ceremonially impure, without being guilty of deadly sin. The Mohammedan of the present day is especially informed that on no account must he here tell lies in it, or even perjure himself. Thus the Rauzah must be respected as much as the interior of the Bait Allah at Meccah.

* This is a stone desk on four pillars, where the *Muballighs* (or clerks) recite the *Ikámah*, the call to divine service.

† I shall have something to say about this pulpit when entering into the history of the Haram.

‡ The afternoon prayers being *Farz*, or obligatory, were recited, because we feared that evening might come on before the ceremony of *Ziyárat* (visitation) concluded, and thus the time for El Asr (afternoon prayers) might pass away. The reader may think this rather a curious forethought in a man who, like Hamid, never prayed except when he found the case urgent. Such, however, is the strict order, and my Musawwir was right to see it executed.

§ This two-prostration prayer, which generally is recited in honor of the mosque, is here, say divines, addressed especially to the Deity by the visitor who intends to beg the intercession of his Prophet. It is only just to confess that the Moslems have done their best by all means in human power, here as well as elsewhere, to inculcate the doctrine of eternal distinction between the creature and the creator. Many of the Maliki school, however, make the ceremony of Ziyarat to precede the prayer to the Deity.

and at the end of them recited the 109th and the 112th chapters of the Koran—the "Kul ya ayyuha'l Kafiruna," and the "Surat El Ikhlas," called also the "Kul Huw Allah," or the declaration of unity; and may be thus translated:

1. "Say, he is the one God!"
2. "The eternal God!"
3. "He begets not, nor is he begot."
4. "And unto him the like is not."

After which was performed a single *Sujdah* of thanks,* in gratitude to Allah for making it my fate to visit so holy a spot. This being the recognised time to give alms, I was besieged by beggars, who spread their napkins before us on the ground sprinkled with a few coppers to excite generosity. But not wishing to be distracted by them, before leaving Hamid's house I had asked change of two dollars, and had given it to the boy Mohammed, who accompanied me, strictly charging him to make that sum last all through the mosque. My answer to the beggars was a reference to my attendant, backed by the simple action of turning my pockets inside out, and whilst he was battling with the beggars, I proceeded to cast my first *coup-d'œil* upon the Rauzah.

The "Garden" is the most elaborate part of the mosque. Little can be said in its praise by day, when it bears the same relation to a second-rate church in Rome as an English chapel-of-ease to Westminster Abbey. It is a space of about eighty feet in length, tawdrily decorated so as to resemble a garden. The carpets are flowered, and the pediments of the columns are cased with bright green tiles, and adorned

* The *Sujdah* is a single "prostration" with the forehead touching the ground. It is performed from a sitting position, after the *Dua* or supplication that concludes the two-prostration prayer.

to the height of a man with gaudy and unnatural vegetation in arabesque. It is disfigured by handsome branched candelabras of cut crystal, the work, I believe, of a London house, and presented to the shrine by the late Abbas Pacha of Egypt.* The only admirable feature of the view is the light cast by the windows of stained glass† in the southern wall. Its peculiar background, the railing of the tomb, a splendid filagree-work of green and polished brass, gilt or made to resemble gold, looks more picturesque near than at a distance, when it suggests the idea of a gigantic bird-cage. But at night the eye, dazzled by oil lamps suspended from the roof,‡ by huge wax candles, and by smaller illuminations falling upon crowds of visitors in handsome attire, with the rich and the noblest of the city sitting in congregation when service is performed, becomes less critical. Still the scene must be viewed with a Moslem's spirit, and until a man is thoroughly embued with the East, the last place the Rauzah will remind him of, is that which the architect primarily intended it to resemble—a garden.

Then with Hamid, professionally solemn, I reassumed the position of prayer, as regards the hands; and retraced my steps. After passing through another small door in the dwarf wall that bounds the *Muwajihah*, we did not turn to the right, which would have led us to the Bab El Salam; our course was in an opposite direction, towards the eastern wall of the temple. Meanwhile we repeated "Verily Allah and his Angels bless§ the Prophet! O ye who believe, bless

* The candles are still sent from Cairo.

† These windows are a present from Kaid-bey, the Mamluk Sultan of Egypt.

‡ These oil lamps are a present from the Sultan.

§ The act of blessing the Prophet is one of peculiar efficacy in a religious point of view. Cases are quoted of sinners being actually snatched from hell by a glorious figure, the personification of the blessings which

him, and salute him with honor!" At the end of this prayer, we arrived at the Mausoleum, which requires some description before the reader can understand the nature of our proceedings there.

The *Hujrah*, or "Chamber" as it is called, from the circumstance of its having been Ayisha's room, is an irregular square of from 50 to 55 feet in the S. E. corner of the building, and separated on all sides from the walls of the mosque by a passage about 26 feet broad on the S. side, and 20 on the eastern. The reason of this isolation has been before explained, and there is a saying of Mohammed's, "O Allah cause not my tomb to become an object of idolatrous adoration! May Allah's wrath fall heavy upon the people who make the tombs of their prophets places of prayer!"* Inside there are, or are supposed to be, three tombs facing the

had been called down by them upon Mohammed's head. This most poetical idea is borrowed, I believe from the ancient Guebres, who fabled that a man's good works assumed a beautiful female shape, which stood to meet his soul when winding its way to judgment. Also when a Moslem blesses Mohammed at El Medinah, his sins are not written down for three days,—thus allowing ample margin for repentance,—by the recording angel. El Malakain (the two Angels), or Kiram el Katibín (the Generous Writers), are mere personifications of the good principle and the evil principle of man's nature: they are fabled to occupy each a shoulder, and to keep a list of words and deeds. This is certainly borrowed from a more ancient faith. In Hermas II. (command 6), we are told that "every man has two angels, one of godliness the other of iniquity," who endeavor to secure his allegiance,—a superstition seemingly founded upon the dualism of the old Persians. Mediæval Europe, which borrowed so much from the East at the time of the Crusades, degraded these angels into good and bad fairies for children's stories.

* Yet Mohammed enjoined his followers to frequent grave-yards. "Visit graves; of a verity they shall make you think of futurity!" and again, "Whoso visiteth the grave of his two parents every Friday, or one of the two, he shall be written a pious child, even though he might have been in the world, before that, disobedient to them."

south, surrounded by stone walls without any aperture, or, as others say, by strong planking.* Whatever this material may be, it is hung outside with a curtain, somewhat like a large four-post bed. The outer railing is separated by a dark narrow passage from the inner one, which it surrounds, and is of iron filagree painted of a vivid grass green,—with a view to the garden,—whilst carefully inserted in the verdure, and doubly bright by contrast, is the gilt or burnished brass work forming the long and graceful letters of the Suls character, and disposed into the Moslem creed, the profession of unity, and similar religious sentences. On the south side, for greater honor, the railing is plated over with silver, and silver letters are interlaced with it. This fence, which connects the columns and forbids passage to all men, may be compared to the baldacchino of Roman churches. It has four gates: that to the south is the Bab el Muwajihah; eastward is the gate of our Lady Fatimah; westward the Bab el Taubah, (of repentance,) opening into the Rauzah or garden, and to the north, the Bab el Shami or Syrian gate. They are constantly kept closed, except the fourth, which admits, into the dark narrow passage above alluded to, the officers who have charge of the treasures there deposited, and the eunuchs who sweep the floor, light the lamps, and carry away the presents sometimes thrown in here by devotees.† In the southern side of the

* The truth is no one knows what is there. I have even heard a learned Persian declare that there is no wall behind the curtain, which hangs so loosely that, when the wind blows against it, it defines the form of a block of marble, or a built-up tomb. I believe this to be wholly apocryphal, for reasons which will presently be offered.

† The peculiar place where the guardians of the tomb sit and confabulate is the Dakkat el Ayhawat (eunuch's bench) or el Mayda—the table—a raised bench of stone and wood, on the north side of the Hujrah. The remaining part of this side is partitioned off from the body of the

fence are three windows, holes about half a foot square, and placed from four to five feet above the ground; they are said to be between three and four cubits distant from the Prophet's head. The most westerly of these is supposed to front Mohammed's tomb, wherefore it is called the Shubák el Nabi, or the Prophet's window. The next, on the right as you front it, is Abubekr's, and the most easterly of the three is Omar's. Above the Hujrah is the Green Dome, surmounted outside by a large gilt crescent springing from a series of globes. The glowing imaginations of the Moslems crown this gem of the building with a pillar of heavenly light, which directs from three days' distance the pilgrims' steps towards El Medinah. But alas! none save holy men, (and perhaps, odylic sensitives,) whose material organs are piercing as their vision spiritual, are allowed the privilege of beholding this poetic splendor.

Arrived at the Shubah el Nabi, Hamid took his stand about six feet or so out of reach of the railing, and at that respectful distance from, and facing* the Hazirah (or presence), with hands raised as in prayer, he recited the following supplication in a low voice, telling me in a stage whisper to repeat it after him with awe, and fear, and love.

"Peace be with thee, O Prophet of Allah, and the mercy of Allah and his blessings! Peace be with thee, O Prophet

mosque by a dwarf wall, inclosing the "Khasafat el Sultan," the place where *Fakihs* are perpetually engaged in *Khitmahs*, or perusals of the Koran, on behalf of the reigning Sultan.

* The ancient practice of El Islam during the recitation of the following benedictions was to face Meccah, the back being turned towards the tomb, and to form a mental image of the Prophet, supposing him to be in front. El Kirmani and other doctors prefer this as the more venerable custom, but in these days it is completely exploded, and the purist would probably be soundly bastinadoed by the eunuchs for attempting it.

of Allah! Peace be with thee, O friend of Allah! Peace be with thee, O best of Allah's creation! Peace be with thee, O pure creature of Allah! Peace be with thee, O chief of Prophets! Peace be with thee, O seal of the Prophets! Peace be with thee, O prince of the pious! Peace be with thee, O Prophet of the Lord of the (three) worlds! Peace be with thee, and with thy family, and with thy pure wives! Peace be with thee, and with all thy companions! Peace be with thee, and with all the Prophets, and with those sent to preach Allah's word! Peace be with thee, and with all Allah's righteous worshippers! Peace be with thee, O thou bringer of glad tidings! Peace be with thee, O bearer of threats! Peace be with thee, O thou bright lamp! Peace be with thee, O thou Prophet of mercy! Peace be with thee, O ruler of thy faith! Peace be with thee, O opener of grief! Peace be with thee! and Allah bless thee! and Allah repay thee for us, O thou Prophet of Allah! the choicest of blessings with which he ever blessed prophet! Allah bless thee as often as mentioners have mentioned thee, and forgetters have forgotten thee! And Allah bless thee among the first and the last, with the best, the highest, and the fullest of blessings ever bestowed on man, even as we escaped error by means of thee, and were made to see after blindness, and after ignorance, were directed into the right way. I bear witness that there is no Allah but Allah, and I testify that thou art his servant, and his prophet, and his faithful follower, and best creature. And I bear witness, O Prophet of Allah! that thou hast delivered thy message, and discharged thy trust, and advised thy faith, and opened grief, and published proofs, and fought valiantly for thy Lord, and worshipped thy God till certainty came to thee (*i. e.* to the hour of death), and we thy friends, O Prophet of Allah! appear before thee travellers from distant lands and far countries, through dangers and difficulties, in the times of darkness, and in the hours of day, longing to give thee thy rights (*i. e.* to honor the Prophet by benediction and visitation), and to obtain the blessings of thine intercession, for our sins have broken our backs, and thou intercedest with the Healer. And Allah said,* 'And though they have injured themselves, they came to thee, and begged thee to secure their pardon, and they found God an acceptor of penitence, and full of compassion.' O Prophet of Allah, intercession! intercession! intercession!† O Allah bless Mohammed and Mohammed's family, and give him superiority and high rank, even as thou didst promise him, and graciously allow us to conclude this visitation. I deposit on this spot, and near thee, O Prophet of God, my everlasting profession (of faith) from this our day, to the day of judgment, that there is no Allah but Allah, and that our Lord Mohammed is his servant, and his Prophet.‡ Amen! O Lord of the (three) worlds!' "§

After which, performing Ziyárat for ourselves,‖ we

* This is the usual introduction to a quotation from the Koran.

† It may easily be conceived how offensive this must be to the Wahhabis, who consider it blasphemy to assert that a mere man can stand between the Creator and the creature on the last day.

‡ This is called the Testification. Like the Fát-háh, it is repeated at every holy place and tomb visited at El Medinah.

§ Burckhardt mentions that in his day, among other favors supplicated in prayer to the Deity, the following request was made,—"Destroy our enemies, and may the torments of hell fire be their lot!" I never heard it at the Prophet's tomb.

As the above benediction is rather a long one, the Zair is allowed to shorten it *à discrétion,* but on no account to say less than "Peace be with thee, O Prophet of Allah"—this being the gist of the ceremony.

‖ Though performing Ziyárat for myself, I had promised my old Shaykh at Cairo to recite a Fát-háh in his name at the Prophet's tomb; so a double recitation fell to my lot. If acting Zair for another person (a common custom we read, even in the days of El Walid, the Caliph of

repeated the Fát-háh or "opening" chapter of the Koran.

"1. In the name of Allah, the merciful, the compassionate!

"2. Praise be to Allah, who the (three) worlds made.

"3. The merciful, the compassionate.

"4. The king of the day of fate.

"5. Thee (alone) do we worship, and of thee (alone) do we ask aid.

"6. Guide us to the path that is straight—

"7. The path of those for whom thy love is great, not those on whom is hate, nor they that deviate.

"Amen! O Lord of Angels, Ginns, and men!"*

After reciting this mentally with upraised hands, the forefinger of the right hand being extended to its full length, we drew our palms down our faces and did almsdeeds, a vital part of the ceremony. Thus concludes the first part of the ceremony of visitation at the Prophet's tomb.

Hamid then stepped about a foot and a half to the right, and I followed his example; so as to place myself exactly opposite the second aperture in the grating called Abubekr's window. There, making a sign towards the mausoleum, we addressed its inmate as follows: "Peace be with thee, O Abubekr, O thou truthful one! Peace be with

Damascus), you are bound to mention your principal's name at the beginning of the benediction, thus: "Peace be with thee, O Prophet of Allah, from such a one, the son of such a one, who wants thine intercession, and begs for pardon and mercy." Most Zairs recite Fát-háhs for all their friends and relations at the tomb.

* I have endeavored in this translation to imitate the imperfect rhyme of the original Arabic. Such an attempt, however, is full of difficulties: the Arabic is a language in which, like Italian, it is almost impossible not to rhyme.

thee, O caliph of Allah's Prophet over his people! Peace be with thee, O Companion of the Cave, and friend in travel! Peace be with thee, O thou banner of the fugitives and the auxiliaries! I testify that thou didst ever stand firm in the right way, and wast a smiter of the infidel, and a benefactor to thine own people. Allah grant thee through his Prophet weal! We pray Almighty God to cause us to die in thy friendship, and to raise us up in company with his Prophet and thyself, even as he hath mercifully vouchsafed to us this visitation."*

After which we closed one more step to the right, and standing opposite Omar's window, the most easterly of the three, after making a sign with our hands, we addressed the just Caliph in these words: "Peace be with thee, O Omar! O thou just one! thou prince of true believers! Peace be with thee, who spakest with truth, and who madest thy word agree with the Strong Book! (the Koran), O thou Faruk.† Thou faithful one! who girdest thy loins with the Prophet, and the first believers, and with them didst make up the full number forty,‡ and thus causedst to be accomplished the Prophet's prayer,§ and then didst return to thy God a martyr leaving the world with praise! Allah grant thee, through his Prophet and his Caliph and his followers, the best of good, and may Allah feel in thee all satisfaction!"

Shaykh Hamid, after wrenching a beggar or two from

* It will not be necessary to inform the reader more than once that all these several divisions of prayer ended with the Testification and the Fát-háh.

† Faruk,—the separator,—a title of Omar.

‡ When the number of the *As-hab* or "Companions" was thirty-nine, they were suddenly joined by Omar, who thus became the fortieth.

§ It is said that Mohammed prayed long for the conversion of Omar to El Islam, knowing his sterling qualities, and the aid he would lend to the establishment of the faith.

my shoulders, then permitted me to draw near to the little window, called the Prophet's, and look in. Here my proceedings were watched with suspicious eyes. The Persians have sometimes managed to pollute the part near Abubekr's and Omar's graves by tossing through the aperture what is externally a handsome shawl intended as a present for the tomb.* After straining my eyes for a time I saw a curtain,† or rather hangings, with three inscriptions in large gold letters, informing readers, that behind them lie Allah's Prophet and the two first caliphs. The exact place of Moham-

* This foolish fanaticism has lost many an innocent life, for the Arabs on these occasions seize their sabres, and cut down every Persian they meet. Still, bigoted Shiahs persist in practising and applauding it, and the man who can boast at Shiraz of having defiled Abubekr's, Omar's, or Osman's tomb becomes at once a lion and a hero.

† Burckhardt, with his usual accuracy, asserts that a new curtain is sent when the old one is decayed, or when a new Sultan ascends the throne, and those authors err who, like Maundrell, declare the curtain to be removed every year.

The Damascus caravan conveys, together with its Mahmal or emblem of royalty, the new Kiswah (or "garment") when required for the tomb. It is put on by the eunuchs, who enter the baldaquin by its northern gate at night time, and there is a superstitious story amongst the people that they guard their eyes with veils against the supernatural splendors which pour from the tomb.

The Kiswah is a black, purple, or green brocade, embroidered with white or with silver letters. A piece in my possession, the gift of Omar Effendi, is a handsome silk and cotton Damascus brocade, with white letters worked in it—manifestly the produce of manual labor, not the poor dull work of machinery. It contains the formula of the Moslem faith in the cursive style of the Suls character, seventy-two varieties of which are enumerated by calligraphers. Nothing can be more elegant or appropriate than its appearance. The old curtain is usually distributed amongst the officers of the mosque, and sold in bits to pilgrims; in some distant Moslem countries, the possessor of such a relic would be considered a saint. When treating of the history of the mosque, some remarks will be offered about the origin of this curtain.

med's tomb is moreover distinguished by a large pearl rosary, and a peculiar ornament, the celebrated Kaukab el Durri, or constellation of pearls, suspended to the curtain breast high.* This is described to be a "brilliant star set in diamonds and pearls," and placed in the dark in order that man's eye may be able to bear its splendors; the vulgar believe it to be a "jewel of the jewels of Paradise." To me it greatly resembled the round stoppers of glass, used for the humbler sort of decanters, but I never saw it quite near enough to judge fairly of it, and did not think fit to pay an exorbitant sum for the privilege of entering the inner passage of the baldaquin.† Altogether the *coup-d'œil* had nothing to recommend it by day. At night, when the lamps hung in this passage shed a dim light upon the mosaic work of the marble floors, upon the glittering inscriptions, and the massive hangings, the scene is more likely to become "ken-speckle."

Never having seen the tomb,‡ I must depict it from

* The place of the Prophet's head is, I was told, marked by a fine Koran hung up to the curtain! This volume is probably a successor to the relic formerly kept there, the Cufic Koran belonging to Osman, the fourth Caliph, which Burckhardt supposes to have perished in the conflagration which destroyed the mosque.

† The eunuchs of the tomb have the privilege of admitting strangers. In this passage are preserved the treasures of the place; they are a "bait Mal el Muslimin," or public treasury of the Moslems; therefore to be employed by the Caliph (*i. e.* the reigning Sultan) for the exigencies of the faith. The amount is said to be enormous, which I doubt.

‡ And I might add, never having seen one who has seen it. Niebuhr is utterly incorrect in his hearsay description of it. It is not "enclosed within iron railings for fear lest the people might superstitiously offer worship to the ashes of the Prophet." The tomb is not "of plain mason-work in the form of a chest," nor does any one believe that it is "placed within or between two other tombs, in which rest the ashes of the two first caliphs." The traveller appears to have lent a credulous ear to the eminent Arab merchant, who told him that a guard was

books, by no means an easy task. Most of the historians are silent after describing the inner walls of the Hujrah. El Kalka-shandi declares "in eo lapidem nobilem continere sepulchra Apostoli, Abubecr et Omar, circumcinctum peribole in modum conclavis fere usque ad tectum assurgente quæ velo serico nigro obligatur." This author, then, agrees with my Persian friends, who declare the sepulchre to be a marble slab. Ibn Jubayr, who travelled A. H. 580, relates that the Prophet's coffin is a box of ebony (abnus) covered with sandal-wood, and plated with silver; it is placed, he says, behind a curtain, and surrounded by an iron grating. El Samanhudi, quoted by Burckhardt, declares that the curtain covers a square building of black stones, in the interior of which are the tombs of Mohammed and his two immediate successors. He adds that the tombs are deep holes, and that the coffin which contains the Prophet is cased with silver, and has on the top a marble slab inscribed "Bismillah! Allahumma salli alayh!" ("In the name of Allah! Allah have mercy upon him!")*

placed over the tomb to prevent the populace scraping dirt from about it, and preserving it as a relic.

* Burckhardt, however, must be in error when he says, "The tombs are also covered with precious stuffs, and in the shape of catafalques, like that of Ibrahim in the great mosque of Meccah." The eunuchs positively declare that no one ever approaches the tomb, and that he who ventured to do so would at once be blinded by the supernatural light. Moreover, the historians of El Medinah all quote tales of certain visions of the Prophet, directing his tomb to be cleared of dust that had fallen upon it from above, in which case some man celebrated for piety and purity was *let through a hole in the roof*, by cords, down to the tomb, with directions to wipe it with his beard. This style of ingress is explained by another assertion of El Samanhudi, quoted by Burckhardt. In A. H. 892, when Kaid-bey rebuilt the mosque, which had been destroyed by lightning, three deep graves were found in the inside, full of rubbish, but the author of this history, who himself entered it,

The Prophet's body, it should be remembered, lies, or is supposed to lie, stretched at full length on the right side, with the right palm supporting the right cheek, the face fronting Meccah, as Moslems are always buried, and consequently the body lies with the head almost to due West and the feet to due East. Close behind him is placed Abubekr, whose face fronts the Prophet's shoulder,* and lastly Omar holds the same position with respect to his predecessor.

It is popularly believed that in the Hujrah there is now spare place for only a single grave, which is reserved for Isa ben Maryam after his second coming. The historians of El Islam are full of tales proving that though many of their early saints, as Osman the Caliph and Hasan the Imam, were desirous of being buried there, and that although Ayisha, to whom the room belonged, willingly acceded to their wishes, son of man has as yet been unable to occupy it.

After the Fát-háh pronounced at Omar's tomb, and the short inspection of the Hujrah, Shaykh Hamid led me round the south-east corner of the baldaquin.† Turning towards

saw no traces of tombs. The original place of Mohammed's tomb was ascertained with great difficulty: the walls of the Hujrah *were then rebuilt*, and the iron railing placed round it, which is now there.

* Upon this point authors greatly disagree. Ibn Jubayr, for instance, says, that Abubekr's head is opposite the Prophet's feet, and that Omar's face is on a level with Abubekr's shoulder.

The vulgar story of the suspended coffin has been explained in two ways. Niebuhr supposes it to have arisen from the rude drawings sold to strangers. Mr. William Bankes (Giovanni Finati, vol. ii. p. 289) more sensibly believes that the mass of rock popularly described as hanging unsupported in the mosque of Omar at Jerusalem, was confounded by Christians, who could not have seen either of these Moslem shrines, with the Prophet's tomb at El Medinah.

† Some Moslems end their Ziyárat at the Prophet's tomb; others, instead of advancing, as I did, return to the Prophet's window, pray, and beg pardon for their parents and themselves, and ask all they desire,

the north we stopped at what is commonly called the Mahbat Jibrail, ("Place of the Archangel Gabriel's Descent with the Heavenly Revelations,") or simply El Malaikah—the Angels. It is a small window in the eastern wall of the mosque; we turned our backs upon it, and fronting the Hujrah, recited the following prayer:—

"Peace be with you, ye Angels of Allah, the Mukarrabin (cherubs), and the Musharrafin (seraphs), the pure, the holy, honored by the dwellers in heaven, and by those who abide upon the earth. O beneficent Lord! O long-suffering! O Almighty! O Pitier! O thou Compassionate One! perfect our light, and pardon our sins, and accept penitence for

concluding with prayers to the Almighty. Thence they repair to the Rauzah or Garden, and standing at the column called after Abu Lubabah, pray a two-prostration prayer there; concluding with the "Dua," or benediction upon the Prophet, and there repeat these words: "O Allah, thou hast said, and thy word is true, 'Say, O Lord, pardon and show mercy; for thou art the best of the Merciful,' (chap. 23). O God, verily we have heard thy word, and we come for intercession to thy Prophet from our own sins, repenting our errors, and confessing our shortcomings and transgressions! O Allah, pity us, and by the dignity of thy Prophet raise our place (in the heavenly kingdom)! O Allah, pardon our brothers who have preceded us in 'the Faith!'" Then the Zair prays for himself, and his parents, and for those he loves. He should repeat, "Allah have mercy upon thee, O Prophet of Allah!" seventy times, when an angel will reply, "Allah bless thee, O thou blesser!" Then he should sit before the pulpit, and mentally conceive in it the Prophet surrounded by the Fugitives and the Auxiliaries. Some place the right hand upon the pulpit, even as Mohammed used to do.

The Zair then returns to the column of Abu Lubabah, and repents his sins there. Secondly, he stands in prayer at Ali's pillar in front of the form. And lastly, he repairs to the Ustuwanat el As-hab, (the Companion's Column,) the fourth distant from the pulpit on the right, and the third from the Hujrah on the left; here he prays, and meditates, and blesses Allah and the Prophet. After which, he proceeds to visit the rest of the holy places.

our offences, and cause us to die among the holy! Peace be with ye, Angels of the Merciful, one and all! And the mercy of God and his blessings be upon you!" after which I was shown the spot in the Hujrah where Sayyidna Isa shall be buried* by Mohammed's side.

Then turning towards the west, at a point where there is a break in the symmetry of the Hujrah, we arrived at the sixth station, the sepulchre or cenotaph of the Lady Fatimah. Her grave is outside the enceinte and the curtain which surrounds her father's remains, so strict is Moslem decorum, and so exalted its opinion of the "Virgin's" delicacy; the eastern side of the Hujrah, here turning a little westward, interrupting the shape of the square, in order to give this spot the appearance of disconnection with the rest of the building. The tomb, seen through a square aperture like those above described, is a long catafalque, covered with a black pall. Though there is great doubt whether the lady be not buried with her son Hasan in the Bakia cemetery, this place is always visited by the pious Moslem.

The following is the prayer opposite the grave of the amiable Fatimah:—

"Peace be with thee, daughter of the Messenger of Allah! Peace be with thee, daughter of the Prophet of Allah! Peace be with thee, thou daughter of Mustafa! Peace be with thee, thou mother of the Shurafa!† Peace be with thee, O Lady amongst women! Peace be with

* It is almost unnecessary to inform the reader that all Moslems deny the personal suffering of Christ, cleaving to the heresy of the Christian Docetes,—certain "beasts in the shape of men," as they are called in the Epistles of Ignatius to the Smyrneans,—who believed that a phantom was crucified in our Savior's place. They also hold to the second coming of the Lord in the flesh, as a forerunner to Mohammed, who shall reappear shortly before the day of judgment.

† Plural of Sherif, a descendant of Mohammed.

thee, O fifth of the Ahl El Kisa!* Peace be with thee, O Zahra and Batúl! † Peace be with thee, O daughter of the Prophet! Peace be with thee, O spouse of our lord Ali El Murtaza! Peace be with thee, O mother of Hassan and Hosayn, the two moons, the two lights, the two pearls, the two princes of the youth of heaven, and gladness of the eyes‡ of true believers! Peace be with thee and with thy sire, El Mustafa, and thy husband, our lord Ali! Allah honor his face, and thy face, and thy father's face in Paradise, and thy two sons the Hasanayn! And the mercy of Allah and his blessings!" (Concluding with the Testification and the Fát-háh.)

We then broke away as we best could from the crowd of female "askers," who have established their Lares and Penates under the shadow of the Lady's wing, and advancing a few paces, we fronted to the north, and recited a prayer in honor of Hamzah, and the martyrs who lie buried at the foot of Mount Ohod.§ We then turned to the right, and, fronting the easterly wall, prayed for the souls of the blessed whose mortal spirits repose within El Bakia's hallowed circuit.‖

* The "people of the garment," so called, because on one occasion the Prophet wrapped his cloak around himself, his daughter, his son-in-law, and his two grandsons, thereby separating them in dignity from other Moslems.

† Burckhardt translates "Zahra" "bright blooming Fatimah." This I believe to be the literal meaning of the epithet. When thus applied, however, it denotes "virginem τα καταμηνια nescientem," in which state of purity the daughter of the Prophet is supposed to have lived. For the same reason she is called El Batúl, the Virgin,—a title given by Eastern Christians to the Mother of our Lord. The perpetual virginity of Fatimah, even after the motherhood, is a point of orthodoxy in El Islam.

‡ Meaning "joy and gladness in the sight of true believers."

§ The prayer is now omitted, in order to avoid the repetition of it when describing a visit to Mount Ohod.

‖ The prayers usually recited here are especially in honor of Abbas,

After this we returned to the southern wall of the mosque, and, facing towards Meccah, we recited the following supplication:—"O Allah! (three times repeated), O Compassionate! O Beneficent! O Requiter (of good and evil)! O Prince! O Ruler! O ancient of Benefits! O Omniscient! O thou who givest when asked, and who aidest when aid is required, accept this our Visitation, and preserve us from dangers, and make easy our affairs, and expand our chests,* and receive our prostration, and requite us according to our good deeds, and turn not our evil deeds against us, and place not over us one who feareth not thee, and one who pitieth not us, and write safety and health upon us and upon thy slaves, the Hujjaj, and the Ghuzat, and the Zawwar,† and the home-dwellers and the wayfarers of the Moslems, by land and by sea, and pardon those of the faith of our lord Mohammed one and all!" (Then the Testification and the Fát-háh.)

From the southern wall we returned to the "Prophet's Window," where we recited the following tetrastich and prayer.

"O Mustafa! verily, I stand at thy door,
A man, weak and fearful, by reason of my sins:
If thou aid me not, O Prophet of Allah!
I die—for in the world there is none generous as thou art!"

"Of a truth, Allah and his Angels bless the Prophet! O

Hasan, (Ali, called) Zayn-El-Abidin, Osman, the Lady Halimah, the Martyrs, and the Mothers of the Moslems (*i. e.* the Prophet's wives), buried in the holy cemetery. When describing a visit to El Bakia, they will be translated at full length.

* That is to say, "gladden our hearts."

† Hujjaj is the plural of Hajj—pilgrims; Ghuzat, of Ghazi—crusaders; and Zawwar of Zäir—visitors to Mohammed's tomb.

ye who believe bless him and salute him with salutation!* O Allah! verily I implore thy pardon, and supplicate therefore thine aid in this world as in the next! O Allah! O Allah! abandon us not in this holy place to the consequences of our sins without pardoning them, or to our griefs without consoling them, or to our fears, O Allah! without removing them. And blessings and salutation to thee, O Prince of Prophets, Commissioned (to preach the word), and praise to Allah the lord of the (three) worlds!" (Then the Testification and the Fát-háh.)

We turned away from the Hujrah, and after gratifying a meek-looking but exceedingly importunate Indian beggar, who insisted on stunning me with the Chapter Y, S,† we fronted southwards, and taking care that our backs should not be in a line with the Prophet's face, stood opposite the niche called Mihrab Osma. There Hamid proceeded with another supplication. "O Allah! (three times repeated), O Safeguard of the fearful, and defenders of those who trust in thee, and pitier of the weak, the poor, and the destitute! accept us, O Beneficent! and pardon us, O Merciful! and receive our penitence, O Compassionate! and have mercy upon us, O Forgiver!—for verily none but thou can remit sin! Of a truth thou alone knowest the hidden and veilest man's transgressions: veil, then, our offences, and pardon our sins, and expand our chests, and cause our last words at the supreme hour of life to be the words, 'There is no God but Allah,‡ and our lord Mohammed is the Pro-

* "Taslím" is "to say Salám" to a person.

† The Ya Sin (Y, S), the 36th chapter of the Koran, frequently recited by those whose profession it is to say such masses for the benefit of living, as well as of dead, sinners. Most educated Moslems commit it to memory.

‡ (Or more correctly, "There is no Ilah but Allah," that is, "There is no *Deity* but God.")

phet of Allah!' O Allah! cause us to live according to this saying, O thou Giver of life! and make us to die in this faith, O thou ruler of death! And the best of blessings and the completest of salutations upon the sole Lord of Intercession, our Lord Mohammed and his family, and his companions one and all!" (Then the Testification and the Fát-háh.)

And, lastly, we returned to the Garden, and prayed another two-prostration prayer, ending, as we began, with the worship of the Creator.

* * * * * *

Unfortunately for me, the boy Mohammed had donned that grand embroidered coat. At the end of the ceremony the Aghas, or eunuchs of the mosque,—a race of men considered respectable by their office, and prone to make themselves respected by the freest administration of club law,—assembled in El Rauzat to offer me the congratulation "Ziyáratak Mubárak"—"blessed be thy visitation," and to demand fees. Then came the Sakka, or water-carrier of the Zemzen,* offering a tinned saucer filled from the holy source. And lastly I was beset by beggars,—some mild beggars and picturesque, who sat upon the ground immersed in the contemplation of their napkins; others angry beggars, who cursed if they were not gratified; and others noisy and petulant beggars, especially the feminine party near the Lady's tomb, who captured me by the skirt of my garment, compelling me to ransom myself. There were, besides, pretty beggars, boys who held out the right hand on the score of good looks; ugly beggars, emaciated rascals, whose long hair, dirt, and leanness, entitled them to charity; and lastly, the blind, the halt, and the diseased,

* This has become a generic name for a well situated within the walls of a mosque.

who, as sons of the Holy City, demanded from the Faithful that support with which they could not provide themselves. Having been compelled by my companions, highly against my inclination, to become a man of rank, I was obliged to pay in proportion, and my almoner in the handsome coat, as usual, took a pride in being profuse. This first visit cost me double what I had intended—four dollars—nearly one pound sterling, and never afterwards could I pay less than half that sum.*

Having now performed all the duties of a good Zair, I was permitted by Shaykh Hamid to wander about and see the sights. We began our circumambulation at the Bab el Salam,—the Gate of Salvation,—in the southern portion of the western long wall of the mosque. It is a fine archway handsomely incrusted with marble and glazed tiles; the number of gilt inscriptions on its sides give it, especially at night-time, an appearance of considerable splendor. The portcullis-like doors are of wood, strengthened with brass plates, and nails of the same metal. Outside this gate is a little Sabil, or public fountain, where those who will not pay for the water, kept ready in large earthen jars by the "Sakka," of the mosque, perform their ablutions gratis. Here all the mendicants congregate in force, sitting on the outer steps and at the entrance of the mosque, up and through which the visitors must pass. About the centre of the western wall is the Bab el Rahmah—the Gate of Pity. It admits the dead bodies of the Faithful when carried to be prayed over in the mosque; there is nothing remarkable in

* As might be expected, the more a man pays, the higher he estimates his own dignity. Some Indians have spent as much as 500 dollars during a first visit. Others have "made maulids," *i. e.*, feasted all the poor connected with the temple with rice, meat, &c., while others brought rare and expensive presents for the officials. Such generosity, however, is becoming rare in these unworthy days.

its appearance; in common with the other gates, it has huge folding doors, iron-bound, an external flight of steps, and a few modern inscriptions. The Bab Mejídi or Gate (of the Sultan Abd el) Mejid stands in the centre of the northern wall; like its portico, it is unfinished, but its present appearance promises that it will eclipse all except the Bab el Salam. The Bab el Nisa is in the eastern wall opposite the Bab el Rahmah, with which it is connected by the "Farsh el Hajar," a broad band of stone, two or three steps below the level of the portico, and slightly raised above the Sahn or the hypæthral portion of the mosque. And lastly, in the southern portion of the same eastern wall is the Bab Jibrail, the Gate of the Archangel Gabriel.* All these entrances are arrived at by short external flights of steps leading from the streets, as the base of the temple, unlike that of Meccah, is a little higher than the foundations of the buildings around it. The doors are closed by the eunuchs in attendance, immediately after night prayers, except during the blessed month El Ramazan, and the pilgrimage season, when a number of pious visitors pay considerable fees to pass the night there in meditation and prayer.

The minarets are five in number; but one, the Shikayliyah, at the north-west angle of the building, has been levelled, and is still in process of being re-built. The Munar Bab el Salam stands by the gate of that name: it is a tall handsome tower surmounted by a large bull, or cow, of

* Most of these entrances have been named and renamed. The Bab Jibrail, for instance, which derives its present appellation from the general belief that the angel once passed through it, is generally called in books Bab el Jabr, the Gate of Repairing (the broken fortunes of a friend or follower). It must not be confounded with the Mahbat Jibrail, or the window near it in the eastern wall, where the archangel usually descended from heaven with the Wahy or Inspiration.

brass gilt or burnished. The Munar Bab el Rahmah, about the centre of the western wall, is of more simple form than the others: it has two galleries with the superior portion circular, and surmounted by the comical "extinguisher" roof so common in Turkey and Egypt. On the north-east angle of the mosque stands the Sulaymaníyah Munar, so named after its founder, Sultan Sulayman the Magnificent. It is a well-built and a substantial stone tower divided into three stages; the two lower portions are polygonal, the upper one circular, and each terminates in a platform with a railed gallery carried all round for the protection of those who ascend. And lastly, from the south-east angle of the mosque, supposed to lie upon the spot where Belal, the Prophet's crier, called the first Moslems to prayer,* springs the Munar Raisiyah, so called because it is appropriated to the Ruasa or chiefs of the Muezzins. Like the Sulamaníyah, it consists of three parts: the first and second stages are polygonal, and the third, a circular one, is furnished like the lower two with a railed gallery. Both the latter minarets end in solid ovals of masonry, from which project a number of wooden triangles.† To these and to the galleries on all festive occasions, such as the arrival of the Damascus caravan, are hung oil lamps—a poor attempt at illumination, which may perhaps rationally explain the origin of the Medinite superstition concerning the column of light which crowns the Prophet's tomb. There is no uniformity in the shape or the size of these four minarets, and at first sight, despite their beauty and grandeur, they appear somewhat

* Belal, the loud-lunged crier, stood, we are informed by Moslem historians, upon a part of the roof on one of the walls of the mosque. The minaret, as the next chapter will show, was the invention of a more tasteful age.

† (As on all the minarets of Cairo.)

bizarre and misplaced. But after a few days I found that my eye grew accustomed to them, and that I had no difficulty in appreciating their massive proportions and lofty forms.

Equally irregular are the Riwaks, or porches, surrounding the hypæthral court. Along the northern wall there will be, when finished, a fine colonnade of granite, paved with marble. The eastern Riwak has three rows of pillars, the western four, and the southern, under which stands the tomb, of course has its columns ranged deeper than all the others. These supports of the building are of different material; some of fine marble, others of rough stone merely plastered over and painted with the most vulgar of arabesques, vermillion and black in irregular patches, and broad streaks like the stage face of a London clown.* Their size moreover is different, the southern colonnade being composed of pillars palpably larger than those in the other parts of the mosque. Scarcely any two shafts have similar capitals; many have no pedestal, and some of them are cut with a painful ignorance of art. I cannot extend my admiration of the minarets to the columns—in *their* "architectural lawlessness" there is not a redeeming point.

Of these unpraisable pillars three are celebrated in the annals of El Islam, for which reason their names are painted upon them, and five others enjoy the honor of distinctive appellations. The first is called El Mukhallak, because, on some occasion of impurity, it was anointed with a perfume called Khaluk. It is near the Mihrab el Nabawi, on the right of the place where the Imam prays, and notes the spot where, before the invention of the pulpit, the Prophet, leaning upon the Ustuwanat el Hannanah—the weeping

* This abomination may be seen in Egypt on many of the tombs,—those outside the Bab el Nasr at Cairo, for instance.

Pillar*—used to recite the Khutbah or Friday sermon. The second stands third from the pulpit, and third from the Hujrah. It is called the Pillar of Ayisha, also the Ustuwanat el Kurah, or the column of Lots, because the Prophet, according to the testimony of his favorite wife, declared that if men knew the value of the place, they would cast lots to pray there: in some books it is known as the pillar of the Muhajirin or Fugitives, and others mention it as El Mukhallak—the Perfumed. Twenty cubits distant from Ayisha's pillar, and the second from the Hujrah, and the fourth from the pulpit, is the Pillar of Repentance, or of Abu Lubabah. It derives its name from the following circumstance. Abu Lubabah was a native of El Medinah, one of the auxiliaries and a companion of Mohammed, originally it is said a Jew, according to others of the Beni Amr ebn Auf of the Aus tribe. Being sent for by his kinsmen or his allies, the Beni Kurayzah, at that time capitulating to Mohammed, he was consulted by the distracted tribe: men, women and children threw themselves at his feet, and begged of him to intercede for them with the offended Prophet. Abu Lubabah swore he would do so: at the same time, he drew his hand across his throat, as much as to say, "Defend yourselves to the last, for if you yield, such is your doom." Afterwards repenting, he bound himself with a huge chain to the date-tree in whose place the column now stands, vowing to continue there until Allah and the Prophet accepted his penitence, a circumstance which did not take place till the tenth day, when his hearing was gone and he had almost lost his sight. The less celebrated pillars are the Ustuwanat Sarí, or column of the Cot, where the Prophet was wont to sit medi-

* The tale of this weeping pillar is well known. Some suppose it to have been buried beneath the pulpit: others—they are few in number—declare that it was inserted in the body of the pulpit.

tating on his humble couch of date-sticks. The Ustuwanat Ali notes the spot where the fourth caliph used to pray and watch his father-in-law at night. At the Ustuwanat el Wufud, as its name denotes, the Prophet received envoys, couriers, and emissaries from foreign places. The Ustuwanat el Tahajjud now stands where Mohammed sitting upon his mat passed the night in prayer. And lastly is the Makam Jibrail (Gabriel's place), for whose other name, Mirbaat el Bair, "the pole of the beast of burden," I have been unable to find an explanation.

The four Riwaks, or porches, of the Medinah mosque open upon a hypæthral court of parallelogrammic shape. The only remarkable object in it * is a square of wooden railing enclosing a place full of well-watered earth, called the Garden of our Lady Fatimah.† It now contains a dozen date-trees—in Ibn Jubayr's time there were fifteen. Their fruit is sent by the eunuchs as presents to the Sultan and the great men of the Islam; it is highly valued by the vulgar, but the Ulema do not think much of its claims to importance. Among the palms are the venerable remains of a Sidr, or Lote tree, whose produce‡ is sold for inordinate

* The little domed building which figures in the native sketches and in all our prints of the El Medinah mosque, was taken down three or four years ago. It occupied part of the centre of the square, and was called Kubbat el Zayt—Dome of Oil—or Kubbat el Shama—Dome of Candles—from its use as a store-room for lamps and wax candles.

† This is its name among the illiterate, who firmly believe the palms to be descendants of trees planted there by the hands of the Prophet's, daughter. As far as I could discover, the tradition has no foundation, and in old times there was no garden in the hypæthral court. The vulgar are in the habit of eating a certain kind of date, "El Say hani," in the mosque, and of throwing the stones about; this practice is violently denounced by the Ulema.

‡ Rhamnus Nabeca Forsk. The fruit, called Nebek, is eaten, and the leaves are used for the purpose of washing dead bodies. The visitor

sums. The enclosure is entered by a dwarf gate in the south-eastern portion of the railing, near the well, and one of the eunuchs is generally to be seen in it: it is under the charge of the Mudir, or chief treasurer. These gardens are not uncommon in Moslem mosques, as the traveller who passes through Cairo can convince himself. They form a pretty and an appropriate feature in a building erected for the worship of Him "who spread the earth with carpets of flowers and drew shady trees from the dead ground." A tradition of the Prophet also declares that "acceptable is devotion in the garden and in the orchard." At the south-east angle of the enclosure, under a wooden roof supported by pillars of the same material, stands the Zemzem, generally called the Bir el Nabi, or "the Prophet's well." My predecessor declares that the brackishness of its produce has stood in the way of its reputation for holiness. Yet a well educated man told me that it was as "light" water* as any in El Medinah,—a fact which he accounted for by supposing a subterraneous passage† which connects it with the great Zemzem at Meccah. Others, again, believe that it is filled by a vein of water springing directly under the Prophet's grave:

is not forbidden to take fruit or water as presents from El Medinah, but it is unlawful for him to carry away earth, or stones, or cakes of dust, made for sale to the ignorant.

* The Arabs, who, like all Orientals, are exceedingly curious about water, take the trouble to weigh the produce of their wells; the lighter the water, the more digestible and wholesome it is considered.

† The common phenomenon of rivers flowing underground in Arabia has, doubtless, suggested to the people these subterraneous passages, with which they connect the most distant places. At El Medinah, amongst other tales of short cuts known only to certain Bedouin families, a man told me of a shaft leading from his native city to Hadramaut: according to him, it existed in the times of the Prophet, and was a journey of only three days!

generally, however, among the learned it is not more revered than our Lady's Garden, nor is it ranked in books among the holy wells of El Medinah. Between this Zemzem and the eastern Riwak is the Stoa, or academia, of the Prophet's city. In the cool mornings and evenings the ground is strewed with professors, who teach, as an eminent orientalist hath it, the young idea to shout rather than to shoot.* A few feet to the south of the palm garden is a movable wooden planking painted green, and about three feet high; it serves to separate the congregation from the Imam when he prays here; and at the north-eastern angle of the enclosure is a Shajar Kanadíl, a large brass chandelier, which completes the furniture of the court.

After this inspection, the shadows of evening began to gather round us. We left the mosque, reverently taking care to issue forth with the left foot, and not to back out of it as in the Sunnat, or practice derived from the Prophet, when taking leave of the Meccan mosque.

To conclude this long chapter. Although every Moslem, learned and simple, firmly believes that Mohammed's remains are interred in the Hujrah at El Medinah, I cannot help suspecting that the place is at least as doubtful as that of the Holy Sepulchre at Jerusalem. It must be remembered that a great tumult followed the announcement of the Prophet's death, when the people, as often happens,†

* The Mosque Library is kept in large chests near the Bab el Salam; the only MS. of any value here is a Koran written in the Sulsi hand. It is nearly four feet long, bound in a wooden cover, and padlocked, so as to require from the curious a "silver key."

† So the peasants in Brittany believe that Napoleon the First is not yet dead; the Prussians expect Frederick the Second; the Swiss, William Tell; the older English, King Arthur; and certain modern fanatics look forward to the re-appearance of Joanna Southcote. Why multiply instances in so well known a branch of the history of popular superstitions?

believing him to be immortal, refused to credit the report, and even Omar threatened destruction to any one that asserted it. Moreover the body was scarcely cold when the contest about the succession arose between the fugitives of Meccah and the auxiliaries of El Medinah: in the ardor of which, according to the Shiahs, the house of Ali and Fatimah,—within a few feet of the spot where the tomb of the Prophet is now placed—was threatened with fire, and that Abubekr was elected caliph that same evening. If any one find cause to wonder that the last resting-place of a personage so important was not fixed for ever, he may find many a parallel case in El Medinah. To quote no other, three places claim the honor of containing the Lady Fatimah's mortal spoils, although one might suppose that the daughter of a Prophet and the mother of the Imams would not be laid in an unknown grave. My reasons for incredulity are the following:

1. From the earliest days the shape of the Prophet's tomb has never been generally known in El Islam. For this reason it is that graves are made convex in some countries, and flat in others: had there been a Sunnat,* this would not have been the case.

2. The discrepant accounts of the learned. El Samanhudi, perhaps the highest authority, contradicts himself. In one place he describes the coffin; in another he expressly declares that he entered the Hujrah when it was being repaired by Kaid-bey, and saw in the inside three deep graves, but no traces of tombs.† Either, then, the mortal

* The Sunnat is the custom or practice of the Prophet, rigidly conformed to by every good and orthodox Moslem.

† The reader will bear in mind that I am quoting from Burckhardt. When in El Hejaz and at Cairo, I vainly endeavored to buy a copy of El Samanhudi. One was shown to me at El Medinah; unhappily, it bore the word Wakf (bequeathed), and belonged to the mosque. I was scarcely allowed time to read it.

remains of the Prophet had—despite Moslem superstition* —mingled with the dust (a probable circumstance after nearly 900 years' interment), or, what is more likely, they had been removed by the Shiah schismatics who for centuries had charge of the sepulchre.

3. And lastly, I cannot but look upon the tale of the blinding light which surrounds the Prophet's tomb, and now universally believed upon the authority of the attendant eunuchs, who must know its falsehood, as a priestly gloss intended to conceal a defect.

I here conclude the subject, committing it to some future and more favored investigator. In offering the above remarks, I am far from wishing to throw a doubt upon an established point of history. But where a suspicion of fable arises from popular "facts," a knowledge of man and of his manners teaches us to regard it with favoring eye.

* In Moslem law, prophets, martyrs, and saints, are not supposed to be dead; their property, therefore, remains their own. The Ulema have confounded themselves in the consideration of the prophetic state after death. Many declare that prophets live and pray for forty days in the tomb; at the expiration of which time, they are taken to the presence of their Maker, where they remain till the last blast of Israfil's trumpet. The common belief, however, leaves the bodies in the graves, but no one would dare to assert that the holy ones are suffered to undergo corruption. On the contrary, their faces are blooming, their eyes bright, and blood would issue from their bodies if wounded.

El Islam, as will afterwards appear, abounds in traditions of the ancient tombs of saints and martyrs, when accidentally opened, exposing to view corpses apparently freshly buried. And it has come to pass that this fact, the result of sanctity, has now become an unerring indication of it. A remarkable case in point is that of the late Sherif Ghalib, the father of the present prince of Meccah. In his lifetime he was reviled as a tyrant. But some years after his death, his body was found undecomposed; he then became a saint, and men now pray at his tomb. Perhaps his tyranny was no drawback to his holy reputation.

# CHAPTER XVI.

## EL MEDINAH.*

It is equally difficult to define, politically or geographically, the limits of El Hejaz. Whilst some authors fix its northern frontier at Aylah and the Desert, making Yemen its southern limit, others include in it only the tract of land lying between Meccah and El Medinah. As the country has no natural boundaries, and its political limits change with every generation, perhaps the best distribution of its frontier would be that which includes all the properly called Holy Land, making Yambu the northern and Jeddah the southern extremes, while a line drawn through El Medinah, Suwayrkiyah, and Jebel Kora, the mountain of Taif, might represent its eastern boundary. Thus El Hejaz would be an irregular parallelogram, about 250 miles in length, with a maximum breadth of 150 miles. Two meanings are assigned to the name of this region; according to most

* Amongst a people who, like the Arabs or the Spaniards, hold a plurality of names to be a sign of dignity, so illustrious a spot as El Medinah could not fail to be rich in nomenclature. A Hadis declares, "to El Medinah belong ten names:" books, however, enumerate nearly a hundred.

authorities, it means the "Separator," or "Barrier," between Nejd and Tehamah;* according to others, the "colligated," (by mountains).

Medinat el Nabi, the Prophet's City, or, as it is usually called for brevity, El Medinah, the City, is situated on the borders of Nejd, upon the vast plateau of high land which forms central Arabia. The limits of the sanctuary called the Hudud el Haram, as defined by the Prophet, may still serve to mark out the city's plain. Northwards, at a distance of about three miles, is Jebel Ohod, or, according to others, Jebel Saur, a hill somewhat beyond Ohod; these are the last ribs of the vast primitive and granitic† chine that, extending from Lebanon to near Aden, and from Aden again to Muscat, fringes the Arabian trapezium. To the S.W. the plain is bounded by ridges of scoriaceous basalt, and by a buttress of rock called Jebel Ayr, like Ohod, about three miles distant from the town. Westward, according to some authors, is the Mosque Zu'l Halifah. On the east there are no natural landmarks, or even artificial, like the "Alamain" at Meccah; an imaginary line, therefore, is drawn, forming an irregular circle, of which the town is the centre, with a diameter of from ten to twelve miles. Such is the sanctuary.‡ Geographically considered, the plain is bounded, on the east, by a thin line of low dark hills, tra-

* Or, according to others, between Yemen and Syria.

† Such is its formation in El Hejaz.

‡ Within the sanctuary all Muharramat, or sins, are forbidden; but the several schools advocate different degrees of strictness. The Imam Malik, for instance, allows no *latrinæ* nearer to El Medinah than Jebel Ayr, a distance of about three miles. He also forbids slaying wild animals, but at the same time he specifies no punishment for the offence. Some do not allow the felling of trees, alleging that the Prophet enjoined their preservation as an ornament to the city, and a pleasure to visitors. El Khattabi, on the contrary, permits people to cut wood, and this is certainly the general practice. All authors strenuously forbid

versed by the Darb el Sharki, or the "eastern road," through Nejd to Meccah: southwards, the plateau is open, and almost perfectly level as far as the eye can see.

El Medinah dates its origin doubtless from ancient times, and the cause of its prosperity is evident in the abundant supply of a necessary generally scarce in Arabia. The formation of the plain is in some places salt sand, but usually a white chalk, and a loamy clay, which even by the roughest manipulation makes tolerable bricks. Lime also abounds. The town is situated upon a gently shelving part of the plain, the lowest portion of which, to judge from the water-shed, is at the southern base of Mount Ohod, hence called El Safilah, and the Awali, or plains about Kuba, and the East. Water is abundant, though rarely of good quality. In the days of the Prophet, the Madani consumed the produce of wells, seven of which are still celebrated by the

within the boundaries slaying man (except invaders, infidels, and the sacrilegious), drinking spirits, and leading an immoral life.

As regards the dignity of the sanctuary, there is but one opinion; a number of Hadis testify to its honor, praise its people, and threaten dreadful things to those who injure it or them. It is certain that on the last day, the Prophet will intercede for, and aid, all those who die, and are buried, at El Medinah. Therefore, the Imam Malik made but one pilgrimage to Meccah, fearing to leave his bones in any other cemetery but El Bakia. There is, however, much debate concerning the comparative sanctity of El Medinah and Meccah. Some say Mohammed preferred the former, blessing it as Abraham did Meccah. Moreover, as a tradition declares that every man's body is drawn from the dust of the ground in which he is buried, El Medinah, it is evident, had the honor of supplying materials for the Prophet's person. Others, like Omar, were uncertain in favor of which city to decide. Others openly assert the pre-eminence of Meccah; the general *consensus* of El Islam preferring El Medinah to Meccah, save only the Bait Allah in the latter city. This last is a *juste-milieu* view, by no means in favor with the inhabitants of either place. In the meanwhile the Meccans claim unlimited superiority over the Madani; the Madani over the Meccans.

people. Historians relate that Omar, the second Caliph, provided the town with drinking-water from the northern parts of the plains by means of an aqueduct. The modern city is supplied by a source called the Ayn El Zarka or Azure spring. During my stay at El Medinah, I always drank this water, which appeared to me, as the citizens declared it to be, sweet and wholesome. There are many wells in the town, as water is found at about 20 feet below the surface of the soil, but few of them produce anything fit for drinking, some being salt, and others bitter. As is usual in the hilly countries of the East, the wide beds and fiumaras, even in the dry season, will supply the travellers for a day or two with an abundance of water, infiltrated into, and, in some cases, flowing beneath the sand.

The climate of the plain is celebrated for a long and comparatively speaking rigorous winter; a popular saying records the opinion of the Prophet "that he who patiently endures the cold of El Medinah and the heat of Meccah, merits a reward in Paradise." Ice is not seen in the town, but may frequently be met with, it is said, on Jebel Ohod; fires are lighted in the houses during winter, and palsies attack those who at this season imprudently bathe in cold water. The fair complexions of the people prove that this account of the wintry rigors is not exaggerated.

And the European reader will observe that the Arabs generally reckon three seasons, including our autumn in their summer. The hot weather at El Medinah appeared to me as extreme as the wintry cold is described to be, but the air was dry, and the open plain prevented the faint stagnant sultriness which distinguishes Meccah. Moreover, though the afternoons were close, the nights and the mornings were cool and dewy. At this season of the year the citizens sleep on the house-tops, or on the ground outside their doors. Strangers must follow this example with circumspection; the open air is safe in the Desert, but in cities it causes to the unaccustomed violent colds and febrile affections.

I collected the following notes upon the diseases and medical treatment of the northern Hejaz. El Medinah has been visited four times by the Rih el Asfar,* or Cholera Morbus, which is said to have committed great ravages, sometimes carrying off whole households. In the Rahmat el Kabirah, the "Great Mercy," as the worst attack is piously called, whenever a man vomited, he was abandoned to his fate; before that he was treated with mint, lime-juice, and copious draughts of coffee. It is still the boast of El Medinah that the Táún or plague has never passed their frontier. The Judari, or small-pox, appears to be indigenous to the countries bordering upon the Red Sea; we read of it there in the earliest works of the Arabs, and even to the present day it sometimes sweeps through Arabia and the Somali country with desolating violence. In the town of El Medinah it is fatal to children, many of whom, however, are in these days inoculated: † amongst the Bedouins old men die of it, but adults are rarely victims, either in the city or in the desert. The nurse closes up the room during the day, and carefully excludes the night-air, believing that, as the disease is "hot,"‡ a breath of wind would kill the patient. During the hours of darkness, a lighted candle or lamp is always placed by the side of the

* Properly meaning the yellow wind or air; the antiquity of the word and its origin are still disputed.

† In Yemen, we are told by Niebuhr, a rude form of inoculation—the mother pricking the child's arm with a thorn—has been known from time immemorial. My Medinah friend assured me that only during the last generation, this practice has been introduced amongst the Bedouins of El Hejaz.

‡ Orientals divide their diseases, as they do remedies and articles of diet, into hot, cold, and temperate.

bed, or the sufferer would die of madness, brought on by evil spirits or fright. Sheep's-wool is burnt in the sick room, as death would follow the inhaling of any perfume. The only remedy I have heard of is pounded Kohl (antimony) drunk in water, and the same is drawn along the breadth of the eyelid, to prevent blindness. The diet is lentils and a peculiar kind of date, called Tamr el Birni. On the 21st day, the patient is washed with salt and tepid water. Ophthalmia is rare.* In the summer,

* Herodotus (Euterpe) has two allusions to eye disease, which seems to have afflicted the Egyptians from the most ancient times. Sesostris the Great died stone-blind; his successor lost his sight for ten years, and the Hermaic books had reason to devote a whole volume to ophthalmic disease. But in the old days of idolatry, the hygienic and prophylactic practices alluded to by Herodotus, the greater cleanliness of the people, and the attention paid to the canals and drainage, probably prevented this malarious disease becoming the scourge which it is now.

The similarity of the soil and the climate of Egypt to that of Upper Sindh, and the prevalence of the complaint in both countries, assist us in investigating the predisposing causes. These are, the nitrous and pungent nature of the soil—what the old Greek calls "acrid matter exuding from the earth,"—and the sudden transition from extreme dryness to excessive damp checking the invisible perspiration of the circum-orbital parts, and flying to an organ which is already weakened by the fierce glare of the sun, and the fine dust raised by the Khamsin or the Chaliho. Glare and dust alone seldom cause eye disease. Every one knows that ophthalmia is unknown in the desert, and the people of El Hejaz, who live in an atmosphere of blaze and sand, seldom lose their sight.

The Egyptian usually catches ophthalmia in his childhood. It begins with simple conjunctivitis, caused by constitutional predisposition, exposure, diet, and allowing the eye to be covered with swarms of flies. He neglects the early symptoms, and cares the less for being a Cyclops, as the infirmity will most probably exempt him from military service. Presently the same organ becomes affected sympathetically. As before, simple disease of the conjunctiva passes into purulent ophthalmia. The man, after waiting a while, will go to the doctor and show a large cica-

quotidian and tertian fevers (Hummah Salis) are not uncommon, and if accompanied by vomitings, they are frequently fatal. The attack generally begins with the Naffazah, or cold fit, and is followed by El Hummah, the hot stage. The principal remedies are cooling drinks, and syrups. After the fever the face and body frequently swell, and indurated lumps appear in the legs and stomach. Jaundice and bilious complaints are common, and the former is popularly cured in a peculiar way. The sick man looks into a pot full of water, whilst the exorciser, reciting a certain spell, draws the heads of two needles from the patient's ears along his eyes, down his face, lastly dipping them into water, which at once becomes yellow. Others have "Mirayat," magic mirrors,* on which the patient looks, and loses the complaint. Dysenteries frequently occur in the fruit season, when the greedy Arabs devour all manner of unripe peaches, grapes, and pomegranates. Hydrophobia is rare, and the people have many superstitions about it. They suppose that a bit of meat falls from the sky, and that the dog who eats it becomes mad. I was assured by respectable persons, that when a man is bitten, they shut him up with food, in a solitary chamber, for four days, and that if at the end of that time he still howls like a dog, they expel the Ghul (Devil)

trix in each eye, the result of an ulcerated cornea. Physic can do nothing for him; he remains blind for life. He is now provided for, either by living with his friends, who seldom refuse him a loaf of bread, or if industriously inclined, by begging, by acting Muezzin, or by engaging himself as "Yemeniyah," or chaunter, at funerals. His children are thus predisposed to the paternal complaint, and gradually the race becomes tender-eyed. Most travellers have observed that imported African slaves seldom become blind either in Egypt or in Sindh.

* This invention dates from the most ancient times, and both in the East and the West has been used by the weird brotherhood to produce the appearance of the absent and the dead, to discover treasure, to detect thieves, to cure disease, and to learn the secrets of the unknown world.

from him, by pouring over him boiling water mixed with ashes—a certain cure I can easily believe. The only description of leprosy known in El Hejaz is that called "Baras;" it appears in white patches on the skin, seldom attacks any but the poorer classes, and is considered incurable. Wounds are treated by Marham, or ointments, especially the Balesan, or Balsam of Meccah; a cloth is tied round the limb, and not removed till the wound heals, which amongst this people of simple life generally takes place by first intention. There is, however, the greatest prejudice against allowing water to touch a wound or a sore.

By the above short account it will be seen that the Arabs are no longer the most skilful physicians in the world. They have, however, one great advantage in their practice, and are sensible enough to make free use of it. As the children of almost all respectable citizens are brought up in the Desert, the camp becomes to them a native village. In all cases of severe wounds or chronic diseases, the patient is ordered off to the black tents, where he lives as a Bedouin, drinking camels' milk, a diet highly cathartic, for the first three or four days, and doing nothing. This has been the practice from time immemorial in Arabia, whereas Europe is only beginning to systematise the adhibition of air, exercise, and simple living. And even now we are obliged to veil it under the garb of charlatanry—to call it a "milk-cure" in Switzerland, a "water-cure" in Silesia, a "grape-cure" in France, a "hunger-cure" in Germany, and other sensible names which act as dust in the public eyes.

El Medinah consists of three parts,—a town, a fort, and a suburb little smaller than the body of the place. The town itself is about one-third larger than Suez, or about half the size of Meccah. It is a walled enclosure forming an irregular oval with four gates. The eastern gates are fine massive buildings, with double towers close together, painted with broad bands of red, yellow, and other colors.* In their shady and well-watered interiors, soldiers find room to keep guard, camel-men dispute, and numerous idlers congregate, to enjoy the luxuries of coolness and companionship. Beyond this gate, in the street leading to the mosque, is the great bazaar. Outside it lie the Suk el Khuzayriyah, or green-grocers' market, and the Suk el Habbabah, or the grain bazaar, with a fair sprinkling of coffee-houses. These markets are long masses of palm-leaf huts, blackened in the sun and wind, of a mean and squalid appearance, detracting greatly from the appearance of the gate. Amongst them there is a little domed and whitewashed building, which I was told is a Sabil or public fountain. In the days of the Prophet the town was not walled. Now, the enceinte is in excellent condition. The walls are well built of granite and lava blocks, in regular layers, cemented with lime; they are provided with long loopholes, and trefoil-shaped crenelles: in order to secure a flanking fire, semicircular towers, also loopholed and crenellated, are disposed in the curtain at short and irregular intervals. Inside, the streets are what they always should be in these torrid lands, deep, dark, and narrow, in few places paved—a thing to be deprecated—and generally covered with black earth well watered and trodden to hardness. The most considerable lines radiate towards the mosques. There are few public buildings. The houses are well built for the East, flat-roofed and double-storied; the materials generally used are a basaltic scoria, burnt brick and palm wood. The best of them enclose spacious court-yards and small gardens with wells, where water basins and date trees gladden the owners' eyes. The latticed balconies, first seen by the European traveller at Alexandria, are

* They may be compared to the gateway towers of the old Norman castles—Arques, for instance.

here common, and the windows are mere apertures in the walls, garnished, as usual in Arab cities, with a shutter of planking. El Medinah fell rapidly under the Wahhabis, but after their retreat, it soon rose again, and now it is probably as comfortable and flourishing a little city as any to be found in the East. It contains between fifty and sixty streets, including the alleys and *culs de sac.* There is about the same number of Harat or quarters. Within the town few houses are in a dilapidated condition. The best authorities estimate the number of habitations at about 1500 within the enceinte, and those in the suburb at 1000. I consider both accounts exaggerated; the former might contain 800, and the Munakhah perhaps 500; at the same time I must confess not to have counted them, and Captain Sadlier (in A.D. 1819) declares that the Turks, who had just made a kind of census, reckoned 6000 houses and a population of 8,000 souls. Assuming the population to be 16,000 (Burckhardt estimates it as high as 20,000), of which 9000 occupy the city, and 7000 the suburbs and fort, this would give little more than twelve inhabitants to each house (taking the total number at 1,300), a fair estimate for an Arab town, where the abodes are large and slaves abound.

The castle joins on to the N.W. angle of the city enceinte, and the wall of its eastern outwork is pierced for a communication between the Munakhah Suburb, through a court strewed with guns and warlike apparatus, and the Bab el Shami, or the Syrian Gate. Having been refused entrance into the fort, I can describe only its exterior. The outer wall resembles that of the city, only its towers are more solid, and the curtain appears better calculated for work. Inside, a donjon, built upon a rock, bears proudly enough the banner of the crescent and the star; its white-washed walls make it a conspicuous object, and guns pointed in all directions, especially upon the town, project from their embrasures. The castle is said to contain wells, bomb proofs, provisions, and munitions of war; if so, it must be a kind of Gibraltar to the Bedouins and the Wahhabis. The garrison consisted of a Nisf Urtah, or half battalion (400 men) of Nizam infantry, commanded by a Pacha; his authority also extends to a Sanjak, or about 500 Kurdish and Albanian irregular cavalry, whose duty it is to escort caravans, to convey treasures, and to be shot in the passes.

The suburbs lie to the S. and W. of the town. Westwards, between El Medinah and its faubourg, lies the plain of El Munakhah, about three quarters of a mile long, by 300 yards broad. The straggling suburbs occupy more ground than the city; fronting the enceinte they are without walls; towards the west, where open country lies, they are enclosed by mud or raw brick ramparts, with little round towers, all falling to decay. A number of small gates lead from the suburb into the country. The suburb contains no buildings of any consequence, except the official residence of the governor, a plain building near the Barr el Munakhah, and the Five Mosques, which every Zair is expected to visit. They are

1. The Prophet's mosque in the Munakhah.
2. Abubekr's, near the Ayn el Zarka.
3. Ali's mosque in the Zukak el Tayyar of the Munakhah.
4. Omar's mosque.
5. Balal's mosque, celebrated in books; I did not see it, and some Madani assured me that it no longer exists.

A description of one of these buildings will suffice, for they are all similar. Mohammed's mosque in the Munakhah stands upon a spot formerly occupied, some say, by the Jami Ghamamah. Others believe it to be founded upon the Musalla el Nabi, a place where the Prophet recited the first Festival prayers after his arrival at El Medinah, and used frequently to pray, and to address those of his followers who lived far from the Haram. It is a trim modern building of cut stone and lime, in regular layers of parallelogrammic shape, surmounted by one large and four smaller cupolas. These are all white-washed, and the principal one is capped with a large crescent, or rather a trident rising from a series of gilt globes. The minaret is the usual Turkish shape, with a conical roof, and a single gallery for the Muezzin. An acacia tree or two on the eastern side, and behind it a wall-like line of mud-houses, finish the *coup d'œil;* the interior of this building is as simple as the exterior. And here I may remark that the Arabs have little idea of splendor, either in their public or in their private architecture. Whatever strikes the traveller's eye in El Hejaz is always either an importation or the work of foreign artists. This arises from the simple tastes of the people, combined, doubtless, with their notable thriftiness. If strangers will build for them, they argue, why should they build for themselves? Moreover, they have scant inducement to lavish money upon grand edifices. Whenever a disturbance takes place, domestic or from without, the principal buildings are sure to suffer. And the climate is inimical to their enduring. Both ground and air at Meccah, as well as at El Medinah, are damp and nitrous in winter, in summer dry and torrid: the lime is poor; palm timber soon decays; even foreign wood-work suffers, and a few years suffice to level the proudest pile with the dust.

The suburbs to the S. of El Medinah are a collection of walled villages, with plantations and gardens between. They are laid out in the form, called here as in Egypt, Hosh—court-yards, with single-storied buildings opening into them. These enclosures contain the cattle of the inhabitants; they have strong wooden doors, shut at night to prevent "lifting," and are capable of being stoutly defended. The inhabitants of the suburb are for the most part Bedouin settlers, and a race of schismatics who will be noticed in another chapter. Beyond these suburbs, to the S., as well as to the N. and N.E., lie gardens and extensive plantations of palm-trees.

## CHAPTER XVII.

### A RIDE TO THE MOSQUE OF KUBA.

THE principal places of pious visitation in the vicinity of El Medinah, are the Mosques of Kuba, the Cemetery El Bakia, and the martyr Hamzah's tomb, at the foot of Mount Ohod. These the Zair is directed by all the Ulema to visit, and on the holy ground to pray Allah for a blessing upon himself, and upon his brethren of the faith.

Early one Saturday morning, I started for Kuba with a motley crowd of devotees. Shaykh Hamid, my Muzawwir, was by my side, mounted upon an ass more miserable than I had yet seen. The boy Mohammed had procured for me a Meccan dromedary, with splendid trappings, a saddle with burnished metal peaks before and behind, covered with a huge sheepskin dyed crimson, and girthed over fine saddle-bags, whose enormous tassels hung almost to the ground The youth himself being too grand to ride a donkey, and unable to borrow a horse, preferred walking. He was proud as a peacock, being habited in a style somewhat resembling the plume of that gorgeous bird, in the coat of many colors—yellow, red, and golden flowers, apparently sewed on a field of bright green silk—which cost me so dear in the Haram. He was armed, as indeed all of us were, in readiness for the Bedouins, and he anxiously awaited opportunities of discharging his pistol. Our course lay from Shaykh Hamid's house in the Munakhah, along and up the fiumara, "El Sayh," and through the Bab Kuba, a little gate in the suburb wall, where, by the by, my mounted companion was nearly trampled down by a rush of half wild camels. Outside the town in this direction, southward, is a plain of clay, mixed with chalk, and here and there with sand, whence protrude blocks and little ridges of basalt.

Presently the Nakhil, or palm plantations began. Nothing lovelier to the eye, weary with hot red glare, than the rich green waving crops and cool shade—for hours I could have sat and looked at it, requiring no other occupation—the "food of vision," as the Arabs call it, and "pure water to the parched throat." The air was soft and balmy, a perfumed breeze, strange luxury in El Hejaz, wandered amongst the date fronds; there were fresh flowers and bright foliage,—in fact at mid-summer, every beautiful feature of spring. Nothing more delightful to the ear than the warbling of the small birds, that sweet familiar sound, the splashing of tiny cascades from the wells into the wooden troughs, and the musical song of the water-wheels. Travellers—young travellers—in the East talk of the "dismal grating," the "mournful monotony," and the "melancholy creaking of these dismal machines." To the veteran wanderer their sound is delightful from association, reminding him of green fields, cool water-courses, hospitable villagers, and plentiful crops. The expatriated Nubian, for instance, listens to the water-wheel with as deep emotion as the Ranz des Vaches ever excited in the hearts of Switzer mercenary at Naples, or "Lochaber no more," among a regiment of Highlanders in the West Indies.

The date-trees of El Medinah merit their celebrity. Their stately columnar stems, here, seem higher than in other lands, and their lower fronds are allowed to tremble in the breeze without mutilation. These enormous palms were loaded with ripening fruit, and the clusters, carefully tied up, must often have weighed upwards of eighty pounds. They hung down between the lower branches by a bright yellow stem, as thick as a man's ankle. Books enumerate 139 varieties of trees; of these between sixty and seventy are well-known, and each is distinguished, as usual among Arabs, by its peculiar name. The best kind is El Shelebi; it is packed in skins, or in flat round boxes covered with paper, somewhat in the manner of French prunes, and sent as presents to the remotest parts of the Moslem world. The fruit is about two inches long, with a small stone, and what appeared to me a peculiar aromatic flavor and smell; it is seldom eaten by the citizens on account of the price, which varies from two to ten piastres the pound. The tree, moreover, is rare, and said to be not so productive as the other species. The Ajwah is eaten, but not sold, because a tradition of the Prophet declares, that whoso breaketh his fast every day with six or seven of the Ajwah-date need fear neither poison nor magic. The third kind, El Hilwah, also a large date, derives a name from its exceeding sweetness: of this tree the Moslems relate that the Prophet planted a stone, which in a few minutes grew up and bore fruit. Next comes El Birni, of which was said "it causeth sickness to depart, and there is no sickness in it." The Wahshi on one occasion bent his head, and salaamed to Mohammed as he ate its fruit, for which reason even now its lofty tuft turns earthwards. The Sayhani is so called, because when the founder of El Islam, holding Ali's hand, happened to pass beneath, it cried, "This is Mohammed the Prince of Prophets, and this is Ali the Prince of the Pious, and the progenitor of the immaculate Imams." Of course the descendants of so intelligent a vegetable hold high rank in the kingdom of palms, and the vulgar were in the habit of eating the Sayhani and of throwing the stones about the Haram. The Khuzayriyah is so called, because it preserves its green color, even when perfectly ripe; it is dried and preserved as a curiosity. The Jebeli is that most usually eaten: the poorest kinds are the "Laun," and the Hilayah, costing from 4 to 7 piastres per mudd (about eleven pounds).

The fruit is prepared in a great variety of ways: perhaps the most favorite dish is a broil with clarified butter, highly distasteful to the European palate. The date is also left upon the tree to dry, and then called "Balah:" this is eaten at dessert as the "Nukliyat," the "quatre mendiants," of Persia. Amongst peculiar preparations must be mentioned the Kulladat el Sham. The unripe fruit is dipped in boiling water to preserve its gamboge color, strung upon a thick thread and hung out in the air to dry. These strings are worn all over El Hejaz as necklaces by children, who seldom fail to munch the ornament when not in fear of slappings, and they are sent as presents to distant countries.

January and February are the time for the masculation of the palm. The "Nakhwali," as he is called, opens the female flower, and having inserted the inverted male flowers, binds them together: this operation is performed as in Egypt upon each cluster. The fruit is ripe about the middle of May, and the gathering of it forms the Arab's "vendemmia." The people make merry the more readily because their favorite fruit is liable to a variety of accidents: droughts injure the tree, locusts destroy the produce, and the date crop, like most productions which men are imprudent enough to adopt singly as the staff of life, is subject to failure. One of the reasons for the excellence of Medinah dates is the quantity of water they obtain: each garden or field has its well, and even in the hottest weather the Persian wheel floods the soil every third day. It has been observed that the date-tree can live in dry and barren spots; but it loves the beds of streams and places where moisture is procurable. The palms scattered over the other parts of the Medinah plain, and depending solely upon rain water, produce less fruit, and that too of an inferior quality.

Verdure is not usually wholesome in Arabia, yet invalids leave the close atmosphere of El Medinah to seek health under the cool shades of Kuba. The gardens are divided by what might almost be called lanes, long narrow lines with tall reed fences on both sides. The graceful branches of the Tamarisk pearled with manna, and cottoned over with dew, and the broad leaves of the castor plant, glistening in the sun, protected us from the morning rays. The ground on both sides of the way was sunken, the earth being disposed in heaps at the foot of the fences, an arrangement which facilitates irrigation, by giving a fall to the water, and in some cases affords a richer soil than the surface. This part of the Medinah plain, however, being higher than the rest, is less subject to the disease of salt and nitre. On the way here and there the earth crumbles and looks dark under the dew of morning, but nowhere has it broken out into that glittering efflorescence which notes the last stage of the attack. The fields and gardens are divided into small oblongs separated from one another by little ridges of mould which form diminutive water courses. Of the cereals there are luxuriant maize, wheat, and barley, but the latter two are in small quantities. Here and there patches of "Barsim," or Egyptian clover, glitter brightly in the sun. The principal vegetables are Badanjan (egg plant), the Bamiyah (a kind of esculent hibiscus, called Bhendi in India), and Mulukhiyah (Corchoris olitorius), a mucilaginous spinage common throughout this part of the East. These three are eaten by citizens of every rank; they are in fact the greens and potatoes of El Medinah. I remarked also onions and leeks in fair quantities, a few beds of carrots and beans, some fijl (radishes), lift (turnips), gourds, cucumbers, and similar plants. Fruit trees abound. There are fine descriptions of vines, the best of which is El Sherifi, a long white grape of a flavor somewhat resembling the produce of Tuscany.* Next to it, and very similar, is El Birni. The Hijazi is a round fruit, sweet, but insipid, which is also the reproach of the Sawadi or black grapes. And lastly, the Raziki is a small white fruit, with a diminutive stone. The Nebek, or Jujube, is here a fine large tree with a dark green leaf, roundish and polished like the olive; it is armed with a short, curved, and sharp thorn,† and bears a pale straw-colored berry about the size of a gooseberry, with red streaks on the side next the sun. Little can be said in favor of the fruit, which has been compared successively by disappointed "Lotus eaters" to a bad plum, an unripe cherry, and an insipid apple. It is, however, a favorite with the people of El Medinah. There are a few peaches, hard like the Egyptian, and almost tasteless, fit only for stewing, but greedily eaten in a half-ripe state, large coarse bananas, lime trees, a few water melons, figs and apples, but neither apricots nor pears. There are three kinds of pomegranates: the best

* The resemblance is probably produced by the similarity of treatment. At El Medinah, as in Italy, the vine is "married" to some tall tree, which, selfish as a husband, appropriates to itself the best of everything,—sun, breeze, and rain.

† This thorn (the Rhamnus Nabeca, or Zizyphus Spina Christi) is supposed to be that which crowned our Saviour's head. There are Mimosas in Syria; but no tree, save the fabled Zakkum, could produce the terrible apparatus with which certain French painters of the modern school have attempted to heighten the terrors of the scene.

is the Shami (Syrian); it is red outside, very sweet, and costs one piastre; the Turki is large and of a white color; and the Misri has a greenish rind, and a somewhat subacid and harsh flavor: these latter are sold four times as cheap as the best. I never saw in the East, except at Meccah, a finer fruit than the Shami: almost stoneless, like those of Muscat, they are delicately perfumed and as large as an infant's head. El Medinah is celebrated for its thick promegranate syrup, drunk with water during the hot weather, and esteemed cooling and wholesome.

After threading our way through the gardens, an operation requiring less time than to describe them, we saw, peeping through the groves, Kuba's simple minaret. Then we came in sight of a confused heap of huts and dwelling-houses, chapels and towers with trees between, and foul lanes, heaps of rubbish and barking dogs,—the usual material of a Hejazi village. Having dismounted, we gave our animals in charge of a dozen infant Bedouins, the produce of the peasant gardeners, who shouted "Bakhshish" the moment they saw us. To this they were urged by their mothers, and I willingly parted with a few paras for the purpose of establishing an intercourse with fellow creatures so fearfully and wonderfully resembling the tail-less baboon. Their bodies, unlike those of Egyptian children, were slim* and straight, but their ribs stood out with a curious distinctness, the color of the skin was that oily lamp-black seen upon the face of a European sweep, and the elf-locks, peeping out of the cocoa-nut heads, had been stained by the sun, wind, and rain to that reddish-brown hue which Hindoo romances have appropriated to their Rakshasas or

* Travellers always remark the curious pot-bellied children on the banks of the Nile. This conformation is admired by the Egyptians, who consider it a sign of strength, and a promise of fine growth.

demons. Each anatomy carried in his arms a stark-naked miniature of himself, fierce-looking babies with faces all eyes, and the strong little wretches were still able to extend the right hand and exert their lungs with direful clamor. Their mothers were fit progenitors for such progeny: long, gaunt, with emaciated limbs, wall-sided, high-shouldered, and straight-backed, with pendulous bosoms, spider-like arms, and splay feet. Their long elf-locks, wrinkled faces, and high cheek-bones, their lips darker than the epidermis, hollow staring eyes, sparkling as if to light up the extreme ugliness around, and voices screaming as if in a perennial rage, invested them with all the "charms of Sycorax." These "houris of hell" were habited in long night-gowns dyed blue to conceal want of washing, and the squalid children had about a yard of the same material wrapped round their waist for all toilette. This is not an overdrawn portrait of the farmer race of Arabs, the most despised by their fellow countrymen, and the most hard-favored, morally as well as physically, of all the breed.

Before entering the mosque of El Kuba it will be necessary to call to mind some passages of its past history. When the Prophet's she camel, El Kaswa, as he was approaching El Medinah after the flight from Meccah, knelt down here, he desired his companions to mount the animal. Abubekr and Omar did so; still she sat upon the ground, but when Ali obeyed the order, she arose. The Prophet bade him loose her halter, for she was directed by Allah, and the mosque walls were built upon the line over which she trod. It was the first place of public prayer in El Islam. Mohammed laid the first brick, and with an "Anzah" or iron-shod javelin, marked out the direction of prayer; each of his successors followed his example. The mosque of El Kuba was much respected by Omar, who once finding it empty, swept it himself with a broom of thorns, and expressed his wonder at the lukewarmness of Moslem piety. It was originally a square building of very small size; Osman enlarged it in the direction of the minaret, making it sixty-six cubits each way. It is no longer "mean and decayed" as in Burckhardt's time: the Sultan Abd el Hamid, father of Mahmoud, erected a neat structure of cut stone, whose crenelles make it look more like a place of defence than of prayer. It has, however, no pretensions to grandeur. The minaret is of the Turkish shape. To the south a small and narrow Riwak, or raised hypostyle, with unpretending columns, looks out northwards upon a little open area simply sanded over; and this is the whole building.

The large Mastabah or stone bench at the entrance of the mosque, was crowded with sitting people: we therefore lost no time, after ablution and the Niyat ("the intention") peculiar to this visitation, in ascending the steps, in pulling off our slippers, and in entering the sacred building. We stood upon the Prophet's place of prayer:* after Shaykh Nur and Hamid had forcibly cleared that auspicious spot of a devout Indian, and had spread a rug upon the dirty matting, we performed a two-prostration prayer, in front of a pillar into which a diminutive marble niche had been inserted by way of memento. Then came the Dua or supplication, which was as follows:

"O Allah! bless and preserve, and increase, and perpetuate, and benefit, and be propitious to, our lord Mohammed, and to his family, and to his companions, and be thou their Preserver! O Allah! this is the mosque Kuba, and the place of the Prophet's prayers. O Allah! pardon our sins, and veil our faults, and place not over us one who

* This is believed to be the spot where the Prophet performed his first Rukat, or bending of the back in prayer.

feareth not thee, and who pitieth not us, and pardon us, and the true believers, men and women, the quick of them and the dead; for verily thou, O Lord, art the hearer, the near to us, the answerer of our supplications." After which we recited the Testification and the Fát-háh, and we drew our palms as usual down our faces.

We then moved away to the south-eastern corner of the edifice, and stood before a niche in the southern wall. It is called "Takat el Kashf" or "niche of disclosure," by those who believe that as the Prophet was standing undecided about the direction of Meccah, the Archangel Gabriel removed all obstructions to his vision. There again we went through the two-prostration prayer, the supplication, the testification, and the Fát-háh, under difficulties, for people crowded us excessively. During our devotions, I vainly attempted to decypher a Cufic inscription fixed in the wall above and on the right of the niche,—my regret, however, at this failure was transitory, the character not being of an ancient date. Then we left the Riwak, and despite the morning sun which shone fiercely with a sickly heat, we went to the open area where stands the "Mabrak el Nakàh," or the "place of kneeling of the she dromedary." This, the exact spot where El Kaswa sat down, is covered with a diminutive dome of cut stone, supported by four stone pillars: the building is about eight feet high and a little less in length and breadth. It has the appearance of being modern. On the floor, which was raised by steps above the level of the ground, lay, as usual, a bit of dirty matting, upon which we again went through the ceremonies above detailed.

Then issuing from the canopy into the sun, a little outside the Riwak and close to the Mabrak, we prayed upon the "Makan el Ayat," or the "place of signs." Here was revealed to Mohammed a passage in the Koran especially alluding to the purity of the place and of the people of Kuba, "a temple founded in purity from its first day:" and again; "there men live who loved to be cleansed, and verily Allah delights in the clean." The Prophet exclaimed in admiration, "O ye sons of Amr! what have ye done to deserve all this praise and beneficence?" when the people offered him an explanation of their personal cleanliness which I do not care to repeat. The mosque of Kuba from that day took a fresh title—Masjid el Takwa, or the "Mosque of Piety."

Having finished our prayers and ceremonies at the mosque of piety, we fought our way out through a crowd of importunate beggars, and turning a few paces to the left, halted near a small chapel adjoining the south-west angle of the larger temple. We there stood at a grated window in the western wall, and recited a supplication, looking the while most reverently at a dark dwarf archway under which the lady Fatimah used to sit grinding grain in a hand mill. The mosque in consequence bears the name of Sittna Fatimah. A surly-looking Khadim, or guardian, stood at the door demanding a dollar in the most authoritative Arab tone—we therefore did not enter. At El Medinah and at Meccah the traveller's hand must be perpetually in his pouch: no stranger in Paris or London is more surely or more severely taken in. Already I began to fear that my eighty pounds would not suffice for all the expenses of sight-seeing, and the apprehension was justified by the sequel. At Meccah, my purse was too low to admit of my paying five dollars for admittance to the Makam Ibrahim; which caused me much regret, as no European has ever entered it. My only friend was the boy Mohammed, who displayed a fiery economy that brought him into considerable dis-repute with his countrymen. They saw with emotion that he was preaching parsimony to me solely that I might have more money to spend at Meccah under his auspices. This being probably the case, I threw all the blame of penuriousness upon the young Machiavel's shoulders, and resolved, as he had taken charge of my finances at El Medinah, so at Meccah to administer them myself.

After praying at the window, to the great disgust of the Khadim, who openly asserted that we were "low fellows," we passed through some lanes lined with beggars and Bedouin children, till we came to a third little mosque situated due south of the larger one. This is called the Masjid Arafat, and is erected upon a mound also named Tall Arafat, because on one occasion the Prophet, being unable to visit the Holy mountain at the pilgrimage season, stood there, saw through the intervening space, and in spirit performed the ceremony. Here also we looked into a window instead of opening the door with a silver key, and the *mesquin* appearance of all within prevented my regretting the necessity of economy. In India or Sindh every village would have a better mosque. Our last visit was to a fourth chapel, the Masjid Ali, so termed because the Prophet's son-in-law had a house upon this spot. After praying there—and terribly hot the little hole was!—we repaired to the last place of visitation at Kuba—a large deep well called the Bir El Aris, in a garden to the west of the Mosque of Piety, with a little oratory adjoining it. A Persian wheel was going drowsily round, and the cool water fell into a tiny pool, whence it whirled and bubbled away in childish mimicry of a river. The music sounded sweet in my ears, I stubbornly refused to do any more praying—though Shaykh Hamid, for form's sake, reiterated with parental emphasis, "how very wrong it was,"—and sat down, as the Prophet himself did not disdain to do, with the resolution of enjoying on the brink of the well a few moments of unwonted "Kaif." The heat was overpowering, though it was only nine o'clock, the sound of the stream was soothing, that water wheel was creaking a lullaby, and the limes and the pomegranates, gently rustling, shed voluptuous fragrance through the morning air. I fell asleep—and wondrous the contrast!—dreamed that I was once more standing

> "By the wall whereon hangeth the crucified vine,"

looking upon the valley of the Lianne, with its glaucous seas and grey skies, and banks here and there white with snow.

The Bir el Aris,* so called after a Jew of El Medinah, is one which the Prophet delighted to visit. He would sit upon its brink with his bare legs hanging over the side, and his companions used to imitate his example. This practice caused a sad disaster; in the sixth year of his caliphate, Osman dropped from his finger Mohammed's seal ring, which, engraved in three lines with "Mohammed—Apostle—(of) Allah," had served to seal the letters sent to neighboring kings, and had descended to the three first successors.† The precious article was not recovered after three days' search, and the well was thenceforward called Bir el Khatim—of the Seal Ring. It is also called the Bir el Taflat—of Saliva‡—because the Prophet honored it by

* Some authors mention a second Bir el Aris, belonging in part to the Caliph Osman.

† Others assert, with less probability, that the article in question was lost by one Maakah, a favorite of Osman. As that ill-fated Caliph's troubles began at the time of this accident, the ring is generally compared to Solomon's. Our popular authors, who assert that Mohammed himself lost the ring, are greatly in error.

‡ According to some authors, Mohammed drew a bucket of water, drank part of the contents, spat into the rest, and poured it back into the well, which instantly became sweet.

expectoration, which, by the by, he seems to have done to almost all the wells in El Medinah. The effect of the operation upon the Bir el Aris, say the historians, was to sweeten the water, which before was salt. Their testimony, however, did not prevent my detecting a pronounced medicinal taste in the lukewarm draught drawn for me by Shaykh Hamid. In the Prophet's day the total number of wells is recorded to have been twenty: most of them have long since disappeared; but there still remain seven, whose waters were drunk by the Prophet, and which, in consequence, the Zair is directed to visit.* After my sleep, which was allowed to last until a pipe or two of latakia had gone round the party, we remounted our animals. On the left of the village returning towards El Medinah, my companions pointed out to me a garden, called El Madshuniyah. It contains a quarry of the yellow loam or bole-earth, called by the Arabs Tafl, the Persians Gili Sarshui, and the Sindhians Metu. It is used as soap in many parts of the East, and, mixed with oil, it is supposed to cool the body, and to render the skin fresh and supple. It is related that the Prophet cured a Bedouin of the Beni Haris tribe of fever by washing him with a pot of Tafl dissolved in water, and hence the earth of El Medinah derived its healing fame. As far as I could learn from the Madani, this clay is no longer valued by them, either medicinally or cosmetically: the only use they could mention was its being eaten by the fair sex, when in the peculiar state described by "chlorosis."

* The pious perform the Lesser Ablution upon the brink of the seven wells, and drink of the remnant of the water in "tabarruk" or to secure the blessing of God.

## CHAPTER XVIII.

### THE VISITATION OF HAMZAH'S TOMB.

On the morning of Sunday, the twenty-third Zu'l Kaadah (28th August 1853), arrived the great caravan from El Sham or Damascus.* It is popularly called Hajj El Shami, or the "Damascus pilgrimage," as the Egyptian Cafala is El Misri,† or the Cairo pilgrimage. It is the main stream which carries off all the small currents that at this season of general movement flow from central Asia towards the great centre of the Islamitic world, and in 1853 amounted to about 7000 souls. It was anxiously expected by the people for several reasons. In the first place, it brought with it a new curtain for the Prophet's Hujrah, the old one being in a tattered condition; secondly, it had charge of the annual stipends and pensions of the citizens; and thirdly, many families expected members returning under its escort to their homes. The popular anxiety was greatly increased by the disordered state of the country round

* This city derives its name, the "Great Gate of Pilgrimage," and the "Key of the Prophet's Tomb," from its being the gathering-place of this caravan.

† The Egyptians corruptly pronounce El Misr—Cairo—" El Masr."

about; and, moreover, the great caravan had been one day late, generally arriving on the morning of the 22nd Zu'l Kaadah.

During the night three of Shaykh Hamid's brothers, who had entered as Muzawwirs with the Haji, came suddenly to the house: they leaped off their camels, and lost not a moment in going through the usual scene of kissing, embracing, and weeping bitterly for joy. I arose in the morning, and looked out from the windows of the *majlis:* the Barr el Munakhah, from a dusty waste dotted with a few Bedouins and hair tents, had assumed all the various shapes and the colors of a kaleidoscope. The eye was bewildered by the shifting of innumerable details, in all parts totally different from one another, thrown confusedly together in one small field; and, however jaded with sight-seeing, it dwelt with delight upon the vivacity, the variety, and the intense picturesqueness of the scene. In one night had sprung up a town of tents of every size, color, and shape,—round, square and oblong,—open and closed,—from the shawl-lined and gilt-topped pavilion of the pacha, with all the luxurious appurtenances of the Haram, to its neighbor the little dirty green "rowtie" of the tobacco-seller. They were pitched in admirable order: here ranged in a long line, where a street was required; there packed in dense masses, where thoroughfares were unnecessary. But how describe the utter confusion in the crowding, the bustling, and the vast variety and volume of sound? Huge white Syrian dromedaries, compared with which those of El Hejaz appeared mere pony-camels, jingling large bells, and bearing shugdufs* like miniature green tents, swaying

* The Syrian shugduf differs entirely from that of El Hejaz. It is composed of two solid wooden cots about four feet in length, slung along the camel's sides and covered over with cloth, in the shape of a tent. They are nearly twice as heavy as the Hejazi litter, and yet a

and tossing upon their backs; gorgeous Takhtrawan, or litters borne between camels or mules with scarlet and brass trappings; Bedouins bestriding naked-backed "Deluls,"* and clinging like apes to the hairy humps; Arnaut, Turkish, and Kurd irregular horsemen, fiercer looking in their mirth than Roman peasants in their rage; fainting Persian pilgrims, forcing their stubborn dromedaries to kneel, or dismounted grumbling from jaded donkeys; Kahwagis, sherbet sellers, and ambulant tobacconists crying their goods; country-people driving flocks of sheep and goats with infinite clamor through lines of horses fiercely snorting and rearing; towns-people seeking their friends; returned travellers exchanging affectionate salutes; devout Hajis jolting one another, running under the legs of camels, and tumbling over the tents' ropes in their hurry to reach the Haram; cannon roaring from the citadel; shopmen, water-carriers and fruit venders fighting over their bargains; boys bullying heretics with loud screams; a well-mounted party of fine old Arab Shaykhs of Hamidah clan, preceded by their varlets, performing the Arzah or war dance,—compared with which the Pyrenean bear's performance is grace itself,—firing their duck guns upwards, or blowing the powder into the calves of those before them, brandishing their swords, leaping frantically the while, with their bright-colored rags floating in the wind, tossing their long spears tufted with ostrich feathers high in the air, reckless where they fall; servants seeking their masters, and masters their tents, with vain cries of Ya Mohammed;† grandees riding

Syrian camel-man would as surely refuse to put one of the latter upon his beast's back, as the Hejazi to carry a Syrian litter.

* This is the Arabic modern word, synonymous with the Egyptian Hajin, namely, a she dromedary. The word "Nakah," at present popular in El Hejaz, means a she dromedary kept for breeding as well as riding.

† One might as sensibly cry out "John" in an English theatre.

mules or stalking on foot, preceded by their crowd-beaters, shouting to clear the way;—here the loud shrieks of women and children, whose litters are bumping and rasping against one another;—there the low moaning of some poor wretch that is seeking a shady corner to die in:—add a thick dust which blurs the outlines like a London fog, with a flaming sun that draws sparkles of fire from the burnished weapons of the crowd, and the brass balls of tent and litter; and—I doubt, gentle reader, that even the length, the jar, and the confusion of this description is adequate to its subject, or that any word-painting of mine can convey a just idea of the scene.

This was the day appointed for our visiting the martyrs of Ohod. After praying the dawn-prayers as directed at the Haram, we mounted our donkeys, and, armed with pistols and knives, set out from the city. Our party was a large one. Saad the Devil had offered to accompany us, and the bustle around kept him in the best of humors; Omar Effendi was also there, quiet looking and humble as usual, leading his ass to avoid the trouble of dismounting every second minute.* I had the boy Mohammed and my "slave," and Shaykh Hamid was attended by half a dozen relations. To avoid the crush of the Barr el Munakhah, we made a detour westwards, over the bridge and down the course of the torrent-bed "el Sayh." During the greater part of the time we were struggling through a living tide; and among dromedaries and chargers, a donkey is by no means a pleasant *monture*. With some difficulty, but without any more serious accident than a fall or two, we found ourselves in the space beyond and northward of the city. This also was covered with travellers and tents, amongst

* Respectable men in El Hejaz, when they meet friends, acquaintances, or superiors, consider it only polite to dismount from a donkey.

which, on an eminence to the left of the road, rose conspicuous the bright green pavilion of the Emir El Hajj, the commandant of the caravan.* Hard by, half its height surrounded by a kanat or tent wall, stood the Syrian or Sultan's Mahmal, all glittering with green and gilding and gold, and around it were pitched the handsome habitations of the principal officers and grandees of the pilgrimage. On the right hand lay extensive palm plantations, and on the left, strewed over the plain, were signs of wells and tanks, built to supply the Hajj with water. We pass two small buildings,—one the Kubbat El Sabak or Dome of Precedence, where the Prophet's warrior friends used to display their horsemanship; the second the *makan* or burial-place of Sayyidna Zaki el Din, one of Mohammed's multitudinous descendants. Then we fall into a plain, resembling that of Kuba, but less fertile. While we are jogging over it, a few words concerning Mount Ohod may not be misplaced. A popular distich says,

"Verily there is healing to the eye that looks
Unto Ohod and the two Harrats† near."

And of this holy hill the Prophet declared, "Ohod is a

* The title of the pacha who has the privilege of conducting the caravan. It is a lucrative as well as an honorable employment, for the emir enjoys the *droit d'aubaine,* becoming heir to the personal property of all pilgrims who die in the holy cities or on the line of march. And no Persian, even of the poorest, would think of undertaking a pilgrimage by this line of country, without having at least 80*l.* in ready money with him.

The first person who bore the title of Emir El Hajj was Abubekr, who in the 9th year of the Hijrah led 300 Moslems from El Medinah to the Meccah pilgrimage. On this occasion idolaters and infidels were for the first time expelled the Holy City.

† "Harrat" from Harr (heat) is the generic name of lava, porous basalt, scoriæ, greenstone, schiste, and others supposed to be of igneous origin. It is also used to denote a ridge or hill of such formation.

mountain which loves us and which we love: it is upon the gate of Heaven;"* adding, "and Ayr is a place which hates us and which we hate: it is upon the gate of Hell." The former sheltered Mohammed in the time of danger, therefore on Resurrection Day it will be raised to paradise: whereas Jebel Ayr, its neighbor, having been so ill-judged as to refuse the Prophet water on an occasion while he thirsted, will be cast incontinently into Hell. Moslem divines, be it observed, ascribe to Mohammed miraculous authority over animals, vegetables, and minerals, as well as over men, angels, and jinns. Hence the speaking wolf, the weeping post, the oil-stone, and the love and hate of these two mountains. It is probably one of the many remains of ancient paganism pulled down and afterwards used to build up the edifice of El Islam.

Jebel Ohod owes its present reputation to a cave which sheltered the Prophet when pursued by his enemies, to certain springs of which he drank, and especially to its being the scene of a battle celebrated in El Islam. On Saturday, the 11th Shawwal, in the 3rd year of the Hijrah (26th January A. D. 625) Mohammed with 700 men engaged 3000 infidels under the command of Abu Sufiyan, ran great personal danger, and lost his uncle Hamzah, the "Lord of Martyrs." On the topmost pinnacle, also, is the Kubbat Harún, the dome erected over Aaron's remains. It is now, I was told, in a ruinous condition.

After half an hour's ride we came to the Mustarah or resting place, so called because the Prophet sat here for a few minutes on his way to the battle of Ohod. It is a newly-built square enclosure of dwarf white-washed walls, within which devotees pray. On the outside fronting El Medinah is a seat like a chair of rough stones. Here I was placed

* Meaning that on that day it shall be so treated.

by my Muzawwir, who recited an insignificant supplication to be repeated after him. At its end with the Fát-háh and accompaniments, we remounted our asses and resumed our way. Travelling onwards, we came in sight of the second harrat or ridge. It lies to the right and left of the road, and resembles lines of lava, but I had not an opportunity to examine it narrowly.* Then we reached the gardens of Ohod, which reflect in miniature those of Kuba, and presently we arrived at what explained the presence of verdure and vegetable life,—a deep fiumara full of loose sand and large stones denoting an impetuous stream. On the south of the fiumara is a village on an eminence, containing some large brick houses now in a ruinous state; these are the villas of opulent and religious citizens who visited the place for change of air, recreation, and worship at Hamzah's tomb. Our donkeys sank fetlock-deep in the loose sand of the torrent-bed. Then reaching the northern side and ascending a gentle slope, we found ourselves upon the battle-field.

This spot, so celebrated in the annals of El Islam, is a shelving strip of land, close to the southern base of Mount Ohod. The army of the infidels advanced from the fiumara in crescent shape, with Abu Sufiyan, the general, and his idols in the centre. It is distant about three miles from El Medinah, in a northerly direction. All the visitor sees is hard gravelly ground, covered with little heaps of various colored granite, red sandstone, and bits of porphyry, to denote the different places where the martyrs fell, and were

* When engaged in such a holy errand as this, to have ridden away for the purpose of inspecting a line of black stone, would have been certain to arouse the suspicions of an Arab. Either, he would argue, you recognise the place of some treasure described in your books, or you are a magician seeking a talisman.

buried.* Seen from this point, there is something appalling in the look of the Holy Mountain. Its seared and jagged flanks rise like masses of iron from the plain, and the crevice into which the Moslem host retired, when the disobedience of the archers in hastening to plunder enabled Khalid bin Walid to fall upon Mohammed's rear, is the only break in the grim wall. Reeking with heat, its surface produces not one green shrub or stunted tree; not a bird or beast appeared upon its inhospitable sides, and the bright blue sky glaring above its bald and sullen brow, made it look only the more repulsive. I was glad to turn my eyes away from it.

To the left of the road N. of the fiumara, and leading to the mountains, stands Hamzah's Mosque, which, like the Haram of El Medinah, is a mausoleum as well as a fane. It is a small square strongly-built edifice of hewn stone, with a dome covering the solitary hypostele to the south, and the usual minaret. On the eastern side of the building a half wing projects, and opens to the south, with a small door upon a Mastabah or stone bench five or six feet high, which completes the square of the edifice. On the right of the road opposite Hamzah's Mosque, is a large erection, now in ruins, containing a deep hole leading to a well, and huge platforms for the accommodation of travellers, and beyond, towards the mountains, are the small edifices presently to be described.

Some Turkish women were sitting veiled upon the shady platform opposite the Martyrs' Mosque. At a little distance their husbands, and the servants holding horses and asses, lay upon the ground, and a large crowd of Bedouins, boys, girls, and old women, had gathered around

* They are said to be seventy, but the heaps appeared to me at least three times more numerous.

to beg, draw water, and sell dry dates. They were awaiting the guardian, who had not yet acknowledged the summons. After half an hour's vain patience, we determined to proceed with the ceremonies. Ascending by its steps the Mastabah subtending half the eastern wall, Shaykh Hamid placed me so as to front the tomb. There, standing in the burning sun, we repeated the following prayer: "Peace be with thee, O our Lord Hamzah! O paternal uncle of Allah's messenger! O paternal uncle of Allah's Prophet! Peace be with thee, O paternal uncle of Mustafa! Peace be with thee, O Prince of the Martyrs! O prince of the happy! Peace be with thee, O Lion of Allah! O Lion of his Prophet!" Concluding with the Testification and the Fát-háh.

After which, we asked Hamzah and his companions to lend us their aid, in obtaining for us and ours pardon, worldly prosperity, and future happiness. Scarcely had we finished when, mounted on a high-trotting dromedary, appeared the emissary of Mohammed Khalifah, descendant of El Abbas, who keeps the key of the mosque, and receives the fees and donations of the devout. It was to be opened for the Turkish pilgrims. I waited to see the interior. The Arab drew forth from his pouch, with abundant solemnity, a bunch of curiously made keys, and sharply directed me to stand away from and out of sight of the door. When I obeyed, grumblingly, he began to rattle the locks, and to snap the padlocks, opening them slowly, shaking them, and making as much noise as possible. The reason of the precaution—it sounded like poetry if not sense—is this. It is believed that the souls of martyrs, leaving the habitations of their senseless clay,* are fond of

* Some historians relate that forty-six years after the battle of Ohod, the tombs were laid bare by a torrent, when the corpses

sitting together in spiritual converse, and profane eye must not fall upon the scene. What grand pictures these imaginative Arabs see! Conceive the majestic figures of the saints—for the soul with Mohammedans is like the old European spirit, a something immaterial in the shape of the body—with long grey beards, earnest faces, and solemn eyes, reposing beneath the palms, and discussing events now buried in the darkness of a thousand years.

I would fain be hard upon this superstition, but shame prevents. When, in Nottingham, eggs may not be carried out after sunset; when Ireland hears Banshees, or apparitional old women, with streaming hair, and dressed in blue mantles; when Scotland sees a shroud about a person, showing his approaching death; when France has her loup-garous, revenants, and poules du Vendredi Saint (*i. e.* hens hatched on Good Friday supposed to change color every year): as long as the Holy Coat cures devotees at Treves, Madonnas wink at Rimini, San Gennaro melts at Naples, and Addolorate and Estatiche make converts to hysteria at Rome—whilst the Virgin manifests herself to children on the Alps, whilst Germany sends forth Psychography, whilst Europe, the civilized, the enlightened, the sceptical, dotes over such puerilities as clairvoyance and table-turning; and whilst even hard-headed America believes in "mediums," in "snail-telegraphs," and "spirit-rappings,"—I must hold the men of El Medinah to be as wise, and their superstition to be as respectable as others.

But the realities of Hamzah's Mosque have little to

appeared in their winding-sheets as if buried the day before. Some had their hands upon their death wounds, from which fresh blood trickled when the pressure was forcibly removed. In opposition to this Moslem theory, we have that of the Modern Greeks, namely, that if the body be not decomposed within a year, it shows that the soul is not where it should be.

recommend them. The building is like that of Kuba, only smaller, and the hypostele is hung with oil lamps and ostrich eggs, the usual paltry furniture of an Arab mausoleum. On the walls are a few modern inscriptions and framed poetry, written in a caligraphic hand. Beneath the Rivak lies Hamzah, under a mass of black basaltic stone, like that of Aden, only more porous and scoriaceous, convex at the top, like a heap of earth, without the Kiswat,* or cover of a saint's tomb, and railed around with wooden bars. At his head or westward, lies Abdullah bin Jaish, a name little known to fame, under a plain white-washed tomb, also convex; and in the court-yard is a similar one, erected over the remains of Shammas bin Usman, another obscure companion. We then passed through a door in the northern part of the western wall, and saw a diminutive palm plantation and a well. After which we left the mosque, and I was under the "fatal necessity" of paying a dollar for the honor of entering it. But the guardian promised that the chapters Y. S. and El Ikhlas should be recited for my benefit—the latter forty times—and if their efficacy be one-twentieth part of what men say it is, the reader cannot quote against me a certain popular proverb, concerning an order of men easily parted from their money.

Issuing from the mosque, we advanced a few paces towards the mountain. On our left we passed by—at a respectable distance, for the Turkish Hajis cried out that their women were engaged in ablution—a large Sehrij or tank, built of cut stone with steps, and intended to detain the overflowing waters of the torrent. The next place we prayed at was a small square, enclosed with dwarf white-washed

* In the common tombs of martyrs, saints, and holy men, this covering is usually of green cloth, with long white letters sewn upon it. I forgot to ask whether it was temporarily absent from Hamzah's grave.

walls, containing a few graves denoted by ovals of loose stones thinly spread upon the ground. This is primitive Arab simplicity. The Bedouins still mark the places of their dead with four stones planted at the head, the feet, and the sides, in the centre the earth is either heaped up Musannam (*i. e.* like the hump of a camel), or more generally left Musattah—level. I therefore suppose that the latter was the original shape of the Prophet's tomb. Within the enclosure certain martyrs of the holy army were buried. After praying there, we repaired to a small building still nearer to the foot of the mountain. It is the usual cupola springing from four square walls, not in the best preservation. Here the Prophet prayed, and it is called the Khubbat El Sanaya, "Dome of the Front Teeth," from the following circumstance. Five infidels were bound by oath to slay Mohammed at the battle of Ohod; one of these, Ibn Kumayyah, threw so many stones and with such good will that two rings of the Prophet's helmet were driven into his cheek, and blood poured from his brow down his mustachios, which he wiped with a cloak to prevent the drops falling to the ground. Then Utbah bin Abi Wakkas hurled a stone at him, which, splitting his lower lip, knocked out one of his front teeth. On the left of the Mihrab, inserted low down in the wall, is a square stone, upon which Shayhk Hamid showed me the impression of a tooth: he kissed it with peculiar reverence, and so did I. But the boy Mohammed being by me objurgated— for I remarked in him a jaunty demeanor combined with neglectfulness of ceremonies—saluted it sulkily, muttering the while hints about the holiness of his birth-place exempting him from the trouble of stooping. Already he had appeared at the Haram without his Jubbeh, and with ungirt loins,—in waistcoat and shirt sleeves. Moreover he had conducted himself indecorously by nudging Shaykh Hamid's sides during divine service. Feeling that the youth's "moral man" was, like his physical, under my charge, and determined to arrest a course of conduct which must have ended in obtaining for me, the master, the reputation of a "son of Belial," I insisted upon his joining us in the customary two-prostration prayers. And Saad the Devil taking my side of the question with his usual alacrity when a disturbance was in prospect, the youth found it necessary to yield. After this little scene, Shaykh Hamid pointed out a sprawling inscription blessing the companions of the Prophet. The unhappy Abubekr's name had been half effaced by some fanatic Shiah, a circumstance which seemed to arouse all the evil in my companion's nature, and looking close at the wall I found a line of Persian verse to this effect:

"I am weary of my life (Umr), because it bears the name of Umar."*

We English wanderers are beginning to be shamed out of our habit of scribbling names and nonsense in noted spots. Yet the practice is both classical and oriental. The Greeks and Persians left their marks everywhere, as Egypt shows, and the paws of the Sphinx bear scratches which, being interpreted, are found to be the same manner of trash as that written upon the remains of Thebes in A. D. 1853. And Easterns never appear to enter a building with a white wall without inditing upon it platitudes in verse and prose. Influenced by these considerations, I drew forth a pencil and inscribed in the Kubbat El Sanaya,

"Abdullah, the servant of Allah."
(A. H. 1269.)

* In the Persian character the word Umr, life, and Umar, the name of the hated caliph, are written exactly in the same way; which explains the pun.

Issuing from the dome we turned a few paces to the left, passed northwards, and blessed the martyrs of Ohod.

Then again we moved a few paces forward and went through a similar ceremony, supposing ourselves to be in the cave that sheltered the Prophet. After which, returning towards the torrent-bed by the way we came, we stood a small distance from a cupola called Kubbat El Masra. We faced towards it and finished the ceremonies of this Ziyarat by a supplication, the Testification, and the Fát-háh.

In the evening I went with my friends to the Haram. The minaret galleries were hung with lamps, and the inside of the temple was illuminated. It was crowded with Hajis, amongst whom were many women, a circumstance which struck me from its being unusual.* Some pious pilgrims, who had duly paid for the privilege, were perched upon ladders trimming wax candles of vast dimensions, others were laying up for themselves rewards in paradise, by performing the same office to the lamps; many were going through the ceremonies of Ziyarat, and not a few were sitting in different parts of the mosque apparently overwhelmed with emotion. The boys and the beggars were inspired with fresh energy, the Aghawat were gruffer and surlier than I had ever seen them, and the young men about town walked and talked with a freer and an easier demeanor than usual. My old friends the Persians—there were about 1200 of them in the Hajj caravan—attracted my attention. The doorkeepers stopped them with curses as they were about to enter, and all claimed from each the sum of five piastres, whilst other Moslems are allowed to

* The Prophet preferred women and young boys to pray privately, and in some parts of El Islam they are not allowed to join a congregation. At El Medinah, however, it is no longer, as in Burckhardt's time, "thought very indecorous in women to enter the mosque."

enter the mosque free. Unhappy men! they had lost all the Shiraz swagger, their mustachios drooped pitiably, their eyes would not look any one in the face, and not a head bore a cap stuck upon it crookedly. Whenever an "Ajemi," whatever might be his rank, stood in the way of an Arab or a Turk, he was rudely thrust aside, with abuse, muttered loud enough to be heard by all around. All eyes followed them as they went through the ceremonies of Ziyarat, especially as they approached the tombs of Abubekr and Omar,—which every man is bound to defile if he can,—and the supposed place of Fatimah's burial. Here they stood in parties, after praying before the Prophet's window: one read from a book the pathetic tale of the Lady's life, sorrows, and mourning death, whilst the others listened to him with breathless attention. Sometimes their emotion was too strong to be repressed. "*Ay Fatimah! Ay Mazlumah! Way! way!*—O Fatimah! O thou injured one! Alas! alas!"—burst involuntarily from their lips, despite the danger of such exclamations, tears trickled down their hairy cheeks, and their brawny bosoms heaved with sobs. A strange sight it was to see rugged fellows, mountaineers, perhaps, or the fierce Iliyat of the plains, sometimes weeping silently like children, sometimes shrieking like hysteric girls, and utterly careless to conceal a grief so coarse and grisly, at the same time so true and real, that we knew not how to behold it. Then the Satanic scowls with which they passed by or pretended to pray at the hated Omar's tomb! With what curses their hearts are belying those mouths full of blessings! How they are internally canonising Fayruz,* and praying for his eternal happiness in the presence of the murdered man! Sticks and stones, however, and not unfrequently the knife and

* The Persian slave who stabbed Omar in the mosque.

the sabre, have taught them the hard lesson of disciplining their feelings, and nothing but a furious contraction of the brow, a roll of the eye, intensely vicious, and a twitching of the muscles about the region of the mouth, denotes the wild storm of wrath within. They generally, too, manage to discharge some part of their passion in words. "Hail Omar thou hog!" exclaims some fanatic Madani as he passes by the heretic—a demand more outraging than requiring a red-hot, black-north Protestant to bless the Pope. "O Allah! *hell* him!" meekly responds the Persian, changing the benediction to a curse most intelligible to, and most delicious in his fellows' ears.†

I found an evening hour in the steamy heat of the Haram, equal to half a dozen afternoons; and left it resolved not to visit it till the Hajj departed from El Medinah. It was only prudent not to see much of the Ajemis; and as I did so somewhat ostentatiously, my companions discovered that the Haj Abdullah, having slain many of those heretics in some war or other, was avoiding them to escape retaliation. In proof of my generalistic qualities, the rolling down of the water jar upon the heads of the Maghribi pilgrims in the "Golden Thread" was quoted, and all offered to fight for me *à l'outrance*. I took care not to contradict the report.

* I have heard of a Persian being beaten to death, because instead of saying "peace be with thee, Ya Omar," he insisted upon saying "peace be with thee, Ya Humár (O ass!)"

## CHAPTER XIX.

### THE PEOPLE OF EL MEDINAH.

El Medinah contains but few families descended from the Prophet's auxiliaries. I heard only four whose genealogy is undoubted. These were,—

1. The Bait el Ansari, or descendants of Abu Ayyub, a most noble race whose tree ramifies through a space of 1500 years. They keep the keys of the Kuba mosque, and are Imams in the Haram, but the family is no longer wealthy or powerful.

2. The Bait Abu Jud: they supply the Haram with Imams and Muezzins. I was told that there are now but two surviving members of this family, a boy and a girl.

3. The Bait el Shaab, a numerous race. Some of the members travel professionally, others trade, and others are employed in the Haram.

4. The Bait el Karrani, who are mostly engaged in commerce.

There is also a race called el Nakhawilah, who, according to some, are descendants of the Ansar, whilst others derive them from Yezid, the son of Muawiyah: the latter opinion is improbable, as the Caliph in question was the

12*

mortal foe to Ali's family, which is inordinately venerated by these people. As far as I could ascertain, they abuse the Shaykhain:* all my informants agreed upon this point, but none could tell me why they neglected to bedevil Osman, the third object of hatred to the Shiah persuasion. They are numerous and warlike, yet they are despised by the townspeople, because they openly profess heresy, and, are moreover of humble degree. They have their own priests and instructors, although subject to the orthodox Kazi, marry in their own sect, are confined to low offices, such as slaughtering animals, sweeping, and gardening, and are not allowed to enter the Haram during life, or to be carried to it after death. Their corpses are taken down an outer street called the Darb el Jenazah—Road of Biers—to their own cemetery near El Bakia. They dress and speak Arabic, like the townspeople; but the Arabs pretend to distinguish them by a peculiar look denoting their degradation,—doubtless the mistake of effect for cause, made about all such

"Tribes of the wandering foot and weary breast."

A number of reports are current about the horrid customs of these people, and their community of women with the Persian pilgrims who pass through the town. It need scarcely be said that such tales coming from the mouths of fanatic foes are not to be credited. I regret not having had an opportunity to become intimate with any of the Nakhawilah, from whom curious information might be elicited. Orthodox Moslems do not like to be questioned about such hateful subjects; when I attempted to learn something from one of my acquaintance, Shaykh Ula el Din, of a Kurd family, settled at El Medinah, a man who

* The "two Shaykhs"—Abubekr and Omar.

had travelled over the East, and who spoke five languages to perfection, he coldly replied that he had never consorted with these heretics. Sayyids and Sherifs, the descendants of the Prophet, here abound.

There are about 200 families of Sayyid Alawiyah,—descendants of Ali by any of his wives but Fatimah,—they bear no distinctive mark in dress or appearance, and are either employed at the temple or engage in trade. Of the Khalifiyyah, or descendants of Abbas, there is, I am told, but one household, who act as Imams in the Haram, and have charge of Hamzah's tomb. Some declare that there are a few of the Siddikiyah, or descendants from Abubekr; others ignored them.

The rest of the population of El Medinah is a motley race composed of offshoots from every nation in El Islam. The sanctity of the city attracts strangers, who, purposing to stay but a short time, become residents: after finding some employment, they marry, have families, die, and are buried there, with an eye to the spiritual advantages of the place. I was much importuned to stay at El Medinah. The only known physician was one Shaykh Abdullah Sahib, an Indian, a learned man, but of so melancholic a temperament, and so ascetic in his habits, that his knowledge was entirely lost to the public. The present ruling race at El Medinah, in consequence of political vicissitudes, are the sons of Turkish fathers by Arab mothers. These half-castes are now numerous, and have managed to secure the highest and most lucrative offices. Besides Turks, there are families originally from the Maghrib, Takruris, Egyptians in considerable numbers, settlers from Yemen and other parts of Arabia, Syrians, Kurds, Afghans, Daghistani from the Caucasus, and a few Jawi—Java Moslems. The Indians are not so numerous in proportion here as at Meccah; still Hindostani is by no means uncommonly heard in the streets.

They preserve their peculiar costume, the women persisting in showing their faces, and in wearing tight, exceedingly tight, pantaloons. This, together with other reasons, secures for them the contempt of the Arabs. At El Medinah they are generally small shopkeepers, especially druggists and sellers of Kumash (cloths), and form a society of their own.

The citizens of El Medinah are a favored race, although their city is not, like Meccah, the grand mart of the Moslem world or the meeting-place of nations. They pay no taxes, and reject the idea of a "Miri," or land-cess, with extreme disdain. "Are we, the children of the Prophet," they exclaim, "to support or to be supported?" The Wahhabis, not understanding the argument, taxed them, as was their wont, in specie and in materials, for which reason the very name of the Puritans is an abomination. As has before been shown, all the numerous attendants at the mosque are paid partly by the Sultan, partly by aukaf, the rents of houses and lands bequeathed to the shrine, and scattered over every part of the Moslem world. When a Madani is inclined to travel, he applies to the Mudir el Haram, and receives from him a paper which entitles him to the receipt of a considerable sum at Constantinople.

The Madani traveller, on arrival at Constantinople, reports his arrival to his consul, the Wakil el Haramain. This "Agent of the two Holy Places" applies to the Nazir el Aukaf, or "Intendant of Bequests;" the latter, after transmitting the demand to the different officers of the treasury, sends the money to the Wakil, who delivers it to the applicant. This gift is sometimes squandered in pleasure, more often invested profitably either in merchandise or in articles of home-use, presents of dress and jewellery for the women, handsome arms, especially pistols and *balas*,* silk tassels, amber pipe-pieces, slippers, and embroidered purses. They are packed up in one or two large sahharahs (chests), and then commences the labor of returning home gratis. I have already described the extent of mental agitation caused during the journey by these precious convoys. Besides the Ikram, most of the Madani, when upon these begging trips, are received as guests by great men at Constantinople. The citizens whose turn it is not to travel, await the Aukaf and Sadakat, forwarded every year by the Damascus caravan; besides which, as has been before explained, the Haram supplies even those not officially employed in it with many perquisites.

Without these advantages El Medinah would soon be abandoned to cultivators and Bedouins. Though commerce is here honorable, as everywhere in the East, business is "slack," because the higher classes prefer the idleness of administering their landed estates, and being servants to the mosque. I heard of only four respectable houses. They all deal in grain, cloth, and provisions, and perhaps the richest have a capital of 20,000 dollars. Caravans in the cold weather are constantly passing between El Medinah and Egypt, but they are rather bodies of visitors to Constantinople than traders travelling for gain. Corn is brought from Jeddah by land, and imported into Yambu or El Rais, a port on the Red Sea, one day and a half's journey from Safra. There is an active provision trade with the neighboring Bedouins, and the Syrian Hajj supplies the citizens with apparel and articles of luxury—tobacco, dried fruits, sweetmeats, knives, and all that is included under the word "notions." There are few storekeepers, and their dealings are petty, because articles of

* The Turkish "yataghan." It is a long dagger, intended for thrusting rather than cutting.

every kind are brought from Egypt, Syria, and Constantinople. As a general rule, labor is exceedingly expensive, and at the visitation time a man will demand fifteen or twenty piastres from a stranger for such a trifling job as mending an umbrella. Handicraftsmen and artisans—carpenters, masons, locksmiths, potters and others, are either slaves or foreigners, mostly Egyptians. This proceeds partly from the pride of the people. They are taught from their childhood that the Madani is a favored being, to be respected however vile or schismatic, and that the vengeance of Allah will fall upon any one who ventures to abuse, much more to strike him. They receive a stranger at the shop window with the haughtiness of Pachas, and take pains to show him by words as well as by looks, that they consider themselves as "good gentlemen as princes, only not so rich." Added to this pride are indolence, and the true Arab prejudice, which, even in the present day, prevents a Bedouin from marrying the daughter of an artisan. Like Castilians they consider labor humiliating to any but a slave; nor is this, as a clever French author remarks, by any means an unreasonable idea, since Heaven, to punish man for disobedience, caused him to eat daily bread by the sweat of his brow. Besides, there *is* degradation, moral and physical, in handiwork compared with the freedom of the desert. The loom and the file do not conserve courtesy and chivalry like the sword and spear; man extending his tongue, to use an Arab phrase, when a cuff and not a stab is to be the consequence of an injurious expression. Even the ruffian becomes polite in California, where his brother ruffian carries a revolver, and those European nations who were most polished when every gentleman wore a rapier have become the rudest since Civilisation disarmed them.

The citizens, despite their being generally in debt, manage to live well. Their cookery, like that of Meccah, has borrowed something from Egypt, Turkey, Syria, Persia, and India; like all Orientals they are exceedingly fond of clarified butter.* I have seen the boy Mohammed drink off nearly a tumbler full, although his friends warned him that it would make him as fat as an elephant. When a man cannot enjoy clarified butter in these countries, it is considered a sign that his stomach is out of order, and all my excuses of a melancholic temperament were required to be in full play to prevent the infliction of fried meat swimming in grease, or that guest-dish, rice saturated with melted—perhaps I should say—rancid butter. The house of a Madani in good circumstances is comfortable, for the building is substantial, and the attendance respectable. Black slave-girls here perform the complicated duties of servant-maids in England; they are taught to sew, to cook, and to wash, besides sweeping the house and drawing water for domestic use. Hasinah (the "Charmer," a decided misnomer) costs from 40 to 50 dollars: if she be a mother, her value is less, but neat-handedness, propriety of demeanor, and skill in feminine accomplishments, raise her to 100 dollars, 25*l*. A little black boy, perfect in all his points, and tolerably intelligent, costs about 1000 piastres; girls are dearer, and eunuchs fetch double that sum. The older the children become, the more their value diminishes, and no one would purchase, save under exceptional circumstances, an adult slave, because he is never parted with but for

* Physiologists have remarked that fat and greasy food, containing a quantity of carbon, is peculiar to cold countries, whereas the inhabitants of the tropics delight in fruits, vegetables, and articles of diet which do not increase caloric. This must be taken *cum grano*. In Italy, Spain, and Greece, the general use of olive oil begins. In Africa and Asia, especially in the hottest parts, the people habitually eat enough clarified butter to satisfy an Esquimaux.

some incurable vice. The Abyssinian, mostly Galla, girls, so much prized because their skins are always cool in the hottest weather, are here rare; they seldom sell for less than 20*l.*, and often fetch 60*l.* I never heard of a Jariyah Bayza, a white slave-girl, being in the market at El Medinah: in Circassia they fetch from 100*l.* to 400*l.* prime cost, and few men in El Hejaz could afford so expensive a luxury. The bazaar at El Medinah is poor, and, as almost all the slaves are brought from Meccah by the Jallabs, or drivers, after exporting the best to Egypt, the town receives only the refuse.*

The personal appearance of the Madani makes the stranger wonder how this mongrel population of settlers has acquired a peculiar and almost an Arab physiognomy. They are remarkably fair, the effect of a cold climate; sometimes the cheeks are lighted up with red, and the hair is a dark chestnut—at El Medinah I was not stared at as a white man. In some points they approach the true Arab type, that is to say, the Bedouins of ancient and noble family. The cheekbones are high and *saillant*, the eye small, more round than long, piercing, fiery, deep-set, and brown rather than black. The head is small, the ears well-cut, the face long and oval, though not unfrequently disfigured by what is popularly called the "lantern-jaw;" the forehead high, bony, broad, and slightly retreating, and the beard and mustachios scanty, consisting of two tufts upon the chin, with, generally speaking, little or no whisker. These are the points of resemblance between the city and the country Arab. The difference is equally remarkable. The temperament of the

* Some of these slaves come from Abyssinia: the greater part are driven from the Galla country, and exported at the harbors of the Somauli coast, Berberah, Tajurrah, and Zayla. As many as 2000 slaves from the former place, and 4000 from the latter, are annually shipped off to Mocha, Jeddah, Suez, and Muscat.

Madani is not purely nervous, like that of the Bedouins, but admits a large admixture of the bilious and, though rarely, the lymphatic. The cheeks are fuller, the jaws project more than in the pure race, the lips are more fleshy, more sensual and ill-fitting, the features are broader, and the limbs are stouter and more bony. The beard is a little thicker, and the young Arabs of the towns are beginning to imitate the Turks in that abomination to their ancestors—shaving. Personal vanity, always a ruling passion among Orientals, and a hopeless wish to emulate the flowing beards of the Turks and the Persians—the only nations in the world who ought not to shave the chin—have overruled even the religious objections to such innovation. I was more frequently appealed to at El Medinah than anywhere else, for some means of removing the opprobrium "Kusah."* They dye the beard with gall nuts, henna, and other preparations. Much refinement of dress is now found at El Medinah, Constantinople, the Paris of the East, supplying it with the newest fashions. The women dress, like the men, handsomely. In-doors they wear, I am told, a boddice of calico and other stuffs, which supports the bosom without the evils of European stays. Over this is a wide shirt, of the white stuff called Halaili or Burunjuk, with enormous sleeves, and flowing down to the feet: the pantaloons are not wide, like the Egyptians, but rather tight, approaching to the Indian cut, without its exaggeration. Abroad, they throw over the head a silk or a cotton Milayah, generally chequered white and blue. Women of all ranks dye the soles of the feet and the palms of the hands black, and trace thin lines down the inside of the fingers, by first applying a plaster of henna and then a mixture, called "Shadar," of gall nuts, alum, and lime. The hair, parted in the centre, is plaited

* A "scant-bearded man."

into about twenty little twists called Jadilah.* Of ornaments, as usual among Orientals, they have a vast variety, ranging from brass and spangles to gold and precious stones; and they delight in strong perfumes—musk, civet, ambergris, attar of rose, oil of jasmine, aloe-wood, and extract of cinnamon. Both sexes wear Constantinople slippers. The women draw on Khuff, inner slippers, of bright yellow leather, serving for socks, and covering the ancle, with papooshes of the same material, sometimes lined with velvet and embroidered with a gold sprig under the hollow of the foot. In mourning the men show no difference of dress, like good Moslems, to whom such display of grief is forbidden. But the women, who cannot dissociate the heart and the toilette, evince their sorrow by wearing white clothes and by doffing their ornaments. This is a modern custom: the accurate Burckhardt informs us that in his day the women of El Medinah did not wear mourning.

The Madani generally appear abroad on foot. Few animals are kept here, on account, I suppose, of the expense of feeding them. The Cavalry are mounted on poor Egyptian nags. The horses ridden by rich men are generally Nejdi, costing from 200 to 300 dollars. Camels are numerous, but those bred in El Hejaz are small, weak, and consequently little prized. Dromedaries of good breed are to be had for any sum between 10 and 400 dollars; they are diminutive but exceedingly swift, sure-footed, sagacious, thorough-bred, with eyes like the antelope, and muzzles that would almost enter a tumbler. Mules are not found at El Medinah, although popular prejudice does not now forbid the people to mount them. Asses come from Egypt and Meccah.

* In the plural called Jedail. It is a most becoming head-dress when the hair is thick, and when—which I regret to say is rare in Arabia—the twists are undone for ablution once a day.

The manners of the Madani are graver and somewhat more pompous than those of any Arabs with whom I ever mixed. This they appear to have borrowed from their rulers, the Turks. But their austerity and ceremoniousness are skin deep. In intimacy or in anger the garb of politeness is thrown off, and the screaming Arab voice, the voluble, copious, and emphatic abuse, and the mania for gesticulation, return in all their deformity. They are great talkers, as the following little trait shows. When a man is opposed to more than his match in disputing or bargaining, instead of patiently saying to himself *s'il crache il est mort*, he interrupts the adversary with a "Sall' ala Mohammed,"—bless the Prophet. Every good Moslem is obliged to obey such requisition by responding, "Allahumma salli alayh,"—O Allah bless him! But the Madani curtails the phrase to "A'n," supposing it to be an equivalent, and proceeds in his loquacity. Then perhaps the baffled opponent will shout out "Wahhid," *i. e.* "Attest the unity of the Deity;" when, instead of employing the usual religious phrases to assert that dogma, he will briefly ejaculate "Al," and hurry on with the course of conversation. As it may be supposed, these wars of words frequently end in violent quarrels. For, to do the Madani justice, they are always ready to fight.

It is not to be believed that in a town garrisoned by Turkish troops, full of travelled traders, and which supports itself by plundering Hajis, the primitive virtues of the Arab could exist. The Meccans, a dark people, say of the Madani that their hearts are black as their skins are white. This is of course exaggerated; but it is not too much to assert that pride, pugnacity, a peculiar point of honor, and a vindictiveness of wonderful force and patience, are the only characteristic traits of Arab character which the citizens of El Medinah habitually display. Here you meet with scant remains of the chivalry of the desert. A man will abuse his guest, even though he will not dine without him, and would protect him bravely against an enemy. And words often pass lightly between individuals which suffice to cause a blood feud amongst Bedouins. The outward appearance of decorum is conspicuous amongst the Madani. There are no places where Corinthians dwell, as at Meccah, Cairo, and Jeddah. Adultery, if detected, would be punished by lapidation according to the rigor of the Koranic law, and simple immorality by religious stripes, or, if of repeated occurrence, by expulsion from the city. But scandals seldom occur, and the women, I am told, behave with great decency. Abroad, they have the usual Moslem pleasures of marriage, lyings-in, circumcision feasts, holy visitations, and funerals. At home, they employ themselves with domestic matters, and especially in scolding "Hasinah" and "Zaaferan." In this occupation they surpass even the notable English house-keeper of the middle orders of society—the latter being confined to "knagging at" her slave, whereas the Arab lady is allowed an unbounded extent of vocabulary. At Shaykh Hamid's house, however, I cannot accuse the women of

> "Swearing into strong shudders
> The immortal gods who heard them."

They abused the black girls with unction, but without any violent expletives. At Meccah, however, the old lady in whose house I was living would, when excited by the melancholy temperament of her eldest son and his irregular hours of eating, scold him in the grossest terms not unfrequently ridiculous in the extreme. For instance, one of her assertions was that he—the son—was the offspring of an immoral mother; which assertion, one might suppose, reflected not indirectly upon herself. So in Egypt I have frequently heard a father, when reproving his boy, address him by "O dog, son of a dog!" and "O spawn of an infidel—of a Jew—of a Christian." Amongst the men of El Medinah I remarked a considerable share of hypocrisy. Their mouths were as full of religious salutations, exclamations, and hacknied quotations from the Koran as of indecency and vile abuse,—a point in which they resemble the Persians. As before observed, they preserve their reputation as the sons of a holy city by praying only in public. At Constantinople they are by no means remarkable for sobriety. Intoxicating liquors, especially araki, are made in El Medinah only by the Turks; the citizens seldom indulge in this way at home, as detection by smell is imminent among a people of water-bibbers. During the whole time of my stay I had to content myself with a single bottle of cognac, colored and scented to resemble medicine. The Madani are, like the Meccans, a curious mixture of generosity and meanness, of profuseness and penuriousness. But the former quality is the result of ostentation, the latter a characteristic of the Semitic race, long ago made familiar to Europe by the Jew. Above all their qualities, personal conceit is remarkable; they show it in their strut, in their looks, and almost in every word. "I am such a one, the son of such a one," is a common expletive, especially in times of danger; and this spirit is not wholly to be condemned, as it certainly acts as an incentive to gallant actions. But it often excites them to vie with one another in expensive entertainments and similar vanities. Upon the whole, though alive to the infirmities of the Madani character, I thought favorably of it, finding among this people more of the redeeming point, manliness, than in most Eastern nations with whom I am acquainted.

The Arabs, like the Egyptians, all marry. Yet, as usual, they are hard and facetious upon that ill-treated subject matrimony. It has exercised not a little the brain of their wits and sages, who have not failed to indite notable things concerning it. Saith "Harikar el Hakim" to his nephew Nadan, whom he would dissuade from taking to himself a wife, "Marriage is joy for a month and sorrow for life, and the paying of settlements and the breaking of back (*i. e.* under the load of misery), and the listening to a woman's tongue!" And again, we have in verse:—

> "They said, 'Marry!' I replied, 'far be it from me
> To take to my bosom a sackful of snakes.
> I am free—why then become a slave?
> May Allah never bless womankind!'"

And the following lines are generally quoted, as affording a kind of bird's-eye view of female existence:—

> "From 10 (years of age) unto 20,
> A repose to the eyes of beholders.
> From 20 unto 30,
> Still fair and full of flesh.
> From 30 unto 40,
> A mother of many boys and girls.
> From 40 unto 50,
> An old woman of the deceitful.
> From 50 unto 60,
> Slay her with a knife.
> From 60 unto 70,
> The curse of Allah upon them, one and all!

Another popular couplet makes a most unsupported assertion:—

> "They declare womankind to be heaven to man,
> I say, 'Allah give me Jehannum, and not this heaven.'"

Yet the fair sex has the laugh on its side, for these railers, at El Medinah as in other places, invariably marry. The ceremony is tedious and expensive. It begins with a Khitbah or betrothal: the father of the young man repairs to the parent or guardian of the marriageable girl, and at the end of his visit exclaims, "The Fát-Háh! we beg of your kindness your daughter for our son." Should the other be favorable to the proposal, his reply is, "Welcome and congratulation to you; but we must perform Istikharah;"* and when consent is given, both pledge themselves to the agreement by reciting the Fát-Háh. Then commence negotiations about the Mahr or sum settled upon the bride;† and after the smoothing of this difficulty follow feastings of friends and relatives, male and female. The marriage itself is called Akd el Nikah or Ziwaj. A Walimah or banquet is prepared by the father of the Aris‡ at his own house, and the Kazi attends to perform the nuptial ceremony, the girl's consent being obtained through her Wakil, any male relation whom she commissions to act for her. Then, with great pomp and circumstance, the Aris visits his Arusah at her father's house; and finally, with a Zuffah or procession and sundry ceremonies at the Haram, the bride is brought to her new home.

Arab funerals are as simple as their marriages are complicated. Neither Naddabah (myriologist or hired keener),

* This means consulting the will of the Deity, by praying for a dream in sleep, by the rosary, by opening the Koran, and other such devices, which bear blame if a negative be deemed necessary. It is a custom throughout the Moslem world, a relic, doubtless, of the Azlam or Kidah (seven divining-arrows) of the Pagan times. At El Medinah it is generally called Khirah.

† Among respectable citizens 400 dollars would be considered a fair average sum; the expense of the ceremony would be about half. This amount of ready money (150*l.*) not being always procurable, many of the Madani marry late in life.

‡ El Aris is the bridegroom, El Arusah the bride.

nor indeed any female, even a relation, is present at burials, as in other parts of the Moslem world,* and it is esteemed disgraceful for a man to weep aloud. The Prophet, who doubtless had heard of those pagan mournings, where an effeminate and unlimited display of woe was often terminated by licentious excesses, like our half-heathen "wakes," forbad aught beyond a decent demonstration of grief. And his strong good sense enabled him to see the folly of professional mourners. At El Medinah the corpse is interred shortly after decease. The bier is carried through the streets at a moderate pace, by the friends and the relatives, these bringing up the rear. Every man who passes lends his shoulder for a minute, a mark of respect to the dead, and also considered a pious and a prayerful act. Arrived at the Haram, they carry the corpse in visitation to the Prophet's window, and pray over it at Osman's niche. Finally, it is interred after the usual Moslem fashion in the cemetery El Bakia.

El Medinah, though pillaged by the Wahhabis, still abounds in books. Near the Haram are two Madrasah or colleges—the Mahmudiyah, so called from Sultan Mahmud, and that of Bashir Agha: both have large stores of theological and other works. I also heard of extensive private collections, particularly of one belonging to the chief of the Sayyids, a certain Mohammed Jemal el Lail, whose father is well known in India. Besides which, there is a large bequest of books presented to the mosque or entailed upon particular families. The celebrated Mohammed Ibn Abdillah El Sannusi has removed his collection, amounting, it is said, to 8000 volumes, from El Medinah to his house in

* Boys are allowed to be present, but they are not permitted to cry. Of their so misdemeaning themselves there is little danger; the Arab in these matters is a man from his cradle.

Jebel Kubays at Meccah. The burial-place of the Prophet no longer lies open to the charge of utter ignorance brought against it by my predecessor. The people now praise their Ulema for learning, and boast a superiority in respect to science over Meccah. Yet many students leave the place for Damascus and Cairo, where the Riwak El Haramain (college of the two shrines) in the Azhar mosque is always crowded, and though Omar Effendi boasted to me that his city was full of lore "as an egg is full of meat," he did not appear the less anxious to attend the lectures of Egyptian professors. But none of my informants claimed for El Medinah any facilities of studying other than the purely religious sciences. Philosophy, medicine, arithmetic, mathematics, and algebra cannot be learnt here. But after denying the Madani the praise of varied learning, it must be owned that their quick observation and retentive memories have stored up for them an abundance of superficial knowledge, culled from conversations in the market and in the camp. I found it impossible here to display those feats which in Sindh, Southern Persia, Eastern Arabia, and many parts of India, would be looked upon as miraculous. Most probably one of the company had witnessed the performance of some Italian conjuror, at Constantinople or Alexandria, and retained a lively recollection of every manœuvre. As linguists they are not equal to the Meccans, who surpass all Orientals excepting only the Armenians; the Madani seldom know Turkish, and more rarely still Persian and Indian. Those only who have studied in Egypt chant the Koran well. The citizens speak and pronounce their language purely: they are not equal to the people of the southern Hejaz, still their Arabic is refreshing after the horrors of Cairo and Muscat.

## CHAPTER XX.

### A VISIT TO THE SAINTS' CEMETERY.

A QUARREL which was renewed about this time between two rival families of the Beni Harb put an end to any lingering possibility of my prosecuting my journey to Muscat, as originally intended. My disappointment was bitter at first, but consolation soon suggested itself. Under the most favorable circumstances, a Bedouin-trip from El Medinah to Muscat, 1500 or 1600 miles, would require at least ten months; whereas, under pain of losing my commission,* I was ordered to be at Bombay before the end of March. Moreover, entering Arabia by El Hejaz, as has before been said, I was obliged to leave behind all my instruments except a watch and a pocket compass, so the benefit rendered to geography by my trip would have been scanty. Still remained to me the comfort of reflecting that possibly at Meccah some opportunity of crossing the Peninsula might present itself. At any rate I had the certainty of seeing the strange wild country of the Hejaz, and of being present at the ceremonies of the Holy City.

* The parliamentary limit of an officer's leave from India is five years: if he overstay that period, he forfeits his commission.

I must request the reader to bear with a Visitation once more: we shall conclude it with a ride to El Bakia. This venerable spot is frequented by the pious every day after the prayer at the Prophet's Tomb, and especially on Fridays. The least we can do is to go there once.

Our party started one morning,—on donkeys, as usual, for my foot was not yet strong,—along the Darb el Jenazah round the southern wall of the town. The locomotives were decidedly slow, principally in consequence of the tent-ropes which the Hajis had pinned down literally over the plain, and falls were by no means infreqnent. At last we arrived at the end of the Darb, where I committed myself by mistaking the decaying place of those miserable schismatics the Nakhawilah for El Bakia, the glorious cemetery of the Saints. Hamid corrected my blunder with tartness, to which I replied as tartly, that in our country—Affghanistan—we burned the body of every heretic upon whom we could lay our hands. This truly Islamitic custom was heard with general applause, and as the little dispute ended, we stood at the open gate of El Bakia. Then having dismounted I sat down on a low Dakkah or stone bench within the walls, to obtain a general view and to prepare for the most fatiguing of the visitations.

The burial-place of the Saints is an irregular oblong surrounded by walls which are connected with the suburb at their S. W. angle. Around it palm plantations seem to flourish. It is small, considering the extensive use made of it: all that die at El Medinah, strangers as well as natives, except only heretics and schismatics, expect to be interred in it. It must be choked with corpses, which it could not contain did not the Moslem style of burial greatly favor rapid decomposition, and it has all the inconveniences of "intramural sepulture." The gate is small and ignoble; a mere doorway in the wall. Inside there are no flower-plots, no tall trees, in fact none of the refinements which lighten the gloom of the Christian burial-place: the buildings are simple, they might even be called mean. Almost all are the common Arab mosque, cleanly white-washed, and looking quite new. The ancient monuments were levelled to the ground by Saad the Wahhabi and his puritan followers, who waged pitiless warfare against what must have appeared to them magnificent mausolea, deeming as they did a loose heap of stones sufficient for a grave. In Burckhardt's time the whole place was a "confused accumulation of heaps of earth, wide pits, and rubbish, without a single regular tomb-stone." The present erections owe their existence, I was told, to the liberality of the Sultans Abd El Hamid and Mahmud.

A poor pilgrim has lately started on his last journey, and his corpse, unattended by friends or mourners, is carried upon the shoulders of hired buriers into the cemetery. Suddenly they stay their rapid steps, and throw the body upon the ground. There is a life-like pliability about it as it falls, and the tight cerements so define the outlines that the action makes me shudder. It looks almost as if the dead pilgrim were conscious of what is about to occur. They have forgotten their tools; one man starts to fetch them, and three sit down to smoke. After a time a shallow grave is hastily scooped out. The corpse is packed into it with such unseemly haste that earth touches it in all directions,—cruel carelessness among Moslems, who believe this to torture the sentient frame. One comfort suggests itself. The poor man being a pilgrim has died Shahid—in martyrdom. Ere long his spirit shall leave El Bakia,

> "And he on honey-dew shall feed,
> And drink the milk of Paradise."

I entered the holy cemetery right foot forwards, as if it

were a mosque, and barefooted, to avoid suspicion of being a heretic. For though the citizens wear their shoes in the Bakia, they are much offended at seeing the Persians follow their example.

Walking down a rough narrow path, which leads from the western to the eastern extremity of El Bakia, we entered the humble mausoleum of the caliph Osman—Osman "El Mazlum," or the "ill-treated," he is called by some Moslem travellers. When he was slain, his friends wished to bury him by the Prophet in the Hujrah, and Ayisha made no objection to the measure. But the people of Egypt became violent, swore that the corpse should neither be buried nor be prayed over, and only permitted it to be removed upon the threat of Habibah (one of the "Mothers" of the Moslems, and daughter of Abu Sufiyan) to expose her countenance. During the night that followed his death Osman was carried out by several of his friends to El Bakia, from which, however, they were driven away, and obliged to deposit their burden in a garden, eastward of and outside the saints' cemetery. It was called Husn Kaukab, and was looked upon as an inauspicious place of sepulture, till Marwan included it in El Bakia.

Then moving a few paces to the north, we faced eastwards, and performed the visitation of Abu Said el Khazari, a Sahib or companion of the Prophet, whose sepulchre lies outside El Bakia. The third place visited was a dome containing the tomb of our lady Halimah, the Bedouin wet-nurse who took charge of Mohammed.*

After which, fronting the north, we stood before a low

* This woman, according to some accounts, also saved Mohammed's life, when an Arab Kahin or diviner, foreseeing that the child was destined to subvert the national faith, urged the bystanders to bury their swords in his bosom.

enclosure, containing ovals of loose stones, disposed side by side. These are the martyrs of El Bakia, who received the crown of glory at the hands of El Muslim, the general of the arch-heretic Yezid. The fifth station is near the centre of the cemetery at the tomb of Ibrahim, who died, to the eternal regret of El Islam, some say six months old, others in his second year. He was the son of Mariyah, the Coptic girl, sent as a present to Mohammed by Jarih, the governor of Alexandria. The Prophet with his own hand piled earth upon the grave, and sprinkled it with water,—a ceremony then first performed,—disposed small stones upon it, and pronounced the final salutation.* Then we visited El Nafi Maula, son of Omar, generally called Imam Nafi el Kari, or the Koran chaunter; and near him the great doctor Imam Malik ibn Anas, a native of El Medinah, and one of the most dutiful of her sons. The eighth station is at the tomb of Ukayl bin Abi Talib, brother of Ali. Then we visited the spot where lie interred all the Prophet's wives, Ayisha included.† After the "Mothers of the Moslems," we prayed at the tombs of Mohammed's daughters, said to be ten in number.

In compliment probably to the Hajj, the beggars mustered strong that morning at El Bakia. Along the walls and at the entrance of each building squatted ancient dames, all engaged in fervent contemplation of every approaching face, and in pointing to dirty cotton napkins spread upon the ground before them, and studded with a few coins, gold, silver, or copper, according to the expec-

* For which reason many holy men were buried in this part of the cemetery, every one being ambitious to lie in ground which had been honored by the Prophet's hands.

† Khadijah, who lies at Meccah, is the only exception. Mohammed married fifteen wives, of whom nine survived him.

tations of the proprietress. They raised their voices to demand largesse: some promised to write Fát-Fáhs, and the most audacious seized visitors by the skirts of their garments. Fakihs, ready to write "Y. S." or anything else demanded of them, covered the little heaps and eminences of the cemetery, all begging lustily, and looking as though they would murder you, when told how beneficent is Allah.* At the doors of the tombs old housewives, and some young ones also, struggled with you for your slippers as you doffed them, and not unfrequently the charge of the pair was divided between two. Inside when the boys were not loud enough or importunate enough for presents, they were urged on by the adults and seniors, the relatives of the "Khadims" and hangers-on. Unfortunately for me, Shaykh Hamid was renowned for taking charge of wealthy pilgrims: the result was, that my purse was lightened of three dollars. I must add that although at least fifty female voices loudly promised that morning, for the sum of ten paras each, to supplicate Allah in behalf of my lameness, no perceptible good came of their efforts.

Before leaving El Bakia, we went to the eleventh station, the Kubbat el Abbasiyah, or Dome of Abbas. Originally built by the Abbaside Caliphs in A. H. 519, it is a larger and a handsomer building than its fellows, and is situated on the right hand side of the gate as you enter in. The crowd of beggars at the door testified to its importance: they were attracted by the Persians who assemble here in force to weep and pray. Crossing the threshold with some difficulty, I walked round a mass of tombs which occupies the centre of the building, leaving but a narrow passage between it and the walls. It is railed round, covered over with several "kiswahs" of green cloth, worked

* A polite form of objecting to be charitable.

with white letters, and looked like a confused heap; but it might have appeared irregular to me by the reason of the mob around. The eastern portion contains the body of El Hasan, the son of Ali, and grandson of the Prophet; the Imam Zayn el Abidin, son of El Hosayn, and great-grandson to the Prophet; the Imam Mohammed El Bakir (fifth Imam), son to Zayn el Abidin; and his son the Imam Jaafar el Sadik—all four descendants of the Prophet, and buried in the same grave with Abbas ibn Abd el Muttaleb, uncle to Mohammed.

We stood opposite this mysterious tomb, and repeated, with difficulty by reason of the Persians weeping, the following supplication:—"Peace be with ye, O family of the Prophet! O Lord Abbas, the free from impurity and uncleanness, and father's brother to the best of men! And thou too, O Lord Hasan, grandson of the Prophet! And thou too, O Lord Zayn el Abidin! Peace be with ye, one and all, for verily God hath been pleased to free you from all guile, and to purify you with all purity. The mercy of Allah and his blessings be upon you, and verily he is the Praised, the Mighty!" After which, freeing ourselves from the hands of greedy boys, we turned round and faced the southern wall, close to which is a tomb attributed to the Lady Fatimah.* I will not repeat the prayer, it being the same as that recited in the Haram.

* Moslem historians seem to delight in the obscurity which hangs over the lady's last resting-place, as if it were an honor even for the receptacle of her ashes to be concealed from the eyes of men. Some place her in the Haram, relying upon this tradition:—Fatimah, feeling about to die, rose up joyfully, performed the greater ablution, dressed herself in pure garments, spread a mat upon the floor of her house near the Prophet's Tomb, lay down fronting the Kiblah, placed her hand under her cheek, and said to her attendant, "I am pure and in a pure dress; now let no one uncover my body, but bury me where I lie!"

Issuing from the hot and crowded dome, we recovered our slippers after much trouble, and found that our garments had suffered from the frantic gesticulations of the Persians. We then walked to the gate of El Bakia, stood facing the cemetery upon an elevated piece of ground, and delivered the general benediction.

After which, issuing from El Bakia,* we advanced northwards, leaving the city gate on the left hand, and came to a small Kubbah close to the road. It is visited as containing the tomb of the Prophet's paternal aunts. Hurrying over our directions here,—for we were tired indeed,—we applied to a Sakka for water, and entered a little coffee-house near the gate of the town, after which we rode home.

I have now described, I fear at a wearying length, the spots visited by every Zair at El Medinah. The guide-books mention altogether between fifty and fifty-five mosques and other holy places, most of which are now unknown even by name to the citizens.

Besides fourteen principal mosques, and which actually have a "local habitation," I find the names, and nothing but the names, of forty mosques. The reader loses little by my unwillingness to offer him a detailed list of such appel-

When Ali returned he found his wife dead, and complied with her last wishes. Omar bin Abd el Aziz believed this tradition, when he included the room in the mosque; and generally in El Islam Fatimah is supposed to be buried in the Haram.

* The other celebrities in El Bakia are, Fatimah bint Asad, mother of Ali. She was buried with great religious pomp. The Prophet shrouded her with his own garment (to prevent hell from touching her), dug her grave, lay down in it (that it might never squeeze or be narrow to her), assisted in carrying the bier, prayed over her, and proclaimed her certain of future felicity. Over her tomb was written, "The grave hath not closed upon one like Fatimah, daughter of Asad."

lations as Masjid Beni Abdel Ashhal, Masjid Beni Harisah, Masjid Beni Haram, Masjid el Fash, Masjid El Sukiya,

"Cum multis aliis quæ nunc perscribere longum est."

The Damascus caravan was to start on the 27th Zu'l Kaadah (1st September). I had intended to stay at El Medinah till the last moment, and to accompany the Kafilat el Tayyarah, or the "Flying Caravan," which usually leaves on the 2nd Zu'l Hijjah, two days after that of Damascus.

Suddenly arose the rumor that there would be no Tayyarah,* and that all pilgrims must proceed with the Damascus caravan, or await the Rakb or dromedary-caravan. The Sherif Zayd, Saad the Robber's only friend, had paid him an unsuccessful visit. Schinderhans demanded back his Shaykh-ship, in return for a safe-conduct through his country: "Otherwise," said he, "I will cut the throat of every hen that ventures into the passes."

The Sherif Zayd returned to El Medinah on the 25th Zu'l Kaadah (30th August). Early on the morning of the next day, Shaykh Hamid returned hurriedly from the bazaar, exclaiming, "You must make ready at once, Effendi! —there will be no Tayyarah—all Hajis start to-morrow— Allah will make it easy to you!—have you your waterskins in order?—you are to travel down the Darb El Sharki, where you will not see water for three days!"

Poor Hamid looked horror-struck as he concluded this fearful announcement, which filled me with joy. Burckhardt had visited and described the Darb El Sultani, the "High" or "Royal road" along the coast. But no European had as yet travelled down by Harun El Rashid's and

* The "Tayyarah," or "Flying Caravan," is lightly laden, and travels by forced marches.

the Lady Zubaydah's celebrated route through the Nejd Desert.

Not a moment, however, was to be lost: we expected to start early the next morning. The boy Mohammed went forth, and bought for eighty piastres a shugduf, which lasted us throughout the pilgrimage, and for fifteen piastres a shibriyah or cot to be occupied by Shaykh Nur, who did not relish sleeping on boxes. The youth was employed all day, with sleeves tucked up and working like a porter, in covering the litter with matting and rugs, in mending broken parts, and in providing it with large pockets for provisions inside and outside, with pouches to contain the gugglets of cooled water.

Meanwhile Shaykh Nur and I, having inspected the water-skins, found that the rats had made considerable rents in two of them. There being no workman procurable at this time for gold, I sat down to patch the damaged articles, whilst Nur was sent to lay in provisions for fourteen days.* By my companion's advice I took wheat-flour, rice, turmeric, onions, dates, unleavened bread of two kinds, cheese, limes, tobacco, sugar, tea and coffee.

Hamid himself started upon the most important part of our business. Faithful camel-men are required upon a road where robberies are frequent and stabbings occasional, and where there is no law to prevent desertion or to limit new and exorbitant demands. After a time he returned, accompanied by a boy and a Bedouin, a short, thin, well-built old man with regular features, a white beard, and a cool clear eye; his limbs, as usual, were scarred with wounds. Masud, of the Rahlah, a sub-family of the Hamidah family of the

* The journey is calculated at eleven days; but provisions are apt to spoil, and the Bedouin camel-men expect to be fed. Besides which, pilferers abound.

Beni Harb, came in with a dignified demeanor, applied his dexter palm to ours, sat down, declined a pipe, accepted coffee, and after drinking it, looked at us to show that he was ready for negotiation. We opened the proceedings with "We want men and not camels," and the conversation proceeded in the purest Hejazi. After much discussion we agreed, if compelled to travel by the Darb El Sharki, to pay twenty dollars for two camels, and to advance *arbun* or earnest-money to half that amount. The Shaykh bound himself to provide us with good animals, which moreover were to be changed in case of accidents; he was also to supply his beasts with water, and to accompany us to Arafat and back. But, absolutely refusing to carry my large box, he declared that the tent under the shugduf was burden enough for one camel, and that the small green case of drugs, the saddle-bags, and the provision-sacks surmounted by Nur's cot, were amply sufficient for the other. On our part we bound ourselves to feed the Shaykh and his son, supplying them either with raw or with cooked provender, and, upon our return to Meccah from Mount Arafat, to pay the remaining hire with a discretionary present.

Hamid then addressed to me flowery praises of the old Bedouin. After which, turning to the latter, he exclaimed, "Thou wilt treat these friends well, O Masud the Harbi!" The ancient replied with a dignity that had no pomposity in it,—"Even as Abu Shawarib—the Father of Mustachios*—behaveth to us, so will we behave to him!" He then arose, bade us be prepared when the departure-

* Most men of the Shafei school clip their mustachios exceedingly short; some clean shave the upper lip, the imperial, and the parts of the beard about the corners of the mouth, and the fore-part of the cheeks. I neglected so to do, which soon won for me the epithet recorded above.

gun sounded, saluted us, and stalked out of the room, followed by his son, who, under pretext of dozing, had mentally made an inventory of every article in the room, ourselves especially included.

When the Bedouins disappeared, Shaykh Hamid shook his head, advising me to give them plenty to eat, and never to allow twenty-four hours to elapse without dipping hand in the same dish with them, in order that the party might always be "málihín,"—on terms of salt. He concluded with a copious lecture upon the villany of Bedouins, and their habit of drinking travellers' water. I was to place the skins on a camel in front, and not behind; to hang the skins with their mouths carefully tied, and turned upwards, contrary to the general practice; always to keep a good store of liquid, and at night to place it under the safeguard of the tent.

In the afternoon, Omar Effendi and others dropped in to take leave. They found me in the midst of preparations, sewing sacks, fitting up a pipe, patching water-bags, and packing medicines. My fellow-traveller had brought me some pencils, and a pen-knife, as "forget-me-nots," for we were by no means sure of meeting again. He hinted, however, at another escape from the paternal abode, and proposed, if possible, to join the Dromedary-Caravan. Shaykh Hamid said the same, but I saw by the expression of his face, that his mother and wife would not give him leave from home so soon after his return.

Towards evening time the Barr el Munakhah became a scene of exceeding confusion. The town of tents lay upon the ground. Camels were being laden, and were roaring under the weight of litters, cots, boxes, and baggage. Horses and mules gallopped about. Men were rushing wildly in all directions on worldly errands, or hurrying to pay a farewell visit to the Prophet's Tomb. Women and children sat screaming on the ground, or ran about distracted, or called their vehicles to escape the danger of being crushed. Every now and then a random shot excited all into the belief that the departure-gun had sounded. At times we heard a volley from the robbers' hills, which elicited a general groan, for the pilgrims were still, to use their own phrase, "between fear and hope," and, consequently, still far from "one of the two comforts."* Then would sound the loud "Jhin-Jhin" of the camels' bells, as the stately animals paced away with some grandee's gilt and emblazoned litter, the sharp grunt of the dromedary, and the loud neighing of excited steeds.

About an hour after sunset all our preparations were concluded, save only the shugduf, at which the boy Mohammed still worked with untiring zeal; he wisely remembered that in it he had to spend the best portion of a week and a half. The evening was hot, we therefore dined outside the house. I was told to repair to the Haram for the "Farewell Visitation;" but my decided objection to this step was that we were all to part,—how soon!—and when to meet again we knew not. My companions smiled consent, assuring me that the ceremony could be performed as well at a distance as in the temple.

Then began the uncomfortable process of paying off little bills. The Eastern creditor always, for divers reasons, waits the last moment before he claims his debt. Shaykh Hamid had frequently hinted at his difficulties; the only means of escape from which, he said, was to rely upon Allah. He had treated me so hospitably, that I could not take back any part of the 5*l.* lent to him at Suez. His three

* The "two comforts" are success and despair; the latter, according to the Arabs, being a more enviable state of feeling than doubt or hope deferred.

brothers received a dollar or two each, and one or two of his cousins hinted to some effect that such a proceeding would meet with their approbation.

The luggage was then carried down, and disposed in packs upon the ground before the house, so as to be ready for loading at a moment's notice. Many flying parties of travellers had almost started on the high road, and late in the evening came a new report that the body of the caravan would march about midnight. We sat up till about 2 A. M., when, having heard no gun, and seen no camels, we lay down to sleep through the sultry remnant of the hours of darkness.

Thus, gentle reader, was spent my last night at El Medinah.

I had reason to congratulate myself upon having passed through the first danger. Meccah is so near the coast, that, in case of detection, the traveller might escape in a few hours to Jeddah, where he would find an English vice-consul, protection from the Turkish authorities, and possibly a British cruiser in the harbor. But at El Medinah discovery would entail more serious consequences. The next risk to run was the journey between the two cities, on which it would be easy for the local officials quietly to dispose of a suspected person by giving a dollar to a Bedouin.

## CHAPTER XXI.

### FROM EL MEDINAH TO EL SUWAYRKIYAH.

Four roads lead from El Medinah to Meccah. The "Darb El Sultani," or "Sultan's Way," follows the line of coast: this "General Passage" has been minutely described by my great predecessor. The "Tarik El Ghabir," a mountain path, is avoided by the Mahmal and the great caravans, on account of its rugged passes; water abounds along the whole line, but there is not a single village; and the Sobh Bedouins, who own the soil, are inveterate plunderers. The route called "Wady El Kura" is a favorite with dromedary-caravans; on this road are two or three small settlements, regular wells, and free passage through the Beni Amr tribe. The Darb El Sharki, or "Eastern road," down which I travelled, owes its existence to the piety of Zubaydah Khatun, wife of Harun el Rashid. That estimable princess dug wells from Baghdad to El Medinah, and built, we are told, a wall to direct pilgrims over the shifting sands. There is a fifth road, or rather mountain path, concerning which I can give no information.

At 8 A. M. on Wednesday, the 26th Zu'l Kaadah (31st August, 1853), as we were sitting at the window of Hamid's house after our early meal, suddenly appeared, in hottest haste, Masud, our Camel-Shaykh. He was accompanied by his son, a bold boy about fourteen years of age, who fought sturdily about the weight of each package as it was thrown over the camel's back; and his nephew, an ugly pock-marked lad, too lazy even to quarrel. We were ordered to lose no time in loading; all started into activity, and at 9 A.M. I found myself standing opposite the "Egyptian Gate," surrounded by my friends, who had accompanied me thus far on foot, to take leave with due honor. After affectionate embraces and parting mementoes, we mounted, the boy Mohammed and I in the shugduf, or litter, and Shaykh Nur in his shibriyah, or cot. Then, in company with some Turks and Meccans, for Masud owned a string of nine camels, we passed through the little gate near the castle, and shaped our course towards the north. On our right lay the palm-groves, which conceal this part of the city; far to the left rose the domes of Hamzah's Mosques at the foot of Mount Ohod; and in front a band of road crowded with motley groups, stretched over a barren stony plain.

After an hour's slow march, we fell into the Nejd road, and came to a place called El Ghadir, or the Basin. There we halted and turned to take a farewell of the Holy City. All the pilgrims dismounted and gazed at the venerable minarets and the Green Dome, spots upon which their memory would ever dwell with a fond and yearning interest.

Remounting at noon we crossed a fiumara which runs, according to my Camel-Shaykh, from N. to S.; we were therefore emerging from the Medinah basin. The sky began to be clouded, and although the air was still full of simoom, cold draughts occasionally poured down from the hills. Arabs fear this

"bitter change
Of fierce extremes, extremes by change more fierce,"

and call that a dangerous climate which is cold in the hot season and hot in the cold. Travelling over a rough and stony path, dotted with thorny acacias, we arrived about 2 P. M. at the bed of lava heard of by Burckhardt. The aspect of the country was volcanic, abounding in basalts and scoriæ, more or less porous. I made diligent enquiries about the existence of active volcanoes in this part of El Hejaz, and heard of none.

At 5 P. M., travelling towards the East, we entered a pass, which follows the course of a wide fiumara, walled in by steep and barren hills—the portals of a region too wild even for Bedouins. The torrent-bed narrowed where the turns were abrupt, and the drift of heavy stones, with a water-mark from 6 to 7 feet high, showed that after rains a violent stream runs from E. and S.E. to W. and N.W. The fertilising fluid is close to the surface, evidenced by a spare growth of acacia, camel-grass, and at some angles of the bed by the Daum, or Theban palm.* I remarked what are technically called "Hufrah," holes dug for water in the sand; and my guide assured me that somewhere near there is a spring flowing from the rocks.

After the long and sultry afternoon, beasts of burden began to sink in considerable numbers. The fresh carcasses of asses, ponies, and camels dotted the way-side: those that had been allowed to die were abandoned to the foul carrion-birds, the Rakham (vulture), and the yellow Ukab; and all whose throats had been properly cut were surrounded by troops of Takruri pilgrims. These half-starved wretches cut steaks from the choice portions, and slung them over their shoulders till an opportunity for cooking might arrive. I never saw men more destitute. They carried wooden

* This is the palm, capped with large fan-shaped leaves, described by every traveller in Egypt and the nearer East.

bowls, which they filled with water by begging; their only weapon was a small knife, tied in a leathern sheath above the elbow; and their costume an old skull-cap, strips of leather tied like sandals under the feet, and a long dirty shirt, or sometimes a mere rag covering the loins. Some were perfect savages, others had been fine-looking men, broad-shouldered and long-limbed; many were lamed by fatigue and thorns; and looking at most of them, I saw death depicted in their forms and features.

After two hours' slow marching up the fiumara eastwards, we saw in front of us a wall of rock, and turning abruptly southwards, we left the bed, and ascended rising ground. Already it was night; an hour, however, elapsed before we saw, at a distance, the twinkling fires, and heard the watch-cries of our camp. It was pitched in a hollow, under hills, in excellent order, the Pacha's pavilion surrounded by his soldiers and guards disposed in tents, with sentinels, regularly posted, protecting the outskirts of the encampment. One of our men, whom we had sent forward, met us on the way, and led us to an open place, where we unloaded the camels, raised our canvas home, lighted fires, and prepared, with supper, for a good night's rest. Living is simple on such marches. The pouches inside and outside the shugduf contain provisions and water, with which you supply yourself when inclined. At certain hours of the day, ambulant vendors offer sherbet, lemonade, hot coffee, and water-pipes admirably prepared.* Chibouques may be smoked in the litter; but few care to do so during the simoom. The first thing, however, called for at the halt-

* The charge for a cup of coffee is one piastre and a half. A pipe-bearer will engage himself for about 1*l.* per mensem; he is always a veteran smoker, and in these regions, it is an axiom that the flavor of your pipe mainly depends on the filler.

ing-place is the pipe, and its delightful soothing influence, followed by a cup of coffee, and a "forty winks" upon the sand, will awaken an appetite not to be roused by other means. How could Waterton, the traveller, abuse the pipe? During the night halt, provisions are cooked: rice, or kichri, a mixture of pulse and rice, are eaten with Chutnee and lime-pickle, varied, occasionally, by tough mutton and indigestible goat.

We arrived at Ja El Sherifah at 8 P. M. after a march of about twenty-two miles.* This halting-place is the rendezvous of caravans: it lies 50° S.E. of El Medinah, and belongs rather to Nejd than to El Hejaz.

At 3 A. M., on Thursday, we started up at the sound of the departure-gun, struck the tent, loaded the camels, mounted, and found ourselves hurrying through a gloomy pass, in the hills, to secure a good place in the caravan. This is an object of some importance, as, during the whole journey, marching order must not be broken. We met with a host of minor accidents, camels falling, shugdufs bumping against one another, and plentiful abuse. Pertinaciously we hurried on till 6 A. M., at which hour we emerged from the black pass. The large crimson sun rose upon us, disclosing, through purple mists, a hollow of coarse yellow gravel, based upon a hard whitish clay. Entering it, we dismounted, prayed, broke our fast, and after half an hour's halt proceeded to cross its breadth. The appearance of the caravan was most striking, as it threaded its

* A day's journey in Arabia is generally reckoned at twenty-four or twenty-five Arab miles. Abulfeda leaves the distance of a Marhalah (or Manzil, a station) undetermined. El Idrisi reckons it at thirty miles, but speaks of short as well as long marches.

The only ideas of distance known to the Bedouin of El Hejaz are the fanciful Saat or hour, and the uncertain Manzil or halt; the former varies from 2 to 3½ miles, the latter from 15 to 25 miles.

slow way over the smooth surface of the low plain. To judge by the eye, there were at least 7,000 souls, on foot, on horseback, in litters, or bestriding the splendid camels of Syria. There were eight gradations of pilgrims. The lowest hobbled with heavy staves. Then came the riders of asses, camels, and mules. Respectable men, especially Arabs, mounted dromedaries, and the soldiers had horses: a led animal was saddled for every grandee, ready whenever he might wish to leave his litter. Women, children, and invalids of the poorer classes sat upon a "haml musattah,"—bits of cloth spread over two large boxes which formed the camel's load. Many occupied shibriyahs, a few, shugdufs, and only the wealthy and the noble rode in Takhtrawan (litters), carried by camels or mules.* The morning beams fell brightly upon the glancing arms which surrounded the stripped Mahmal,† and upon the scarlet and gilt litters of the grandees. Not the least beauty of the spectacle was its wondrous variety of detail: no man was dressed like his neighbor, no camel was caparisoned, nor horse clothed in uniform, as it were. And nothing stranger than the contrast;—a band of half-naked Takruri marching with the Pacha's equipage, and long-capped, bearded Persians conversing with Tarbushed and shaven Turks.

* The vehicle mainly regulates the expense, as it evidences a man's means. I have heard of a husband and wife leaving Alexandria with three months' provision and the sum of 5*l*. They would mount a camel, lodge in public buildings, when possible, probably be reduced to beggary, and possibly starve on the road. On the other hand the minimum expenditure,—for necessaries, not donations and luxuries,—of a man who rides in a Takhtrawan from Damascus and back, would be about 1200*l*.

† On the line of march the Mahmal, stripped of its embroidered cover, is carried on camel-back, a mere framewood. Even the gilt silver balls and crescent are exchanged for similar articles in brass.

The plain even at an early hour reeked with vapors distilled by the fires of the simoom: about noon, however, the air became cloudy, and nothing of color remained, save that white haze, dull, but glaring withal, which is the prevailing day-tint in these regions. At mid-day we reached a narrowing of the basin, where, from both sides, "Irk," or low hills, stretch their last spurs into the plain. But after half a mile, it again widened to upwards of two miles. At 2 P. M. we turned towards the S.W., ascended stony ground, and found ourselves one hour afterwards in a desolate rocky flat, distant about twenty-four miles of unusually winding road from our last station.

After pitching the tent, we prepared to recruit our supply of water; for Masud warned me that his camels had not drunk for ninety hours, and that they would soon sink under the privation. The boy Mohammed, mounting a dromedary, set off with the Shaykh and many water-bags, giving me an opportunity of writing out my journal. They did not return home till after nightfall, a delay caused by many adventures. The wells are in a fiumara, as usual, about two miles distant from the halting-place, and the soldiers, regular as well as irregular, occupied the water and exacted hard coin in exchange for it. The men are not to blame; they would die of starvation, but for this resource. The boy Mohammed had been engaged in several quarrels; but after snapping his pistol at a Persian pilgrim's head, he came forth triumphant with two skins of sweetish water, for which we paid ten piastres. He was in his glory. There were many Meccans in the caravan, among them his elder brother and several friends; the Sherif Zayd had sent, he said, to ask why he did not travel with his compatriots. That evening he drank so copiously of clarified butter, and ate dates mashed with flour and other abominations to such an extent, that at night he prepared to give up the ghost. We passed a pleasant hour or two before sleeping. I began to like the old Shaykh Masud, who, seeing it, entertained me with his genealogy, his battles, and his family affairs. The rest of the party could not prevent expressing contempt when they heard me putting frequent questions about torrents, hills, Bedouins, and the directions of places. "Let the Father of Mustachios ask and learn," said the old man; "he is friendly with the Bedouins, and knows better than you all." This reproof was intended to be bitter as the poet's satire,—

> "All fools have still an itching to deride,
> And fain would be upon the laughing side."

It called forth, however, another burst of merriment, for the jeerers remembered my nickname to have belonged to that pestilent heretic, Saud the Wahhabi.

On Saturday, the 3rd September, that hateful signal-gun awoke us at 1 A. M. In Arab travel there is nothing more disagreeable than the Sariyah or night-march, and yet the people are inexorable about it. "Choose early darkness (Daljah) for your wayfarings," said the Prophet, "as the calamities of the earth—serpents and wild beasts—appear not at night." I can scarcely find words to express the weary horrors of a long night's march, during which the hapless traveller, fuming, if a European, with disappointment in his hopes of "seeing the country," is compelled to sit upon the back of a creeping camel. The day sleep too is a kind of lethargy, and it is all but impossible to preserve an appetite during the hours of heat.

At half-past 5 A. M., after drowsily stumbling through hours of outer darkness, we entered a spacious basin at least six miles broad, and limited by a circlet of low hill. It was overgrown with camel-grass and acacia trees—mere vegetable mummies;—in many places the water had left a mark;

and here and there the ground was pitted with mud-flakes, the remains of recently dried pools. After an hour's rapid march we toiled over a rugged ridge, composed of broken and detached blocks of basalt and scoriæ, fantastically piled together, and dotted with thorny trees. It was wonderful to see the camels stepping from block to block with the sagacity of mountaineers; assuring themselves of their fore-feet before trusting all their weight to advance. Not a camel fell, either here or on any other ridge: they moaned, however, piteously, for the sudden turns of the path puzzled them; the ascents were painful, the descents were still more so; the rocks were sharp, deep holes yawned between the blocks, and occasionally an acacia caught the shugduf, almost overthrowing the hapless bearer by the suddenness and the tenacity of its clutch.

Descending the ridge, we entered another hill-encircled basin of gravel and clay. In many places basalt in piles and crumbling strata of hornblende schiste, disposed edgeways, green within, and without blackened by sun and rain, cropped out of the ground. At half-past ten we found ourselves in an "acacia-barren," one of the things which pilgrims dread. Here shugdufs are bodily pulled off the camel's back and broken upon the hard ground; the animals drop upon their knees, the whole line is deranged, and every one, losing his temper, attacks his Moslem Brother. The road was flanked on the left by an iron wall of black basalt. Noon brought us to another ridge, whence we descended into a second wooden basin surrounded by hills.

Here the air was filled with those pillars of sand so graphically described by Abyssinian Bruce. They scudded on the wings of the whirlwind over the plain—huge yellow shafts, with lofty heads, horizontally bent backwards, in the form of clouds; and on more than one occasion camels were overthrown by them. It required little stretch of fancy to enter into the Arab's superstition. These sand-columns are supposed to be genii of the waste, which cannot be caught—a notion arising from the fitful movements of the wind-eddy that raises them—and, as they advance, the pious Moslem stretches out his finger, exclaiming, "Iron! O thou ill-omened one!"

During the forenoon we were troubled with simoom, which, instead of promoting perspiration, chokes up and hardens the skin. The Arabs complain greatly of its violence on this line of road. Here I first remarked the difficulty with which the Bedouins bear thirst. Ya Latif—O! Merciful Lord—they exclaimed at times, and yet they behaved like men.* I had ordered them to place the water-camel in front, so as to exercise due supervision. Shaykh Masud and his son made only an occasional reference to the skins. But his nephew, a short, thin, pock-marked lad of eighteen, whose black skin and woolly head suggested the idea of a semi-African and ignoble origin, was always drinking; except when he climbed the camel's back, and, dozing upon the damp load, forgot his thirst. In vain we ordered, we taunted, and we abused him: he would drink, he would sleep, but he would not work.

* The Eastern Arabs allay the torments of thirst by a spoonful of clarified butter, carried on journeys in a leathern bottle. Every European traveller has some recipe of his own. One chews a musket-bullet or a small stone. A second smears his legs with butter. Another eats a crust of dry bread, which exacerbates the torments, and afterwards brings relief. A fourth throws water over his face and hands or his legs and feet; a fifth smokes, and a sixth turns his dorsal region (raising his coat-tail) to the fire. I have always found that the only remedy is to be patient and not to talk. The more you drink, the more you require to drink—water or strong waters. But after the first two hours' abstinence you have mastered the overpowering feeling of thirst, and then to refrain is easy.

Early in the afternoon we reached a diminutive flat, on a fiumara bank. Beyond it lies a Mahjar or stony ground, black as usual in El Hejaz, and over its length lay the road, white with dust and the sand deposited by the camels' feet. Having arrived before the Pacha, we did not know where to pitch; many opining that the caravan would traverse the Mahjar and halt beyond it. We soon alighted, however, pitched the tent under a burning sun, and were imitated by the rest of the party.

We loitered on Sunday, the 4th September, at El Hijriyah, although the Shaykh forewarned us of a long march. But there is a kind of discipline in these great caravans. A gun sounds the order to strike the tents, and a second bids you march off with all speed. There are short halts of half an hour each at dawn, noon, the afternoon, and sunset, for devotional purposes, and these are regulated by a cannon or a culverin. At such times the Syrian and Persian servants, who are admirably expert in their calling, pitch the large green tents, with gilt crescents, for the dignitaries and their hareems. The last resting-place is known by the hurrying forward of these "Farrash,"* who are determined to be the first on the ground and at the well. A discharge of three guns denotes the station, and when the caravan moves by night, a single cannon sounds three or four halts at irregular intervals.

Leaving our camp at seven A.M., we passed over the grim stone-field by a detestable footpath, and at nine o'clock struck into a broad fiumara, which runs from the east towards the north-west. Up this line we travelled the whole day. About six P.M., we came upon a basin at least twelve miles broad, which absorbs the water of the adjacent hills. Accustomed as I have been to mirage, a long thin

* Tent-pitchers, &c.

line of salt efflorescence appearing at some distance on the plain below us, when the shades of evening invested the view, completely deceived me. Even the Arabs were divided in opinion, some thinking it was the effects of the rain which fell the day before: others were more acute.* Upon the horizon beyond the plain rose dark, fort-like masses of rock which I mistook for buildings, the more readily as the Shaykh had warned me that we were approaching a populous place. At last descending a long steep hill, we entered upon the level ground, and discovered our error by the crunching sound of the camels' feet upon large curling flakes of nitrous salt overlying caked mud. Those civilised birds, the kite and the crow, warned us that we were in the vicinity of man. It was not, however, before eleven P.M., that we entered the confines of El Suwayrkiyah. The fact was made patent to us by the stumbling and the falling of our dromedaries over the little ridges of dried clay disposed in squares upon the fields. There were other obstacles, such as garden walls, wells, and hovels, so that midnight had sped before our weary camels reached the resting-place. A rumor that we were to halt here the next day, made us think lightly of present troubles; it proved, however, to be false.

During the last four days I attentively observed the general face of the country. This line is a succession of low plains and basins, here quasi-circular, there irregularly oblong, surrounded by rolling hills and cut by fiumaras which passed through the higher ground. The basins are divided by ridges and flats of basalt and greenstone ave-

* It is said that beasts are never deceived by the mirage, and this, as far as my experience goes, is correct. May not the reason be that most of them know the vicinity of water rather by smell than by sight?

raging from 100 to 200 feet in height. The general form is a huge prism; sometimes there is a table on the top. From El Medinah to El Suwayrkiyah the low beds of sandy fiumaras abound. Water obtained by digging is good where rain is fresh in the fiumaras; saltish, so as to taste at first unnaturally sweet, in the plains, and bitter in the basins and lowlands where nitre effloresces and rain has had time to become tainted. The landward faces of the hills are disposed at a sloping angle, contrasting strongly with the perpendicularity of their seaward sides, and I saw no inner range corresponding with, and parallel to, the maritime chain. Nowhere is there a land in which Earth's anatomy lies so barren, or one richer in volcanic and primary formations. Especially towards the south, the hills are abrupt and highly vertical, with black and barren flanks, ribbed with furrows and fissures, with wide and formidable precipices and castellated summits like the work of man. The predominant formation was basalt, called by the Arabs Hell-stone; here and there it is porous and cellular; in some places compact and black; and in others coarse and gritty, of a tarry color, and when fractured, shining with bright points. Hornblende abounds at El Medinah and throughout this part of El Hejaz: it crops out of the ground edgeways, black and brittle. Greenstone, diorite, and actinolite are found, though not so abundantly as those above mentioned. The granites, called in Arabic Suwan,* abound. Some are large grained, of a pink color, and appear in blocks, which, flaking off under the influence of the atmosphere, form into oöidal blocks and

* The Arabic language has a copious terminology for the mineral as well as the botanical productions of the country: with little alteration it might be made to express all the requirements of our modern geology.

boulders piled in irregular heaps. Others are grey and compact enough to take a high polish when cut. The syenite is generally coarse, although there is occasionally found a rich red variety of that stone. I have never seen Eurite or Euritic porphyry except in small pieces, and the same may be said of the petrosilex and the milky quartz. In some parts, particularly between Yambu and El Medinah, there is an abundance of tawny yellow gneiss markedly stratified. The transition formations are represented by a fine calcareous sandstone of a bright ochre color; it is used at Meccah to adorn the exteriors of houses, bands of this stone being here and there inserted into the courses of masonry. There is also a small admixture of the greenish sandstone which abounds at Aden. The secondary formation is represented by a fine limestone, in some places almost fit for the purposes of lithography, and a coarse gypsum often of a tufaceous nature. The maritime towns are mostly built of coralline. For the superficial accumulations of the country, I may refer the reader to any description of the Desert between Cairo and Suez.

## CHAPTER XXII.

### THE BEDOUINS OF EL HEJAZ.

I WILL not apologize for entering into details concerning the *personale* of the Bedouins: a precise physical portrait of race, it has justly been remarked, is the sole deficiency in the otherwise perfect pages of Bruce and Burckhardt.

The temperament of the Hejazi is not unfrequently the pure nervous, as the height of the forehead and the fine texture of the hair prove. Sometimes the bilious, and rarely the sanguine, elements predominate: the lymphatic I never saw. He has large nervous centres, and well formed spine and brain, a conformation favorable to longevity. Bartema well describes his color as a "dark leonine:" it varies from the deepest Spanish to a chocolate hue, and its varieties are attributed by the people to blood. The skin is hard, dry, and soon wrinkled by exposure. The xanthous complexion is rare, though not unknown in cities, but the leucous does not exist. The crinal hair is frequently lightened by bleaching, and the pilar is generally browner than the crinal. The voice is strong and clear, but rather barytone than bass: in anger it becomes a shrill chattering like the cry of a wild animal. The look of a chief is dignified and grave, even to pensiveness; the "respectable man's" is self-sufficient and fierce; the lower orders look ferocious or stupid and inquisitive. Yet there is not much difference in this point between men of the same tribe, who have similar pursuits which engender similar passions. "Expression" is the grand diversifier of appearance among civilized people: in the desert it knows few varieties.

The Bedouin cranium is small, oöidal, long, high, narrow, and remarkable in the occiput for the development of Gall's second propensity: the crown slopes upwards towards the region of firmness, which is elevated; whilst the sides are flat to a fault. The hair, exposed to sun, wind, and rain, acquires a coarseness not natural to it: worn in ragged elf-locks, hanging down to the breast, or shaved in the form "Shushah," nothing can be wilder than its appearance. The face is made to be a long oval, but want of flesh detracts from its regularity. The forehead is high, broad, and retreating: the upper portion is moderately developed; but nothing can be finer than the lower brow, and the frontal sinuses stand out, indicating bodily strength and activity of character. The eyebrows are long, bushy, and crooked, broken, as it were, at the angle where "order" is supposed to be, and bent in sign of thoughtfulness. Most popular writers, following De Page, describe the Arab eye as large, ardent, and black. The Bedouin of the Hejaz, and indeed the race generally, has a small eye, round, restless, deep-set and fiery, denoting keen inspection with an ardent temperament and an impassioned character. Its color is dark brown or green brown, and the pupil is often speckled. The habit of pursing up the skin below the orbits and half closing the lids to prevent dazzle, plants the outer angles with premature crow's feet. Another peculiarity is the sudden way in which the eye opens, especially under excitement. This, combined with its fixity of gaze, forms an expression now of lively fierceness, then of exceeding sternness; whilst the narrow space between the orbits impresses the countenance in repose with an intelligence not destitute of cunning. As a general rule, however, the expression of the Bedouin's face is rather dignity than that of cunning, for which the Semitic race is celebrated, and there are lines about the mouth in variance with the stern or the fierce look of the brow. The ears are like those of Arab horses, small, well-cut, "castey" and elaborate, with many elevations and depressions. His nose is pronounced, generally aquiline, but sometimes straight like those Greek statues which have been treated as prodigious exaggerations of the facial angle. For the most part, it is a well-made feature with delicate nostrils below which the septum appears: in anger they swell and open like a perfectly bred mare's. I have, however, seen, in not a few instances, pert and offensive "pugs." Deep furrows descend from the wings of the nose, showing an uncertain temper, now too grave, then too gay. The mouth is irregular. The lips are either *bordés*, denoting rudeness and want of taste, or they form a mere line. In the latter case there is an appearance of undue development in the upper portion of the countenance, especially when the jaws are ascetically thin, and the chin weakly retreats. The latter feature, however, is generally well and strongly made. The teeth, as usual among Orientals, are white, even, short, and broad—indications of strength. Some tribes trim their moustachios according to the "Sunnat;" the Shafei often shave them, and many allow them to hang Persian-like over the lips. The beard is represented by two tangled tufts upon the chin; where whisker should be, the place is either bare or thinly covered with straggling pile.

The Bedouins of El Hejaz are short men, about the

height of the Indians near Bombay, but weighing on an average a stone more. As usual in this stage of society, stature varies little; you rarely see a giant, and scarcely ever a dwarf. Deformity is checked by the Spartan restraint upon population, and no weakly infant can live through a Bedouin life. The figure, though spare, is square and well knit, fulness of limb never appears but about spring when milk abounds: I have seen two or three muscular figures, but never a fat man. The neck is sinewy, the chest broad, the flank thin, and the stomach in-drawn; the legs, though fleshless, are well-made, especially when the knee and ankle are not bowed by too early riding. The shins seldom bend to the front as in the African race. The arms are thin, with muscles like whip-cords, and the hands and feet are, in point of size and delicacy, a link between Europe and India. As in the Celt, the Arab thumb is remarkably long, extending almost to the first joint of the index, which, with its easy rotation, makes it a perfect prehensile instrument: the palm also is fleshless, small-boned, and elastic. With his small active figure it is not strange that the wildest Bedouin's gait should be pleasing; he neither unfits himself for walking, nor distorts his ankles by turning out his toes according to the farcical rule of fashion, and his shoulders are not dressed like a drill sergeant's, to throw all the weight of the body upon the heels. Yet there is no slouch in his walk; it is light and springy, and errs only in one point, sometimes becoming a kind of strut.

Such is the Bedouin, and such he has been for ages. The national type has been preserved by systematic intermarriage. The wild men do not refuse their daughters to a stranger, but the son-in-law would be forced to settle among them, and this life, which has charms for a while, ends in becoming wearisome. Here no evil results are anticipated from the union of first cousins, and the experience of ages and of a nation may be trusted. Every Bedouin has a right to marry his father's brother's daughter before she is given to a stranger; hence "cousin" in polite phrase signifies a "wife." Our physiologists* adduce the Sangre Azul of Spain and the case of the lower animals to prove that degeneracy inevitably follows "breeding-in."† Either they have theorised from insufficient facts, or civilisation and artificial living exercise some peculiar influence, or Arabia is a solitary exception to a general rule. The fact which I have mentioned is patent to every Eastern traveller.

After this weary description, the reader will perceive with pleasure that we are approaching an interesting theme, the first question of mankind to the wanderer—"What are the women like?" Truth compels me to state that the women of the Hejazi Bedouins are by no means comely. Although the Beni Amur boast of some pretty girls, yet they are far inferior to the high-bosomed beauties of Nejd. The Hejazi woman's eyes are fierce, her features harsh, and her face haggard; like all people of the South, she soon fades, and in old age her appearance is truly witch-like. Withered crones abound in the camps, where old men are seldom seen.

The manners of the Bedouins are free and simple: "vulgarity" and affectation, awkwardness and embarrass-

* Dr. Howe (Report on Idiotcy in Massachusetts, 1848,) asserts that "the law against the marriage of relations is made out as clearly as though it were written on tables of stone." He proceeds to show that in seventeen households where the parents were connected by blood, of ninety-five children one was a dwarf, one deaf, twelve scrofulous, and forty-four idiots—total fifty-eight diseased!

† Yet the celebrated "Flying Childers" and all his race were remarkably bred in. There is still, in my humble opinion, much mystery about the subject, to be cleared up only by the studies of physiologists.

ment, are weeds of civilised growth, unknown to the people of the desert. Yet their manners are sometimes dashed with a strange ceremoniousness. When two friends meet, they either embrace, or both extend their right hands, clapping palm to palm; their foreheads are either pressed together, or their heads moved from side to side, whilst for minutes together mutual inquiries are made and answered. It is a breach of decorum, even when eating, to turn the back upon a person, and when a Bedouin does it he intends an insult. When a friend approaches the camp—it is not done to strangers for fear of startling them—those who catch sight of him shout out his name, and gallop up saluting with lances or firing matchlocks in the air. This is the well-known gunpowder play. As a general rule the Bedouins are polite in language, but in anger temper is soon shown, and although life may not be in peril, the foulest epithets, dog, drunkard, liar and infidel, are discharged like pistol shots by both parties.

The best character of the Bedouin is a truly noble compound of determination, gentleness, and generosity. Usually they are a mixture of worldly cunning and great simplicity, sensitive to touchiness, good-tempered souls, solemn and dignified withal, fond of a jest yet of a grave turn of mind, easily managed by a laugh and a soft word, and placable after passion, though madly revengeful after injury. The reader will inquire, like the critics of a certain modern humorist, how the fabric of society can be supported by such material. In the first place, it is a kind of "*société léonine*," in which the fiercest, the strongest, the craftiest obtains complete mastery over his fellows, and this gives a key-stone to the arch. Secondly, there is the terrible blood-feud, which even the most reckless fear for their posterity. And, thirdly, though the revealed law of the Koran, being insufficient for the desert, is openly disregarded, the immemorial customs of the "Kazi el Arab"* form a system stringent in the extreme.

The valor of the Bedouin is fitful and uncertain, and his ideas of bravery do not prepossess us. His romances, full of foolhardy feats and impossible exploits, might charm for a time, but would not become the standard works of a really fighting people. Nor would a truly valorous race admire the timid freebooters who safely fire down upon caravans from their eyries. Arab wars, too, are a succession of skirmishes, in which 500 men will retreat after losing a dozen of their number. In this partisan fighting the first charge secures a victory, and the vanquished fly till covered by the shades of night. Then come cries of women, deep oaths, wild poetry, excitement, and reprisals, which will probably end in the flight of the former victor. When peace is to be made, both parties count up their dead, and the usual blood-money is paid for excess on either side. Generally, however, the feud endures till all becoming weary of it, some great man, as the sherif of Meccah, is called upon to settle the terms of a treaty, which is nothing but an armistice. After a few months' peace, a glance or a word will draw blood, for these hates are old things, and new dissensions easily shoot up from them.

But, contemptible though their battles be, the Bedouins are not cowards. The habit of danger in raids and blood-feuds, the continual uncertainty of existence, the desert, the chase, the hard life and exposure to the air, blunting the nervous system; the presence and the practice of weapons of horsemanship, sharpshooting, and martial exercises, habituate them to look death in the face like men,

* The "Kazi el Arab" (Judge of the Arabs) was in distinction to the Kazi el Shara, or the Kazi of the Koran. The former was, almost always, some sharp-witted greybeard, with a minute knowledge of genealogy and precedents, a retentive memory and an eloquent tongue.

and powerful motives will make them heroes. The English, it is said, fight willingly for liberty, our neighbors for glory; the Spaniard fights, or rather fought, for religion and the "Pundonor," and the Irishman fights for the fun of fighting. Gain and revenge draw the Arab's sword: yet then he uses it fitfully enough, without the gay gallantry of the French or the persistency of the Anglo-Saxon. To become desperate he must have the all powerful stimulants of honor and fanaticism. Frenzied by the taunts of his women, or by the fear of being branded as a coward, he is capable of any mad deed. And the obstinacy produced by strong religious impressions gives a steadfastness to his spirit unknown to mere enthusiasm.

There are two things which tend to soften the ferocity of Bedouin life. These are, in the first place, intercourse with citizens, who frequently visit and entrust their children to the people of the Black tents; and, secondly, the social position of the women.

The author of certain "Lectures on Poetry, addressed to Working Men," asserts that Passion became Love under the influence of Christianity, and that the idea of a virgin mother spread over the sex a sanctity unknown to the poetry or the philosophy of Greece and Rome. Passing over the objections of deified Eros and Immortal Psyche and of the virgin mother,—symbol of moral purity,—being common to all old and material faiths, I believe that all the noble tribes of savages display the principle. Thus we might expect to find wherever the fancy, the imagination, and the ideality are strong, some traces of a sentiment innate in the human organization. It exists, says Mr. Catlin, amongst the North American Indians, and even the Gallas and the Somal of Africa are not wholly destitute of it. But when the barbarian becomes a semi-barbarian, as are the most polished Orientals, or as were the classical authors of Greece and Rome, then women fall from their proper place in society, become mere articles of luxury, and sink into the lowest moral condition.* In the next stage, "civilization," they rise again to be "highly accomplished," and not a little frivolous.

Were it not evident that the spiritualising of sexuality by imagination is universal among the highest orders of

* Miss Martineau, when travelling through Egypt, once visited a Harem, and there found, among many things, especially in their ignorance of books and book-making, materials for a heart-broken wail over the degradation of her sex. The learned lady indulges, too, in sundry strong and unsavory comparisons between the harem and certain haunts of vice in Europe.

On the other hand, male travellers generally speak lovingly of the harem. Sonnini, no admirer of Egypt, expatiates on "the generous virtues, the examples of magnanimity and affectionate attachment, the sentiments ardent, yet gentle, forming a delightful unison with personal charms in the harems of the Mamelukes."

As usual, the truth lies somewhere between the two extremes. Human nature, all the world over, differs but in degree. Everywhere women may be "capricious, coy, and hard to please" in common conjunctures: in the hour of need they will display devoted heroism. Any chronicler of the Afghan war will bear witness that warm hearts, noble sentiments, and an overflowing kindness to the poor, the weak, and the unhappy, are found even in a harem. Europe now knows that the Moslem husband provides separate apartments and a distinct establishment for each of his wives, unless, as sometimes happens, one be an old woman and the other a child. And, confessing that envy, hatred, and malice often flourish in polygamy, the Moslem asks, Is monogamy open to no objections? As far as my limited observations go, polyandry is the only state of society in which jealousy and quarrels about the sex are the exception and not the rule of life.

In quality of doctor I have seen a little and heard much of the harem. It very much resembles a European home composed of a man, his wife, and his mother. And I have seen in the West many a "happy fire-side" fitter to make Miss Martineau's heart ache than any harem in Grand Cairo.

mankind, I should attribute the origin of love to the influence of the Arabs' poetry and chivalry upon European ideas rather than to mediæval Christianity.

In pastoral life, tribes often meet for a time, live together whilst pasturage lasts, and then separate perhaps for a generation. Under such circumstance youths will lose heart to maidens, whom possibly, by the laws of the clan, they may not marry,* and the light o' love will fly her home. The fugitives must brave every danger, for revenge, at all times the Bedouin's idol, now becomes the lode-star of his existence. But the Arab lover will dare all consequences. "Men have died and the worms have eaten them, but not for love," may be true in the West; it is false in the East. This is attested in every tale where love, and not ambition, is the groundwork of the narrative.† And nothing can be more tender, more pathetic than the use made of these separations and long absences by the old Arab poets. Whoever peruses the Suspended Poem of Lebid, will find thoughts at once so plaintive and so noble, that even Dr. Carlyle's learned verse cannot wholly deface their charm. The author returns from afar. He looks upon the traces of hearth and home still furrowing the desert ground. In bitterness of spirit

* There is no objection to intermarriage between equal clans, but the higher will not give their daughters to the lower in dignity.

† For instance: "A certain religious man was so deeply affected with the love of a king's daughter, that he was brought to the brink of the grave," is a favorite inscriptive formula. Usually the hero "sickens in consequence of the heroine's absence, and continues to the hour of his death in the utmost grief and anxiety." He rarely kills himself, but sometimes, when in love with a pretty infidel, he drinks wine and he burns the Koran. The "hated rival" is not a formidable person; but there are for good reasons great jealousy of female friends, and not a little fear of the beloved's kinsmen. Such are the material sentiments; the spiritual part is a thread of mysticism, upon which all the pearls of adventure and accident are strung.

he checks himself from calling aloud upon his lovers and his friends. He melts at the remembrance of their departure, and long indulges in the absorbing theme. Then he strengthens himself by the thought of Nawara's inconstancy, how she left him and never thought of him again. He impatiently dwells upon the charms of the places which detain her, advocates flight from the changing lover and the false friend, and, in the exultation with which he feels his swift dromedary start under him upon her rapid course, he seems to find some consolation for woman's perfidy and forgetfulness. Yet he cannot abandon Nawara's name or memory. Again he dwells with yearning upon scenes of past felicity, and he boasts of his prowess—a fresh reproach to her—of his gentle birth, and of his hospitality. He ends with an encomium upon his clan, to which he attributes, as a noble Arab should, all the virtues of man. This is Goldsmith's deserted village in El Hejaz. But the Arab, with equal simplicity and pathos, has a fire, a force of language, and a depth of feeling, which the Irishman, admirable as his verse is, could never rival.

In the early days of El Islam, if history be credible, Arabia had a race of heroines. Within the last century, Ghaliyah, the wife of a Wahhabi chief, opposed Mohammed Ali himself in many a bloody field. A few years ago, when Ibn Asm, popularly called Ibn Rumi, chief of the Zabayd clan about Rabigh, was treacherously slain by the Turkish general, Kurdi Usman, his sister, a fair young girl, determined to revenge him. She fixed upon the "Arafat-day" of pilgrimage for the accomplishment of her designs, disguised herself in male attire, drew her kerchief in the form "lisam" over the lower part of her face, and with lighted match awaited her enemy. The Turk, however, was not present, and the girl was arrested to win for herself a local reputation equal to the maid of Salamanca. Thus it is that the Arab has learned to swear that great oath "by the honor of my women."

The Bedouins are not without a certain Platonic affection, which they call "Hawa uzri,"—pardonable love. They draw the fine line between *amant* and *amoureux:* this is derided by the townspeople, little suspecting how much such a custom says in favor of the wild men. In the cities, however, it could not prevail. Arabs, like other Orientals, hold that, in such matters, man is saved, not by faith, but by want of faith. They have also a saying, not unlike ours—

> "She partly is to blame who has been tried,
> He comes too near who comes to be denied."

The evil of this system is that they, like certain southerns, *pensano sempre al male*—always suspect, which may be worldly wise, and also always show their suspicions, which is assuredly foolish. For thus they demoralize their women, who might be kept in the way of right by self-respect and a sense of duty.

From ancient periods of the Arab's history we find him practising "knight-errantry," the wildest form of chivalry. "The Songs of Antar," says the author of the "Crescent and the Cross," "show little of the true chivalric spirit." What thinks the reader of sentiments like these? "This valiant man," remarks Antar (who was "ever interested for the weaker sex"), "hath defended the honor of women." We read in another place, "Mercy, my lord, is the noblest qnality of the noble." Again, "It is the most ignominious of deeds to take free-born women prisoners." "Bear not malice, O Shibub," quoth the hero, "for of malice good never came." Is there no true greatness in this sentiment? —"Birth is the boast of the *fainéant;* noble is the youth who beareth every ill, who clotheth himself in mail during the noon-tide heat, and who wandereth through the outer darkness of night." And why does the "knight of knights" love Ibla? Because "she is blooming as the sun at dawn, with hair black as the midnight shades, with Paradise in her eye, her bosom an enchantment, and a form waving like the tamarisk when the soft wind blows from the hills of Nejd?" Yes, but his chest expands also with the thoughts of her "faith, purity, and affection,"—it is her moral as well as her material excellence that makes her the hero's "hope, and hearing, and sight." Briefly, in Antar I discern

> "—A love exalted high,
> By all the glow of chivalry;"

and I lament to see so many intelligent travellers misjudging the Arab after a superficial experience of a few debased Syrians or Sinaites. The true children of Antar have *not* "ceased to be gentlemen."

In the days of ignorance, it was the custom for Bedouins, when tormented by the tender passion, which seems to have attacked them in the form of "possession," for long years to sigh and wail and wander, doing the most truculent deeds to melt the obdurate fair. When Arabia Islamized, the practice changed its element for proselytism. The Fourth Caliph is fabled to have travelled far, redressing the injured, punishing the injurer, preaching to the infidel, and especially protecting women—the chief end and aim of knighthood. The Caliph El Mutasem heard in the assembly of his courtiers that a woman of Sayyid family had been taken prisoner by a "Greek barbarian" of Ammoria. The man on one occasion struck her, when she cried, "Help me, O Mutasem!" and the clown said derisively, "Wait till he cometh upon his pied steed!" The chivalrous prince arose, sealed up the wine cup which he held in his hand, took oath to do his knightly *devoir*, and on the morrow started for Ammoria, with 70,000 men, each mounted on a piebald charger. Having taken the place, he entered it, exclaiming, "Labbayki, Labbayki!"—Here am I at thy call. He struck off the caitiff's head, released the lady with his own hands, ordered the cupbearer to bring the sealed bowl, and drank from it, exclaiming, "Now, indeed, wine is good!"

It is the existence of this chivalry among the "Children of Antar" which makes the society of Bedouins ("damned saints," perchance, and "honorable villains,") so delightful to the traveller who understands and is understood by them. Your guide will protect you with blade and spear, even against his kindred, and he expects you to do the same for him. You may give a man the lie, but you must lose no time in baring your sword. If involved in dispute with overwhelming numbers, you address some elder, "Dakhilak ya Shaykh!"—(I am) thy protected, O Sir,—and he will espouse your quarrel, and, indeed, with greater heat and energy than if it were his own. But why multiply instances?

The language of love and war and all excitement is poetry, and here, again, the Bedouin excels. Travellers complain that the wild men cease to sing. This is true if "poet" be limited to a few authors whose existence everywhere depends upon the accidents of patronage or political occurrences. A far stronger evidence of poetic feeling is afforded by the phraseology of the Arab, and the highly imaginative turn of his commonest expressions. Destitute of the poetic taste, as we define it, he certainly is: as in the Milesian, wit and fancy, vivacity and passion, are too strong for reason and judgment, the reins which guide Apollo's car. And although the Bedouins no longer boast a Lebid or a Maisunah, yet they are passionately fond of their ancient bards.* A man skilful in reading El Mutanabi and the Suspended Poems would be received by them with the honors paid by civilization to the travelling millionnaire.†

I cannot well explain the effect of Arab poetry to one who has not visited the Desert.‡ Apart from the pomp of words and the music of the sound, there is a dreaminess of idea and a haze thrown over the object, infinitely attractive, but indescribable. Description, indeed, would rob the song of indistinctness, its essence. To borrow a simile from a sister art, the Arab poet sets before the mental eye the dim grand outlines of a picture,—which must be filled up by the reader, guided only by a few glorious touches, powerfully standing out, and the sentiment which the scene is intended to express;—whereas, we Europeans and moderns,

* I am informed that the Beni Kahtan still improvise, but I never heard them. The traveller in Arabia will always be told that some remote clan still produces mighty bards, and uses in conversation the terminal vowels of the classic tongue, but he will not believe these assertions till personally convinced of their truth.

The Bedouin dialect, however, though debased, is still, as of yore, purer than the language of the citizens. During the days when philology was a passion in the East, those Stephens and Johnsons of Semitic lore, Firuzabadi and El Zamakhshari, wandered from tribe to tribe and tent to tent, collecting words and elucidating disputed significations. Their grammatical adventures are still remembered, and are favorite stories with scholars.

† I say "skilful in reading," because the Arabs, like the Spaniards, hate to hear their language mangled by mispronunciation. When Burckhardt, who spoke badly, began to read verse to the Bedouins, they could not refrain from a movement of impatience, and used to snatch the book out of his hands.

‡ The civilised poets of the Arab cities throw the charm of the Desert over their verse, by images borrowed from its scenery—the dromedary, the mirage, and the well—as naturally as certain of our songsters, confessedly haters of the country, babble of distant kine, shady groves, spring showers, and purling rills.

by stippling and minute touches, produce a miniature on a large scale so objective as to exhaust rather than to arouse reflection. As the poet is a creator, the Arab's is poetry, the European's versical description. The language leaves a mysterious vagueness between the relation of word to word, which materially assists the sentiment, not the sense, of the poem. When verbs and nouns have—each one—many different significations, only the radical or general idea suggests itself. Rich and varied synonyms, illustrating the finest shades of meaning, are artfully used; now scattered to startle us by distinctness, now to form as it were a star about which dimly seen satellites revolve. There is in the Semitic dialect a copiousness of rhyme which leaves the poet almost unfettered to choose the desired expression. Hence it is that a stranger speaking Arabic becomes poetical as naturally as he would be witty in French and philosophic in German. Truly spake Mohammed el Damiri, "Wisdom hath alighted upon three things—the brain of the Franks, the hands of the Chinese, and the tongues of the Arabs."

The name of "harami"—brigand—is still honorable among the Hejazi Bedouins. Slain in raid or foray, a man is said to die "ghandûr," or a brave. He, on the other hand, who is lucky enough, as we should express it, to die in his bed, is called "fatis" (carrion), his weeping mother will exclaim, "O that my son had perished of a cut throat!" and her attendant crones will suggest, with deference, that such evil came of the will of Allah. It is told of the Lahabah, a sub-family of the Auf near Rabigh, that a girl will refuse even her cousin unless, in the absence of other opportunities, he plunder some article from the Hajj caravan in front of the Pacha's links. Detected twenty years ago, the delinquent would have been impaled; now he escapes with a rib-roasting. Fear of the blood-feud, and the certainty of a shut road to future travellers, prevent the Turks proceeding to extremes. They conceal their weakness by pretending that the Sultan hesitates to wage a war of extermination with the thieves of the Holy Land. Hence, petty pilfering has re-appeared in El-Hejaz.

The true Bedouin style of plundering, with its numerous niceties of honor and gentlemanly manners, gives the robber a consciousness of moral rectitude. "Strip off that coat, O certain person! and that turban," exclaims the highwayman, "they are wanted by my lady-cousin." You will (of course if necessary) lend ready ear to an order thus politely attributed to the wants of the fair sex. If you will add a few obliging expressions to the bundle, and offer *Latro* a cup of coffee and a pipe, you will talk half your toilette back to your person; and if you can quote a little poetry, you will part the best of friends, leaving perhaps only a pair of sandals behind you. But should you hesitate, *Latro*, lamenting the painful necessity, touches up your back with the heel of his spear. If this hint suffice not, he will make things plain by the lance's point, and when blood shows, the tiger-part of humanity appears.

I omit general details about the often described Sar (Thar), or Vendetta. The price of blood is 800 dollars (=200*l.*), or rather that sum imperfectly expressed by live-stock. All the blood relations of the slayer assist to make up the required amount, rating each animal at three or four times its proper value. On such occasions violent scenes arise from the conflict of the Arab's two pet passions, avarice and revenge.

The "avenger of blood" longs to cut the foe's throat. On the other hand, how let slip an opportunity of enriching himself? His covetousness is intense, as are all his passions. He has always a project of buying a new dromedary, or of investing capital in some marvellous colt; the consequence is, that he is insatiable. Still he receives blood-money with a feeling of shame; and if it be offered to an old woman—the most revengeful variety of our species, be it remarked,—she will dash it to the ground, and clutch her knife, and fiercely swear by Allah that she will not eat her son's blood.

The Bedouin considers himself a man only when mounted on horseback, lance in hand, bound for a foray or a fray, carolling some such gaiety as—

> "A steede! a steede of matchlesse speede!
> A sword of metal keene!
> All else to noble minds is drosse,
> All else on earth is meane."

Even in his sports he affects those that imitate war. Preserving the instinctive qualities which lie dormant in civilisation, he is an admirable "Venator." The children, men in miniature, begin a rude system of gymnastics when they can walk. "My young ones play upon the backs of camels," was the reply made to me by a Jehayni Bedouin when offered some Egyptian plaything. The men pass their time principally in hawking, shooting, and riding. The "Sakr," I am told, is the only falcon in general use; they train it to pursue the gazelle, which greyhounds pull down when fatigued. I have heard much of their excellent marksmanship, but saw only moderate practice with a long matchlock rested and fired at standing objects. Double-barrelled guns are rare amongst them.* Their principal weapons are matchlocks and firelocks, pistols, javelins, spears, swords, and the dagger called "Jambiyah;" the sling and the bow have long been given up. The guns come from Egypt, Syria, and Turkey; for the Bedouin

* Here called "bandukiyah bi ruhayn," or the two-mouthed gun.

cannot make, although he can repair, this arm. He particularly values a good old barrel seven spans long, and would rather keep it than his coat; consequently, a family often boasts of four or five guns, which descend from generation to generation. The price of a gun varies from two to sixty dollars. The Bedouins collect nitre in the country, make excellent charcoal, and import sulphur from Egypt and India; their powder, however, is coarse and weak. For hares and birds they cut up into slugs a bar of lead hammered out to a convenient size, and they cast bullets in moulds. They are fond of ball-practice, firing, as every sensible man does, at short distances, and striving at extreme precision. They are fond of backing themselves with wagers, and will shoot for a sheep, the loser inviting his friends to a feast. On festivals they boil a sheep's head, and use it as mark and prize. Those who affect excellence are said to fire at a bullet hanging by a thread; curious, however, to relate, the Bedouins of El Hejaz have but just learned the art, general in Persia and Barbary, of shooting from horseback at speed.

Pistols have been lately introduced into the Hejaz, and are not common amongst the Bedouins. The citizens are fond of this weapon, as it is derived from Constantinople.

The spears, called Kanat, or reeds, are made of male bamboos imported from India. They are about twelve feet long, iron shod, with a long tapering point, beneath which are one or two tufts of black ostrich feathers. Besides the Mirzak, or javelin, they have a spear called "Shalfah," a bamboo or palmstick garnished with a head about the breadth of a man's hand.

No good swords are fabricated in El Hejaz. The Khelawiyah and other Desert clans have made some poor attempts at blades. They are brought from Persia, India, and Egypt; but I never saw anything of value.

The Darakah, or shield, also comes from India. It is the common Cutch article, supposed to be made of rhinoceros hide, and displaying as much brass knob and gold wash as possible. The Bedouins still use in the remoter parts Diraa, or coats of mail, worn by horsemen over buff jackets.

The dagger is made in Yemen and other places; it has a vast variety of shapes, each of which, as usual, has its proper name. Generally they are but little curved (whereas the gadaymi of Yemen and Hazramaut is almost a semicircle), with tapering blade, wooden handle, and scabbard of the same material overlaid with brass. At the point of the scabbard is a round knob, and the weapon is so long, that a man when walking cannot swing his right arm. In narrow places he must enter sideways. But it is the mode always to appear in dagger, and the weapon, like the French soldier's *coupe-choux*, is really useful for such bloodless purposes as cutting wood and gathering grass. In price they vary from one to thirty dollars.

The Hejazi Bedouins have no game of chance, and dare not, I am told, ferment the juice of the Daum palm, as proximity to Aden has taught the wild men of Yemen. Their music is in a rude state. The principal instrument is the tabl or kettle-drum, which is of two kinds; one, the smaller, used at festivals; the other a large copper "tom-tom," for martial purposes, covered with leather, and played upon, pulpit-like, with fist and not with stick. Besides which, they have the one-stringed Rubabah, or guitar, that "monotonous, but charming instrument of the Desert." In another place I have described their dancing, which is an ignoble spectacle.

The Bedouins of El Hejaz have all the knowledge necessary for procuring and protecting the riches of savage life. They are perfect in the breeding, the training, and the selling of cattle. They know sufficient of astronomy to guide themselves by night, and are acquainted with the names of the principal stars. Their local memory is wonderful. Such is their instinct in the art of Asar, or tracking, that it is popularly said of the Zubayd clan, which lives between Meccah and El Medinah, a man will lose a she camel and know her four-year-old colt by its foot. Always engaged in rough exercises and perilous journeys, they have learned a kind of farriery and a simple system of surgery. In cases of fracture they bind on splints with cloth bands, and the patient drinks camel's milk and clarified butter till he is cured. Cut-wounds are washed carefully, sprinkled with meal gunpowder, and sewn up. They dress gunshot wounds with raw camels' flesh, and rely entirely upon nature and diet. When bitten by snakes or stung by scorpions they scarify the wound with a razor, recite a charm, and apply to it a dressing of garlic. The wealthy have "fiss," or ring-stones, brought from India, and used with a formula of prayer to extract venom. Some few possess the "Teriyak" (Theriack) of El Irak—the great counter-poison, internal as well as external, of the East. The poorer classes all wear the "hibas" of Yemen; two yarns of black sheep's wool tied round the leg, under the knee and above the ankle. When bitten, the sufferer tightens these cords above the injured part, which he immediately scarifies; thus they act as tourniquets. The Bedouin's knowledge of medicine is unusually limited in this part of Arabia, where even simples are not required by a people who rise with dawn, eat little, always breathe desert air, and "at night make the camels their curfew." The great tonic is clarified butter, and the "kay," or actual cautery, is used even for rheumatism. This counter-irritant, together with a curious and artful phlebotomy, blood being taken, as by the Italians, from the toes, the fingers, and other parts of the body, are the Arab panaceas. Mules' teeth, roasted and imperfectly pounded, cure cataract. Teeth are extracted by the farrier's pincers, and the worm which throughout the East is supposed to produce tooth-ache, falls by fumigation. And, finally, after great fatigue, or when suffering from cold, the body is copiously greased with clarified butter and exposed to a blazing fire.

Mohammed and his followers conquered only the more civilised Bedouins; and there is even to this day little or no religion amongst the wild people, except amongst those on the coast or in the vicinity of cities. The faith of the Bedouin comes from El Islam, whose hold is weak. But his customs and institutions, the growth of his climate, his nature, and his wants, are still those of his ancestors, cherished ere Meccah had sent forth a Prophet, and likely to survive the day when every vestige of the Kaabah shall have disappeared. Of this nature are the Hejazi's pagan oaths, their heathenish names (few being Moslem except "Mohammed"), their ordeal of licking red-hot iron, their Salkh, or scarification, proof of manliness, their blood revenge, their eating carrion (*i. e.* the body of an animal killed without the usual formula), and their lending wives to strangers. All these I hold to be remnants of some old creed; nor should I despair of finding among the Bedouins bordering upon the Great Desert some lingering system of idolatry.

The Bedouins of El Hejaz call themselves Shafei; but what is put into the mouths of their brethren in the West applies equally well here. "We pray not, because we must drink the water of ablution; we give no alms, because we ask them; we fast not the Ramazan month, because we starve throughout the year; and we do no pilgrimage, because the world is the House of Allah." Their blunders in religious matters supply the citizens with many droll stories. And it is to be observed that they do not, like the Greek pirates or the Italian bandits, preserve a religious element in their plunderings: they make no vows and carefully avoid offerings.

The ceremonies of Bedouin life are few and simple—circumcisions, marriages, and funerals.

Women being a marketable commodity in barbarism as in civilisation, youths in El Hejaz are not married till the father can afford to pay for a bride. There is little pomp or ceremony save firing of guns, dancing, singing, and eating mutton. The "settlement" is usually about thirty sound Spanish dollars, half paid down, and the other half owed by the bridegroom to the fathers, the brothers, or the kindred of his spouse. Some tribes will take animals in lieu of ready money. A man of wrath not contented with his bride, puts her away at once. If peaceably inclined, by a short delay he avoids scandal. Divorces are very frequent among Bedouins, and if the settlement money be duly paid, no evil comes of them.

The funerals of the wild men resemble those of the citizens, only they are more simple; the dead are buried where they die. The corpse, after being washed, is shrouded in any rags procurable, and, women and hired weepers not being permitted to attend, is carried to the grave by men only. A hole is dug, according to Moslem custom; dry wood, which everywhere abounds, is disposed to cover the corpse, and an oval of stones surrounding a mound of earth keeps out jackals and denotes the spot. These Bedouins have not, like the wild Sindhis and Belochis, favorite cemeteries, to which they transport their dead from afar.

The traveller will find no difficulty in living amongst the Hejazi Bedouins. "Trust to their honor and you are safe," as was said of the Crow Indians, "to their honesty, and they will steal the hair off your head." Only the wanderer must adopt the wild man's motto, "*omnia mea mecum porto*," he must have good nerves, be capable of fatigue and hardship, and possess some knowledge of drugs, shoot and ride well, speak Arabic and Turkish, know by reading the customs, and avoid offending against local prejudices, by causing himself, for instance, to be called "Taggaa." Caution must be exercised in choosing a companion who has not too many blood feuds. There is no objection to carrying a copper watch and a pocket compass, and a Koran could be fitted with secret pockets for notes and pencil. Strangers should especially avoid handsome weapons: these tempt the Bedouins' cupidity more than gold. The other extreme, defencelessness, is equally objectionable. It is needless to say that the traveller must never be seen writing anything but charms, and on no account sketch in public. He should be careful in questioning, and rather lead up to information than ask directly. It offends some Bedouins, besides denoting ignorance and curiosity, to be asked their names or those of their clans: a man may be living incognito, and the tribes distinguish themselves when they desire to do so by dress, personal appearance, voice, dialect, and accentuation, points of difference plain to the initiated. A few dollars suffice for the road, and if you would be "respectable," a taste which I dare not deprecate, some such presents as razors and Tarbushes are required for the chiefs.

The government of the Arabs may be called almost an autonomy. The tribes never obey their shaykhs, unless for personal considerations, and, as in a civilised army, there generally is some sharp-witted and brazen-faced individual whose voice is louder than the general's. In their leonine society the sword is the great administrator of law.

The Arab's dress marks his simplicity; it gives him a nationality, as, according to John Evelyn, "prodigious breeches" did to the Swiss. It is remarkably picturesque, and with sorrow we see it now confined to the wildest Bedouins and a few Sherifs. The necessary dress of a man is his Saub (Tobe), a blue calico shirt, reaching from neck to ankles, tight or loose-sleeved, opening at the chest in front, and rather narrow below; so that the wearer, when running, must either hold it up or tuck it into his belt. The latter article, called Hakw, is a plaited leathern thong, twisted round the waist very tightly, so as to support the back. The trowsers and the "Futah," or loin cloth of cities, are looked upon as signs of effeminacy. In cold weather the chiefs wear over the shirt an Aba, or cloak. These garments are made in Nejd and the eastern districts; they are of four colors, white, black, red, and brown-striped. The best are of camel's-hair, and may cost fifteen dollars; the worst, of sheep's wool, are worth only three; both are cheap, as they last for years. The Mahramah (head-cloth) comes from Syria; which, with Nejd, supplies also the Kufiyah, or head-kerchief. The "Ukal," fillets bound over the kerchief, are of many kinds; the Bisher tribe near Meccah make a kind of crown like the gloria round a saint's head, with bits of wood, in which are set pieces of mother-o'-pearl. Sandals, too, are of every description, from the simple sole of leather tied on with thongs, to the handsome and elaborate chaussure of Meccah; the price varies from a piastre to a dollar, and the very poor walk bare-footed. A leathern bandoleer, called Majdal, passed over the left shoulder, and reaching to the right hip, supports a line of brass cylinders for cartridges. The other cross-belt (El Masdar), made of leather, ornamented with brass rings, hangs down at the left side, and carries a Kharizah, or hide-case for bullets. And finally, the Hizam, or waist-belt, holds the dagger and extra cartridge cases. A Bedouin never appears in public unarmed.

The women wear, like their masters, dark blue cotton Tobes, but larger and looser. When abroad they cover the head with a yashmak of black stuff, or poppy-colored Burka of the Egyptian shape. They wear no pantaloons, and rarely slippers or sandals. The hair is twisted into "Majdul," little pig-tails, and copiously anointed with clarified butter. The rich perfume the skin with rose and cinnamon-scented oils, and wear in their hair El Shayh, sweetest herb of the desert; their ornaments are bracelets, collars, ear and nose-rings of gold, silver, or silver-gilt. The poorer classes wear strings of silver coins hung round the neck.

The true Bedouin is an abstemious man, capable of living for six months on ten ounces of food per diem; the milk of a single camel, and a handful of dates dry, or fried in clarified butter, suffice for his wants. He despises the obese and all who require regular and plentiful meals, sleeps on a mat, and knows neither luxury nor comfort, freezing during one quarter and frying three quarters of the year. But though he can endure hunger like all savages, he will gorge when an opportunity offers. I never saw the man who could refrain from water upon the line of march. They are still "acridophagi," and even the citizens far prefer a dish of locusts to the "fasikh," which act as anchovies, sardines, and herrings in Egypt. They light a fire at night, and as the insects fall dead they quote this couplet to justify their being eaten—

> "We are allowed two carrions and two bloods,
> The fish and locusts, the liver and the spleen."

Where they have no crops to lose, the people are thankful for a fall of locusts. In El Hejaz the flights are uncertain; during the last five years El Medinah has seen but few. They are prepared for eating by boiling in salt water and drying four or five days in the sun: a "wet" locust to an Arab is as a snail to a Briton. The head is plucked off, the stomach drawn, the wings and the prickly part of the legs are plucked, and the insect is ready for the table. Locusts are never eaten with sweet things, which would be nauseous; the dish is always "hot" with salt and pepper, or onions fried in clarified butter, when it tastes nearly as well as a plate of stale shrimps.

The favorite food on journeys is meat cut into strips and sun-dried. This, with a bag of milk-balls and a little coffee, must suffice for journey or campaign. The Bedouins know neither fermented nor distilled liquors, although fie upon thee, drunkard! is a popular phrase, preserving the memory of a better state of things. Some clans, though not all, smoke tobacco. It is generally the growth of the country called Hejazi or Kazimiyah; a green weed, very strong, with a foul smell, and costing about one piastre per pound.

The tribes of El Hejaz are tediously numerous. The Beni Harb, however, is now the ruling clan in the Holy Land.

## CHAPTER XXIII.

### FROM EL SUWAYRKIYAH TO MECCAH.

WE have now left the territory of El Medinah. El Suwayrkiyah, which belongs to the Sherif of Meccah, is by dead reckoning about ninety-nine miles along the road from the Prophet's burial-place. The town, consisting of about 100 houses, is built at the base and on the sides of a basaltic mass, which rises abruptly from the hard clayey plain. There is little to describe in the narrow streets and the mud houses, which are essentially Arab. The fields around are divided into little square plots by earthen ridges and stone walls; some of the palms are fine grown trees, and the wells appeared numerous. The water is near the surface and plentiful, but it has a brackish taste, highly disagreeable after a few days' use, and the effects are the reverse of chalybeate.

The morning after our arrival at El Suwayrkiyah witnessed a commotion in our little party: hitherto they had kept together in fear of the road. Among the number was one Ali bin Ya Sin, a perfect "old man of the sea." By profession he was a "Zem Zemi," or dispenser of water from the Holy Well,* and he had a handsome "palazzo" at the foot of Abu Kubays in Meccah, which he periodically converted into a boarding house. Though past sixty, very decrepit, bent by age, white-bearded, and toothless, he still acted cicerone to pilgrims, and for that purpose travelled once every year to El Medinah. These trips had given him the cunning of a veteran voyager. He lived well and cheaply; his home-made shugduf, the model of comfort, was garnished with soft cushions and pillars, whilst from the pockets protruded select bottles of pickled limes and similar luxuries; he had his travelling shishah,† and at the halting-place, disdaining the crowded, reeking tent, he had a contrivance for converting his vehicle into a habitation. He was a type of the Arab old man. He mumbled all day and three-quarters of the night, for he had *des insomnies.* His nerves were so fine, that if any one mounted his shugduf, the unfortunate was condemned to lie like a statue. Fidgety and priggishly neat, nothing annoyed him so much as a moment's delay or an article out of place, a rag removed from his water-gugglet, or a cooking pot imperfectly free from soot; and I judged his avarice by observing that he made a point of picking up and eating the grains scattered from our pomegranates, exclaiming that the heavenly seed (located there by Arab superstition) might be one of those so wantonly wasted.

* There are certain officers called Zem Zemi, who distribute the holy water. In the case of a respectable pilgrim they have a large jar marked with his names and titles, and sent every morning to his lodgings. If he be generous, one or more will be placed in the Haram, that men may drink in his honor. The Zem Zemi expects a present varying from five to eleven dollars.

† The shishah, smoked on the camel, is a tin canister divided into two compartments, the lower half for the water, the upper one for the tobacco. The cover is pierced with holes to feed the fire, and a short hooka-snake projects from one side.

Ali bin Ya Sin, returning to his native city, had not been happy in his choice of a companion this time. The other occupant of the handsome shugduf was an ignoble-faced Egyptian from El Medinah. This ill-suited pair clave together for awhile, but at El Suwayrkiyah some dispute about a copper coin made them permanent foes. With threats and abuse such as none but an Egyptian could tamely hear, Ali kicked his quondam friend out of the vehicle. But terrified, after reflection, by the possibility that the man now his enemy might combine with two or three Syrians of our party to do him a harm, and frightened by a few black looks, the senior determined to fortify himself by a friend. Connected with the boy Mohammed's family, he easily obtained an introduction to me; he kissed my hand with great servility, declared that his servant had behaved disgracefully, and begged my protection, together with the occasional attendance of my "slave."

This was readily granted in pity for the old man, who became immensely grateful. He offered at once to take Shaykh Nur into his shugduf. The Indian boy had already reduced to ruins the frail structure of his shibriyah, by lying upon it lengthways, whereas prudent travellers sit in it cross-legged and facing the camel. Moreover, he had been laughed to scorn by the Bedouins, who, seeing him pull up his dromedary to mount and dismount, had questioned his sex, and determined him to be a woman of the "Miyan."* I could not rebuke them; the poor fellow's timidity was a ridiculous contrast to the Bedouin's style of mounting; a pull at the camel's head, the left foot placed on the neck, an agile spring, and a scramble into the saddle. Shaykh Nur, elated by the sight of old Ali's

* The Hindostani word for "sir." Bedouins address it slightingly to Indians.

luxuries, promised himself some joyous hours; but next morning he owned with a sigh that he had purchased splendor at the extravagant price of happiness—the senior's tongue never rested throughout the livelong night.

During one half-halt at El Sawayrkiyah we determined to have a small feast; we bought some fresh dates, and paid a dollar and a half for a sheep. Hungry travellers consider "liver and fry" a dish to set before a shaykh. On this occasion, however, our enjoyment was marred by the water; even Soyer's dinners would scarcely charm if washed down with cups of a certain mineral-spring found at Epsom.

We started at 10 A. M. in a south-easterly direction, and travelled over a flat thinly dotted with desert vegetation. At 1 P. M. we passed a basaltic ridge, and then, entering a long depressed line of country, a kind of valley, paced down it five tedious hours. The simoom as usual was blowing hard, and it seemed to affect the traveller's temper. In one place I saw a Turk who could not speak a word of Arabic, violently disputing with an Arab who could not speak a word of Turkish. The pilgrim insisted upon adding to the camel's load a few dry sticks, such as are picked up for cooking. The camel man as perseveringly threw off the extra burden. They screamed with rage, hustled each other, and at last the Turk dealt the Arab a heavy blow. I afterwards heard that the pilgrim was mortally wounded that night, his stomach being ripped open with a dagger. On inquiring what had become of him, I was assured that he had been comfortably wrapped up in his shroud and placed in a half-dug grave. This is the general practice in the case of the poor and solitary, whom illness or accident incapacitates from proceeding. It is impossible to contemplate such a fate without horror: the torturing thirst of a wound,* the burning sun heating the brain to madness, and—worst of all, for they do not wait till death—the attacks of the jackal, the vulture, and the raven of the wild.

At 8 P.M. the camels began to stumble over the dwarf dykes of the wheat and barley fields, and presently we arrived at our halting-place, a large village called El Sufayna. The plain was already dotted with tents and lights. We found the Baghdad caravan, whose route here falls into the Darb el Sharki. It consists of a few Persians and Kurds, and collects the people of north-eastern Arabia, Wahhabis, and others. They are escorted by the Agayl tribe and the fierce mountaineers of Jebel Shamar. Scarcely was our tent pitched when the distant pattering of musketry and an ominous tapping of the kettle-drum sent all my companions in different directions to inquire what was the cause of quarrel. The Baghdad Cafila, though not more than 2000 in number, men, women, and children, had been proving to the Damascus caravan, that, being perfectly ready to fight, they were not going to yield any point of precedence. From that time the two bodies encamped in different places. I never saw a more pugnacious assembly: a look sufficed for a quarrel. Once a Wahhabi stood in front of us, and by pointing with his finger and other insulting gestures, showed his hatred to the chibouque, in which I was peaceably indulging. It was impossible to refrain from chastising his insolence by a polite and smiling offer of the offending pipe. This made him draw his dagger without a thought; but it was sheathed again, for we all cocked our pistols, and these gentry prefer steel to lead. Though it was night when we encamped,

* When Indians would say, "he was killed upon the spot," they use the picturesque phrase, "he asked not for water."

Shaykh Masud set out to water his moaning camels: they had not quenched their thirst for three days. He returned in a depressed state, having been bled by the soldiery at the well to the extent of forty piastres, or about eight shillings.

After supper we spread our rugs and prepared to rest. And here I first remarked the coolness of the nights, proving at this season of the year a considerable altitude above the sea. As a general rule the atmosphere stagnated between sunrise and 10 A.M., when a light wind rose. During the forenoon the breeze strengthened, and it gradually diminished through the afternoon. Often about sunset there was a gale accompanied by dry storms of dust. At El Sufayna, though there was no night-breeze and little dew, a blanket was necessary, and the hours of darkness were invigorating enough to mitigate the effect of the sand and simoom-ridden day. Before sleeping I was introduced to a namesake, one Shaykh Abdullah of Meccah. Having committed his shugduf to his son, a lad of fourteen, he had ridden forward on a dromedary, and had suddenly fallen ill. His objects in meeting me were to ask for some medicine, and a temporary seat in my shugduf; the latter I offered with pleasure, as the boy Mohammed was longing to mount a camel. The shaykh's illness was nothing but weakness brought on by the hardships of the journey: he attributed it to the hot wind, and the weight of a bag of dollars, which he had attached to his waist-belt. He was a man about forty, long, thin, pale, and of a purely nervous temperament: and a few questions elicited the fact, that he had lately and suddenly given up his daily opium pill. I prepared one for him, placed him in my litter, and persuaded him to stow away his burden in some place where it would be less troublesome. He was my companion for two marches, at the end of which he found his own shugduf, and I never met amongst the Arab citizens a better bred or better informed man. At Constantinople he had learned a little French, Italian, and Greek; and from the properties of a shrub to the varieties of honey,* he was full of "useful knowledge," and open as a dictionary. We parted near Meccah, where I met him only once, and then accidentally, in the Valley of Muna.

At half-past 5 A. M., on the 5th of September, we arose refreshed by the cool, comfortable night, and loaded the camels.

We travelled towards the south-east, and entered a country destitute of the low ranges of hill, which from El Medinah southwards had bounded the horizon. After two miles' march, our camels climbed up a precipitous ridge, and then descended into a broad gravel plain. From 10 to 11 A. M. our course was southerly, over a high table-land, and we afterwards traversed for five hours and a half a plain which bore signs of standing water. This day's march was peculiarly Arabian. It was a desert peopled only with echoes,—a place of death for what little there is to die in it,—a wilderness, where, to use my companion's phrase, there is nothing but He.† Nature, scalped, flayed, discovered her anatomy to the gazer's eye. The horizon was a sea of mirage; gigantic sand columns whirled over the plain; and on both sides of our road were huge piles of bare rock, standing detached upon the surface of sand and clay. Here they appeared in oval lumps, heaped up with a semblance

* The Arabs are curious in and fond of honey: Meccah alone affords eight or nine different varieties. The best, and in Arab parlance the "coldest," is the green kind, produced by bees that feed upon a thorny plant called "sihhah." The white and red honeys rank next. The worst is the Asal Asmar (brown honey), which sells for something under a piastre per pound.

† "La Siwa Hu," *i. e.* where there is none but Allah.

of symmetry; there a single boulder stood, with its narrow foundation based upon a pedestal of low, dome-shaped rock. All are of a pink coarse-grained granite, which flakes off in large crusts under the influence of the atmosphere. I remarked one block which could not measure less than thirty feet in height. Through these scenes we travelled till about half-past 4 P. M., when the guns suddenly roared a halt. There was not a trace of human habitation around us: a few parched shrubs and the granite heaps were the only objects diversifying the hard clayey plain. Shaykh Masud correctly guessed the cause of our detention at the inhospitable "halting place of the Mutayr" (Bedouins). "Cook your bread and boil your coffee," said the old man, "the camels will rest for awhile and the gun sound at nightfall."

At half-past ten that evening we heard the signal for departure, and as the moon was still young we prepared for a hard night's work. We took a south-westerly course through what is called a Waar—rough ground covered with thicket. Darkness fell upon us like a pall. The camels tripped and stumbled, tossing their litters like cock-boats in a short sea; at times the shugdufs were well nigh torn off their backs. When we came to a ridge worse than usual, old Masud would seize my camel's halter, and, accompanied by his son and nephew bearing lights, encourage the animals with gesture and voice. It was a strange, wild scene. The black basaltic field was dotted with the huge and doubtful forms of spongy-footed camels with silent tread, looming like phantoms in the midnight air; the hot wind moaned, and whirled from the torches sheets of flame and fiery smoke, whilst ever and anon a swift travelling Takhtrawan, drawn by mules, and surrounded by runners bearing gigantic mashals,* threw a passing glow of

* This article, an iron cylinder with bands, mounted on a long pole, corresponds with the European cresset of the fifteenth century.

red light upon the dark road and the dusky multitude. On this occasion the rule was "every man for himself." Each pressed forward into the best path, thinking only of preceding others. The Syrians, amongst whom our little party had become entangled, proved most unpleasant companions; they often stopped the way, insisting upon their right to precedence. On one occasion a horseman had the audacity to untie the halter of my dromedary, and thus to cast us adrift, as it were to make room for some secluded friend. I seized my sword; but Shaykh Abdullah stayed my hand, and addressed the intruder in terms sufficiently violent to make him slink away. Nor was this the only occasion on which my companion was successful with the Syrians. He would begin with a mild "Move a little, O my father!" followed, if fruitless, by "Out of the way, O father of Syria!*" and if still ineffectual, concluding with a "Begone, O he!" This ranged between civility and sternness. If without effect, it was followed by revilings to the "Abusers of the Salt," the "Yezid," the "offspring of Shimr." Another remark which I made about my companion's conduct well illustrates the difference between the Eastern and Western man. When traversing a dangerous place, Shaykh Abdullah the European attended to his camel with loud cries of "Hai! Hai!"† and an occasional switching. Shaykh Abdullah the Asiatic commended himself to Allah by repeated ejaculations of "Ya Sátir! Ya Sattár!"

The morning of Wednesday (Sept. 6th) broke as we entered a wide plain. In many places were signs of water; lines of basalt here and there seamed the surface, and wide sheets of the tufaceous gypsum called by the Arabs "sab-

* "Abu Sham," a familiar address in El Hejaz to Syrians.

† There is a regular language to camels. "Ikh! ikh!" makes them kneel; "Yakh! Yakh!" urges them on; "Hai! Hai!" induces caution, and so on.

khah" shone like mirrors set in russet frame-work of the flat. This substance is found in cakes, often a foot long by an inch in depth, curled by the sun's rays and overlying clay into which water had sunk. After our harassing night, day came on with a sad feeling of oppression, greatly increased by the unnatural glare.

At 10 A. M. we pitched the tent in the first convenient spot, and lost no time in stretching our cramped limbs upon the bosom of mother Earth.

In our anxiety to rest we had strayed from the Damascus caravan into the mountaineers of Shamar. Our Shaykh Masud manifestly did not like the company; for shortly after 3 P.M. he insisted upon our striking the tent and rejoining the Hajj, which lay encamped about two miles distant in the western part of the basin. We loaded, therefore, and half an hour before sunset found ourselves in more congenial society. To my great disappointment a stir was observable in the caravan. I at once understood that another night-march was in store for us.

At 6 P.M. we again mounted and turned towards the eastern plain. A heavy shower was falling upon the western hills, whence came damp and dangerous blasts. Between 9 P.M. and the dawn of the next day we had a repetition of the last night's scenes, over a road so rugged and dangerous, that I wondered how men could prefer to travel in the darkness. But the camels of Damascus were now worn out with fatigue; they could not endure the sun, and our time was too precious for a halt. My night was spent perched upon the front bar of my shugduf, encouraging the dromedary, and that we had not one fall excited my extreme astonishment. At 5 A.M. we entered a wide plain thickly clothed with the usual thorny trees, in whose strong grasp many a shugduf lost its covering, and not a few were dragged with their screaming inmates to the ground.

About five hours afterwards we crossed a high ridge, and saw below us the camp of the caravan not more than two miles distant.

At 11 A.M. we had reached our station. It is called El Birkat (the Tank), from a large and now ruinous cistern built of hewn stone by the Caliph Harun. The land belongs to the Utaybah Bedouins, the bravest and most ferocious clan in El Hejaz; and the citizens denote their dread of these banditti by asserting, that to increase their courage they drink their enemy's blood.* My companions shook their heads when questioned upon the subject, and prayed that we might not become too well acquainted with them—an ill-omened speech.

As we were now near the Holy City, all the Meccans were busy canvassing for lodgers and offering their services to pilgrims. Quarrels, too, were of hourly occurrence. In our party was an Arnaut, a white-bearded old man, so decrepit that he could scarcely stand, and yet so violent that no one could manage him but his African slave, a brazen-faced little wretch about fourteen years of age. Words were bandied between this angry senior and Shaykh Masud, when the latter insinuated, sarcastically, that if the former had teeth he would be more intelligible. The Arnaut in his rage seized a pole, raised it, and delivered a blow which missed the camel man, but brought the striker headlong to the ground. Masud exclaimed, with shrieks of rage, "Have we come to this, that every old dastard Turk smites us?" Our party had the greatest trouble to quiet the quarrellers. The Arab listened to us when we threatened him with the Pacha. But the Arnaut, whose

* Some believe this literally, others consider it a phrase expressive of blood-thirstiness. It is the only suspicion of cannibalism, if I may use the word, now attaching to El Hejaz.

rage was "like red-hot steel," would hear nothing but our repeated declarations, that unless he behaved more like a pilgrim, we should be compelled to leave him and his slave behind.

On the 7th September, at 4 P.M., we left El Birkat, and travelled eastwards over rolling ground thickly wooded. About 2 A.M. we began ascending hills in a south-westerly direction, and presently fell into the bed of a large rock-girt fiumara, which runs from east to west. The sands were overgrown with saline and salsolaceous plants. At 6 A.M. we left the fiumara, and, turning to the west, arrived about an hour afterwards at the station. El Zaribah, "the valley," is an undulating plain amongst high granite hills. In many parts it was faintly green; water was close to the surface, and rain stood upon the ground. During the night we had travelled about twenty-three miles.

Having pitched the tent, and eaten and slept, we prepared to perform the ceremony of El Ihram (assuming the pilgrim-garb), as El Zaribah is the mikat, or the appointed place.* Between the noonday and the afternoon prayers a barber attended to shave our heads, cut our nails, and trim our mustachios. Then, having bathed and perfumed ourselves—the latter is a questionable point—we donned the attire, which is nothing but two new cotton cloths, each six feet long by three and a half broad, white, with narrow red stripes and fringes; in fact, the costume called "El Eddeh" in the baths at Cairo.† Our

* "El Ihram" literally meaning "prohibition" or "making unlawful," equivalent to our "mortification," is applied to the ceremony of the toilette, and also to the dress itself.

† These sheets are not positively necessary; any clean cotton cloth not sewn in any part will serve equally well. Servants and attendants expect the master to present them with an "ihram."

heads were bare, and nothing was allowed upon the instep.*

After the toilet we were placed with our faces in the direction of Meccah, and ordered to say aloud, "I vow this ihram of hajj (the pilgrimage) and the umrah (the little pilgrimage) to Allah Almighty!" Having thus performed a two-prostration prayer, we repeated, without rising from the sitting position, these words, "O Allah! verily I purpose the hajj and the umrah, then enable me to accomplish the two, and accept them both of me, and make both blessed to me!" When these ceremonies had been duly performed, our friend Shaykh Abdullah, who acted as director of our consciences, bade us be good pilgrims, avoiding quarrels, bad language, immorality, and light conversation. We must so reverence life that we should avoid killing game, causing an animal to fly, and even pointing it out for destruction;† nor should we scratch ourselves, save with the open palm, lest vermin be destroyed, or a hair uprooted by the nail. We were to respect the sanctuary by sparing the trees, and not to pluck a single blade of grass. As regards personal considerations, we were to abstain from all oils, perfumes, and unguents; from washing the head with mallow or lote leaves; from dyeing, shaving, cutting, or vellicating a single pile or hair; and though we might take advantage of shade, and even form it with upraised hands, we must by no means cover our sconces. For each infraction of

* Sandals are made at Meccah expressly for the pilgrimage: the poorer classes cut off the upper leathers of an old pair of shoes.

† The object of these ordinances is clearly to inculcate the strictest observance of the "truce of God." Pilgrims, however, are allowed to slay, if necessary, "the five noxious," viz., a crow, a kite, a scorpion, a rat, and a biting dog.

these ordinances we must sacrifice a sheep;* and it is commonly said by Moslems, that none but the Prophet could be perfect in the intricacies of pilgrimage.

The wife and daughters of a Turkish pilgrim of our party assumed the ihram at the same time as ourselves. They appeared dressed in white garments; and they had exchanged the lisam, that coquettish fold of muslin which veils without concealing the lower part of the face, for a hideous mask, made of split, dried, and plaited palm leaves, with two "bull's-eyes," for light.† I could not help laughing when these strange figures met my sight, and, to judge from the shaking of their shoulders, they were not less susceptible to the merriment which they had caused.

At 3 P. M. we left El Zaribah, travelling towards the S. W., and a wondrously picturesque scene met the eye. Crowds hurried along, habited in the pilgrim garb, whose whiteness contrasted strangely with their black skins, their newly shaven heads glistening in the sun, and long black hair streaming in the wind. The rocks rang with shouts of "Labbayk! Labbayk!" At a pass we fell in with the Wahhabis, accompanying the Baghdad caravan, screaming "here am I;" and, guided by a large, loud kettle-drum, they followed in double file the camel of a standard-bearer, whose green flag bore in huge white letters the formula of the Moslem creed. They were wild-looking mountaineers, dark and fierce, with hair twisted into thin dalik or plaits: each was armed with a long spear, a matchlock, or a dagger. They were seated upon coarse wooden saddles, without cushions or stirrups, a fine saddle-cloth alone denoting

* The victim is sacrificed as a confession that the offender deems himself worthy of death; the offerer is not allowed to taste any portion of his offering.

† The reason why this "ugly" must be worn, is, that a woman's veil during the pilgrimage ceremonies is not allowed to touch her face.

a chief. The women emulated the men; they either guided their own dromedaries, or, sitting in pillion, they clung to their husbands; veils they disdained, and their countenances certainly belonged not to a "soft sex." These Wahhabis were by no means pleasant companions. Most of them were followed by spare dromedaries, either unladen or carrying water-skins, fodder, fuel, and other necessaries for the march. The beasts delighted in dashing furiously through one file, which being colligated, was thrown each time into the greatest confusion. And whenever we were observed smoking, we were cursed aloud for infidels and idolaters.

At about half-past 5 P. M. we entered a suspicious-looking place. On the right was a stony buttress, along whose base the stream, when there is one, flows; and to this depression was our road limited by the rocks and thorn trees, which filled the other half of the channel. The left side was a precipice, grim and barren, but not so abrupt as its brother. Opposite us the way seemed barred by piles of hills, crest rising above crest into the far blue distance. Day still smiled upon the upper peaks, but the lower slopes and the fiumara bed were already curtained with grey sombre shade.

A damp seemed to fall upon our spirits as we approached this Valley Perilous. I remarked with wonder that the voices of the women and children sank into silence, and the loud Labbaykas of the pilgrims were gradually stilled. Whilst still speculating upon the cause of this phenomenon it became apparent. A small curl of smoke, like a lady's ringlet, on the summit of the right-hand precipice caught my eye, and simultaneous with the echoing crack of the matchlock a high-trotting dromedary in front of me rolled over the sands—a bullet had split his heart—throwing his rider a goodly somerset of five or six yards.

Ensued terrible confusion; women screamed, children shrieked, and men vociferated, each one striving with might and main to urge his animal out of the place of death. But the road being narrow, they only managed to jam the vehicles in a solid immovable mass. At every matchlock shot a shudder ran through the huge body, as when the surgeon's scalpel touches some more sensitive nerve. The irregular horsemen, perfectly useless, galloped up and down over the stones, shouting to and ordering one another. The Pacha of the army had his carpet spread at the foot of the left-hand precipice, and debated over his pipe with the officers what ought to be done. No good genius whispered "crown the heights."

Then it was that the conduct of the Wahhabis found favor in my eyes. They came up, galloping their camels, with their elf-locks tossing in the wind, and their flaring matches casting a strange lurid light over their features. Taking up a position, one body began to fire upon the Utaybah robbers, whilst two or three hundred, dismounting, swarmed up the hill under the guidance of the Sherif Zayd. I had remarked this nobleman at El Medinah as a model specimen of the pure Arab. Like all Sherifs, he is celebrated for bravery, and has killed many with his own hand. When urged at El Zaribah to ride into Meccah, he swore that he would not leave the caravan till in sight of the walls; and, fortunately for the pilgrims, he kept his word. Presently the firing was heard far in our rear—the robbers having fled; the head of the column advanced, and the dense body of pilgrims opened out. Our forced halt was now exchanged for a flight. It required much management to steer our desert-craft clear of danger; but Shaykh Masud was equal to the occasion. That many were lost was evident by the boxes and baggage that strewed the shingles. I had no means of ascertaining the number of men killed and wounded: reports were contradictory, and exaggeration unanimous. The robbers were said to be 150 in number: their object was plunder, and they would eat the shot camels. But their principal ambition was the boast, "We, the Utaybah, on such and such a night stopped the Sultan's mahmal one whole hour in the pass."

As we advanced our escort took care to fire every large dry asclepias, to disperse the shades which buried us. Again the scene became wondrous wild.

At the beginning of the skirmish I had primed my pistols, and sat with them ready for use. But soon seeing that there was nothing to be done, and, wishing to make an impression,—nowhere does Bobadil now "go down" but in the East,—I called aloud for my supper. Shaykh Nur, exanimate with fear, could not move. The boy Mohammed ejaculated only an "Oh, sir!" and the people around exclaimed in disgust, "By Allah! he eats!" Shaykh Abdullah, the Meccan, being a man of spirit, was amused by the spectacle. "Are these Afghan manners, Effendim?" he inquired from the shugduf behind me. "Yes," I replied aloud, "in my country we always dine before an attack of robbers, because that gentry is in the habit of sending men to bed supperless." The Shaykh laughed aloud, but those around him looked offended. I thought the bravado this time *mal placé;* but a little event which took place on my way to Jeddah proved that it was not quite a failure.

On either side were ribbed precipices, dark, angry, and towering above, till their summits mingled with the glooms of night; and between them formidable looked the chasm, down which our host hurried with shouts and discharges of matchlocks. The torch-smoke and the night-fires of flaming asclepias formed a canopy, sable above and livid red below, which hung over our heads like a sheet, and divided the cliffs into two equal parts. Here the fire flashed fiercely from a tall thorn, that crackled and shot up showers of sparks into the air; there it died away in lurid gleams, which lit up a truly Stygian scnee. As usual, however, the picturesque had its inconveniences. There was no path. Rocks, stone-banks, and trees obstructed our passage. The camels, now blind in darkness, then dazzled by a flood of light, stumbled frequently; in some places slipping down a steep descent, in others sliding over a sheet of mud. There were furious quarrels and fierce language between camel-men and their hirers, and threats to fellow-travellers; in fact, we were united in discord. I passed that night crying, "Hai Hai!" switching the camel, and fruitlessly endeavoring to fustigate Masud's nephew, who resolutely slept on the water-bags. During the hours of darkness we made four or five halts, when we boiled coffee and smoked pipes, but men and beasts were beginning to suffer from a deadly fatigue.

Dawn found us still travelling down the fiumara, which here is about 100 yards broad.

We then turned northward, and sighted El Mazik, more generally known as Wady Laymun, the Valley of Limes. On the right bank of the fiumara stood the Meccan Sherif's state pavilion, green and gold: it was surrounded by his attendants, and prepared to receive the Pacha of the caravan. We advanced half a mile, and encamped temporarily in a hill-girt bulge of the fiumara bed.

Shaykh Masud allowed us only four hours' halt; he wished to precede the main body. After breaking our fast joyously upon limes, pomegranates, and fresh dates, we sallied forth to admire the beauties of the place. We are once more on classic ground, and this wady, celebrated for the purity of its air, has from remote ages been a favorite resort of the Meccans.

Exactly at noon Masud seized the halter of the foremost

camel, and we started down the fiumara. Troops of Bedouin girls looked over the orchard walls laughingly, and children came out to offer us fresh fruit and sweet water. In some places were clumps of trees, and scattered villages warned us that we were approaching a city. Far to the left rose the blue peaks of Taif, and the mountain road, a white thread upon the nearer heights, was pointed out to me. Here I first saw the tree, or rather shrub, which bears the balm of Gilead, erst so celebrated for its tonic and stomachic properties. I told Shaykh Masud to break off a twig, which he did heedlessly. The act was witnessed by our party with a roar of laughter, and the astounded shaykh was warned that he had become subject to an atoning sacrifice.* Of course he denounced me as the instigator, and I could not fairly refuse assistance. The tree has of late years been carefully described by many botanists; I will only say that the bark resembled in color a cherry-stick pipe, the inside was a light yellow, and the juice made my fingers stick together.

As we jogged on we were passed by the cavalcade of no less a personage than the Sherif of Meccah. Abd el Muttalib bin Ghalib is a dark, beardless old man, with African features, derived from his mother. He was plainly dressed in white garments and a white muslin turban, which made him look jet black; he rode an ambling mule, and the only emblem of his dignity was the large green satin umbrella borne by an attendant on foot.† Scattered

* This being one of the "Muharrimat," or actions forbidden to a pilgrim. At all times, say the Moslems, there are three vile trades, viz., those of the Harak el Hajar (stone-burner), the Kati el Shajar (tree-cutter), and the Bayi el Bashar (man-seller).

† From India to Abyssinia the umbrella is the sign of royalty: the Arabs of Meccah and Sennaa probably derived the custom from the Hindus.

around him were about forty matchlock-men, mostly slaves.

We halted as evening approached, and strained our eyes, but all in vain, to catch sight of Meccah, which lies in a winding valley. By Shaykh Abdullah's direction I recited, after the usual devotions, the following prayer. The reader is forewarned that it is difficult to preserve the flowers of Oriental rhetoric in a European tongue.

"O Allah! verily this is thy safeguard (Amn) and thy Sanctuary (Haram)! Into it whoso entereth becometh safe (Amin). So deny (Harrim) my flesh and blood, my bones and skin, to hell-fire. O Allah! save me from thy wrath on the day when thy servants shall be raised from the dead. I conjure thee by this that thou art Allah, besides whom is none (thou only), the merciful, the compassionate. And have mercy upon our lord Mohammed, and upon the progeny of our lord Mohammed, and upon his followers, one and all!" This was concluded with the "Talbiyat," and with an especial prayer for myself.

We again mounted, and night completed our disappointment. About 1 A.M. I was aroused by general excitement. "Meccah! Meccah!" cried some voices; "The Sanctuary! O the Sanctuary!" exclaimed others; and all burst into loud "Labbayk," not unfrequently broken by sobs. I looked out from my litter, and saw by the light of the southern stars the dim outlines of a large city, a shade darker than the surrounding plain. We were passing over the last ridge by a "winding path" flanked on both sides by watch-towers, which command the "Darb el Maala," or road leading from the north into Meccah. Thence we passed into the Maabidah (northern suburb), where the Sherif's palace is built. After this, on the left hand, came the deserted abode of the Sherif bin Aun, now said to be a "haunted house."* Opposite to it lies the Jannat el Maala, the holy cemetery of Meccah. Thence, turning to the right, we entered the Sulaymaniyah or Afghan quarter. Here the boy Mohammed, being an inhabitant of the Shamiyah or Syrian ward, thought proper to display some apprehension. These two are on bad terms; children never meet without exchanging volleys of stones, and men fight furiously with quarter-staves. Sometimes, despite the terrors of religion, the knife and sabre are drawn. But these hostilities have their code. If a citizen be killed, there is a subscription for blood-money. An inhabitant of one quarter, passing singly through another, becomes a guest; once beyond the walls, he is likely to be beaten to insensibility by his hospitable foes.

At the Sulaymaniyah we turned off the main road into a bye-way, and ascended by narrow lanes the rough heights of Jebel Hindi, upon which stands a small whitewashed and crenellated building called a "fort." Thence descending, we threaded dark streets, in places crowded with rude cots and dusky figures, and finally at 2 A. M. we found ourselves at the door of the boy Mohammed's house.

We arrived on the morning of Sunday the 7th Zu'l Hijjah (11th September, 1853), and had one day before the beginning of the pilgrimage to repose and visit the Haram. From El Medinah to Meccah the distance, according to my calculation, was 248 English miles, which was accomplished in eleven marches.

* I cannot conceive what made the accurate Niebuhr fall into the strange error that "apparitions are unknown in Arabia." Arabs fear to sleep alone, to enter the bath at night, to pass by cemeteries during dark, and to sit amongst ruins, simply for fear of apparitions. And Arabia, together with Persia, has supplied half the Western World —Southern Europe—with its ghost stories and tales of angels, demons, and fairies. To quote Milton, the land is struck "with superstition as with a planet."

## CHAPTER XXIV.

### THE HOUSE OF ALLAH.

THE House of Allah has been so fully described by my predecessors, that there is little inducement to attempt a new portrait. Readers, however, may desire a view of the great sanctuary, and, indeed, without a plan and its explanation, the ceremonies of the Haram would be scarcely intelligible. I will do homage to the memory of the accurate Burckhardt, and extract from his pages a description which may be illustrated by a few notes.

"The Kaabah stands in an oblong square (enclosed by a great wall) 250 paces long, and 200 broad, none of the sides of which run quite in a straight line, though at first sight the whole appears to be of a regular shape. This open square is enclosed on the eastern side by a colonnade. The pillars stand in a quadruple row; they are three deep on the other sides, and united by pointed arches, every four of which support a small dome plastered and whitened on the outside. These domes, according to Kotobeddyn, are 152 in number.* The pillars are above twenty feet in height,

* On each short side I counted 24 domes; on the long 35. This would give a total of 118 along the cloisters. The Arabs reckon in all

and generally from one foot and a half to one foot and three quarters in diameter; but little regularity has been observed in regard to them. Some are of white marble, granite or porphyry; but the greater number are of common stone of the Meccah mountains. El Fasy states the whole at 589, and says they are all of marble excepting 126, which are of common stone, and three of composition. Kotobeddyn reckons 555, of which, according to him, 311 are of marble, and the rest of the stone taken from the neighboring mountains; but neither of these authors lived to see the latest repairs of the mosque, after the destruction occasioned by a torrent in A. D. 1626.* Between every three or four columns stands an octagonal one, about four feet in thickness. On the east side are two shafts of reddish grey granite in one piece, and one fine grey porphyry with slabs of white feldspath. On the north side is one red granite column, and one of fine-grained red porphyry; these are probably the columns which Kotobeddyn states to have been brought from Egypt, and principally from Akhmin (Panopolis), when the chief (Caliph) El Mohdy enlarged the mosque in A. H. 163. Among the 450 or 500 columns which form the enclosure I found not any two capitals or bases exactly alike. The capitals are of coarse Saracen workmanship; some of them, which had served for former buildings, by the igno-

152; viz. 24 on the east side, on the north 36, on the south 36; one on the mosque corner, near the Zarurah minaret; 16 at the porch of the Bab el Ziyadah; and 15 at the Bab Ibrahim. The shape of these domes is the usual "Media-Naranja," and the superstition of the Meccans informs the pilgrim that they cannot be counted. Books reckon 1352 pinnacles or battlements on the temple wall.

* I counted in the temple 554 pillars. It is, however, difficult to be accurate, as the four colonnades and the porticos about the two great gates are irregular; topographical observations, moreover, must here be much under difficulties. Ali Bey numbers them roughly at "plus de 500 colonnes et pilastres."

rance of the workmen, have been placed upside down upon the shafts. I observed about half a dozen marble bases of good Grecian workmanship. A few of the marble columns bear Arabic or Cufic inscriptions, in which I read the dates 863 and 762 (A. H.)* A column on the east side exhibits a very ancient Cufic inscription, somewhat defaced, which I could neither read nor copy. Some of the columns are strengthened with broad iron rings or bands,† as in many other Saracen buildings of the East.

"Some parts of the walls and arches are gaudily painted in stripes of yellow, red, and blue, as are also minarets. Paintings of flowers, in the usual Muselman style, are nowhere seen; the floors of the colonnades are paved with large stones badly cemented together."

"Some paved causeways lead from the colonnades towards the Kaabah, or Holy House, in the centre. They are of sufficient breadth to admit four or five persons to walk abreast, and they are elevated about nine inches above the ground. Between these causeways, which are covered with fine gravel or sand, grass appears growing in several places, produced by the Zem Zem water oozing out of the jars placed in (*on*) the ground in long rows during the day.‡ There is a descent of eight or ten steps from the gates on the north side into the platform of the colonnade,

* The author afterwards informs us, that "the temple has been so often ruined and repaired, that no traces of remote antiquity are to be found about it." He mentions some modern and unimportant inscriptions upon the walls and over the gates. Knowing that many of the pillars were sent in ships from Syria and Egypt by the Caliph El Mahdi, a traveller would have expected better things.

† The reason being, that "those shafts formed of the Meccan stone are mostly in three pieces; but the marble shafts are in one piece."

‡ The jars are little amphoræ, each inscribed with the name of the donor and a peculiar cypher.

and of three or four steps from the gates on the south side."

"Towards the middle of this area stands the Kaabah; it is 115 paces from the north colonnade, and 88 from the south. For this want of symmetry we may readily account, the Kaabah having existed prior to the mosque, which was built around it, and enlarged at different periods. The Kaabah is an oblong massive structure, 18 paces in length, 14 in breadth, and from 35 to 40 feet in height. It is constructed of the grey Mekka stone, in large blocks of different sizes joined together, in a very rough manner, with bad cement.* It was entirely rebuilt, as it now stands, in A. D. 1627. The torrent in the preceding year had thrown down three of its sides, and, preparatory to its re-erection, the fourth side was, according to Asamy, pulled down, after the Olemas, or learned divines, had been consulted on the question whether mortals might be permitted to destroy any part of the holy edifice without incurring the charge of sacrilege and infidelity."

"The Kaabah stands upon a base two feet in height, which presents a sharp inclined plane.† Its roof being flat, it has at a distance the appearance of a perfect cube. The

* I would alter this sentence thus:—"It is built of fine grey granite in horizontal courses of masonry of irregular depth; the stones are tolerably fitted together, and held by excellent mortar like Roman cement." The lines are also straight.

† This base is called El Shazarwan, from the Persian Shadarwan, a cornice, eaves, or canopy. It is in pent-house shape, projecting about a foot beyond the wall, and composed of fine white marble slabs, polished like glass; there are two breaks in it, one opposite and under the doorway, and another in front of Ishmael's tomb. Pilgrims are directed, during circumambulation, to keep their bodies outside of the Shazarwan; this would imply it to be part of the building, but its only use appears in the large brass rings welded into it, for the purpose of holding down the Kaabah covering.

only door which affords entrance, and which is opened but two or three times a year,* is on the north side and about seven feet above the ground. In the first periods of Islam, however, when it was rebuilt in A. H. 64 by Ibn Zebeyr, chief of Mecca, it had two doors even with the ground-floor of the mosque. The present door (which, according to Azraky, was brought hither from Constantinople in A. D. 1633) is wholly coated with silver, and has several gilt ornaments; upon its threshold are placed every night various small lighted wax candles, and perfuming pans, filled with musk, aloe-wood, &c."†

"At the north-east (south-east) corner of the Kaabah, near the door, is the famous 'Black Stone;'‡ it forms a part of

* In Ibn Jubair's time the Kaabah was opened every day in Rajab, and in other months on every Monday and Friday. The house may now be entered ten or twelve times a year gratis; and by pilgrims as often as they can collect, amongst parties, a sum sufficient to tempt the guardians' cupidity.

† Pilgrims and ignorant devotees collect the drippings of wax, the ashes of the aloe-wood, and the dust from the "Atabah," or threshold of the Kaabah, either to rub upon their foreheads or to preserve as relics. These superstitious practices are sternly rebuked by the Ulema.

‡ I will not enter into the fabulous origin of the Hajar el Aswad. Some of the traditions connected with it are truly absurd. "When Allah," says Ali, "made covenant with the sons of Adam on the Day of Fealty, he placed the paper inside the stone;" it will, therefore, appear at the judgment, and bear witness to all who have touched it. Moslems agree that it was originally white, and became black by reason of men's sins. It appeared to me a common aërolite covered with a thick shaggy coating, glossy and pitch-like, worn and polished. Dr. Wilson of Bombay showed me a specimen in his possession, which externally appeared to be a black slag, with the inside of a bright and sparkling greyish-white, the result of admixture of nickel with the iron. This might possibly, as the learned Orientalist then suggested, account for the mythic change of color, its appearance on earth after a thunder-storm, and its being originally a material part of the heavens. Kutb el

the sharp angle of the building* at four or five feet above the ground.† It is an irregular oval, about seven inches in diameter, with an undulating surface, composed of about a dozen smaller stones of different sizes and shapes, well joined together with a small quantity of cement, and perfectly well smoothed: it looks as if the whole had been broken into many pieces by a violent blow, and then united again. It is very difficult to determine accurately the quality of this stone, which has been worn to its present surface by the millions of touches and kisses it has received. It appeared to me like a lava, containing several small extraneous particles of a whitish and of a yellowish substance. Its color is now a deep reddish brown, approaching to black. It is surrounded on all sides by a border composed of a substance which I took to be a close cement of pitch and gravel of a similar, but not quite the same brownish color.‡ This border serves to support its detached

Din expressly declares that, when the Karamitah restored it after twenty-two years to the Meccans, men kissed it and rubbed it upon their brows; and remarked that the blackness was only superficial, the inside being white.

* Presenting this appearance in profile. The Hajar has suffered from the iconoclastic principle of Islam, having once narrowly escaped destruction by order of El Hakim of Egypt. In these days the metal rim serves as a protection as well as an ornament.

† The height of the Hajar from the ground, according to my measurement, is four feet nine inches; Ali Bey places it forty-two inches above the pavement.

‡ The color appeared to me black and metallic, and the centre of the stone was sunk about two inches below the metal circle. Round the sides was a reddish brown cement, almost level with the metal, and sloping down to the middle of the stone.

Ibn Jubair declares the depth of the stone unknown, but that most people believe it to extend two cubits into the wall. In his day it was three "Shibr" (the large span from the thumb to the little finger tip) broad, and one span long, with knobs, and a joining of four pieces,

pieces; it is two or three inches in breadth, and rises a little above the surface of the stone. Both the border and the stone itself are encircled by a silver band,* broader below than above, and on the two sides, with a considerable swelling below, as if a part of the stone were hidden under it. The lower part of the border is studded with silver nails."

"In the south-east corner of the Kaabah, or, as the Arabs call it, Rokn el Yemany, there is another stone about five feet from the ground; it is one foot and a half in length, and two inches in breadth, placed upright, and of the common Meccah stone. This the people walking round the Kaabah touch only with the right hand; they do not kiss it.†

"On the north side of the Kaabah, just by its door, and close to the wall, is a slight hollow in the ground, lined with marble, and sufficiently large to admit of three persons sitting. Here it is thought meritorious to pray: the spot is called El Maajan, and supposed to be where Abraham and his son Ismail kneaded the chalk and mud which they used in building the Kaabah; and near this Maajan the former is said to have placed the large stone upon which he stood while working at the masonry. On the basis of the Kaabah, just over the Maajan, is an ancient Cufic inscription; but this I was unable to decipher, and had no opportunity of copying it."

"On the west (north-west) side of the Kaabah, about two feet below its summit, is the famous Myzab, or water-

which the Karamitah had broken. The stone was set in a silver band. Its softness and moisture were such, says Ibn Jubair, "that the sinner never would remove his mouth from it, which phenomenon made the Prophet declare it to be the covenant of Allah on earth."

* The band is now a massive arch of gold or silver gilt. I found the aperture in which the stone is, one span and three fingers long.

† I have frequently seen it kissed by men and women.

spout,* through which the rain-water collected on the roof of the building is discharged, so as to fall upon the ground; it is about four feet in length, and six inches in breadth, as well as I could judge from below, with borders equal in height to its breadth. At the mouth hangs what is called the beard of the Myzab: a gilt board, over which the water flows. This spout was sent hither from Constantinople in A. H. 981, and is *reported* to be of pure gold. The pavement round the Kaabah, below the Myzab, was laid down in A. H. 826, and consists of various colored stones, forming a very handsome specimen of mosaic. There are two large slabs of fine *verde antico* in the centre, which, according to Makrizi, were sent thither, as presents from Cairo, in A. H. 241. This is the spot where, according to Mohammedan tradition, Ismayl the son of Ibrahim, and his mother Hijirah are buried; and here it is meritorious for the pilgrim to recite a prayer of two Rikats. On this side is a semicircular wall, the two extremities of which are in a line with the sides of the Kaabah, and distant from it three or four feet, leaving an opening, which leads to the burial-place of Ismayl. The wall bears the name of El Hatym; and the area which it encloses is called Hedjer, on account of its being separated from the Kaabah: the wall itself also is sometimes so called."

"Tradition says that the Kaabah once extended as far as the Hatym, and that this side having fallen down just at the time of the Hadj, the expenses of repairing it were demanded from the pilgrims, under a pretence that the revenues of government were not acquired in a manner sufficiently pure to admit of their application towards a pur-

* Generally called Myzab el Rahmah (of mercy). It carries rain from the roof, and discharges it upon Ishmael's grave, where pilgrims stand fighting to catch it. In El Edrisi's time it was of wood; now it is said to be gold, but it looks very dingy.

pose so sacred. The sum, however, obtained proved very inadequate; all that could be done, therefore, was to raise a wall, which marked the space formerly occupied by the Kaabah. This tradition, although current among the Metowefs (cicerones), is at variance with history; which declares that the Hedjer was built by the Beni Koreish, who contracted the dimensions of the Kaabah: that it was united to the building by Hadjadj, and again separated from it by Ibn Zebeyr. It is asserted by Fasy, that a part of the Hedjer as it now stands was never comprehended within the Kaabah. The law regards it as a portion of the Kaabah, inasmuch as it is esteemed equally meritorious to pray in the Hedjer as in the Kaabah itself; and the pilgrims who have not an opportunity of entering the latter are permitted to affirm upon oath that they have prayed in the Kaabah, although they have only prostrated themselves within the enclosure of the Hatym. The wall is built of solid stone, about five feet in height, and four in thickness, cased all over with white marble, and inscribed with prayers and invocations neatly sculptured upon the stone in modern characters. These and the casing, are the work of El Ghoury, the Egyptian sultan, in A. H. 917. The walk round the Kaabah is performed on the outside of the wall—the nearer to it the better."

"Round the Kaabah is a good pavement of marble* about eight inches below the level of the great square; it was laid in A. H. 981, by order of the sultan, and describes an irregular oval; it is surrounded by thirty-two slender gilt pillars, or rather poles, between every two of which are suspended seven glass lamps, always lighted after sunset.†

* It is a fine, close, grey granite, polished like glass by the feet of the faithful; the walk is called El Mataf, or the place of circumambulation.

† These are now iron posts, very numerous, supporting cross rods, and of tolerably elegant shape. In Ali Bey's time there were "trente-

Beyond the poles is a second pavement, about eight paces broad, somewhat elevated above the first, but of coarser work; then another six inches higher, and eighteen paces broad, upon which stand several small buildings; beyond this is the gravelled ground; so that two broad steps may be said to lead from the square down to the Kaabah. The small buildings just mentioned which surround the Kaabah are the five Makams, with the well of Zem Zem, the arch called Bab es Salam, and the Mambar."

"Opposite the four sides of the Kaabah stand four other small buildings, where the Imaums of the orthodox Mohammedan sects, the Hanefy, Shafey, Hanbaly, and Maleky take their station, and guide the congregation in their prayers. The Makam el Maleky on the south, and that of Hanbaly opposite the Black Stone, are small pavilions open on all sides, and supported by four slender pillars, with a light sloping roof, terminating in a point, exactly in the style of Indian pagodas. The Makam el Hanefy, which is the largest, being fifteen paces by eight, is open on all sides, and supported by twelve small pillars; it has an upper story, also open, where the Mueddin who calls to prayers takes his stand. This was first built in A. H. 923, by Sultan Selim I.; it was afterwards rebuilt by Khoshgeldy, governor of Djidda, in 947; but all the four Makams, as they now stand, were built in A. H. 1074. The Makam-es'-Shafey is over the well Zem Zem, to which it serves as an upper chamber.*

une colonnes minces en piliers en bronze." Some native works say thirty-three, including two marble columns. Between each two hang several white or green glass globe-lamps, with wicks and oil floating on water; their light is faint and dismal. The whole of the lamps in the Haram is said to be more than 1000, yet they serve but to "make darkness visible."

* Only the Muezzin takes his stand here, and the Shafeis pray behind their Imam on the pavement round the Kaabah, between the

"Near their respective Makams the adherents of the four different sects seat themselves for prayers. During my stay at Meccah the Hanefys always began their prayer first; but, according to Muselman custom, the Shafeys should pray first in the mosque; then the Hamefys, Malekys, and Hanbalys. The prayer of the Maghreb is an exception, which they are all enjoined to utter together.* The Makam el Hanbaly is the place where the officers of government and other great people are seated during prayers; here the Pacha and the sherif are placed, and in their absence the eunuchs of the temple. These fill the space under this Makam in front, and behind it the female Hadjys who visit the temple have their places assigned, to which they repair principally for the two evening prayers, few of them being seen in the mosque at the three other daily prayers: they also perform the Towaf, or walk round the Kaabah, but generally at night, though it is not uncommon to see them walking in the day-time among the men."

"The present building which encloses Zem Zem stands close by the Makam Hanbaly, and was erected in A. H. 1072: it is of a square shape, and of massive construction, with an

corner of the well Zem Zem, and the Makam Ibrahim. This place is forty cubits from the Kaabah, that is to say, eight cubits nearer than the northern and southern "Makams." Thus the pavement forms an irregular oval ring round the house.

* In Burckhardt's time the schools prayed according to the seniority of their founders, and they uttered the Azan of El Maghrib together, because that is a peculiarly delicate hour, which easily passes by unnoticed. In the twelfth century, at all times but the evening, the Shafei began, then came the Maliki and Hanbali simultaneously, and, lastly, the Hanafi. Now the Shaykh el Muezzin begins the call, which is taken up by the others. He is a Hanafi; as indeed are all the principal people at Meccah, only a few wild Sherifs of the hills being Shafei.

entrance to the north, opening into the room which contains the well. This room is beautifully ornamented with marbles of various colors; and adjoining to it, but having a separate door, is a small room with a stone reservoir, which is always full of Zem Zem water. This the Hadjys get to drink by passing their hand with a cup through an iron grated opening, which serves as a window, into the reservoir, without entering the room. The mouth of the well is surrounded by a wall five feet in height and about ten feet in diameter. Upon this the people stand who draw up the water in leathern buckets, an iron railing being so placed as to prevent their falling in. In El Fasy's time there were eight marble basins in this room, for the purpose of ablution.

"On the north-east (south-east) side of Zem Zem stand two small buildings, one behind the other, called El Kobbateyn; they are covered by domes painted in the same manner as the mosque, and in them are kept water-jars, lamps, carpets, mats, brooms, and other articles used in the very mosque. These two ugly buildings are injurious to the interior appearance of the building, their heavy forms and structure being very disadvantageously contrasted with the light and airy shape of the Makams. I heard some Hadjys from Greece, men of better taste than the Arabs, express their regret that the Kobbateyn should be allowed to disfigure the mosque. They were built by Khoshgeldy, governor of Djidda A. H. 947; one is called Kobbert el Abbas, from having been placed on the site of a small tank said to have been formed by Abbas, the uncle of Mohammed."

"A few paces west (north-west) of Zem Zem, and directly opposite to the door of the Kaabah, stands a ladder or staircase, which is moved up to the wall of the Kaabah on days when that building is opened, and by which the visitors ascend to the door. It is of wood, with some carved ornaments, moves on low wheels, and is sufficiently broad to admit of four persons ascending abreast. The first ladder was sent hither from Cairo in A. H. 818 by Moyaed Abou el Naser, king of Egypt."

"In the same line with the ladder and close by it stands a lightly built insulated and circular arch, about fifteen feet wide, and eighteen feet high, called Bab-es-Salam, which must not be confounded with the great gate of the mosque, bearing the same name. Those who enter the Bait Ullah for the first time are enjoined to do so by the outer and inner Bab-es-Salam; in passing under the latter they are to exclaim, 'O God, may it be a happy entrance.' I do not know by whom this arch was built, but it appears to be modern."

"Nearly in front of the Bab-es-Salam and nearer than the Kaabah than any of the other surrounding buildings, stands the Makam Ibrahim.* This is a small building supported by six pillars about eight feet high, four of which are surrounded from top to bottom by a fine iron railing, while they leave the space beyond the two hind pillars open; within the railing is a frame about five feet square, terminating in a pyramidal top, and said to contain the sacred stone upon which Ibrahim stood when he built the Kaabah, and which with the help of his son Ismayl he had removed from hence to the place called Maajen, already mentioned. The stone is said to have yielded under the weight of the Patriarch, and to preserve the impression of his foot still visible upon it; but no hadjy has ever seen it,† as the frame

* "The (praying) place of Abraham." Readers will remember that the Meccan Mosque is peculiarly connected with Ibrahim, whom Moslems prefer to all prophets except Mohammed.

† This I believe to be incorrect. I was asked five dollars for permission to enter; but the sum was too high for my finances. Learned men told me that the stone shows the impress of two feet, especially the

is always entirely covered with a brocade of red silk richly embroidered. Persons are constantly seen before the railing invoking the good offices of Ibrahim; and a short prayer must be uttered by the side of the Makam after the walk round the Kaabah is completed. In this part of the area the Khalif Soleyman built a fine reservoir in A. H. 97, which was filled from a spring east of Arafat; but the Mekkawys destroyed it after his death, on the pretence that the water of Zem Zem was preferable."

"On the side of Makam Ibrahim, facing the middle part of the front of the Kaabah, stands the Mambar, or pulpit of the mosque; it is elegantly formed of fine white marble, with many sculptured ornaments; and was sent as a present to the mosque in A. H. 969 by Sultan Soleyman Ibn Selym. A straight, narrow staircase leads up to the post of the Khatyb, or preacher, which is surmounted by a gilt polygonal pointed steeple, resembling an obelisk. Here a sermon is preached on Fridays and on certain festivals. These, like the Friday sermons of all mosques in the Mohammedan countries, are usually of the same turn, with some slight alterations upon extraordinary occasions."

"I have now described all the buildings within the inclosure of the temple."

"The gates of the mosque are nineteen in number, and are distributed about it without any order or symmetry."

Burckhardt's description of the gates is short and imperfect. On the eastern side of the mosque there are four principal entrances, seven on the southern side, three in the western, and five in the northern wall.

The eastern gates are the Greater Bab el Salam, through which the pilgrim enters the mosque; it is close to

big toes, and devout pilgrims fill the cavities with water, which they rub over their eyes and faces.

the north-east angle. Next to it the Lesser Bab el Salam, with two small arches; thirdly, the Bab el Nabi, where the Prophet used to pass through from Khadijah's house; and, lastly, near the south-east corner, the Bab Ali, or of the Beni Hashem, opening upon the street between Safa and Marwah.

Beyond the north-eastern corner, in the northern wall, is the Bab Duraybah, a small entrance with one arch. Next to it, almost fronting the Kaabah, is the grand adit, "Bab el Ziyadah," also known as Bab el Nadwah. Here the colonnade, projecting far beyond the normal line, forms a small square or hall supported by pillars, and a false colonnade of sixty-one columns leads to the true cloister of the mosque. This portion of the building being cool and shady, is crowded by the poor, the diseased, and the dying, during divine worship, and at other times by idlers, schoolboys, and merchants. Passing through three external arches, pilgrims descend by a flight of steps into the hall, where they deposit their slippers, it not being considered decorous to hold them when circumambulating the Kaabah.* A broad pavement, in the shape of an irregular triangle, whose base is the cloister, leads to the circuit of the house.

In the western wall are three entrances. The single-arched gate nearest to the north angle is called Bab Beni Saham or Bab el Umrah, because pilgrims pass through it to the Tanim and the ceremony El Umrah (Little Pilgrimage). In the centre of the wall is the Bab Ibrahim, or Bab el Khayyatin (the Tailor's Gate); a single arch leading into a large projecting square, like that of the Ziyadah en-

* An old pair of slippers is here what the "shocking bad hat" is at a crowded house in Europe, a self-preserver. Burckhardt lost three pair. I, more fortunate or less wealthy, only one.

trance, but somewhat smaller. Near the south-west corner is a double-arched adit, the Bab el Widaa ("of Farewell"): hence departing pilgrims issue forth from the temple.

At the western end of the southern wall is the two-arched Bab Umm Hani, so called after the lady's residence, when included in the mosque. Next to it is a similar building, which derives its name from the large college "Madrasat Ujlan;" some call it Bab el Sherif, because it is opposite one of the palaces. After which, and also pierced with two arches, is the Bab el Jiyad, the gate leading to Jebel Jiyad. The next is also double arched, and called the Bab el Mujahid or el Rahmah ("of Mercy"). Nearly opposite the Kaabah, and connected with the pavement by a raised line of stone, is the Bab el Safa, through which pilgrims now issue to perform the ceremony "El Sai;" it is a small and unconspicuous erection. Next to it is the Bab el Baglah with two arches, and close to the south-east angle of the mosque the Bab Yunus, alias Bab Bazan, alias Bab el Zayt, alias Bab el Asharah, "of the ten," because a favorite with the ten first Sahabah, or Companions of the Prophet. "Most of these gates," says Burckhardt, "have high pointed arches; but a few round arches are seen among them, which, like all arches of this kind in the Hejar, are nearly semicircular. They are without ornament, except the inscription on the exterior, which commemorates the name of the builder, and they are all posterior in date to the fourteenth century. As each gate consists of two or three arches, or divisions, separated by narrow walls, these divisions are counted in the enumeration of the gates leading into the Kaabah, and they make up the number thirty-nine. There being no doors to the gates, the mosque is consequently open at all times. I have crossed at every hour of the night, and always found people there, either at prayers or walking about."*

"The outside walls of the mosques are those of the houses which surround it on all sides. These houses belonged originally to the mosque; the greater part are now the property of individuals. They are let out to the richest Hadjys, at very high prices, as much as 500 piastres being given during the pilgrimage for a good apartment with windows opening into the mosque. Windows have in consequence been opened in many parts of the walls on a level with the street, and above that of the floor of the colonnades. Hadjys living in these apartments are allowed to perform the Friday's prayers at home; because, having the Kaabah in view from the windows, they are supposed to be in the mosque itself, and to join in prayer those assembled within the temple. Upon a level with the ground floor of the colonnades and opening into them are small apartments formed in the walls, having the appearance of dungeons; these have remained the property of the mosque while the houses above them belong to private individuals. They are let out to watermen, who deposit in them the Zem Zem jars, or to less opulent Hadjys who wish to live in the mosque. Some of the surrounding houses still belong to the mosque, and were originally intended for public schools, as their name of Medresa implies; they are now all let out to Hadjys."

"The exterior of the mosque is adorned with seven minarets irregularly distributed. They are quadrangular or round steeples, in no way differing from other minarets. The entrance to them is from the different buildings round the mosque, which they adjoin. A beautiful view of the

* The Meccans love to boast that at no hour of the day or night is the Kaabah ever seen without a devotee to perform "Tawaf."

busy crowd below is attained by ascending the most northern one."*

Having described at length the establishment attached to the mosque of El Medinah, I spare my readers a detailed account of the crowd of idlers that hang about the Meccan temple. The Naib el Haram, or vice-intendant, is one Sayyid Ali, said to be of Indian extraction; he is superior to all the attendants. There are about eighty eunuchs, whose chief, Serur Agha, was a slave of Mohammed Ali Pacha. Their pay varies from 100 to 1000 piastres per mensem; it is, however, inferior to the Medinah salaries. The Imams, Muezzins, Khatibs, Zem Zemis, &c., &c., are under their respective Shaykhs who are of the Ulema.

Briefly to relate the history of the Kaabah.

The "House of Allah" is supposed to have been built and rebuilt ten times.

1. The first origin of the idea is manifestly a symbolical allusion to the angels standing before the Almighty and praising his name. When Allah, it is said, informed the celestial throng that he was about to send a viceregent on earth, they deprecated the design. Being reproved in these words, "God knoweth what ye know not," and dreading eternal anger, they compassed the Arsh, or throne, in adoration. Upon this Allah created the Bait el Maamur, four jasper pillars with a ruby roof, and the angels circumambulated it, crying, "Praise to Allah, and exalted be Allah, and there is no Allah but Allah, and Allah is omnipotent!" The Creator then ordered them to build a simi-

* A stranger must be careful how he appears at a minaret window, unless he would have a bullet whizzing past his head. Arabs are especially jealous of being overlooked, and have no fellow-feeling for votaries of "beautiful views." For this reason here, as in Egypt, a blind Muezzin is preferred, and many ridiculous stories are told about men who for years have counterfeited cecity to live in idleness.

lar house for man on earth. This, according to Ali, took place 40, according to Abu Horayrah, 2000 years before the creation; both authorities, however, are agreed that the firmaments were spread above and the seven earths beneath this Bait el Maamur.

2. There is considerable contradiction concerning the second house. Kaab related that Allah sent down with Adam* a Khaymah, or tabernacle of hollow ruby, which the angels raised on stone pillars. This was also called Bait el Maamur. Adam received an order to compass it about; after which, he begged a reward for obedience, and was promised a pardon to himself and all his progeny who repent.

Others declare that Adam, expelled from Paradise, and lamenting that he no longer heard the prayers of the angels, was ordered by Allah to take the stones of five hills, Lebanon, Sinai, Tur Zayt, Ararat, and Hira, which afforded the first stone. Gabriel, smiting his wing upon earth, opened a foundation to the seventh layer, and the position of the building is exactly below the heavenly Bait el Maamur,—a Moslem corruption of the legends concerning the heavenly and the earthly Jerusalem. Our first father compassed it as he had seen the angels, and was by them taught the formula of prayer and the number of circuits.

According to others, again, this second house was not erected till after the "angelic foundation" was destroyed by time.

3. The history of the third house is also somewhat confused. When the Bait el Maamur, or, as others say, the tabernacle, was removed to heaven after Adam's death, a

* It must be remembered that the Moslems, like many of the Jews, hold that Paradise was not on earth, but in the lowest firmament, which is, as it were, a reflection of earth.

stone-and-mud building was placed in its stead by his son Shays (Seth). For this reason it is respected by the Sabæans, or Christians of St. John, as well as the Moslems. This Kaabah, according to some, was destroyed by the deluge, which materially altered its site. Others believe that it was raised to heaven. Others, again, declare that only the pillars supporting the heavenly tabernacle were allowed to remain. Most authorities agree in asserting that the Black Stone was stored up in Abu Kubays, whence that "first created of mountains" is called El Amin, "the Honest."

4. Abraham and his son were ordered to build the fourth house upon the old foundations: its materials, according to some, were taken from the five hills which supplied the second; others give the names Ohob, Kuds, Warka, Sinai, Hira, and a sixth, Abu Kubays. There was no roof; two doors, level with the ground, were pierced in the eastern and western walls; and inside, on the right hand, near the present entrance, a hole for treasure was dug. Gabriel restored the Black Stone, which Abraham, by his direction, placed in its present corner, as a sign where circumambulation is to begin; and the patriarch then learned all the complicated rites of pilgrimage. When this house was completed, Abraham, by Allah's order, ascended Jebel Sabir, and called the world to visit the sanctified spot; and all earth's sons heard him, even those "in their father's loins or in their mother's womb, from that day unto the day of resurrection."

5. The Amalikah (descended from Imlik, great-grandson of Sam, son of Noah), who first settled near Meccah, founded the fifth house.

6. The sixth Kaabah was built about the beginning of the Christian era by the Beni Jurham, the children of Kahtan, fifth descendant from Noah. The Jurham in-

habited the higher parts of Meccah, especially Jebel Kaakaan, so called from their clashing arms; whereas the Amalikah dwelt in the lower grounds, which obtained the name of Jiyad, from their generous horses.

7. Kusay bin Kilab, governor of Meccah and fifth forefather of the Prophet, built the seventh house, according to Abraham's plan. He roofed it over with palm leaves, stocked it with idols, and persuaded his tribe to settle near the Haram.

8. Kusay's house was burnt down by a woman's censer, which accidentally set fire to the Kiswat, or covering, and the walls were destroyed by a torrent. A merchant-ship belonging to a Greek trader, being wrecked at Jeddah, afforded material for the roof, and the crew were employed as masons. In digging the foundation they came to a green stone, like a camel's hunch, which, struck with a pickaxe, sent forth blinding lightning, and prevented further excavation.

When the eighth house was being built Mohammed was in his twenty-fifth year. His surname of El Amin, the Honest, probably induced the tribes to make him their umpire for the decision of a dispute about the position of the Black Stone, and who should have the honor of raising it to its place. He decided for the corner chosen by Abraham, and distributed the "Kudos" amongst the clans.

9. Abdullah bin Zubayr, nephew of Ayisha, re-built the Kaabah in A. H. 64. It had been weakened by fire, which burnt the covering, besides splitting the Black Stone into three pieces. Abdullah, hoping to fulfil a prophecy,* and seeing that the people of Meccah fled in alarm, pulled down

* As will afterwards be mentioned, almost every Meccan knows the prophecy of Mohammed that the birthplace of his fate will be destroyed by an army from Abyssinia.

the building by means of "thin-calved Abyssinian slaves;" and when they came to Abraham's foundation he saw that it included El Hijr, which part the Kuraysh had been unablo to build. The building was made of cut stone and fine limo brought from Yemen. During the building, a curtain was stretched round the walls, and pilgrims compassed them outside. When finished, it was perfumed inside and outside, and invested with brocade. Then Abdullah and all the citizens went forth to Tanim in procession, returned to perform Umrah, slew 100 victims, and rejoiced with great festivities.

The Caliph Abd el Malik bin Marwan besieged Abdullah bin Zubayr, who, after a brave defence, was slain. In A. H. 74 Hajjaj bin Yusuf, general of Abd el Malik's troops, wrote to the prince, informing him that Abdullah had made unauthorised additions to and changes in the Haram: the reply brought an order to rebuild the house. He gave the house a double roof, closed the western door, and raised the eastern four cubits and a span above the Mataf, or circuit, which he paved over. The Haram was enlarged and beautified by the Abbasides, especially by el Mehdi, El Mutamid, and El Mutazid. Some authors reckon, as an eleventh house, the repairs made by Sultan Murad Khan. On the night of Tuesday 20th Shaaban, A. H. 1030, a violent torrent swept the Haram; it rose one cubit above the threshold of the Kaabah, carried away the lamp-posts and the Makam Ibrahim, all the northern wall of the house, half of the eastern, and one-third of the western side. It subsided on Wednesday night. The repairs were not finished till A. H. 1040. The greater part, however, of the building dates from the time of El Hajjaj; and Moslems, who never mention his name without a curse, knowingly circumambulate his work.

The present proofs of the Kaabah's sanctity, as adduced by the learned, are puerile enough, but curious. The Ulema have made much of the verselet: "Verily the first house built for mankind (to worship in) is that in Beccah (Meccah), blessed and a salvation to the three worlds. Therein (fihi) are manifest signs, the standing-place of Abraham, which whoso entereth shall be safe," (Kor. ch. 3.) The word "therein" is interpreted to mean Meccah, and the "manifest signs" the Kaabah, which contains such marvels as the foot-prints on Abraham's platform and the spiritual safeguard of all who enter the Sanctuary. The other "signs," historical, psychical, and physical, are briefly these: The preservation of the Hajar el Aswad and the Makam Ibrahim from many foes, and the miracles put forth (as in the War of the Elephant), to defend the house; the violent and terrible deaths of the sacrilegious; and the fact that, in the Deluge, the large fish did not eat the little fish in the Haram. A wonderful desire and love impel men from distant regions to visit the holy spot, and the first sight of the Kaabah causes awe and fear, horripilation and tears. Furthermore, ravenous beasts will not destroy their prey in the Sanctuary land, and the pigeons and other birds never perch upon the house, except to be cured of sickness, for fear of defiling the roof. The Kaabah, though small, can contain any number of devotees; no one is ever hurt in it,* and invalids recover their health by rubbing themselves against the Kiswah and the Black Stone. Finally, it is observed that every day 100,000 mercies descend upon the house, and especially that if rain come up from the northern corner there is plenty in Irak; if from the south, there is plenty in Yemen; if from the east, plenty in India; if from the western, there is plenty in Syria; and if from all four angles, general plenty is presignified.

* This is an audacious falsehood; the Kaabah is scarcely ever opened without some accident happening.

## CHAPTER XXV.

### THE FIRST VISIT TO THE HOUSE OF ALLAH.

SCARCELY had the first smile of morning beamed upon the rugged head of Abu Kubays * when we arose, bathed, and proceeded in our pilgrim garb to the Sanctuary. We entered by the Bab el Ziyadah, or principal northern door, descended two long flights of steps, traversed the cloister, and stood in sight of the Bait Allah.

There at last it lay, the bourn of my long and weary pilgrimage, realizing the plans and hopes of many and many a year. The mirage medium of Fancy invested the huge

* This hill bounds Meccah on the east. According to many Moslems, Adam, with his wife and his son Seth, lie buried in a cave here. Others place his tomb at Muna; the majority at Najaf. The early Christians had a tradition that our first parents were interred under Mount Calvary; the Jews place their grave near Hebron. Habil (Abel), it is well known, is supposed to be entombed at Damascus! and Kabil (Cain) rests at last under Jebel Shamsan, the highest wall of the Aden crater, where he and his progeny, tempted by Iblis, erected the first fire-temple. It certainly deserves to be the sepulchre of the first murderer. The worship, however, was probably imported from India, where Agni (the fire god) was, as the Vedas prove, the object of man's earliest adoration.

catafalque and its gloomy pall with peculiar charms. There were no giant fragments of hoar antiquity as in Egypt, no remains of graceful and harmonious beauty as in Greece and Italy, no barbaric gorgeousness as in the buildings of India; yet the view was strange, unique, and how few have looked upon the celebrated shrine! I may truly say that, of all the worshippers who clung weeping to the curtain, or who pressed their beating hearts to the stone, none felt for the moment a deeper emotion than did the Haji from the far north. It was as if the poetical legend of the Arab spoke truth, and that waving wings of angels, not the sweet breeze of morning, were agitating and swelling the black coverings of the shrine. But, to confess humbling truth, theirs was the high feeling of religious enthusiasm, mine was the ecstasy of gratified pride.

Few Moslems contemplate for the first time the Kaabah without fear and awe; there is a popular jest against new comers, that they generally inquire the direction of prayer.* The boy Mohammed therefore left me for a few minutes to myself, but presently he warned me that it was time to begin. Advancing, we entered through the Bab Beni Shaybah, the "Gate of the Sons of the Old Woman."† There we raised our hands, repeated the Labbayk, the Takbir, and the Tahlil; after which we uttered certain supplications,

* This being the Kiblah, or fronting place, Moslems can pray all around it; a circumstance which of course cannot take place in any spot of El Islam but the Haram.

† The popular legend of this gate is, that when Abraham and his son were ordered to rebuild the Kaabah, they found the spot occupied by an old woman. She consented to remove her house on condition that the key of the new temple should be entrusted to her and to her descendants for ever and ever. The origin of this is, that Beni Shaybah means the "sons of an old woman" as well as "descendants of Shaybah." According to others, the Kaabah key was committed to the charge of Usman bin Talhah by the Prophet.

and drew our hands down our faces. Then we proceeded to the Shafei's place of prayer—the open pavement between the Makam Ibrahim and the well Zem Zem,—where we performed the usual two prostrations in honor of the mosque. This was followed by a cup of holy water * and a present to the Sakkas, or carriers, who for the consideration distributed a large earthen vaseful in my name to poor pilgrims. We then advanced towards the eastern angle of the Kaabah, in which is inserted the Black Stone, and standing about ten yards from it, repeated with upraised hands, "There is no god but Allah alone, whose covenant is truth, and whose servant is victorious. There is no god but Allah, without sharer, his is the kingdom; to him be praise, and he over all things is potent." After which we approached as close as we could to the stone. A crowd of

* The word Zem Zem has a doubtful origin. Some derive it from Zam Zam, or murmuring of its waters, others from Zam! Zam! (fill! fill! *i. e.* the bottle), Hagar's exclamation when she saw the stream. Sale translates it stay! stay! and says, that Hagar called out in the Egyptian language, to prevent her son wandering.

The produce of Zem Zem is held in great esteem. It is used for drinking and ablution, but for no baser purposes; and the Meccans advise pilgrims always to break their fast with it. It is apt to cause diarrhœa and boils, and I never saw a stranger drink it without a wry face. Sale is decidedly correct in his assertion; the flavor is a salt-bitter, much resembling an infusion of a tea-spoonful of Epsom salts in a large tumbler of tepid water. Moreover it is exceedingly "heavy" to the taste. For this reason Turks and other strangers prefer rain-water collected in cisterns and sold for five farthings a gugglet. It was a favorite amusement with me to watch them whilst they drank the holy water, and to taunt their scant irreverent potations.

The water is transmitted to distant regions in glazed earthen jars covered with basket work, and sealed by the Zem Zemis. Religious men break their lenten fast with it, apply it to their eyes to brighten vision, and imbibe a few drops at the hour of death, when Satan stands by holding a bowl of purest water, the price of the departing soul.

pilgrims preventing our touching it that time, we raised our hands to our ears in the first position of prayer, and then lowering them, exclaimed, "O Allah (I do this), in thy belief, and in verification of thy book, and in pursuance of thy Prophet's example—may Allah bless him and preserve! O Allah, I extend my hand to thee, and great is my desire to thee! O accept thou my supplication, and diminish my obstacles, and pity my humiliation, and graciously grant me thy pardon." After which, as we were still unable to reach the stone, we raised our hands to our ears, the palms facing the stone, as if touching it, recited the Takbir, the Tahlil, and the Hamdilah, blessed the Prophet, and kissed the finger-tips of the right hand.

Then commenced the ceremony of "Tawaf," or circumambulation, our route being the "Mataf," or low oval of polished granite immediately surrounding the Kaabah. I repeated, after my Mutawwif, or cicerone,* the Niyat of Tawaf. Then we began the prayer, "O Allah (I do this), in thy belief, and in verification of thy book, and in faithfulness to thy covenant, and in pursuance of the example of the Prophet Mohammed—may Allah bless him and preserve!" till we reached the place El Multazem, between the corner of the Black Stone and the Kaabah door. Here we ejaculated "O Allah, thou hast rights, so pardon my transgressing them." Opposite the door we repeated, "O Allah, verily the house is thy house, and the Sanctuary thy Sanctuary, and the safeguard thy safeguard, and this is the place of him who flies to thee from (hell) fire!" At the little building called Makam Ibrahim we said, "O Allah, verily this is the place of Abraham, who took refuge with and fled to thee from the fire!—O deny my flesh and blood, my skin and bones to the (eternal) flames!" As we paced slowly

* The Mutawwif, or Dalil, is the guide at Meccah.

round the north or Irak corner of the Kaabah we exclaimed, "O Allah, verily I take refuge with thee from polytheism and disobedience, hypocrisy and evil conversation, and evil thoughts concerning family, and property, and progeny!" When fronting the Mizab, or spout, we repeated the words, "O Allah, verily I beg of thee faith which shall not decline and a certainty which shall not perish, and the good aid of thy Prophet Mohammed—may Allah bless him and preserve! O Allah, shadow me in thy shadow on that day when there is no shade but thy shadow, and cause me to drink from the cup of thy Prophet Mohammed—may Allah," &c.!—"that pleasant draught after which is no thirst to all eternity, O Lord of honor and glory!" Turning the west corner, or the Rukn el Shami, we exclaimed, "O Allah, make it an acceptable pilgrimage, and a forgiveness of sins, and laudable endeavor, and a pleasant action (in thy sight), and a store which perisheth not, O thou glorious! O thou pardoner!" This was repeated thrice, till we arrived at the Yemani, or southern corner, where, the crowd being less importunate, we touched the wall with the right hand, after the example of the Prophet, and kissed the finger-tips. Between the south angle and that of the Black Stone, where our circuit would be completed, we said, "O Allah, verily I take refuge with thee from infidelity, and I take refuge with thee from want, and from the tortures of the tomb, and from the troubles of life and death. And I fly to thee from ignominy in this world and the next, and implore thy pardon for the present and for the future. O Lord, grant to me in this life prosperity, and in the next life prosperity, and save me from punishment of fire."

Thus finished a Shaut, or single course round the house. Of these we performed the three first at the pace called Harwalah, very similar to the French "*pas gymnastique*," or Tarammul, that is to say, "moving the shoulders as if walking in sand." The four latter are performed in Taammul, slowly and leisurely; the reverse of the Sai, or running. The Moslem origin of this custom is too well known to require mention. After each Taufah, or circuit, we being unable to kiss or even to touch the Black Stone, fronted towards it, raised our hands to our ears, exclaimed "In the name of Allah, and Allah is omnipotent!" kissed our fingers, and resumed the ceremony of circumambulation, as before, with "Allah, in thy belief," &c.!

At the conclusion of the Tawaf it was deemed advisable to attempt to kiss the stone. For a time I stood looking in despair at the swarming crowd of Bedouin and other pilgrims that besieged it. But the boy Mohammed was equal to the occasion. During our circuit he had displayed a fiery zeal against heresy and schism, by foully abusing every Persian in his path; * and the inopportune introduction of hard words into his prayers made the latter a strange patchwork; as "Ave Maria purissima—arrah, don't ye be letting the pig at the pot—sanctissima," and so forth. He might, for instance, be repeating "and I take refuge with thee from ignominy in this world," when "O thou rejected one, son of the rejected!" would be the interpolation addressed to some long-bearded Khorasani,—"and in that to come—O hog and brother of a hoggess!" And so he continued till I wondered that no one dared to

* In A.D. 1674, some wretch smeared the Black Stone with impurity, and every one who kissed it retired with a sullied beard. The Persians, says Burckhardt, were suspected of this sacrilege, and now their ill-fame has spread far; at Alexandria they were described to me as a people who defile the Kaabah. It is scarcely necessary to say, that a Shiah as well as a Sunni would look upon such an action with lively horror. The defilement of the Black Stone was probably the work of some Jew or Greek, who risked his life to gratify a furious bigotry.

turn and rend him. After vainly addressing the pilgrims, of whom nothing could be seen but a mosaic of occiputs and shoulder-blades, the boy Mohâmmed collected about half a dozen stalwart Meccans, with whose assistance, by sheer strength, we wedged our way into the thin and light-legged crowd. The Bedouins turned round upon us like wild cats, but they had no daggers. The season being autumn, they had not swelled themselves with milk for six months; and they had become such living mummies, that I could have managed single-handed half a dozen of them. After thus reaching the stone, despite popular indignation, testified by impatient shouts, we monopolised the use of it for at least ten minutes. Whilst kissing it and rubbing hands and forehead upon it I narrowly observed it, and came away persuaded that it is a big aërolite.*

Having kissed the stone, we fought our way through the crowd to the place called El Multazem.

After embracing the Multazem we repaired to the Shafei's place of prayer near the Makam Ibrahim, and there recited two prostrations, technically called "Sunnat el Tawaf," or the (Prophet's) practice of circumambulation. The chapter repeated in the first was "Say thou, O ye infidels:" in the second, "Say thou he is the one God." We then went to the door of the building in which is Zem Zem: there I was condemned to another nauseous draught, and was deluged with two or three skinfuls of water dashed

* It is curious that almost all travellers agree upon one point, namely, that the stone is volcanic. Ali Bey calls it "mineralogically" a "block of volcanic basalt, whose circumference is sprinkled with little crystals, pointed and straw-like, with rhombs of tile-red feldspath upon a dark background, like velvet or charcoal, except one of its protuberances, which is reddish." Burckhardt thought it was "a lava containing several small extraneous particles of a whitish and of a yellowish substance."

over my head *en douche*. This ablution causes sins to fall from the spirit like dust.* During the potation we prayed, "O Allah, verily I beg of thee plentiful daily bread, and profitable learning, and the healing of every disease!" Then we returned towards the Black Stone, stood far away opposite, because unable to touch it, ejaculated the Tekbir, the Tahlil, and the Hamdilah, and thoroughly worn out, with scorched feet and a burning head—both extremities, it must be remembered, were bare, and various delays had detained us till ten A.M.—I left the mosque.

In the evening, accompanied by the boy Mohammed, and followed by Shaykh Nur, who carried a lantern and a praying-rug, I again repaired to the "Navel of the World;"† this time æsthetically to enjoy the delights of the hour after the "gaudy, babbling, and remorseful day." The moon, now approaching the full, tipped the brow of Abu Kubays, and lit up the spectacle with a more solemn light. In the midst stood the huge bier-like erection,—

"Black as the wings
Which some spirit of ill o'er a sepulchre flings,"—

except where the moonbeams streaked it like jets of silver falling upon the darkest marble. It formed the point of rest for the eye; the little pagoda-like buildings and domes around it, with all their gilding and fretwork, vanished. One object, unique in appearance, stood in view—the

* These superstitions, I must remark in fairness, belong only to the vulgar.

† Ibn Haukal begins his cosmography with Meccah "because the temple of the Lord is situated there, and the holy Kaabah is the navel of the earth, and Meccah is styled in sacred writ the parent city, or the mother of towns." Unfortunately, Ibn Haukal, like most other Mohammedan travellers and geographers, says no more about Meccah.

temple of the one Allah, the God of Abraham, of Ishmael, and his posterity. Sublime it was, and expressing by all the eloquence of fancy the grandeur of the One Idea which vitalised El Islam, and the sternness and steadfastness of its votaries.

The oval pavement around the Kaabah was crowded with men, women, and children, mostly divided into parties, which followed a Mutawwif; some walking steadily, and others running, whilst many stood in groups to prayer. What a scene of contrast! Here stalked the Bedouin woman, in her long black robe like a nun's serge, and poppy-colored face-veil, pierced to show two fiercely flashing orbs. There an Indian woman, with her semi-Tartar features, nakedly hideous, and her thin parenthetical legs, encased in wrinkled tights, hurried round the fane. Every now and then a corpse, borne upon its wooden shell, circuited the shrine by means of four bearers, whom other Moslems, as is the custom, occasionally relieved. A few fair-skinned Turks lounged about, looking cold and repulsive, as their wont is. In one place a fast Calcutta "Khitmugar" stood, with turban awry and arms akimbo, contemplating the view jauntily, as those gentlemen's gentlemen will do. In another, some poor wretch, with arms thrown on high, so that every part of his person might touch the Kaabah, was clinging to the curtain and sobbing as though his heart would break.

From this spectacle my eyes turned towards Abu Kubays. The city extends in that direction half way up the grim hill. Some writers liken it to Florence; but conceive a Florence without beauty! To the south lay Jebel Jiyad the greater, also partly built over and crowned with a fort, which at a distance looks less useful than romantic: a flood of pale light was sparkling upon its stony surface. Below, the minarets became pillars of silver, and the cloisters dimly streaked by oil lamps, bounded the view of the temple with horizontal lines of shade.

Before nightfall the boy Mohammed rose to feed the pigeons,* for whom he had brought a pocketful of barley. He went to the place where these birds flock; the line of pavement leading from the isolated arch to the eastern cloisters. During the day women and children are to be seen sitting here, with small piles of grain upon little plaited trays of basket-work. For each they demand a copper piece; and religious pilgrims consider it their duty to provide the revered blue rooks with a plentiful meal.

Late in the evening I saw a negro in the state called Malbus—religious phrenzy. To all appearance a Takruri, he was a fine and powerful man, as the numbers required to hold him testified. He threw his arms widely about him, uttering shrill cries, which sounded like lé! lé! lé! lé! and when held, he swayed his body, and waved his head from side to side, like a chained and furious elephant, straining out the deepest groans. The Africans appear unusually subject to this nervous state, which, seen by the ignorant, and the imagination would at once suggest a "demoniacal possession."† Either their organisation is more impressionable, or more probably the hardships, privations,

* The Moslems connect the pigeon on two occasions with their faith; first, when that bird appeared to whisper in Mohammed's ear, and, secondly, during the flight to El Medinah. Moreover, in many countries they are called "Allah's proclaimers," because their movement when cooing resembles prostration.

At Meccah they are called the doves of the Kaabah, and never appear at table. They are remarkable for propriety when sitting upon the holy building. This may be a minor miracle: I would rather believe that there is some contrivance on the roof.

† In the Mandal, or palm-divination, a black slave is considered the best subject. European travellers have frequently remarked their nervous sensibility.

and fatigues endured whilst wearily traversing inhospitable wilds and perilous seas, have exalted their imaginations to a pitch bordering upon frenzy. Often they are seen prostrate on the pavement, or clinging to the curtain, or rubbing their foreheads upon the stones, weeping bitterly, and pouring forth the wildest ejaculations.

That night I stayed in the Haram till 2 A. M., wishing to see if it would be empty. But the morrow was to witness the egress to Arafat; many, therefore, passed the hours of darkness in the Haram. Numerous parties of pilgrims sat upon their rugs, with lanterns in front of them, conversing, praying, and contemplating the Kaabah. The cloisters were full of merchants, who resorted there to "talk shop" and vend such holy goods as combs, tooth-sticks, and rosaries. Before 10 P. M. I found no opportunity of praying the usual two prostrations over the grave of Ishmael. After waiting long and patiently, at last I was stepping into the vacant place, when another pilgrim rushed forward; the boy Mohammed, assisted by me, instantly seized him, and, despite his cries and struggles, taught him to wait. Till midnight we sat chatting with the different ciceroni, who came up to offer their services. I could not help remarking their shabby and dirty clothes, and was informed that, during pilgrimage, when splendor is liable to be spoiled, they wear out old dresses, and appear *endimanchés* for the Muharram fête, when most travellers have left the city. Presently, my two companions, exhausted with fatigue, fell asleep; I went up to the Kaabah, with the intention of "obtaining" a bit of the torn, old Kiswat or curtain, but too many eyes were looking on.* The opportunity, how-

* At this season of the year the Kiswat is much tattered at the base, partly by pilgrims' fingers, and partly by the strain of the cord which confines it when the wind is blowing. It is considered a mere peccadillo to purloin a bit of the venerable stuff: but as the officers of the temple

ever, was favorable for a survey, and with a piece of tape, and the simple processes of stepping and spanning, I managed to measure all the objects concerning which I was curious.

At last sleep began to weigh heavily upon my eyelids. I awoke my companions, and in the dizziness of slumber they walked with me through the tall, narrow street, to our home in the Shamiyah. The brilliant moonshine prevented our complaining, as other travellers have had reason to do, of the darkness and the difficulty of Meccah's streets. The town, too, appeared safe; there were no watchmen, and yet people slept everywhere upon cots placed opposite their open doors. Arrived at the house, we made some brief preparations for snatching a few hours' sleep upon the Mastabah—a place so stifling, that nothing but utter exhaustion could induce lethargy there.

make money by selling it, they certainly would visit detection with an unmerciful application of the quarter-staff. The piece in my possession was given to me by the boy Mohammed before I left Meccah. Waistcoats made of the Kiswat still make the combatant invulnerable in battle, and are considered presents fit for princes. The Moslems generally try to secure a strip of this cloth as a mark for the Koran, &c., &c.

## CHAPTER XXVI.

### OF HAJJ, OR PILGRIMAGE.

THE word Hajj is explained by Moslem divines to mean "Kasd," or aspiration, and to express man's sentiment that he is but a wayfarer on earth wending towards another and a nobler world. This explains the origin and the belief that the greater the hardships the higher will be the reward of the pious wanderer. He is urged by the voice of his soul: "O thou who toilest so hard for worldly pleasures and perishable profit, wilt thou endure nothing to win a more lasting reward?" Hence it is that pilgrimage is common to all old faiths. The Hindus still wander to Egypt, to Tibet, and to the inhospitable Caucasus; the classic philosophers visited Egypt; the Jews annually flocked to Jerusalem; and the Tartars and Mongols—Buddhists—journey to distant Lamaserais.

Every Moslem is bound, under certain conditions,* to

* The two extremes, between which lie many gradations, are these: Abu Hanifah directs every Moslem and Moslemah to perform the pilgrimage if they have health and money for the road and the support of their families; moreover, he allows a deputy-pilgrim, whose expenses must be paid by the principal. Ibn Malik, on the contrary, enjoins

pay at least one visit to the Holy City. This constitutes the Hajjat el Farz (the one obligatory pilgrimage), or Hajjat el Islam, of the Mohammedan faith. Repetitions become mere Sunnats, or practices of the Prophet, and are therefore supererogatory. Some European writers have of late years labored to represent the Meccan pilgrimage as a fair, a pretext to collect merchants and to afford Arabia the benefits of purchase and barter. It would be vain to speculate whether the secular or the spiritual element originally prevailed; most probably each had its portion. But those who peruse this volume will see that, despite the comparatively lukewarm piety of the age, the Meccan pilgrimage is religious essentially, accidentally an affair of commerce.

Moslem pilgrimage is of three kinds.

every follower to visit Meccah, if able to walk, and to earn his bread on the way.

As a general rule, in El Islam there are four Shurut el Wujub, or necessary conditions, viz.:—

1. Islam, the being a Moslem.
2. Bulugh, adolescence.
3. Hurriyat, the being a free man.
4. Akl, or mental sanity.

Other authorities increase the conditions to eight, viz.:—

5. Wujud el Zad, sufficiency of provision.
6. El Rahlah, having a beast of burden, if living two days' journey from Meccah.
7. Takhliyat el Tarik, the road being open; and
8. Imkan el Masir, the being able to walk two stages, if the pilgrim hath no beast.

Others, again, include all conditions under two heads —

1. Sihhat, health.
2. Istitaat, ability.

These subjects have exercised not a little the casuistic talents of the Arab doctors: a folio volume might be filled with differences of opinion on the subject, "Is a blind man sound?"

1. El Mukarinah (the uniting) is when the votary performs the Hajj and the Umrah together, as was done by the Prophet in his last visit to Meccah.

2. El Ifrad (singulation) is when either the Hajj or the Umrah is performed singularly, the former preceding the latter. The pilgrim may be either El Mufrid b'il Hajj (one who is performing only the Hajj), or *vice versâ*, El Mufrid b'il Umrah. According to Abu Hanifah, this form is more efficacious than the following.

3. El Tamattu ("possession") is when the pilgrim assumes the Ihram, and preserves it throughout the months of Shawwal, Z'ul Kaadah, and nine days (ten nights) in Zu'l Hijjah,* performing Hajj and Umrah the while.

There is another threefold division of pilgrimage:—

1. Umrah (the little pilgrimage), performed at any time except the pilgrimage season. It differs in some of its forms from Hajj, as will afterwards appear.

2. Hajj (or simple pilgrimage), performed at the proper season.

3. Hajj el Akbar (the great pilgrimage) is when the "day of Arafat" happens to fall upon a Friday. This is a most auspicious occasion.

The following compendium of the Shafei pilgrim rites is translated from a little treatise by Mohammed of Shirbin, surnamed El Khatib, a learned doctor, whose work is generally read in Egypt and the countries adjoining.

### Chapter I.—Of Pilgrimage.†

"Know," says the theologist, with scant preamble, "that the acts of El Hajj, or pilgrimage, are of three kinds:—

* At any other time of the year Ihram is considered Makruh, or objectionable, without being absolutely sinful.

† In other books the following directions are given to the intended

"1. El Arkan or Faraiz; those made obligatory by Koranic precepts, and therefore essentially necessary, and not admitting expiatory or vicarious atonement, either in Hajj or Umrah.

"2. El Wajibat (requisites); the omission of which may, according to some schools, be compensated for the Fidyat, or atoning sacrifice: and—

"3. El Sunan (pl. of Sunnat), the practice of the Prophet, which may be departed from without positive sin.

"Now, the Arkan, the 'pillars' upon which the rite stands, are six in number, viz.:—

pilgrim:—Before leaving home he must pray two prostrations, concluding the orisons with a long supplication and blessings upon relatives, friends, and neighbors, and he must distribute not less than seven silver pieces to the poor. The day should be either a Thursday or a Saturday; some, however, say

"Allah hath honored the Monday and the Thursday."

If possible, the first of the month should be chosen, and the hour early dawn. Moreover, the pilgrim should not start without a Rafik, or companion, who should be a pious as well as a travelled man. The other preambles to journeying, are the following. Istikharah, consulting the rosary and friends. Khulus el Niyat, vowing pilgrimage to the Lord (not for lucre or revenge). Settling worldly affairs, paying debts, drawing up a will, and making arrangements for the support of one's family. Hiring animals from a pious person. The best *monture* is a camel, because preferred by the Prophet; an ass is not commendable; a man should not walk if he can afford to ride; and the palanquin or litter is, according to some doctors, limited to invalids. Reciting long prayers when mounting, halting, dismounting, and at nightfall. On hills the Takbir should be used: the Tasbih is properest for vales and plains; and Meccah should be blessed when first sighted. Avoiding abuse, curses, or quarrels. Sleeping like the Prophet, namely, in early night (when prayer hour is distant), with "Iftirash," or lying at length with the right cheek on the palm of the dexter hand; and near dawn with "Ittaka," *i. e.* propping the head upon the hand, with the arm resting upon the elbow. And, lastly, travelling with collyrium-pot, looking-glass and comb, needle and thread for sewing, scissors and tooth-stick, staff and razor.

"1. El Ihram ('rendering unlawful'), or the wearing pilgrim garb and avoiding certain actions.

"2. El Wukuf, the 'standing' upon Mount Arafat.

"3. The Tawaf el Ifazah, or circumambulation of impetuosity.*

"4. The Sai, or course between Mounts Safa and Marwah.

"5. El Halk; tonsure (of the whole or part) of the head for men; or taksir, cutting the hair (for men and women).†

"6. El Tartib, or the due order of the ceremonies, as above enumerated.

"Now, the Wajibat (requisites of pilgrimage, also called 'Nusuk') are five in number, viz.:—

"1. El Ihram, or assuming pilgrim garb, from the Mikat, or fixed limit.

"2. The Mabit, or nighting at Muzdalifah: for this a short portion, generally in the latter watch, preceding the Yaum el Nahr, or victim day, suffices.

"3. The spending at Muna the three nights of the 'Ayyan el Tashrik,' or days of drying flesh: of these, the first is the most important.

"4. The Ramy el Jimar, or casting stones at the devil: and—

"5. The avoiding all things forbidden to the pilgrim when in a state of Ihram.

"Some writers reduce these requisites by omitting the second and third."

## Section I.—*Of Ihram.*

"Before doffing his laical garment, the Pilgrim performs a total ablution, shaves, and perfumes himself. He then puts on a 'Rida' and an 'Izar,' both new, clean, and of a white color: after which he

* The Ifazah is the impetuous descent from Mount Arafat. Its Tawaf is that performed immediately after throwing the stones and resuming the laical dress on the victim day at Mount Muna.

† Shaving is better for man, cutting for women. A razor must be passed over the bald head; but it is sufficient to burn, pluck, shave, or clip three hairs when the *chevelure* is long.

performs a two-prostration prayer (the 'Sunnat' of El Ihram), with a *sotto voce* Niyat, specifying which rite he intends.

"When Muhrim (*i. e.* in Ihram), the Moslem is forbidden (unless in case of sickness, necessity, over-heat, or unendurable cold, when a victim must expiate the transgression),—

"1. To cover his head with aught which may be deemed a covering, as a cap or turban; but he may carry an umbrella, dive under water, stand in the shade, and even place his hands upon his head. A woman may wear sewn clothes, white or light blue (not black), but her face-veil should be kept at a distance from her face.

"2. To wear anything sewn or with seams, as shirt, trowsers, or slippers, anything knotted or woven, as chain armor; but the pilgrim may use, for instance, a torn-up shirt or trowsers bound round his loins or thrown over his shoulders, he may knot his 'Izar,' and tie it with a cord, and he may gird his waist.

"3. To knot the Rida, or shoulder-cloth.

"4. To deviate from absolute chastity, even kissing being forbidden to the Muhrim. Marriage cannot be contracted during the pilgrimage season.

"5. To use perfumes, oil, curling the locks, or removing the nails and hair by paring, cutting, plucking, or burning. The nails may be employed to remove pediculi from the hair and clothes, but with care, that no pile fall off.

"6. To hunt wild animals, or to kill those which were such originally. But he may destroy the 'five noxious,' a kite, a crow, a rat, a scorpion, and a dog given to biting. He must not cut down a tree, or pluck up a self-growing plant; but he is permitted to reap and to cut grass.

"When assuming the pilgrim garb, and before entering Meccah, 'Ghusl,' or total ablution, should be performed; but if water be not procurable, the Tayammum, or sand ablution, suffices. The pilgrim should enter the Holy City by day and on foot. When his glance falls upon the Kaabah he should say, 'O Allah, increase this (thy) house in degree, and greatness, and honor, and awfulness, and increase all those who have honored it and glorified it with degree, and greatness, and honor, and dignity!' Entering the outer Bab el Salam, he must exclaim, 'O Allah, thou art the safety, and from thee is the safety!' And then passing into the mosque, he should repair to the 'Black Stone,' touch it with his right hand, kiss it, and commence his circumambulation.

"Now, the victims of El Ihram are five in number, viz:—

"1. The 'Victim of Requisites,' when a pilgrim accidentally or willingly omits to perform a requisite, such as the assumption of the pilgrim garb at the proper place. This victim is a sheep, or, in lieu of it, ten days' fast.

"2. The 'Victim of Luxuries' (Turfah), such as shaving the head or using perfumes. This is a sheep, or a three days' fast, or alms, consisting of three saa measures of grain, distributed among six paupers.

"3. The 'Victim of suddenly returning to Laical Life;' that is to say, before the proper time. It is also a sheep, after the sacrifice of which the pilgrim shaves his head.

"4. The 'Victim of killing game.' If the animal slain be one for which the tame equivalent be procurable (a camel for an ostrich, a cow for a wild ass or cow, and a goat for a gazelle), the pilgrim should sacrifice it, or distribute its value, or purchase with it grain for the poor, or fast one day for each 'Mudd' measure. If the equivalent be not procurable, the offender must buy its value of grain for alms-deeds, or fast a day for every measure.

"5. The 'Victim of Incontinence.' This offering is either a male or a female camel: these failing, a cow or seven sheep, or the value of a camel in grain distributed to the poor, or a day's fast for each measure."

## Section II.—*Of Tawaf, or Circumambulation.*

"Of this ceremony there are five Wajibat, or requisites, viz.:—Concealing 'the shame,'* as in prayer. Ceremonial purity of body, garments, and place. Circumambulation inside the mosque. Seven circuits of the house. Commencement of circuit from the Black Stone. Circumambulating the house with the left shoulder presented

* A man's "Aurat" is from the navel to the knee; in the case of a free woman the whole of her face and person are "shame."

to it. Circuiting the house outside its Shazarwan, or marble basement. And, lastly, the Niyat, or intention of Tawaf, specifying whether it be for Hajj or for Umrah.

"Of the same ceremony the principal Sunnat, or practices, are to walk on foot; to touch, kiss, and place his forehead upon the Black Stone, if possible after each circuit to place the hand upon the south corner, but not to kiss it; to pray during each circuit for what is best for man (pardon of sins); to quote lengthily from the Koran, and often to say 'Subhan Allah!' and to mention none but Allah; to walk slowly during the three first circuits, and trotting the last four, all the while maintaining an humble and contrite demeanor with downcast eyes.

"After the sevenfold circumambulation the pilgrim should recite a two-prostration prayer. If unable to pray there, he may take any other part of the mosque. These devotions are performed silently by day and aloud by night. And after prayer the pilgrim should return to the Black Stone, and kiss it."

## Section III.—*Of Sai, or Course between Mounts Safa and Marwah.*

"After performing Tawaf, the pilgrim should issue from the gate 'El Safa' (or another, if necessary), and ascend the steps of Mount Safa, about a man's height from the street. There he raises the cry Tekbir, and implores pardon for his sins. He then descends, and turns towards Mount Marwah at a slow pace. Arrived within six cubits of the Mil el Akhzar (the 'green pillars,' planted in the corner of the temple on the left hand), he runs swiftly till he reaches the 'two green pillars,' the left one of which is fixed in the corner of the temple, and the other close to the Dar el Abbas. Thence he again walks slowly up to Marwah, and ascends it as he did Safa. This concludes a single course. The pilgrim then starts from Marwah, and walks, runs, and walks again through the same limits, till the seventh course is concluded.

"There are four requisites of Sai. The pilgrim must pass over all the space between Safa and Marwah; he must begin with Safa, and end with Marwah; he must traverse the distance seven times; and he must perform the rite after some important Tawaf, as that of arrival, or that of return from Arafat.

"The practices of Sai are, briefly, to walk, if possible, to be in a state of ceremonial purity, to quote lengthily from the Koran, and to be abundant in praise of Allah."

## Section IV.—*Of Wukuf, or standing upon Mount Arafat.*

"The days of pilgrimage are three in number; namely, the 8th, the 9th, and the 10th of the month Zu'l Hijjah.*

"On the first day (8th), called Yaum el Tarwiyah, the pilgrim should start from Meccah after the dawn-prayer and sunrise, perform his noontide, afternoon, and evening devotions at Muna, where it is a Sunnat that he should sleep.†

"On the second day (9th), the 'Yaum Arafat,' after performing the early prayer at 'Ghalas' (*i. e.* when a man cannot see his neighbor's face) on Mount Sabir, near Muna, the pilgrim should start

* The Arab legend is, that the angels asking the Almighty why Ibrahim was called El Khalil (or God's friend), they were told that all his thoughts were fixed on heaven; and when they called to mind that he had a wife and children, Allah convinced them of the Patriarch's sanctity by a trial. One night Ibrahim saw, in a vision, a speaker, who said to him, "Allah orders thee to draw near him with a victim!" He awoke, and not comprehending the scope of the dream, took especial notice of it; hence the first day of pilgrimage is called Yaum el Tarwiyah. The same speaker visited him on the next night, saying, "Sacrifice what is dearest to thee!' From the Patriarch's knowing what the first vision meant, the second day is called Yaum Arafat. On the third night he was ordered to sacrifice Ismail; hence that day is called Yaum Nahr (of "throat-cutting"). The English reader will bear in mind that the Moslem day begins at sunset.

† The present generation of pilgrims, finding the delay inconvenient, always pass on to Arafat without halting, and generally arrive at the mountain late in the afternoon of the 8th, that is to say, the first day of pilgrimage. Consequently, they pray the morning prayer of the 9th at Arafat.

when the sun is risen, proceed to the 'Mountain of Mercy,' encamp there, and after performing the noontide and afternoon devotions at the Masjid Ibrahim, joining and shortening them,* he should take his station upon the mountain, which is all standing ground. But the best position is that preferred by the Prophet, near the great rocks lying at the lower slope of Arafat. He must be present at the sermon,† and be abundant in Talbiyat (supplication), Thalil (recitations of the chapter 'Say he is the one God!' ‡), and weeping, for that is the place for the outpouring of tears. There he should stay till sunset, and then decamp and return hastily to Muzdalifah, where he should pass a portion of the night. After a visit to the mosque 'Mashar el Haram,' he should collect seven pebbles, and proceed to Muna.

"Yaum el Nahr, the third day of pilgrimage (10th Zu'l Hijjah), is the great festival of the Moslem year. Amongst its many names, 'Ed el Kurban' is the best known, as expressive of Abraham's sacrifice in lieu of Ismail. Most pilgrims, after casting stones at the Akabah, or 'Great Devil,' hurry to Meccah. Some enter the Kaabah, whilst others content themselves with performing the Tawaf el Ifazah, or circumambulation of impetuosity, round the house. The pilgrim should then return to Muna, sacrifice a sheep, and sleep there. Strictly speaking, this day concludes the pilgrimage.

"The second set of 'trois jours,' namely, the 11th, the 12th, and the 13th of Zu'l Hijjah, are called the 'days of drying flesh in the sun.'§ The pilgrim should spend that time at Muna, and each day throw seven pebbles at each of the three pillars.

* The Shafei when engaged on a journey which takes up a night and day, is allowed to shorten his prayers, and to "join" the noon with the afternoon, and the evening with the night devotions; thus reducing the number of times from five to three per diem.

† If the pilgrim be too late for the sermon, his labor is irretrievably lost.

‡ Ibn Abbas relates a tradition, that whoever recites this short chapter 11,000 times on the Arafat day shall obtain from Allah all he desires.

§ "The days of drying flesh," because at this period pilgrims prepare provisions for their return, by cutting up their victims, and exposing to the sun large slices slung upon long lines of cord.

"When throwing the stones, it is desirable that the pilgrim should cast them far from himself, although he is allowed to place them upon the pillar. The act also should be performed after the Zawal, or declension of the sun. If unable to cast the stones during the daytime, he is allowed to do it at night.

"The 'throwing' over—the pilgrim returns to Meccah, and when his journey is fixed, performs the Tawaf el Widaa ('of farewell'). On this occasion it is a Sunnat to drink the water of Zem Zem, to enter the temple with more than usual respect and reverence, and bidding it adieu, to depart from the Holy City.

"The Moslem is especially forbidden to take with him cakes made of the earth or dust of the Haram, and similar mementos, as they savor of idolatry."

## CHAP. II.—OF UMRAH, OR THE LITTLE PILGRIMAGE.

"The word 'Umrah' denotes a pilgrimage performed at any time except the pilgrim season (the 8th, 9th, and 10th of Zu'l Hijjah).

## CHAP. III.—OF ZIYARAT, OR THE VISIT TO THE PROPHET'S TOMB.

"El Ziyarat is a practice of the faith, and the most effectual way of drawing near to Allah through his Prophet Mohammed.

"As the Zair arrives at El Medinah, when his eyes fall upon the trees of the city, he must bless the Prophet with a loud voice. Then he should enter the mosque, and sit in the Holy Garden, which is between the pulpit and the tomb, and pray a two-prostration prayer in honor of the Masjid. After this he should supplicate pardon for his sins. Then, approaching the sepulchre, and standing four cubits away from it, recite this prayer:—

"'Peace be with thee, O thou T. H. and Y. S.,* peace be with thee, and upon thy descendants, and thy companions, one and all,

* The 20th and 36th chapters of the Koran.

and upon all the prophets, and those inspired to instruct mankind. And I bear witness that thou hast delivered thy message, and performed thy trust, and advised thy followers, and swept away darkness, and fought in Allah's path the good fight; may Allah requite thee from us the best with which he ever requited prophet from his followers!'

"Let the visitor stand the while before the tomb with respect, and reverence, and singleness of mind, and fear, and awe. After which, let him retreat one cubit, and salute Abubekr the Truthful in these words:—

"'Peace be with thee, O Caliph of Allah's Prophet over his people, and aider in the defence of his faith!'

"After this, again retreating another cubit, let him bless in the same way Umar the Just. After which, returning to his former station opposite the Prophet's tomb, he should implore intercession for himself and all dearest to him. He should not neglect to visit the Bakia Cemetery and the Kuba Mosque, where he should pray for himself and his brethren of the Muslimin and the Muslimat, the Muminín and the Muminat,* the quick of them and the dead. When ready to depart, let the Zair take leave of the mosque with a two-prostration prayer, and visit the tomb and salute it, and again beg intercession for himself and for those he loves. And the Zair is forbidden to circumambulate the tomb, or to carry away the cakes of clay made by the ignorant with the earth and dust of the Haram."

* These second words are the feminines of the first; they prove that the Moslem is not above praying for what Europe supposed he did not believe in, namely, the souls of women.

## CHAPTER XXVII.

### THE CEREMONIES OF THE YAUM EL TARWIYAH.

At 10 A. M. on Monday, the 12th Sept. 1853, habited in our Ihram, or pilgrim garbs, we mounted the litter.

We followed the road by which we entered Meccah. It was covered with white-robed pilgrims, some few wending their way on foot, others riding, and all men barefooted and bareheaded. Most of the wealthier classes mounted asses. The scene was, as usual, one of strange contrasts: Bedouins bestriding swift dromedaries; Turkish dignitaries on fine horses; the most picturesque beggars, and the most uninteresting looking Nizam. Not a little wrangling mingled with the loud bursts of "Talbiyat." Dead animals dotted the ground, and carcases had been cast into a dry tank, the "Birkat el Shami," which caused every Bedouin to hold his nose, and show disgust.* Here, on the right of the road, the poorer pilgrims, who could not find houses, had erected huts, and pitched their ragged tents. At 11 A. M. ascending a Mudaraj, or flight of stone steps, about thirty

* The true Bedouin, when in the tainted atmosphere of towns, is always known by bits of cotton in his nostrils, or his kerchief tightly drawn over his nose, and a heavy frown marking extreme disgust.

yards broad, we passed without difficulty, for we were in advance of the caravans, over the Akabah, or steeps, and the narrow hill-girt entrance, to the low gravel basin in which Muna lies.

Muna, more classically called Mina, is a place of considerable sanctity. Its three standing miracles are these:—The pebbles thrown at "the devil" return by angelic agency to whence they came; during the three days of drying meat rapacious beasts and birds cannot prey there; and flies do not settle upon the articles of food exposed so abundantly in the bazaars.* During pilgrimage houses are let for an exorbitant sum, and it becomes a "world's fair" of Moslem merchants. At all other seasons it is almost deserted, in consequence, says popular superstition, of the Rajm or diabolical lapidation.* Distant about three miles from Meccah, it is a long, narrow, straggling village, composed of mud and stone houses of one or stories, built in the common Arab style. Traversing a narrow street, we passed on the left the Great Devil, which shall be described at a future time. After a quarter of an hour's halt, spent over pipes and coffee, we came to an open space, where stands the mosque "El Khayf." Here, according to some Arabs, Adam lies, his head being at one end of the long wall, and his feet at another, whilst the dome covers his omphalic region. Grand preparations for fireworks were being made in this square; I especially marked a fire-ship, which savored strongly of Stamboul.

* According to Mohammed the pebbles of the accepted are removed by angels;. as, however, each man and woman has to throw 49 or 70 stones, it is fair to suspect the intervention of something more material. Animals are frightened away by the bustling crowd, and flies are found in myriads.

† This demoniacal practice is still as firmly believed in Arabia as it formerly was in Europe.

At noon we reached the mosque Muzdalifah, also called Mashar el Haram, the "Place dedicated to Religious Ceremonies." It is known in El Islam as "the minaret without the mosque," opposed to Masjid Nimrah, which is the "mosque without the minaret." Half way between Muna and Arafat—about three miles from both—there is something peculiarly striking in the distant appearance of the tall, solitary tower, rising abruptly from the desolate valley of gravel, flanked with buttresses of yellow rock. No wonder that the ancient Arabs loved to give the high-sounding name of this oratory to distant places in their giant empire.

Here, as we halted to perform the mid-day prayer, we were overtaken by the Damascus caravan. It was a grand spectacle. The Mahmal, no longer naked, as upon the line of march, flashed in the sun all green and gold. Around the moving host of white-robed pilgrims hovered a crowd of Bedouins, male and female, all mounted on swift dromedaries, and many of them armed to the teeth. As their drapery floated in the wind, and their faces were veiled with the "lisam," it was frequently difficult to distinguish the sex of the wild being flogging its animal to speed, as they passed. These people, as has been said, often resort to Arafat for blood-revenge, in hopes of finding the victim unprepared. Nothing can be more sinful in El Islam than such a deed,—it is murder "made sicker" by sacrilege; yet the prevalence of the practice proves how feeble is the religion's hold upon the race. The women are as unscrupulous: I remarked many of them emulating the men in reckless riding, and striking with their sticks every animal in the way.

Travelling eastwards up the Arafat fiumara, after about half an hour we came to a narrow pass called El Akhshabayn, or the "two rugged hills." Here the spurs of the hill limit the road to about 100 paces, and it is generally a scene of great confusion. After this we arrived at El Bazan (the Basin), a widening of the plain; and another half hour brought us to the Alamain (the "Twin Signs"), two whitewashed pillars, or rather thin, narrow walls, surmounted with pinnacles, which denote the precincts of the Arafat plain. Here, in full sight of the Holy Hill, standing quietly out from the fair blue sky, the host of pilgrims broke into loud Labbayks.

Arafat is about a six hours' march, or twelve miles, on the Taif road, due east of Meccah. We arrived there in a shorter time, but our weary camels, during the last third of the way, frequently threw themselves upon the ground. Human beings suffered more. Between Muna and Arafat I saw no less than five men fall down and die upon the highway; exhausted and moribund, they had dragged themselves out to give up the ghost where it departs to instant beatitude.* The spectacle showed how easy it is to die in these latitudes;† each man suddenly staggered, fell as if shot, and after a brief convulsion, lay still as marble. The corpses were carefully taken up, and carelessly buried that same evening, in a vacant space amongst the crowds encamped upon the Arafat plain.‡

The boy Mohammed who had long chafed at my pertinacious claim to dervishhood, resolved on this occasion to be grand. To swell the party, he had invited Umar Effendi, whom we accidentally met in the streets of Meccah, to join

* Those who die on a pilgrimage become martyrs.

† I cannot help believing that some unknown cause renders death easier to man in hot than in cold climates; certain it is that in Europe rare are the quiet and painless deathbeds so common in the East.

‡ We bury our dead, to preserve them as it were; the Moslem tries to secure rapid decomposition, and makes the grave-yard a dangerous as well as a disagreeable place.

us; but failing therein, he brought with him two cousins, fat youths of sixteen and seventeen, and his mother's ground-floor servants. These were four Indians; an old man; his wife, a middle-aged woman of most ordinary appearance; their son, a sharp boy, who spoke excellent Arabic; and a family friend, a stout fellow about thirty years old. They were Panjabis, and the bachelor's history was instructive. He was gaining an honest livelihood in his own country, when suddenly one night Hazrat Ali, dressed in green, and mounted upon his charger Duldul—at least, so said the narrator—appeared, crying in a terrible voice, "How long wilt thou toil for this world, and be idle about the life to come?" From that moment, like an English murderer, he knew no peace, conscience and Hazrat Ali haunted him. Finding life unendurable at home, he sold everything, raised the sum of 20*l.*, and started for the Holy Land. He reached Jeddah with a few rupees in his pocket, and came to Meccah, where, everything being exorbitantly dear, and charity all but unknown, he might have starved, had he not been received by his old friend. The married pair and their son had been taken as house-servants by the boy Mohammed's mother, who generously allowed them shelter and a pound of rice per diem to each, but not a farthing of pay. They were even expected to provide their own turmeric and onions. Yet these poor people were anxiously awaiting the opportunity to visit El Medinah, without which their pilgrimage would not, they believed, be complete. They would beg their way through the terrible desert and its Bedouins—an old man, a boy, and a woman! What were their chances of returning to their homes? Such, I believe, is too often the history of those wretches whom a fit of religious enthusiasm, likest to insanity, hurries away to the Holy Land.

With the Indians' assistance the boy Mohammed removed the handsome Persian rugs with which he had covered the shugduf, pitched the tent, carpeted the ground, disposed a diwan of silk and satin cushions round the interior, and strewed the centre with new chibouques and highly polished shishas. At the doorway was placed a Mankal, a large copper fire-pan, with coffee-pots singing a welcome to visitors. In front of us were the litters, and by divers similar arrangements our establishment was made to look grand. The youth also insisted upon my removing the Rida, or upper cotton cloth, which had become way-soiled, and he supplied its place by a fine cashmere, left with him, some years before, by a son of the king of Delhi. Little thought I that this bravery of attire would lose me every word of the Arafat sermon next day.

Arafat is a mass of coarse granite split into large blocks with a thin coat of withered thorns, about one mile in circumference and rising abruptly from the low gravelly plain —a dwarf wall at the southern base forming the line of demarcation—to the height of 180 or 200 feet. Nothing can be more picturesque than the view it affords of the blue peaks behind, and the vast encampment scattered over the barren yellow plain below. On the north lay the regularly pitched camp of the guards that defend the unarmed pilgrims. To the eastward was the Sherif's encampment with the bright mahmals and the gilt knobs of the grander pavilions; whilst, on the southern and western sides, the tents of the vulgar crowded the ground, disposed in dowars, or circles, for penning cattle. After many calculations, I estimated the number to be not less than 50,000, of all ages and sexes; a sad falling off, it is true, but still considerable.*

* Ali Bey (A.D. 1807) calculates 83,000 pilgrims; Burckhardt (1814), 70,000. I reduce it, in 1853, to 50,000, and in A.D. 1854, owing to

The Holy Hill owes its name* and honors to a well-known legend. When our first parents forfeited heaven by eating wheat, which deprived them of their primeval purity, they were cast down upon earth. The serpent descended at Ispahan, the peacock at Cabul, Satan at Bilbays (others say Semnan and Seistan), Eve upon Arafat, and Adam at Ceylon. The latter, determining to seek his wife, began a journey, to which earth owes its present mottled appearance. Wherever our first father placed his foot —which was large—a town afterwards arose; between the strides will always be "country." Wandering for many years, he came to the Mountain of Mercy, where our common mother was continually calling upon his name, and their *recognition* gave the place the name of Arafat. Upon its summit Adam, instructed by the archangel, erected a "Madaa," or place of prayer; and between this spot and the Nimrah mosque the pair abode till death.

From the Holy Hill I walked down to look at the camp arrangements. The main street of tents and booths, huts and shops, was bright with lanterns, and the bazaars were crowded with people and stocked with all manner of eastern delicacies. Some anomalous spectacles met the eye. Many pilgrims, especially the soldiers, were in laical cos-

political causes, it fell to about 25,000. Of these at least 10,000 are Meccans, as every one who can leave the city does so at pilgrimage-time. The Arabs have a superstition that the numbers at Arafat cannot be counted, and that if less than 600,000 mortals stand upon the hill to hear the sermon, the angels descend and complete the number. Even this year my Arab friends declared that 150,000 spirits were present in human shape.

* The word is explained in many ways. One derivation has already been mentioned. Others assert that when Gabriel taught Abraham the ceremonies, he ended by saying "A'*arafta* manasik'ak?"—hast thou learned thy pilgrim rites? To which the Friend of Allah replied, "*Araftu!*"—I have learned them.

tume. In one place a half-drunken Arnaut stalked down the road, elbowing peaceful passengers and frowning fiercely in hopes of a quarrel. In another, a huge dimly lit tent, reeking hot, and garnished with cane-seats, contained knots of Egyptians, as their red tarbushes, white turbans, and black zaabuts showed, noisily intoxicating themselves with forbidden hemp. There were frequent brawls and great confusion; many men had lost their parties, and, mixed with loud Labbayks, rose the shouted names of women as well as men. I was surprised at the disproportion of female nomenclature,—the missing number of fair ones seemed to double that of the other sex,—and at a practice so opposed to the customs of the Moslem world. At length the boy Mohammed enlightened me. Egyptian and other bold women, when unable to join the pilgrimage, will pay or persuade a friend to shout their names in hearing of the Holy Hill, with a view of ensuring a real presence at the desired spot next year. So the welkin rang with the indecent sounds of O Fatimah! O Zaynab! O Khayzaran!* Plunderers, too, were abroad. As we returned to the tent we found a crowd assembled near it; a woman had seized a thief as he was beginning operations, and had the courage to hold his beard till men ran to her assistauce. And we were obliged to defend by force our position against a knot of grave-diggers, who would bury a little heap of bodies within a yard or two of our tent.

One point struck me at once, the difference in point of cleanliness between an encampment of citizens and Be-

* The latter name, "Ratan," is servile. Respectable women are never publicly addressed by Moslems except as "daughter," "female pilgrim," after some male relation, "O mother of Mohammed," "O sister of Umar," or, *tout bonnement*, by a man's name. It would be ill-omened and dangerous were the true name known. So most women, when travelling, adopt an alias.

douins. Poor Masud sat holding his nose in ineffable disgust; for which he was derided by the Meccans. I consoled him with quoting the celebrated song of Maysunah.*

"O take these purple robes away,
  Give back my cloak of camel's hair,
And bear me from this tow'ring pile
  To where the Black Tents flap i' the air.
The camel's colt with falt'ring tread,
  The dog that bays at all but me,
Delight me more than ambling mules—
  Than every art of minstrelsy.
And any cousin, poor but free,
  Might take me, fatted ass! from thee."†

The old man, delighted, clapped my shoulder, and exclaimed, "Verily, O Father of Mustachios, I will show thee the black tents of my tribe this year!"

At length night came, and we threw ourselves upon our

* The beautiful Bedouin wife of the Caliph Muawiyah. Nothing can be more charming in its own Arabic than this little song: the Bedouins never heard it without screams of joy.

† The British reader will be shocked to hear that by the term "fatted ass" the intellectual lady alluded to her husband. The story is, that Muawiyah, overhearing the song, sent back the singer to her cousins and beloved wilds. Maysunah departed, with her son Yezid, and did not return to Damascus till the "fatted ass" had joined his forefathers.

Yezid inherited, with his mother's talents, all her contempt for his father; at least the following quatrain, addressed to Muawiyah, and generally known in El Islam, would appear to argue anything but reverence:—

"I drank the water of the vine—that draught had power to rouse
 Thy wrath, grim father! now, indeed, 'tis joyous to carouse!
I'll drink!—Be wrath!—I reck not!—Ah! dear to this heart of mine
It is to scoff a sire's command—to quaff forbidden wine."

rugs, but not to sleep. Close by, to our bane, was a prayerful old gentleman, who began his devotions at a late hour and concluded them not before dawn. He reminded me of the undergraduate my neighbor at college, who would spout Æschylus at 2 A.M. Sometimes the chaunt would grow drowsy, and my ears would hear a dull retreating sound; presently, as if in self-reproach, it would rise to a sharp treble, and proceed at a rate perfectly appalling. The coffee-houses, too, were by no means silent; deep into the night I heard the clapping of hands accompanying merry Arab songs, and the loud shouts of laughter of the Egyptian hemp-drinkers. And the guards and protectors of the camp were not "Charleys" or night-nurses.

## CHAPTER XXVIII.

### THE CEREMONIES OF THE DAY OF ARAFAT.

THE morning of the 13th Sept. was ushered in by military sounds; a loud discharge of cannon warned us to arise and to prepare for the ceremonies of this eventful day.

After ablution and prayer, I proceeded with the boy Mohammed to inspect the numerous consecrated sites on the "Mountain of Mercy." In the first place, we repaired to a spot on rising ground to the south-east, and within a hundred yards of the hill. It is called "Jami el Sakhrah" —the assembling place of the rock—from two granite boulders upon which the Prophet stood to perform "Talbiyat." There is nothing but a small enclosure of dwarf and white-washed stone walls, divided into halves by a similar partition, aud provided with a niche to direct prayer towards Meccah. Entering by steps we found crowds of devotees and guardians, who for a consideration offered mats and praying carpets. After two prostrations and a long supplication opposite the niche, we retired to the inner compartment, stood upon a boulder and shouted the Labbayk.

Thence, threading our way through many obstacles of tents and stone, we ascended the broad flight of rugged steps which winds up the southern face of the rocky hill. Even at this early hour it is crowded with pilgrims, principally Bedouins and Wahhabis, who had secured favorable positions for hearing the sermon. Already their green flag was planted upon the summit close to Adam's place of prayer. About half-way up I counted sixty-six steps, and remarked that they became narrower and steeper. Crowds of beggars instantly seized the pilgrims' robes and strove to prevent our entering a second enclosure. This place, which resembles the former, except that it has but one compartment and no boulders, is that whence Mohammed used to address his followers, and here, to the present day, the Khatib, or preacher, in imitation of the "Last of Prophets," sitting upon a dromedary, recites the Arafat sermon. Here, also, we prayed a two-prostration prayer, and gave a small sum to the guardian.

Thence ascending with increased difficulty to the hill-top, we arrived at a large stuccoed platform, with prayer-niche and a kind of obelisk, mean and badly built of lime and granite stone, whitewashed, and conspicuous from afar. It is called the Makam, or Madaa Sayyidna Adam. Here we performed the customary ceremonies amongst a crowd of pilgrims, and then descended the little hill. Close to the plain we saw the place where the Egyptian and Damascus Mahmals stand during the sermon; and descending the wall that surrounds Arafat by a steep and narrow flight of coarse stone steps, on my right was the fountain which supplies the place with water.

Our excursion employed us longer than the description requires,—nine o'clock had struck before we reached the plain. All were in a state of excitement. Guns fired furiously. Horsemen and camel-riders galloped about without apparent object. Even the women and the children stood and walked, too restless even to sleep. Arrived at the tent,

I was unpleasantly surprised to find a new visitor in an old acquaintance, Ali ibn Ya Sin the Zem Zemi. He had lost his mule, and, wandering in search of its keeper, he unfortunately fell in with our party. I had solid reasons to regret the mishap—he was far too curious and observant to suit my tastes. On the present occasion he, being uncomfortable, made us equally so. Accustomed to all the terrible "neatness" of an elderly damsel in Great Britain, a few specks of dirt upon the rugs, and half-a-dozen bits of cinder upon the ground, sufficed to give him attacks of "nerves."

That day we breakfasted late, for night must come before we could eat again. After midday prayer we performed ablutions, some the greater, others the less, in preparation for the "wukuf," or standing. From noon onwards the hum and murmur of the multitude increased, and people were seen swarming about in all directions.

A second discharge of cannon (about P. M. 3 15) announced the approach of El Asr, the afternoon prayer, and almost immediately we heard the Naubat, or band, preceding the Sherif's procession as he wended his way towards the mountain. Fortunately my tent was pitched close to the road, so that without trouble I had a perfect view of the scene. First came a cloud of mace-bearers, who, as usual on such occasions, cleared the path with scant ceremony. They were followed by the horsemen of the desert, wielding long and tufted spears. Immediately behind them came the led horses of the Sherif, upon which I fixed a curious eye. All were highly bred, and one, a brown Nejdi with black points, struck me as the perfection of an Arab. They were small, and apparently of the northern race.* Of their old

* In Solomon's time the Egyptian horse cost 150 silver shekels, which, if the greater shekel be meant, would still be about the average price, 18*l*. Abbas, the late Pacha, did his best to buy first-rate Arab stallions: on one occasion he sent a mission to El Medinah for the sole

crimson-velvet caparisons the less said the better; no little Indian Nawab would show aught so shabby on state occasions. After the chargers came a band of black slaves on foot, bearing huge matchlocks; and immediately preceded by three green and two red flags, was the Sherif, riding in front of his family and courtiers. The prince, habited in a simple white Ihram, and bareheaded, mounted a mule; the only sign of his rank was a large green and gold-embroidered umbrella, held over him by a slave. The rear was brought up by another troop of Bedouins on horses and camels. Behind this procession were the tents, whose doors and walls were scarcely visible for the crowd; and the picturesque background was the granite hill covered wherever standing-room was to be found with white-robed pilgrims shouting Labbayks and waving the skirts of their glistening garments violently over their heads.

Slowly the procession advanced towards the hill. Exactly at the hour El Asr the two Mahmals had taken their

purpose of fetching a rare work on farriery. Yet it is doubted whether he ever had a first-rate Nejdi. A Bedouin sent to Cairo by one of the chiefs of Nejd, being shown by the viceroy's order over the stables, on being asked his opinion of the blood, replied bluntly, to the great man's disgust, that they did not contain a single thoroughbred. He added an apology on the part of his laird for the animals he had brought from Arabia, saying, that neither Sultan nor shaykh could procure colts of the best strain.

For none of these horses would a staunch admirer of the long-legged monster called in England a thorough-bred give twenty pounds. They are mere "rats," short and stunted, ragged and fleshless, with rough coats and a slouching walk. But the experienced glance notes at once the fine snake-like head, ears like reeds, wide and projecting nostrils, large eyes, fiery and soft alternately, broad brow, deep base of skull, wide chest, crooked tail, limbs padded with muscle, and long elastic pasterns. And the animal put out to speed soon displays the wondrous force of blood. In fact, when buying Arabs, there are only three things to be considered—blood, blood, and again blood.

station side by side on a platform in the lower slope. That of Damascus could be distinguished as the narrower and the more ornamented of the pair. The Sherif placed himself with his standard-bearers and retinue a little above the Mahmals, within hearing of the preacher. The pilgrims crowded up to the foot of the mountain; the loud Labbayks of the Bedouins and Wahhabis fell to a solemn silence, and the waving of white robes ceased—a sign that the preacher had begun the Khutbat el Wakfah. From my tent I could distinguish the form of the old man upon his camel, but the distance was too great for ear to reach.

But how came I to be at the tent?

A short confession will explain. They will shrive me who believe in inspired Spenser's lines:—

> "And every spirit, as it is more pure,
> And hath in it the more of heavenly light,
> So it the fairer body doth procure
> To habit in."——

The evil came of a "fairer body." I had prepared *en cachette* a slip of paper, and had hid in my Ihram a pencil destined to put down the heads of this rarely heard discourse. But unhappily that red cashmere shawl was upon my shoulders. Close to us sat a party of fair Meccans, apparently belonging to the higher classes, and one of these I had already several times remarked. She was a tall girl, about eighteen years old, with regular features, a skin somewhat citrine-colored, but soft and clear, symmetrical eyebrows, the most beautiful eyes, and a figure all grace. There was no head thrown back, no straightened neck, no flat shoulders, nor toes turned out—in fact, no elegant barbarisms; but the shape was what the Arabs love,—soft, bending, and relaxed, as a woman's figure ought to be. Unhappily she wore, instead of the usual veil, a "Yashmak" of transparent muslin, bound round the face; and the chaperone, mother, or duenna, by whose side she stood, was apparently a very unsuspicious or compliant old person. Flirtilla fixed a glance of admiration upon my cashmere. I directed a reply with interest at her eyes. She then, by the usual coquettish gesture, threw back an inch or two of head-veil, disclosing broad bands of jetty hair, crowning a lovely oval. My palpable admiration of the new charm was rewarded by a partial removal of the Yashmak; when a dimpled mouth and a rounded chin stood out from the envious muslin. Seeing that my companions were safely employed, I ventured upon the dangerous ground of raising hand to forehead. She smiled almost imperceptibly, and turned away. The pilgrim was in ecstasy.

The sermon was then half over. I resolved to stay upon the plain and see what Flirtilla would do. Grace to the cashmere, we came to a good understanding. The next page will record my disappointment:—that evening the pilgrim resumed his soiled cotton cloth, and testily returned the red shawl to the boy Mohammed.

The sermon always lasts till near sunset, or about three hours. At first it was spoken amid profound silence. Then loud, scattered "Amins" (Amen) and volleys of Labbayks exploded at uncertain intervals. At last the breeze brought to our ears a purgatorial chorus of cries, sobs, and shrieks. Even my party thought proper to be affected: old Ali rubbed his eyes, which in no case unconnected with dollars could by any amount of straining be made to shed even a crocodile's tear; and the boy Mohammed wisely his hid face in the skirt of his Rida. Presently the people, exhausted by emotion, began to descend the hill in small parties; and those below struck their tents and commenced loading their camels, although at least an hour's sermon remained.

On this occasion, however, all hurry to be foremost, as the race from Arafat is enjoyed by none but the Bedouins.

Although we worked with a will, our animals were not ready to move before sunset, when the preacher gave the signal of "israf," or permission to depart. The pilgrims,

> " —— swaying to and fro,
> Like waves of a great sea, that in mid shock
> Confound each other, white with foam and fear,"

rushed down the hill with a Labbayk, sounding like a blast, and took the road to Muna. Then I saw the scene which has given to this part of the ceremonies the name of El Dafa min Arafat,—the "Hurry from Arafat." Every man urged his beast with might and main: it was sunset; the plain bristled with tent-pegs, litters were crushed, pedestrians trampled, and camels overthrown: single combats with sticks and other weapons took place;—here a woman, there a child, and there an animal were lost; briefly, it was a state of chaotic confusion.

To my disgust, old Ali insisted upon bestowing his company upon me. He gave over his newly found mule to the boy Mohammed, bidding him take care of the beast, and mounted with me in the shugduf. I had persuaded Shaykh Masud, with a dollar, to keep close in the rear of the pretty Meccan; and I wanted to sketch the Holy Hill. The Senior began to give orders about the camel—I, counter orders. The camel was halted. I urged it on, old Ali directed it to be stopped. Meanwhile the charming face that smiled at me from the litter grew dimmer and dimmer; the more I stormed, the less I was listened to—a string of camels crossed our path—I lost sight of the beauty. Then we began to advance. Now my determination to sketch seemed likely to fail before the Zem Zemi's little snake's eye. After a few minutes' angry search for expe dients, one suggested itself. "Effendi!" said old Ali, "sit quiet; there is danger here." I tossed about like one suffering from evil conscience or the colic. "Effendi!" shrieked the Senior, "what are you doing? You will be the death of us." "Wallah!" I replied, with a violent plunge, "it is all your fault! There! (another plunge)—put your beard out of the other opening, and Allah will make it easy to us." In the ecstasy of fear my tormentor turned his face, as he was bidden, towards the camel's head. A second halt ensued, when I looked out of the aperture in rear, and made a rough drawing of the Mountain of Mercy.

At the Akhshabayn, double lines of camels, bristling with litters, clashed, and gave a shock more noisy than the meeting of torrents. It was already dark: no man knew what he was doing. The guns roared their brazen notes, re-echoed far and wide by the voices of the stony hills. A shower of rockets bursting in the air threw into still greater confusion the timorous mob of women and children. At the same time martial music rose from the masses of Nizam, and the stouter-hearted pilgrims were not sparing of their Labbayks, and "Eed kum Mubarak"—may your festival be happy!

After the pass of the two rugged hills, the road widened, and old Ali, who, during the bumping, had been in a silent convulsion of terror, recovered speech and spirits. This change he evidenced by beginning to be troublesome once more. Again I resolved to be his equal. Exclaiming, "My eyes are yellow with hunger!" I seized a pot full of savory meat which the old man had previously stored for supper, and, without further preamble, began to eat it greedily, at the same time ready to shout with laughter at the mumbling and grumbling sounds that proceeded from the darkness of the litter. We were at least three hours on the road before reaching Muzdalifah, and, being fatigued, we resolved to pass the night there. The Mosque was brilliantly illuminated, but my hungry companions apparently thought more of supper and sleep than devotion. Whilst the tent was raised, the Indians prepared our food, boiled our coffee, filled pipes, and spread the rugs. Before sleeping, each man collected for himself seven bits of granite, the size of a small bean. Then, weary with emotion and exertion, all lay down except the boy Mohammed, who preceded us to find encamping ground at Muna. Old Ali, in lending his mule, made the most stringent arrangements with the youth about the exact place and the exact hour of meeting—an act of simplicity at which I could not but smile. The night was by no means peaceful or silent. Lines of camels passed us every ten minutes, and the shouting of travellers continued till near dawn. Pilgrims ought to have nighted at the Mosque, but, as in Burckhardt's time, so in mine, baggage was considered to be in danger hereabouts, and consequently most of the devotees spent the sermon hours in brooding over their boxes.

## CHAPTER XXIX.

### THE CEREMONIES OF THE DAY OF VICTIMS.

At dawn, on Wednesday, 14th Sept., a gun warned us to lose no time; we arose hurriedly and started up the Batn Muhassir to Muna. By this means we lost at Muzdalifah the "Salat el Eed," or "Festival Prayers," the great solemnity of the Moslem year, performed by all the community at day-break. My companion was so anxious to reach Meccah, that he would not hear of devotions. About 8 A. M. we entered the village, and looked for the boy Mohammed in vain. Old Ali was dreadfully perplexed: a host of high-born Turkish pilgrims were, he said, expecting him; his mule was missing,—could never appear,—he must be late,—should probably never reach Meccah,—what *would* become of him? I began by administering admonition to the mind diseased; but signally failing in a cure, amused myself with contemplating the world from my shugduf, leaving the office of directing it to old Ali. Now he stopped, then he pressed forward; here he thought he saw Mohammed, there he discovered our tent; at one time he would "nakh" the camel to await, in patience, his supreme hour; at another, half mad with nervousness, he would urge the excellent

Masud to hopeless inquiries. Finally, by good fortune, we found one of the boy Mohammed's cousins, who led us to an enclosure called Hosh el Uzem, in the southern portion of the Muna Basin, at the base of Mount Sabir.* There we pitched the tent, refreshed ourselves, and awaited the truant's return. Old Ali, failing to disturb my equanimity, attempted, as those who consort with philosophers often will do, to quarrel with me. But, finding no material wherewith to build a dispute in such fragments as "Ah!"—"Hem!"—"Wallah!" he hinted desperate intentions against the boy Mohammed. When, however, the youth appeared, with even more jauntiness of mien than usual, Ali bin Ya Sin lost heart, brushed by him, mounted his mule, and, doubtless cursing us "under his tongue," rode away, frowning viciously, with his heels playing upon the beast's sides.

Mohammed had been delayed, he said, by the difficulty of finding asses. We were now to mount for "the throwing,"†—as a preliminary to which, we washed "with seven waters" the seven pebbles brought from Muzdalifah, and bound them in our Ihrams. Our first destination was the entrance to the western end of the long line which composes the Muna village. We found a swarming crowd in the narrow road opposite the "Jamrat el Akabah,"‡ or, as it is vulgarly called, the Shaytan el Kabir—the "Great Devil." These names distinguish it from another pillar, the "Wusta," or "central place" (of stoning), built in the middle of Muna, and a third at the eastern end, "El Ula," or the "first place."§

* Even pitching ground here is charged to pilgrims.

† Some authorities advise that this rite of "Ramy" be performed on foot.

‡ The word "Jamrat" is applied to the place of stoning, as well as to the stones.

§ These numbers mark the successive spots where the Devil, in the

The "Shaytan el Kabir" is a dwarf buttress of rude masonry, about eight feet high by two and a half broad, placed against a rough wall of stones, at the Meccan entrance to Muna. As the ceremony of "Ramy," or. Lapidation, must be performed on the first day by all the pilgrims between sunrise and sunset, and as the fiend was malicious enough to appear in a rugged pass, the crowd makes the place dangerous. On one side of the road, which is not forty feet broad, stood a row of shops belonging principally to barbers. On the other side is the rugged wall of the pillar, with a chevaux de frise of Bedouins and naked boys. The narrow space was crowded with pilgrims, all struggling like drowning men to approach as near as possible to the Devil;—it would have been easy to run over the heads of the mass. Amongst them were horsemen with rearing chargers. Bedouins on wild camels, and grandees on mules and asses, with outrunners, were breaking a way by assault and battery. I had read Ali Bey's self-felicitations upon escaping this place with "only two wounds in the left leg," and had duly provided myself with a hidden dagger. The precaution was not useless. Scarcely had my donkey entered the crowd than he was overthrown by a dromedary, and I found myself under the stamping and roaring beast's stomach. By a judicious use of the knife, I avoided being trampled upon, and lost no time in escaping from a place so ignobly dangerous. Some Moslem travellers assert, in proof of the sanctity of the spot, that no Moslem is ever killed here: I was assured by Meccans that accidents are by no means rare.

Presently the boy Mohammed fought his way out of the

shape of an old Shaykh, appeared to Adam, Abraham, and Ishmael, and was driven back by the simple process taught by Gabriel, of throwing stones about the size of a bean.

crowd with a bleeding nose. We both sat down upon a bench before a barber's booth, and, schooled by adversity, awaited with patience an opportunity. Finding an opening, we approached within about five cubits of the place, and holding each stone between the thumb and the forefinger* of the right hand, cast it at the pillar, exclaiming, "In the name of Allah, and Allah is Almighty! (I do this) in hatred of the fiend and to his shame." After which came the Tahlil and the "Sana," or praise to Allah. The seven stones being duly thrown, we retired, and entering the barber's booth, took our places upon one of the earthen benches around it. This was the time to remove the Ihram or pilgrim's garb, and to return to Ihlal, the normal state of El Islam. The barber shaved our heads,† and, after trimming our beards and cutting our nails, made us repeat these words: "I purpose loosening my Ihram according to the practice of the Prophet, whom may Allah bless and preserve! O Allah, make unto me in every hair, a light, a purity, and a generous reward! In the name of Allah, and Allah is Almighty!" At the conclusion of his labor the barber politely addressed to us a "Naiman"—Pleasure to you! To which we as ceremoniously replied, "Allah give thee pleasure!" We had no clothes with us, but we could use our cloths to cover our heads and defend our feet from

* Some hold the pebble as a schoolboy does a marble, others between the thumb and forefinger extended, others shoot them from the thumb knuckle, and most men consult their own convenience.

† The barber removed all my hair. Hanifis shave at least a quarter of the head, Shafeis a few hairs on the right side. The prayer is, as usual, differently worded, some saying, "O Allah, this my forelock is in thy hand, then grant me for every hair a light on Resurrection-day, by thy mercy, O most Merciful of the Merciful!" I remarked that the hair was allowed to lie upon the ground, whereas strict Moslems, with that reverence for man's body—the Temple of the Supreme—which characterises their creed, carefully bury it in the earth.

the fiery sun; and we now could safely twirl our mustachios and stroke our beards,—placid enjoyments of which we had been deprived by the laws of pilgrimage. After resting about an hour in the booth, which, though crowded with sitting customers, was delightfully cool compared with the burning glare of the road, we mounted our asses, and at eleven A. M. started Meccah-wards.

This return from Muna to Meccah is called El Nafr, or the Flight: we did not fail to keep our asses at speed, with a few halts to refresh ourselves with gugglets of water. There was nothing remarkable in the scene: our ride in was a repetition of our ride out. In about half an hour we entered the city, and repaired to the boy Mohammed's house for the purpose of bathing and preparing to enter the Kaabah.

Shortly after our arrival, the youth returned home in a state of excitement, exclaiming, "Rise, Effendi! bathe, dress, and follow me!" The Kaabah, though open, would for a time be empty, so that we should escape the crowd. My pilgrim's garb, which had not been removed, was made to look neat and somewhat Indian, and we sallied forth together without loss of time.

A crowd had gathered round the Kaabah, and I had no wish to stand bareheaded and barefooted in the midday September sun. At the cry of "Open a path for the Haji who would enter the House," the gazers made way. Two stout Meccans, who stood below the door, raised me in their arms, whilst a third drew me from above into the building. At the entrance I was accosted by several officials, dark-looking Meccans, of whom the darkest and plainest was a youth of the Beni Shaybah family, the true *sangre azul* of El Hejaz. He held in his hand the huge silver-gilt padlock of the Kaabah, and presently taking his seat upon a kind of wooden press in the left corner of the hall, he officially inquired my name, nation, and other particulars. The replies were satisfactory, and the boy Mohammed was authoritatively ordered to conduct me round the building, and recite the prayers. I will not deny that, looking at the windowless walls, the officials at the door, and the crowd below—

> "And the place death, considering who I was," *

my feelings were of the trapped-rat description acknowledged by the immortal nephew of his uncle Perez. This did not, however, prevent my carefully observing the scene during our long prayers, and making a rough plan with a pencil upon my white Ihram.

Nothing is more simple than the interior of this celebrated building. The pavement, which is level with the ground, is composed of slabs of fine and various colored marbles, mostly however white, disposed chequer-wise. The walls, as far as they can be seen, are of the same material, but the pieces are irregularly shaped, and many of them are engraved with long inscriptions in the Suls and other modern characters. The upper part of the walls, together with the ceiling, at which it is considered disrespectful to look,† are covered with handsome red damask, flowered over with gold,‡ and tucked up about six feet high, so as to

* However safe a Christian might be at Meccah, nothing could preserve him from the ready knives of enraged fanatics if detected in the House. The very idea is pollution to a Moslem.

† I do not know the origin of this superstition; but it would be unsafe for a pilgrim to look fixedly at the Kaabah ceiling. Under the arras I was told is a strong planking of Saj, or Indian teak, and above it a stuccoed Sath, or flat roof.

‡ Exactly realising the description of our English bard:—

> "Goodly arras of great majesty,
> Woven with gold and silk so close and nere,
> That the rich metal lurked pr vily,
> As feigning to be hid from envious eye."

be removed from pilgrims' hands. The ceiling is upheld by three cross-beams, whose shapes appear under the arras: they rest upon the eastern and western walls, and are supported in the centre by three columns about twenty inches in diameter, covered with carved and ornamented aloe wood. At the Iraki corner there is a dwarf door, called Bab el Taubah (of repentance), leading into a narrow passage built for the staircase by which the servants ascend to the roof: it is never opened except for working purposes. The "Aswad" or "As'ad" corner is occupied by a flat-topped and quadrant-shaped press or safe in which at times is placed the key of the Kaabah. Both door and safe are of aloe wood. Between the columns and about nine feet from the ground ran bars of a metal which I could not distinguish, and hanging to them were many lamps said to be of gold. This completes the upholstery work of the hall.

Although there were in the Kaabah but a few attendants engaged in preparing it for the entrance of pilgrims, the windowless stone walls and the choked-up door made it worse than the Piombi of Venice; the perspiration trickled in large drops, and I thought with horror what it must be when filled with a mass of jostling and crushing fanatics. Our devotions consisted of a two-prostration prayer, followed by long supplications at the Shami (west) corner, the Iraki (north) angle, the Yemani (south), and, lastly, opposite the southern third of the back wall. These concluded, I returned to the door, where payment is made. The boy Mohammed told me that the total expense would be seven dollars. At the same time he had been indulging aloud in his favorite rhodomontade, boasting of my greatness, and had declared me to be an Indian pilgrim, a race still supposed at Meccah to be made of gold.* When seven

* These Indians are ever in extremes, paupers or millionaires, and like all Moslems, the more they pay at Meccah the higher become

dollars were tendered they were rejected with instance. Expecting something of the kind, I had been careful to bring no more than eight. Being pulled and interpellated by half a dozen attendants, my course was to look stupid, and to pretend ignorance of the language. Presently the Shaybah youth bethought him of a contrivance. Drawing forth from the press the key of the Kaabah, he partly bared it of its green-silk gold-lettered *étui*,* and rubbed a golden knob quatrefoil-shaped upon my eyes, in order to brighten them. I submitted to the operation with good grace, and added a dollar—my last—to the former offering. The Sherif received it with a hopeless glance, and, to my satisfaction, would not put forth his hand to be kissed. Then the attendants began to demand vails. I replied by opening my empty pouch. When let down from the door by the two brawny Meccans I was expected to pay them, and accordingly appointed to meet them at the boy Mohammed's house; an arrangement to which they grumblingly assented. When delivered from these troubles, I was congratulated by my sharp companion thus: "Wallah, Effendi! thou hast escaped well! some men have left their skins behind."

All pilgrims do not enter the Kaabah, and may refuse to do so for religious reasons. Umar Effendi, for instance,

their character and religious titles. A Turkish Pacha seldom squanders so much money as does a Moslem merchant from the far East. Khudabaksh, the Lahore shawl-dealer, owned to have spent 800*l.* in feastings and presents. He appeared to consider that sum a trifle, although, had a debtor carried off one tithe of it, his health would have been seriously affected.

* The cover of the key is made, like Abraham's veil, of three colors, red, black, or green. It is of silk, embroidered with golden letters, and upon it are written the Bismillah, the name of the reigning Sultan, "Bag of the key of the holy Kaabah," and a verselet from the "Family of Amran" (Koran, ch. 3).

who never missed a pilgrimage, had never seen the interior. Those who tread the hallowed floor are bound, among many other things, never again to walk barefooted, to take up fire with the fingers, or to tell lies. Most really conscientious men cannot afford the luxuries of slippers, tongs, and truth. Lying to the Oriental is meat and drink, and the roof that covers him.

The Kaabah had been dressed in her new attire when we entered.* The covering, however, instead of being secured at the bottom to the metal rings in the basement, was tucked up by ropes from the roof and depended over each face in two long tongues. It was of a brilliant black, and the Hizam—the zone or golden band running round the upper portion of the building—as well as the Burka (face-veil) were of dazzling brightness.

The origin of this custom must be sought in the ancient practice of typifying the church visible by a virgin or bride. The poet Ab el Rahim el Burai, in one of his Gnostic effusions, has embodied the idea:—

> "And Meccah's bride (*i. e.* the Kaabah) appeareth decked with (miraculous) signs."

This idea doubtless led to the face-veil, the covering, and the guardianship of eunuchs.

The Meccan temple was first dressed as a mark of honor by Tubba the Himyarite when he Judaised. If we accept this fact, which is vouched for by oriental history, we are led to the conclusion that the children of Israel settled at

* The use of the feminine pronoun is explained below. When unclothed, the Kaabah is called Uryanah (naked), in opposition to its normal state, "Muhramah," or clad in Ihram. In Burckhardt's time the house remained naked for fifteen days; and now the investiture is effected in a few hours.

Meccah had connected the temple with their own faith, and as a corollary, that the prophet of El Islam introduced their apocryphal traditions into his creed. The pagan Arabs did not remove the coverings: the old and torn Kiswah was covered with a new cloth, and the weight threatened to crush the building. From the time of Kusay, the Kaabah was veiled by subscription, till Abu Rabiat el Mughayrah bin Abdullah, who having acquired great wealth by commerce, offered to provide the Kiswah on alternate years, and thereby gained the name of El Adl. The Prophet preferred a covering of fine Yemen cloth, and directed the expense to be defrayed by the Bait el Mal, or public treasury. Umar chose Egyptian linen, ordering the Kiswah to be renewed every year, and the old covering to be distributed among the pilgrims. In the reign of Usman the Kaabah was twice clothed, in winter and summer. For the former season it received a Kamis, or Tobe (shirt of brocade), with an Izar, or veil; for the latter a suit of fine linen. Muawiyah at first supplied linen and brocade; he afterwards exchanged the former for striped Yemen stuff, and ordered Shaybah bin Usman to strip the Kaabah, and perfume the walls with Khaluk. Shaybah divided the old Kiswah among the pilgrims, and Abdullah bin Abbas did not object to this distribution.* The Caliph Maamum (9th century) ordered the dress to be changed three times a year. In his day it was red brocade on the 10th Muharram; fine linen on the 1st Rajab; and white brocade on the 1st Shawwal. At last he was informed that the veil applied on the 10th of Muharram was

* Ayisha also, when Shaybah proposed to bury the old Kiswah, that it might not be worn by the impure, directed him to sell it, and to distribute the proceeds to the poor. The Meccans still follow the first half, but neglect the other part of the order given by the "Mother of the Moslems." To the present day they continue to sell it.

too closely followed by the red brocade in the next month, and that it required renewing on the 1st of Shawwal. This he ordered to be done. El Mutawakkil (9th century), when informed that the dress was spoiled by pilgrims, at first ordered two to be given, and the brocade shirt to be let down as far as the pavement; at last he sent a new veil every two months. During the Caliphat of the Abassides this investiture came to signify sovereignty in El Hejaz, which passed alternately from Baghdad to Egypt and Yemen. When the Holy Land fell under the power of the Usmanli, Sultan Selim ordered the Kiswah to be black, and his son, Sultan Sulayman the magnificent (10th century), devoted considerable sums to the purpose. In El Idrisi's time (12th century) the Kiswah was composed of black silk, and renewed every year by the Caliph of Baghdad. Ibn Jubair writes that it was green and gold. The Kiswah remained with Egypt when Sultan Kalaun (13th century) conveyed the rents of two villages, "Baysus" and "Sindbus," to the expense of providing an outer black and inner red curtain for the Kaabah, and hangings for the Prophet's tomb at El Medinah. The Kiswah was afterwards renewed at the accession of each Sultan. And the Wahhabi, during the first year of their conquest, covered the Kaabah with a red Kiswah of the same stuff as the fine Arabian Aba or cloak, and made at El Hasa.

The Kiswah is now worked at a cotton manufactory called El Khurunfish, of the Tumn Bab el Shaariyah, Cairo. It is made by a hereditary family, called the Bait el Sadi, and, as the specimen in my possession proves, it is a coarse tissue of silk and cotton mixed. The Kiswah is composed of eight pieces—two for each face of the Kaabah—the seams being concealed by the Hizam, a broad band, which at a distance looks like gold; it is lined with white calico, and supplied with cotton ropes. Anciently it is said all the Koran was interwoven into it. Now, it is inscribed, "Verily, the first of houses founded for mankind (to worship in) is that at Bekkah; blessed and a direction to all creatures;" together with seven chapters, namely, the Cave, Mariam, the Family of Amran, Repentance, T. H. with Y. S. and Tabarak. The character is that called Tumar, the largest style of Eastern calligraphy, legible from a considerable distance. The Hizam is a band about two feet broad, and surrounding the Kaabah at two-thirds of its height. It is divided into four pieces, which are sewn together. On the first and second is inscribed the "Throne verselet," and on the third and fourth the titles of the reigning Sultan. These inscriptions are, like the Burka, or door curtain, gold worked into red silk, by the Bait el Sadi. When the Kiswah is ready at Khurunfish, it is carried in procession to the Mosque El Hasanayn, where it is lined, sewn, and prepared for the journey.

After quitting the Kaabah, I returned home exhausted, and washed with henna and warm water, to mitigate the pain of the sun-scalds upon my arms, shoulders, and breast. The house was empty, all the Turkish pilgrims being still at Muna, and the old lady received me with peculiar attention. I was ushered into an upper room, whose teak wainscotings, covered with Cufic and other inscriptions, large carpets, and ample diwans, still showed a ragged splendor. The family had "seen better days," the Sherif Ghalib having confiscated three of its houses; but it is still proud, and cannot merge the past into the present. In the "drawing-room," which the Turkish colonel occupied when at Meccah, the Kabirah supplied me with a pipe, coffee, cold water, and breakfast. I won her heart by praising the graceless boy Mohammed; like all mothers, she dearly loved the scamp of the family. When he entered, and saw his maternal parent standing near me, with only the end of her veil drawn over her mouth, he began to scold her with divers insinuations. "Soon thou wilt sit amongst the men in the hall!" he exclaimed. "O, my son," rejoined the Kabirah, "fear Allah, thy mother is in years!"—and truly she was so, being at least fifty. "A-a-h!" sneered the youth, who had formed, as boys of the world must do, or appear to do, a very low estimate of the sex. The old lady understood the drift of the exclamation, and departed with a half-laughing "may Allah disappoint thee!" She soon, however, returned, bringing me water for ablution; and having heard that I had not yet sacrificed a sheep at Muna, enjoined me to return and perform without delay that important rite.

After resuming our laical toilette, and dressing gaily for the great festival, we mounted our asses about the cool of the afternoon, and returning to Muna, found the tent full of visitors. We sat down, and chatted together for an hour; and I afterwards learned from the boy Mohammed, that all had pronounced me to be an "Ajemi." After their departure we debated about the victim, which is only a Sunnat, or Practice of the Prophet. It is generally sacrificed immediately after the first lapidation, and we had already been guilty of delay. Under these circumstances, and considering the meagre condition of my purse, I would not buy a sheep, but contented myself with watching my neighbors. They gave themselves great trouble, especially a large party of Indians pitched near us, to buy the victim cheap; but the Bedouins were not less acute, and he was happy who paid less than a dollar and a quarter. Some preferred contributing to buy a lean ox. None but the Sherif and the principal dignitaries slaughtered camels. The pilgrims dragged their victims to a smooth rock near the Akabah, above which stands a small open pavilion, whose sides, red with fresh blood, showed that the prince and his attendants had been busy at sacrifice. Others stood before their tents, and, directing the victim's face towards the Kaabah, cut its throat, ejaculating "Bismillah! Allahu Akbar!" The boy Mohammed sneeringly directed my attention to the Indians, who, being a mild race, had hired an Arab butcher to do the deed of blood; and he aroused all Shaykh Nur's ire by his taunting comments upon the chicken-heartedness of the men of Hind. It is considered a meritorious act to give away the victim without eating any portion of its flesh. Parties of Takruri might be seen, sitting vulture-like, contemplating the sheep and goats; and no sooner was the signal given, than they fell upon the bodies, and cut them up without removing them. The surface of the valley soon came to resemble the dirtiest slaughter-house, and my prescient soul drew bad auguries for the future.

We had spent a sultry afternoon in the basin of Muna, which is not unlike a volcanic crater. Towards night the occasional puffs of simoom ceased, and through the air of deadly stillness a mass of purple nimbus, bisected by a thin grey line of mist-cloud, rolled down upon us from the Taif hills. When darkness gave the signal, most of the pilgrims pressed towards the square in front of the Muna mosque, to enjoy the pyrotechnics and the discharge of cannon. But during the spectacle came on a windy storm, whose lightnings, flashing their fire from pole to pole, paled the rockets, and whose thunderings, re-echoed by the rocky hills, drowned the puny artillery of man. We were disappointed in our hopes of rain. A few huge drops pattered upon the plain and sank into its thirsty entrails; all the rest was thunder and lightning, dust-clouds and whirlwind.

## CHAPTER XXX.

### THE DAYS OF DRYING FLESH.

All was dull after the excitement of the Great Festival. The heat of the night succeeding rendered every effort to sleep abortive; and as our little camp required a guard in a place so celebrated for plunderers, I spent the great part of the time sitting in the clear pure moonlight.

After midnight* we again repaired to the Devils, and, beginning with the Ula, or first pillar, at the eastern extremity of Muna, threw at each 7 stones (making a total of 21), with the ceremonies before described.

On Thursday we arose before dawn, and prepared with a light breakfast for the fatigues of a climbing walk. After half an hour spent in hopping from boulder to boulder, we arrived at a place situated on the lower declivity of Jebel

* It is not safe to perform this ceremony at an early hour, although the ritual forbids it being deferred after sunset. A crowd of women, however, assembled at the Devils in the earlier part of the 11th night (our 10th); and these dames, despite the oriental modesty of face-veils, attack a stranger with hands and stones as heartily as English hop-gatherers hasten to duck the Acteon who falls in their way. Hence, popular usage allows stones to be thrown by the men until the morning prayers of the 11th Zu'l Hijjah.

Sabir, the northern wall of the Muna basin. Here is the Majarr el Kabsh, "the Draggigg-place of the Ram;" a small whitewashed square, divided into two compartments. In the N.E. corner is a block of granite, in which a huge gash, several inches broad, some feet deep, and completely splitting the stone in knife-shape, notes the spot where Ibrahim's blade fell when the archangel Gabriel forbade him to slay Ismail his son. We descended by a flight of steps, and under the stifling ledge of rock found mats and praying rugs, which, at this early hour, were not over crowded. We followed the example of the patriarchs, and prayed a two-prostration prayer in each of the enclosures. After distributing the usual gratification, we left the place, and proceeded to mount the hill, in hope of seeing some of the apes said still to haunt the heights. These animals are supposed by the Meccans to have been Jews, thus transformed for having broken the Sabbath by hunting. They abound in the elevated regions about Arafat and Taif, where they are caught by mixing the juice of the asclepias and narcotics with dates and other sweet bait. The Hejazi ape is a hideous cynocephalus, with small eyes placed close together, and almost hidden by a disproportionate snout; a greenish-brown coat, long arms, and a stern of lively pink, like fresh meat. They are docile, and are said to be fond of spirituous liquors, and to display an inordinate affection for women. El Masud tells about them a variety of anecdotes. According to him, their principal use in Hind and Chin was to protect kings from poison by eating suspected dishes. The Bedouins have many tales concerning them. It is universally believed that they catch and kill kites by exposing the pink portion of their persons and concealing the rest: the bird pounces upon what appears to be raw meat, and presently finds himself viciously plucked alive. Throughout Arabia an old story is told of them. A merchant was once plundered during his absence by a troop of these apes: they tore open his bales, and charmed with the scarlet hue of the tarbushes began applying those articles of dress to uses quite opposite to their normal purpose. The merchant was in despair, when his slave offered for a consideration to recover the goods. Placing himself in front, like a fugleman to the ape-company, he went through a variety of manœuvres with a tarbush, and concluded with throwing it far away. The recruits carefully imitated him, and the drill concluded with his firing a shot: the plunderers decamped and the caps were regained.

Failing to see any apes, we retired to the tent ere the sun waxed hot, in anticipation of a terrible day. Nor were we far wrong. In addition to the heat, we had swarms of flies, and the blood-stained earth began to reek with noisome vapors. Nought moved in the air except kites and vultures, speckling the deep blue sky: the denizens of earth seemed paralysed by the sun. I spent the time between breakfast and nightfall lying half-dressed upon a mat, moving round the tent-pole to escape the glare, and watching my numerous neighbors, male and female. The Indians were particularly kind, filling my pipe, offering cooled water, and performing similar little offices. I repaid them with a supply of provisions, which, at Muna market-prices, these unfortunates could ill-afford.

When the moon arose the boy Mohammed and I walked out into the town, performed our second day's lapidation, and visited the coffee-houses. The shops were closed early, but business was transacted in places of public resort till midnight. We entered the houses of numerous acquaintances, who accosted my companion, and were hospitably welcomed with pipes and coffee. The first question always was "Who is this pilgrim?" and more than once the reply, "An Afghan," elicited the language of my own country, which I could no longer speak. Of this phenomenon, however, nothing was thought: many Afghans settled in India know not a word of Pushtu, and even above the Passes many of the townspeople are imperfectly acquainted with it. The Meccans, in consequence of their extensive intercourse with strangers and habits of travelling, are admirable conversational linguists. They speak Arabic remarkably well, and with a volubility surpassing the most lively of our continental nations. Persian, Turkish, and Hindostani are generally known; and the Mutawwifs, who devote themselves to particular races of pilgrims, soon become masters of the language.

Returning homewards, we were called to a spot by the clapping of hands and the loud sound of song. We found a crowd of Bedouins surrounding a group engaged in their favorite occupation of dancing. The performance is wild in the extreme, resembling rather the hopping of bears than the inspirations of Terpsichore. The bystanders joined in the song; an interminable recitative, as usual in the minor key, and as Orientals are admirable timists, it sounded like one voice. The refrain appeared to be—

"Lá Yayhá! Lá Yayhá!"

to which no one could assign a meaning. At other times they sang something intelligible.

The style of the saltation, called Rufayhah, rivalled the song. The dancers raised both arms high above their heads, brandishing a dagger, pistol, or some other small weapon. They followed each other by hops, on one or both feet, sometimes indulging in the most demented leaps; whilst the bystanders clapped with their palms a more enlivening measure. This I was told is especially their war-dance. They have other forms, which my eyes were not fated to see.

Amongst the Bedouins of El Hejaz, unlike the Somali and other African races, the sexes never mingle: the girls may dance together, but it would be disgraceful to perform in the company of men.

After so much excitement we retired to rest, and slept soundly.

On Friday, the 12th Zu'l Hijjah, the camels appeared, according to order, at early dawn, and they were loaded with little delay. We were anxious to enter Meccah in time for the sermon, and I for one was eager to escape the now pestilential air of Muna.

Literally, the land stank. Five or six thousand animals had been slain and cut up in this Devil's Punch-bowl. I leave the reader to imagine the rest. The evil might be avoided by building "abattoirs," or, more easily still, by digging long trenches, or by ordering all pilgrims, under pain of mulct, to sacrifice in the same place. Unhappily, the spirit of El Islam is opposed to these precautions of common sense. "Inshallah" and "Kismat" take the place of prevention and cure. And at Meccah, the head-quarters of the faith, a desolating attack of cholera is preferred to the impiety of "flying in the face of Providence," and the folly of endeavoring to avert inevitable decrees.

Mounting our camels, and led by Masud, we entered Muna by the eastern end, and from the litter threw the remaining twenty-one stones. I could now see the principal lines of shops, and, having been led to expect a grand display of merchandise, was surprised to find only mat-booths and sheds, stocked chiefly with provisions. The exit from Muna was crowded, for many, like ourselves, had fled from the revolting scene. I could not think without pity of those whom religious scruples detained another day and a half in this foul spot.

After entering Meccah we bathed, and when the noon drew nigh we repaired to the Haram for the purpose of hearing the sermon. Descending to the cloisters below the Bab el Ziyadah, I stood wonderstruck by the scene before me. The vast quadrangle was crowded with worshippers sitting in long rows, and everywhere facing the central black tower: the showy colors of their dresses were not to be surpassed by a garden of the most brilliant flowers, and such diversity of detail would probably not be seen massed together in any other building upon earth. The women, a dull and sombre-looking group, sat apart in their peculiar place. The Pacha stood on the roof of Zem Zem, surrounded by guards in Nizam uniform. Where the principal ulema stationed themselves the crowd was thicker; and in the more auspicious spots nought was to be seen but a pavement of heads and shoulders. Nothing seemed to move but a few dervishes, who, censer in hand, sidled through the rows and received the unsolicited alms of the faithful. Apparently in the midst, and raised above the crowd by the tall, pointed pulpit, whose gilt spire flamed in the sun, sat the preacher, an old man with snowy beard. The style of headdress called "Taylasan"* covered his turban, which was white as his robes, and a short staff supported his left hand. Presently he arose, took the staff in his right hand, pronounced a few inaudible words, and sat down again on one of the lower steps, whilst a Muezzin, at the foot of the pulpit, recited the call to sermon. Then the old man stood up and began to preach. As the majestic figure began to exert itself there was a deep silence. Presently a general "Amin" was intoned by the crowd at the conclusion of some long sentence. And at last, towards the

* A scarf thrown over the head, with one end brought round under the chin and passed over the left shoulder, composes the "Taylasan."

end of the sermon, every third or fourth word was followed by the simultaneous rise and fall of thousands of voices.

I have seen the religious ceremonies of many lands, but never—nowhere—aught so solemn, so impressive as this spectacle.

# CHAPTER XXXI.

## LIFE AT MECCAH, AND THE LITTLE PILGRIMAGE.

My few remaining days at Meccah sped pleasantly. Umar Effendi visited me regularly, and arranged to accompany me furtively to Cairo. I had already consulted Mohammed Shiklibbha,—who suddenly appeared at Muna, having dropped down from Suez to Jeddah, and reached Meccah in time for pilgrimage,—about the possibility of proceeding eastward. The honest fellow's eyebrows rose till they almost touched his turban, and he exclaimed in a roaring voice, "Wallah! Effendi! thou art surely mad." Every day he brought me news of the different caravans. The Bedouins of El Hejaz were, he said, in a ferment caused by reports of the Holy War, want of money, and rumors of quarrels between the Sherif and the Pacha: already they spoke of an attack upon Jeddah. Shaykh Masud, the camel-man, with whom I parted on the best of terms, seriously advised my remaining at Meccah for some months even before proceeding to Sanaa. Others gave the same counsel. Briefly I saw that my star was not then in the ascendant, and resolved to reserve myself for a more propitious conjuncture by returning to Egypt.

The Turkish colonel and I had become as friendly as two men ignoring each other's speech could be. He had derived benefit from some prescription; but, like all his countrymen, he was pining to leave Meccah.* Whilst the pilgrimage lasted, said they, no *mal de pays* came to trouble them; but, its excitement over, they could think of nothing but their wives and children. Long-drawn faces and continual sighs evidenced nostalgia. At last the house became a scene of preparation. Blue china-ware and basketed bottles of Zem Zem water appeared standing in solid columns, and pilgrims occupied themselves in hunting for mementos of Meccah, drawings, combs, balm, henna, tooth-sticks, aloe-wood, turquoises, coral and mother-o'-pearl rosaries, shreds of Kiswah-cloth and fine Abas, or cloaks of camels'-wool. It was not safe to mount the stairs without shouting "Tarik"—out of the way!—at every step, on peril of meeting face to face some excited fair.* The lower floor was crowded with provision-vendors; and the staple article of conversation seemed to be the chance of a steamer from Jeddah to Suez.

Weary of the wrangling and chaffering of the hall below, I had persuaded my kind hostess, in spite of the surly skeleton her brother, partially to clear out a small store-room in the first floor, and to abandon it to me between the hours of ten and four. During the heat of the day clothing is unendurable at Meccah. The city is so "compacted together" by hills, that even the simoom can scarcely sweep it, the heat reverberated by the bare rocks is intense, and the nor-

* Not more than one-quarter of the pilgrims who appear at Arafat go on to El Medinah; the expense, the hardships, and the dangers of the journey account for the smallness of the number.

† When respectable married men live together in the same house, a rare occurrence, except on journeys, this most ungallant practice of clearing the way is and must be kept up in the East.

mal atmosphere of an eastern town communicates a faint lassitude to the body and irritability to the mind. The houses being unusually strong and well-built, might by some art of thermantidote be rendered cool enough in the hottest weather: they are now ovens.* It was my habit to retire immediately after the late breakfast to the little room upstairs, to sprinkle it with water, and lie down upon a mat. In the few precious moments of privacy notes were committed to paper, but one eye was ever fixed on the door. Sometimes a patient would interrupt me, but a doctor is far less popular in El Hejaz than in Egypt. The people, being more healthy, have less faith in physic: Shaykh Masud and his son had never tasted in their lives aught more medicinal than green dates and camels' milk. Occasionally the black slave girls came into the room, asking if the pilgrim wanted a pipe or a cup of coffee: they generally retired in a state of delight, attempting vainly to conceal with a corner of tattered veil a grand display of ivory consequent upon some small and innocent facetiousness. The most frequent of my visitors was Abdullah, the Kabirah's eldest son. This melancholy Jacques had joined our caravan at El Hamra, on the Yambu road, accompanied us to El Medinah, lived there, and journeyed to Meccah with the Syrian pilgrimage; yet he had not once come to visit me or to see his brother, the boy Mohammed. When gently reproached for this omission he declared it to be his way—that

* I regret being unable to offer the reader a sketch of Meccah, or of the Great Temple. The stranger who would do this should visit the city out of the pilgrimage season, and hire a room looking into the quadrangle of the Haram. This addition to our knowledge is the more required, as our popular sketches (generally taken from D'Ohsson) are utterly incorrect. The Kaabah is always a recognisable building; but the "View of Meccah" known to Europe is not more like Meccah than like Cairo or Bombay.

he never called upon strangers until sent for. He was a perfect Saudawi (melancholist) in mind, manners, and personal appearance, and this class of humanity in the East is almost as uncomfortable to the household as the idiot of Europe. I was frequently obliged to share my meals with him, as his mother—though most filially and reverentially entreated—would not supply him with breakfast two hours after the proper time, or with a dinner served up forty minutes before the rest of the household. Often, too, I had to curb, by polite deprecation, the impetuosity of the fiery old Kabirah's tongue. Thus Abdullah and I became friends, after a fashion. He purchased several little articles required, and never failed to pass hours in my closet, giving me much information about the country, deploring the laxity of Meccan morals, and lamenting that in these evil days his countrymen had forfeited their name at Cairo and Constantinople. His curiosity about the English in India was great, and I satisfied it by praising, as a Moslem would, their "politike," their even-handed justice, and their good star. Then he would inquire into the truth of a fable extensively known on the shores of the Mediterranean and the Red Sea. The English, it is said, sent a mission to Mohammed, inquiring into his doctrines, and begging that Khalid bin Walid might be sent to proselytise them. Unfortunately, the envoys arrived too late—the Prophet's soul had winged its way to Paradise. An abstract of the Moslem scheme was, however, sent to the "Ingreez," who declined, as the founder of the new faith was no more, to abandon their own religion; but the refusal was accompanied with expressions of regard. For this reason many Moslems in Barbary and other countries hold the English to be, of all "People of the Books," the best inclined towards them.

Late in the afternoon I used to rise, perform ablution, and repair to the Haram, or wander about the bazaars till sunset. After this it was necessary to return home and prepare for supper—dinner it would be called in the West. The meal concluded, I used to sit for a time outside the street door in great dignity, upon a broken-backed black-wood chair, traditionally said to have been left in the house by one of the princes of Delhi, smoking a hookah, and drinking sundry cups of strong green tea with a slice of lime, a fair substitute for milk. At this hour the seat was as in a theatre, but the words of the actors were of a nature somewhat too Fescennine for the public. After nightfall we either returned to the Haram or retired to rest. Our common dormitory was the flat roof of the house; under each cot stood a water-gugglet; and all slept, as must be done in the torrid lands, on and not in bed.

I sojourned at Meccah but a short time, and, as usual with travellers, did not see the best specimens of the population. The citizens appeared to me more civilised and more vicious than those of El Medinah. They often leave—

"Home, where small experience grows,"

and—"*qui multum peregrinatur, raro sanctificatur*"—become a worldly-wise, God-forgetting, and Mammonish sort of folk. The pilgrim is forbidden, or rather dissuaded, from abiding at Meccah after the rites, and wisely. Great emotions must be followed by a reaction. And he who stands struck by the first aspect of Allah's house, after a few months, the marvel becoming stale, sweeps past it with indifference or something worse.

There is, however, little at Meccah to offend the eye. Like certain other nations further west, a layer of ashes overspreads the fire: the mine is concealed by a green turf fair to look upon. It is only when wandering by starlight through the northern outskirts of the town that men may be seen with light complexions and delicate limbs, coarse turbans and Egyptian woollen robes, speaking disguise and the purpose of disguise. No one within the memory of man has suffered the penalty of immorality. Spirituous liquors are no longer sold, as in Burckhardt's day, in shops; and some Arnaut officers assured me that they found considerable difficulty in smuggling flasks of "raki" from Jeddah.

The Meccan is a darker man than the Medinite. The people explain this by the heat of the climate. I rather believe it to be caused by the number of female slaves that find their way into the market. Gallas, Sawahilis, a few Somalis, and Abyssinians, are embarked at Suakin, Zayla, Tajurrah, and Berbera, carried in thousands to Jeddah, and the Holy City has the pick of each batch. Thence the stream sets northward, a small current towards El Medinah, and the main line to Egypt and Turkey. Most Meccans have black concubines, and, as has been said, the appearance of the Sherif is almost that of a negro. I did not see one handsome man in the Holy City, although some of the women appeared to me beautiful. The male profile is high and bony, the forehead recedes, and the head rises unpleasantly towards the region of firmness. In most families male children, when forty days old, are taken to the Kaabah, prayed over, and carried home, where the barber draws with a razor three parallel gashes down the fleshy portion of each cheek, from the exterior angles of the eyes almost to the corners of the mouth. These "mashali," as they are called,* may be of modern date: the citizens

* The act is called "Tashrit," or gashing. The body is also marked, but with smaller cuts, so that the child is covered with blood. Ali Bey was told by some Meccans that the face-gashes served for the purpose of phlebotomy, by others that they were signs that the scarred was the servant of Allah's house. He attributes this male-gashing, like female

declare that the custom was unknown to their ancestors. I am tempted to assign to it a high antiquity." In point of figure the Meccan is somewhat coarse and lymphatic. The young men are rather stout and athletic, but in middle age—when man "swills and swells"—they are apt to degenerate into corpulence.

The Meccan is a covetous spendthrift. His wealth, lightly won, is lightly prized. Pay, pension, stipends, presents, and the "Ikram" here, as at El Medinah, supply the citizen with the means of idleness. With him everything is on the most expensive scale, his marriage, his religious ceremonies, and his household expenses. His house is luxuriously furnished, entertainments are frequent, and the junketings of the women make up a heavy bill at the end of the year. It is a common practice for the citizen to anticipate the pilgrimage season by falling into the hands of the usurer. If he be in luck, he catches and "skins" one or more of the richest Hajis. On the other hand, should fortune fail him, he will feel for life the effect of interest running on at the rate of at least 50 per cent., the simple and the compound forms of which are equally familiar to the wily Sarraf.*

tattooing, to coquetry. The citizens told me that the custom arose from the necessity of preserving children from the kidnapping Persians, and that it is preserved as a mark of the Holy City. But its wide diffusion denotes an earlier origin. Mohammed expressly forbad his followers to mark the skin with scars. These "beauty-marks" are common to the nations in the regions to the west of the Red Sea. The Barabarah of Upper Egypt adorn their faces with scars exactly like the Meccans. The Abyssinians moxa themselves in hecatombs for fashion's sake. I have seen cheeks gashed, as in the Holy City, among the Gallas. Certain races of the Sawahil trace around the head a corona of little cuts, like those of a cupping instrument. And, to quote no other instances, some Somalis raise ghastly seams upon their chocolate-colored skins.

* The Indian "Shroff"—banker, money-changer, and usurer.

The most unpleasant peculiarities of the Meccans are their pride and coarseness of language. They look upon themselves as the cream of earth's sons, and resent with extreme asperity the least slighting word concerning the Holy City and its denizens. They plume themselves upon their holy descent, their exclusion of infidels, their strict fastings, their learned men, and their purity of language. In fact, their pride shows itself at every moment; but it is not the pride which makes a man too proud to do a dirty action. My predecessor did not remark their scurrility: he seems, on the contrary, rather to commend them for respectability in this point. If he be correct, the present generation has degenerated. The Meccans appeared to me distinguished, even in this foul-mouthed East, by the superior licentiousness of their language. Abuse was bad enough in the streets, but in the house it became intolerable. The Turkish pilgrims remarked, but they were too proud to take notice of it. The boy Mohammed and one of his tall cousins at last transgressed the limits of my endurance. They had been abusing each other vilely one day at the house-door about dawn, when I administered the most open reprimand: "In my country (Afghanistan) we hold this to be the hour of prayer, the season of good thoughts, when men remember Allah; even the Kafir doth not begin the day with curses and abuse." The people around approved, and even the offenders could not refrain from saying, "Thou hast spoken truth, O Effendi!" Then the bystanders began, as usual, to "improve the occasion." "See," they exclaimed, "this Sulaymani gentleman, he is not the son of a Holy City, and yet he teacheth you—ye, the children of the Prophet!—repent and fear Allah!" They replied, "Verily we do repent, and Allah is a pardoner and the merciful!"—were silent for an hour, and then abused each other more foully than before. Yet it is a good point in the Meccan character, that it is open to reason, can confess itself in error, and displays none of that doggedness of vice which distinguishes the sinner of a more stolid race. Like the people of Southern Europe, the Semite is easily managed by a jest: though grave and thoughtful, he is by no means deficient in the sly wit which we call humor, and the solemn gravity of his words contrasts amusingly with his ideas. He particularly excels in the Cervantic art, the spirit of which, says Sterne, is to clothe low subjects in sublime language. In Mohammed's life we find that he by no means disdained a joke, sometimes a little *hasardé*, as in the case of the Paradise-coveting old woman. The other redeeming qualities of the Meccan are his courage, his *bonhomie*, his manly suavity of manners, his fiery sense of honor, his strong family affections, his near approach to what we call patriotism, and his general knowledge: the reproach of extreme ignorance which Burckhardt directs against the Holy City has long ago sped to the limbo of things that were. The dark half of the picture is pride, bigotry, irreligion, greed of gain, immorality, and prodigal ostentation.

Of the pilgrimage ceremonies I cannot speak harshly. It may be true that "the rites of the Kaabah, emasculated of every idolatrous tendency, still hang a strange unmeaning shroud around the living theism of Islam." But what nation, either in the West or the East, has been able to cast out from its ceremonies every suspicion of its old idolatry? What are the English mistletoe, the Irish wake, the Pardon of Brittany, the Carnival and the Worship at Iserna? Better far to consider the Meccan pilgrimage rites in the light of Evil-worship turned into lessons of Good than to philosophise about their strangeness, and to err in asserting them to be insignificant. Even the Bedouin circumambulating the Kaabah fortifies his wild belief by the fond thought that he treads the path of "Allah's friend." At Arafat the good Moslem worships in imitation of the "Pure of Allah;"* and when hurling stones and curses at three senseless little buttresses which commemorate the appearance of the fiend, the materialism of the action gives to its sentiment all the strength and endurance of reality. The supernatural agencies of pilgrimage are carefully and sparingly distributed. The angels who restore the stones from Muna to Muzdalifah, the heavenly host whose pinions cause the Kaabah's veil to rise and wave, and the mysterious complement of the pilgrims' total at the Arafat sermon, all belong to the category of spiritual creatures walking earth unseen,--a poetical tenet, not condemned by Christianity. The Meccans are, it is true, to be reproached with their open Mammon worship, at times and at places the most sacred and venerable; but this has no other effect upon the pilgrims than to excite disgust and open reprehension. Here, however, we see no such silly frauds as heavenly fire drawn from a phosphor-match; nor do two rival churches fight in the flesh with teeth and nails, requiring the contemptuous interference of an infidel power to keep order.

As regards the Meccan and Moslem belief that Abraham and his son built the Kaabah, it may be observed that the Genesitic account of the Great Patriarch has suggested to learned men the idea of two Abrahams, one the son of Terah, another the son of Azar (fire), a Prometheus, who imported civilisation and knowledge into Arabia from Harran, the sacred centre of Sabæan learning. Moslem historians all agree in representing Abraham as a star-worshipper in youth, and Eusebius calls the patriarch son of Athar; his father's name, therefore, is no Arab invention. Whether Ishmael

* Adam.

or his sire ever visited Meccah to build the Kaabah is, in my humble opinion, an open question. The Jewish Scripture informs us only that the patriarch dwelt at Beersheba and Gerar, in the S.W. of Palestine, without any allusion to the annual visit which Moslems declare he paid to their Holy City. At the same time Arab tradition speaks clearly and consistently upon the subject, and generally omits those miraculous and superstitious adjuncts which cast shadows of sore doubts upon the philosopher's mind. Those who know the habits of the expatriated Jews and Christians of the East—their practice of connecting all remarkable spots with their old traditions—will readily believe that the children of Israel settled in pagan Meccah saw in its idolatry some perverted form of their own worship.

The amount of risk which a stranger must encounter at the pilgrimage rites is still considerable. A learned Orientalist and divine intimated his intention, in a work published but a few years ago, of visiting Meccah without disguise. He was assured that the Turkish governor would now offer no obstacle to a European traveller. I would strongly dissuade a friend from making the attempt. It is true that the Frank is no longer insulted when he ventures out of the Meccan Gate of Jeddah; and that our vice-consuls and travellers are allowed, on condition that their glance do not pollute the shrine, to visit Taif and the regions lying eastward of the Holy City. Neither the Pacha nor the Sherif would, in these days, dare to enforce, in the case of an Englishman, the old law, a choice thrice offered between circumcision and death. But the first Bedouin who caught sight of the Frank's hat would not deem himself a man if he did not drive a bullet through the wearer's head. At the pilgrimage season disguise is easy, on account of the vast and varied multitudes which visit Meccah, exposing the traveller only to "stand the buffet with knaves who smell of sweat." But woe to the unfortunate who happens to be recognised in public as an infidel,—unless at least he could throw himself at once upon the protection of the government.* Amidst, however, a crowd of pilgrims, whose fanaticism is worked up to the highest pitch, detection would probably ensure his dismissal at once *al numero de' piu.* Those who find danger the salt of pleasure may visit Meccah; but if asked whether the results justify the risk, I should reply in the negative. And the vice-consul at Jeddah would only do his duty in peremptorily forbidding European travellers to attempt Meccah without disguise, until the day comes when such steps can be taken in the certainty of not causing a mishap, which would not redound to our reputation, as we could not in justice revenge it.

On the 14th Zu'l Hijjah we started to perform the rite of Umrah, or Little Pilgrimage. After performing ablution, and resuming the Ihram with the usual ceremonies, I set out, accompanied by the boy Mohammed and his brother Abdullah. Mounting asses, which resembled mules in size and speed,† we rode to the Haram, and prayed there. Again

* The best way would be to rush, if possible, into a house; and the owner would then, for his own interest, as well as honor, defend a stranger till assistance could be procured.

† Pliny is certainly right about this useful quadruped and its congeners, the zebra and the wild ass, in describing it as "animal frigoris maxime impatiens." It degenerates in cold regions, unless, as in Afghanistan and Barbary, there be a long, hot, and dry summer. Aden, Cutch, and Baghdad have fine breeds, whereas those of India and south-eastern Africa are poor and weak. The best and the highest-priced come from the Maghrib, and second to them ranks the Egyptian race. At Meccah careful feeding and kind usage transform the dull slave into an active and symmetrical friend of man: he knows his owner's kind voice, and if one of the two fast, it is generally the biped. The asses of the Holy City are tall and plump, with sleek coats, generally ash or grey-colored, the eyes of deers heads gracefully carried, an ambling gait, and ex-

remounting, we issued through the Bab el Safa towards the open country N.E. of the city. The way was crowded with pilgrims, on foot as well as mounted, and their loud Labbayks distinguished those engaged in the Umrah rite from the many whose business was with the camp of the Damascus caravan. At about half a mile from the city we passed on the left a huge heap of stones, where my companions stood and cursed. This grim-looking cairn is popularly believed to note the place of the well where Abu Lahab laid an ambuscade for the Prophet. This wicked uncle stationed there a slave, with orders to throw headlong into the pit the first person who approached him, and privily persuaded his nephew to visit the spot at night: after a time, anxiously hoping to hear that the deed had been done, Abu Lahab incautiously drew nigh, and was precipitated by his own bravo into the place of destruction. Hence the well-known saying in Islam, "Whoso diggeth a well for his brother shall fall into it himself." We added our quota of stones, and proceeding, saw the Jeddah road spanning the plain like a white ribbon. In front of us the highway was now lined with coffee-tents, before which effeminate dancing-boys performed to admiring Syrians: a small whitewashed "bungalow," the palace of the Emir el Hajj, lay on the left, and all around it clustered the motley encampment of his pilgrims. After cantering about three miles from the city, we reached the Alamain, or two pillars that limit the sanctuary; and a little beyond it, is the small settlement, popularly called El Umrah. Dismounting here, we sat down on rugs outside a coffee-tent to enjoy the beauty of the moonlight night, and an hour of "Kaif" in the sweet air of the desert.

Presently the coffee-tent keeper, after receiving payment,

tremely sure-footed. They are equal to great fatigue, and the stallions have been known, in their ferocity, to kill the groom. The price varies from 25 to 150 dollars.

brought us water for ablution. This preamble over, we entered the principal chapel; an unpretending building, badly lighted, spread with dirty rugs, full of pilgrims, and offensively close. Here we prayed the Isha, or night devotions, and then a two-prostration prayer in honor of the Ihram, after which we distributed gratuities to the guardians, and alms to the importunate beggars. And now I perceived the object of Abdullah's companionship. The melancholy man assured me that he had ridden out for love of me, and in order to perform as Wakil (substitute) a vicarious pilgrimage for my parents. Vainly I assured him that they had been strict in the exercises of their faith. He would take no denial, and I perceived that love of me meant love of my dollars. With a surly assent, he was at last permitted to act for the "pious pilgrims Yusuf (Joseph) bin Ahmed and Fatimah bint Yunus," my progenitors. It was impossible to prevent smiling at contrasts, as Abdullah, gravely raising his hands, and directing his face to the Kaabah, intoned, "I do vow this Ihram of Umrah in the name of Yusuf son of Ahmed, and Fatimah daughter of Yunus; then render it attainable to them, and accept it of them! Bismillah! Allahu Akbar!"

Remounting, we galloped towards Meccah, shouting Labbayk, and halting at every half mile to smoke and drink coffee. In a short time we entered the city, and repairing to the Haram by the Safa Gate, performed the Tawaf, or circumambulation of Umrah. After this dull round and necessary repose we left the temple by the same exit, and mounting once more, turned towards the hill El Safa, which stands about 100 yards S. E. of the Mosque, and as little deserves its name of "mountain" as do those that undulate the face of modern Rome. The Safa end is closed by a mean-looking building, composed of three round arches, with a dwarf flight of steps leading up to them out of a narrow road. Without dismounting, we wheeled our donkeys round, "left shoulders forward"—no easy task in the crowd,—and vainly striving to sight the Kaabah through the Bab el Safa, performed the Niyat, or the running.

After Tahlil, Takbir, and Talbiyat, we raised our hands in the supplicatory position, and twice repeated, "There is no god but Allah, alone without partner; his is the kingdom, unto him be praise; he giveth life and death, he is alive and perisheth not; in his hand is good, and he over all things is omnipotent." Then, with the donkey-boys leading our animals and a stout fellow preceding us with a lantern and a quarter-staff to keep off the running Bedouins, camel-men, and riders of asses, we descended Safa, and slowly walked down the street El Masaa, towards Marwah. During our descent we recited aloud, "O Allah, cause me to act according to the Sunnat of thy Prophet, and to die in his faith, and defend me from errors and disobedience by thy mercy, O most merciful of the merciful!" Arrived at what is called the Batn el Wady (belly of the vale), a place now denoted by the Milain el Akhzarain (the two green pillars), one fixed in the eastern course of the Haram, the other in a house on the right side, we began the running by urging on our beasts. At length we reached Marwah. The houses cluster in amphitheatre shape above it, and from the Masaa, or street below, a short flight of steps leads to a platform, bounded on three sides like a tennis court, by tall walls without arches. The street, seen from above, has a bowstring curve: it is between 800 and 900 feet long, with high houses on both sides, and small lanes branching off from it. At the foot of the platform we brought the "right shoulder forward," so as to face the Kaabah, and raising hands to ears, thrice exclaimed, "Allahu Akbar."

This concluded the first course, and, of these, seven compose the ceremony El Sai, or the running.

There was a startling contrast with the origin of this ceremony,—

> "When the poor outcast on the cheerless wild,
> Arabia's parent, clasped her fainting child,"—

as the Turkish infantry marched, in European dress, with sloped arms, down the Masaa to relieve guard. By the side of the half-naked, running Bedouins, they looked as if epochs, disconnected by long centuries, had met. A laxity, too, there was in the frequent appearance of dogs upon this holy and most memorial ground, which said little in favor of the religious strictness of the administration.

Our Sai ended at Mount Marwah. There we dismounted, and sat outside a barber's shop, on the right-hand of the street. He operated upon our heads, causing us to repeat, "O Allah, this my forelock is in thy hand, then grant me for every hair a light on the resurrection-day, O most merciful of the merciful!" This, and the praying for it, constituted the fourth portion of the Umrah, or Little Pilgrimage.

Throwing the skirts of our garments over our heads, to show that our "Ihram" was now exchanged for the normal state, "Ihlal," we cantered to the Haram, prayed there a two-prostration prayer, and returned home not a little fatigued.

## CHAPTER XXXII.

### PLACES OF PIOUS VISITATION AT MECCAH.

THE lionizer has little work at the Holy City. With the exceptions of Jebel Nur and Jebel Saur, all the places of pious visitation lie inside or close outside the city. It is well worth the traveller's while to ascend Abu Kubays; not so much to inspect the Makan el Hajar and the Shakk el Kamar,* as to obtain an excellent bird's-eye view of the Haram and the parts adjacent.

The boy Mohammed had applied himself sedulously to commerce after his return home; and had actually been seen by Shaykh Nur sitting in a shop and selling small curiosities. With my plenary consent I was made over to Abdullah, his brother. On the morning of the 19th Sept. he hired two asses, and accompanied me as guide to the holy places.

* The tradition of these places is related by every historian. The former is the repository of the Black Stone during the Deluge. The latter, "splitting of the moon," is the spot where the Prophet stood when, to convert the idolatrous Kuraysh, he caused half of the orb of night to rise from behind Abu Kubays, and the other from Jebel Kaykaan, on the western horizon. This silly legend appears unknown to Mohammed's day.

Mounting our animals, we followed the road before described to the Jannat el Maala, the sacred cemetery of Meccah. A rough wall, with a poor gateway, encloses a patch of barren and grim-looking ground at the foot of the chain which bounds the city's western suburb. Inside are a few ignoble, whitewashed domes; all are of modern construction, for here, as at El Bakia, further north, the Wahabis indulged their levelling propensities. The rest of the ground shows some small enclosures belonging to particular houses—equivalent to our family vaults—and the ruins of humble tombs, lying in confusion, whilst a few parched aloes spring from between the bricks and stones.*

This cemetery is celebrated in local history: here the body of Abdullah bin Zubayr was exposed by order of Hajjaj bin Yusuf; and the number of saints buried in it has been so numerous, that even in the twelfth century many had fallen into oblivion. It is visited by the citizens on Fridays, and by women on Thursdays, to prevent that meeting of sexes which in the East is so detrimental to public decorum.

After a long supplication, pronounced standing at the doorway, we entered, and sauntered about the burial-ground. On the left of the road stood an enclosure, which, according to Abdullah, belonged to his family. The door and stone slabs, being valuable to the poor, had been removed, and the graves of his forefathers appeared to have been invaded by the jackal. He sighed, recited a Fat-hah with tears in his eyes, and hurried me away from the spot.

The first dome which we visited covered the remains of Abdel Rahman, the son of Abubekr, one of the worthies

* The aloe here, as in Egypt, is hung, like the dried crocodile, over houses as a talisman against evil spirits.

of El Islam, equally respected by Sunni and Shiah. The tomb was a simple catafalque, covered with the usual cloth. After performing our devotions at this grave, and distributing a few piastres to guardians and beggars, we crossed the main path, and found ourselves at the door of the cupola, beneath which sleeps the venerable Khadijah, Mohammed's first wife. The tomb was covered with a green cloth, and the walls of the little building were decorated with written specimens of religious poetry. A little beyond it, we were shown into another dome, the resting-place of Sitt Aminah, the Prophet's mother.* Burckhardt chronicles its ill usage by the fanatic Wahhabis: it has now been rebuilt in that frugal style which characterises the architecture of El Hejaz. An old woman exceedingly garrulous came to the door, invited us in, and superintended our devotions; at the end of which she sprinkled rose-water upon my face. When asked for a cool draught she handed me a metal saucer, whose contents smelt strongly of mastic, earnestly directing me to drink it in a sitting posture. This tomb she informed us is the property of a single woman, who visits it every evening, receives the contributions of the Faithful, prays, sweeps the pavement, and dusts the furniture. We left five piastres for this respectable maiden, and gratified the officious crone with another shilling. She repaid us by signalling to some score of beggars that a rich pilgrim had entered the Maala, and their importunities fairly drove me out of the hallowed walls.

Leaving the Jannat el Maala, we returned towards

* Burckhardt mentions the "Tomb of Umna, the mother of Mohammed," in the Maala at Meccah; and all the ciceroni agree about the locality. Yet historians place it at Abwa, where she died, after visiting El Medinah to introduce her son to his relations. And the learned believe that the Prophet refused to pray over or to intercede for his mother, she having died before El Islam was revealed.

the town, and halted on the left side of the road, at a mean building called the Masjid el Jinn (of the Genii). Here was revealed the seventy-second chapter of the Koran, called after the name of the mysterious firedrakes who paid fealty to the Prophet. Descending a flight of steps,—for this mosque, like all ancient localities at Meccah, is as much below as above ground,—we entered a small apartment containing water-pots for drinking and all the appurtenances of ablution. In it is show the Mauza el Khatt (place of the writing), where Mohammed wrote a letter to Abu Masud after the homage of the genii. A second and interior flight of stone steps led to another diminutive oratory, where the Prophet used to pray and receive the archangel Gabriel. Having performed a pair of prostrations, which caused the perspiration to burst forth as if in a Russian bath, I paid a few piastres, and issued from the building with much satisfaction.

We had some difficulty in urging our donkeys through the crowded street, called the Zukak el Hajar. Presently we arrived at the Bait el Naby, the Prophet's old house, in which he lived with the Sitt Khadijah. Here, says Burckhardt, the Lady Fatimah first saw the light; and here, according to Ibn Jubair, Hasan and Husayn were born. Dismounting at the entrance we descended a deep flight of steps, and found ourselves in a spacious hall, vaulted, and of better appearance than most of the sacred edifices at Meccah. In the centre, and well railed round, stood a closet of rich green and gold stuffs, in shape not unlike an umbrella tent. A surly porter guarded the closed door, which some respectable people vainly attempted to open by honeyed words: a whisper from Abdullah solved the difficulty. I was directed to lie at full length upon my stomach, and to kiss a black-looking stone—said to be the lower half of the Lady Fatimah's quern—fixed at the bottom of a basin of the same material. Thence we repaired to a corner, and recited a two-prostration at the place where the Prophet used to pray the Sunnat and the Nafilah, or supererogatory devotions.

Again remounting, we proceeded at a leisurely pace homewards, and on the way we passed through the principal slave-market. It is a large street, roofed with matting and full of coffee-houses. The merchandise sits in rows, parallel with the walls. The prettiest girls occupied the highest benches, below them were the plain, and lowest of all the boys. They were all gaily dressed in pink and other light-colored muslins, with transparent veils over their heads; and, whether from the effect of such unusual splendor, or from the reaction succeeding to their terrible land-journey and sea-voyage, they appeared perfectly happy, laughing loudly, talking unknown tongues, and quizzing purchasers, even during the delicate operation of purchasing. There were some pretty Gallas, *douce*-looking Abyssinians, and Africans of various degrees of hideousness, from the half-Arab Somal to the baboon-like Sawahili. The highest price of which I could hear was 60*l.* And here I matured a resolve to strike, if favored by fortune, a death-blow at a trade which is eating into the vitals of industry in Eastern Africa. The reflection was pleasant,—the idea that the humble Haji, contemplating the scene from his donkey, might become the instrument of the total abolition of this pernicious traffic.* What would have become of

* About a year since writing the above I was informed that a firman has been issued by the Porte suppressing the traffic from central Africa. Hitherto we have respected slavery in the Red Sea, because the Turk thence drew his supplies; we are now destitute of an excuse. A single steamer would destroy the trade, and if we delay to take active measures, the people of England, who have spent millions in keep-

that pilgrim had the crowd in the slave-market guessed his intentions?

Passing through the large bazaar, called the Suk el Lail, I saw the palace of Mohammed bin Aun, quondam Prince of Meccah. It has a certain look of rude magnificence, the effect of huge hanging balconies scattered in profusion over lofty walls, *claire-voies* of brick-work, and courses of various-colored stone. The owner is highly popular among the Bedouins, and feared by the citizens on account of his fierce looks, courage, and treachery. They described him to me as "vir bonus, bene strangulando peritus;" but Mr. Cole, who knew him personally, gave him a high character for generosity and freedom from fanaticism. He seems to have some idea of the state which should "hedge in" a ruler. His palaces at Meccah, and that now turned into a Wakalah at Jeddah, are the only places in the country that can be called princely. He is now a state prisoner at Constantinople, and the Bedouins pray for his return in vain.*

ing up a West African squadron, will not hold us guiltless of negligence.

* This man was first invested with the Sherifat by Mohammed Ali of Egypt in A.D. 1827, when Yahya, Prince of Meccah, fled, after stabbing his nephew in the Kaabah, to the Beni Harb Bedouins. He was supported by Ahmed Pacha of Meccah, with a large army; but after the battle of Tarabah, in which Ibrahim Pacha was worsted by the Bedouins, Mohammed bin Aun, accused of acting as Sylla, was sent in honorable bondage to Cairo. He again returned to Meccah, where the rapacity of his eldest son Abdullah, who would rob pilgrims, caused fresh misfortunes. In A.D. 1851, when Abd el Muttaleb was appointed Sherif, the Pacha was ordered to send Bin Aun to Stamboul; no easy task. The Turk succeeded by a manœuvre. Mohammed's two sons happening to be at Jeddah, were invited to inspect a man-of-war, and were there made prisoners. Thereupon the father yielded himself up; although, it is said, the flashing of the Bedouin's sabre during his embarkation made the Turks rejoice that they had won the day by state-

The other places of pious visitation at Meccah are briefly these:—

1. Natak el Naby, a small oratory in the Zukah el Hajar. It derives its name from the following circumstance: —As the Prophet was knocking at the door of Abubekr's shop, a stone gave him God-speed, and told him that the master was not at home. This wonderful mineral is of a reddish-black color, about a foot in dimension, and fixed in the wall somewhat higher than a man's head. There are servants attached to it, and the street sides are spread, as usual, with the napkins of importunate beggars.

2. Maulid el Naby, or the Prophet's birth-place. This is a little chapel in the Suk el Lail, not far from Mohammed bin Aun's palace. It is below the present level of the ground, and in the centre is a kind of tent, concealing, it is said, a hole in the floor upon which Aminah sat to be delivered.

3. In the quarter "Shaab Ali," near the Maulid el Naby, is the birthplace of Ali, another oratory below the ground.

4. Near Khadijah's house and the Natak el Naby is a place called El Muttaka, from a stone against which the Prophet leaned when worn out with fatigue. It is much visited by devotees; and some declare that, on one occasion, when the Father of Lies appeared to the Prophet in the form of an elderly gentleman and tempted him to sin by asserting that the mosque-prayers were over, this stone, disclosing the fraud, caused the fiend to flee.

5. Maulid Hamzah, a little building near the Shebayki cemetery. Here was the Bazan, or channel down which

craft. The wild men of El Hejaz still sing songs in honor of this Sherif, and the Sultan will probably never dismiss a prisoner who, though old, is still able and willing to cause him trouble.

the Ayn Honayn ran into the Birkat Majid. Many author ities doubt that Hamzah was born at this place.*

The reader must now be as tired of "pious visitations" as I was.

Before leaving Meccah I was urgently invited to dine by old Ali, a proof that he entertained inordinate expectations, excited, it appeared, by the boy Mohammed, for the simple purpose of exalting his own dignity. One day we were hurriedly summoned about 3 P.M. to the senior's house, a large building in the Zukah el Hajar. We found it full of pilgrims, amongst whom we had no trouble to recognise our fellow-travellers the quarrelsome old Arnaut and his impudent slave-boy. Ali met us upon the staircase and conducted us into an upper room, where we sat upon divans and with pipes and coffee prepared for dinner. Presently the semicircle arose to receive a eunuch, who lodged somewhere in the house. He was a person of importance, being the guardian of some dames of high degree at Cairo or Constantinople: the highest place and the best pipe were unhesitatingly offered to and accepted by him. He sat down with dignity, answered diplomatically certain mysterious questions about the dames, and then glued his blubber lips to a handsome mouthpiece of lemon-colored amber. It was a fair lesson of humility for a man to find himself ranked beneath this high-shouldered, spindle-shanked, beardless bit of neutrality, and as such I took it duly to heart.

The dinner was served up in a "Sini," a plated copper tray about six feet in circumference, and handsomely ornamented with arabesques and inscriptions. Under this was the usual Kursi, or stool, composed of mother-o'-pearl facets

* The reader is warned that I did not see the five places above enumerated. The ciceroni and books mention twelve other visitations, several of which are known only by name.

set in sandal wood; and upon it a well-tinned and clean-looking service of the same material as the Sini. We began with a variety of stews; stews with spinach, stews with bamiyah (hibiscus), and rich vegetable stews. These being removed, we dipped hands in "Biryani," a meat pillaw, abounding in clarified butter; "Kimah," finely chopped meat; "Warak Mahshi," vine leaves filled with chopped and spiced mutton, and folded into small triangles; "Kabab," or bits of *roti* spitted in mouthfuls upon a splinter of wood; together with a "Salatah" of the crispest cucumber, and various dishes of watermelon cut up into squares. Bread was represented by the eastern scone; but it was of superior flavor and far better than the ill-famed Chapati of India. Our drink was water perfumed with mastic. After the meat came a "Kunafah," fine vermicelli sweetened with honey and sprinkled with powdered white sugar; several stews of apples and quinces; "Nuhallibah," a thin jelly made of rice, flour, milk, starch, and a little perfume; together with squares of Rahah,* a confiture highly prized in these regions, because it comes from Constantinople. Fruits were then placed upon the table; plates full of pomegranate grains and dates of the finest flavor. The dinner concluded with a pillaw of boiled rice and butter; for the easier discussion of which we were provided with carved wooden spoons.

Orientals ignore the delightful French art of prolonging a dinner. After washing your hands, you sit down, throw

* Familiar for "Rahat el Hulkum,"—the pleasure of the throat,—a name which has sorely puzzled our tourists.

This sweetmeat would be pleasant did it not smell so strongly of the perruquier's shop. Rosewater tempts to many culinary sins in the East; and Europeans cannot dissociate it from the idea of a lotion. However, if a guest is to be honored, rosewater must often take the place of the pure element, even in tea.

an embroidered napkin over your knees, and with a "Bismillah," by way of grace, plunge your hand into the attractive dish, changing *ab libitum*, occasionally sucking your finger-tips as boys do lollipops, and varying that diversion by cramming a chosen morsel into a friend's mouth. When your hunger is satisfied you do not sit for your companions; you exclaim "Al Hamd!" edge away from the tray, wash your hands and mouth with soap, display signs of repletion, otherwise you will be pressed to eat more, seize your pipe, sip your coffee, and take your "Kaif."

Nor is it customary, in these benighted lands, to sit together after dinner—the evening prayer cuts short the *séance*. Before we arose to take leave of Ali a boy ran into the room, and displayed those infantine civilities which in the East are equivalent to begging for a present. I slipped a dollar into his hand; at sight of which he, veritable little Meccan, could not contain his joy. "The Riyal!" he exclaimed; "the Riyal! look, grandpa', the good Effendi has given me a Riyal!" The old gentleman's eyes twinkled with emotion: he saw how easily money had slipped from my fingers, and he fondly hoped that he had not seen the last piece. "Verily thou art a good young man!" he ejaculated, adding fervently, as prayers cost nothing, "May Allah further all thy desires." A gentle patting of the back evidenced high approval.

I never saw Ali after that evening, but entrusted to the boy Mohammed what was considered a just equivalent for his services.

## CHAPTER XXXIII.

### TO JEDDAH.

A GENERAL plunge into worldly pursuits and pleasures announced the end of the pilgrimage ceremonies. All the devotees were now "whitewashed," the book of their sins was a *tabula rasa:* too many of them lost no time in making a new departure "down south," and in opening a fresh account.*

The Moslem's "Holy Week" over, nothing detained me at Meccah. For reasons before stated, I resolved upon returning to Cairo, resting there for awhile, and starting a second time for the interior, *viâ* Muwaylah.†

* The faith must not bear the blame of the irregularities. They may be equally observed in the Calvinist, after a Sunday of prayer, sinning through Monday with a zest, and the Romanist falling back with new fervor upon the causes of his confession and penance, as in the Moslem who washes his soul clean by running and circumambulation; and, in fairness, it must be observed that, as amongst Christians, so in the Moslem persuasion, there are many notable exceptions to this rule of extremes. Several of my friends and acquaintances date their reformation from their first sight of the Kaabah.

† This second plan was defeated by bad health, which detained me in Egypt till a return to India became imperative.

The Meccans are as fond of little presents as are nuns: the Kabirah took an affectionate leave of me; begged me to be careful of her boy, who was to accompany me to Jeddah, and laid friendly but firm hands upon a brass pestle and mortar, upon which she had long cast the eye of concupiscence.

Having hired two camels for thirty-five piastres, and paid half the sum in advance, I sent on my heavy boxes with Shaykh, now Haji Nur, to Jeddah.* Umar Effendi was to wait at Meccah till his father had started, in command of the dromedary caravan, when he would privily take ass, join me at the port, and return to his beloved Cairo. I bade a long farewell to all my friends, embracing the Turkish pilgrims, and mounting on donkeys, the boy Mohammed and I left the house. Abdullah the Melancholy followed us on foot through the city, and took leave of me, though without embracing, at the Shebayki quarter.

Issuing into the open plain, I felt a thrill of pleasure—such pleasure as only the captive delivered from his dungeon can experience. The sunbeams warmed me into renewed life and vigor, the air of the desert was a perfume, and the homely face of nature was as the smile of an old friend. I contemplated the Syrian caravan, lying on the right of our road, without any of the sadness usually suggested by a last look.

It is not my intention minutely to describe the line down which we travelled that night: the pages of Burckhardt give full information about the country. Leaving Meccah, we fell into the direct road running south of Wady Fatimah, and traversed for about an hour a flat surrounded by hills. Then we entered a valley by a flight

* The usual hire is thirty piastres, but in the pilgrimage season a dollar is often paid. The hire of an ass varies from one to three riyals.

of rough stone steps, dangerously slippery and zigzag, intended to facilitate the descent for camels and laden beasts. About midnight we passed into a hill-girt Wady, now covered with deep sands, now hard with gravelly clay; and finally, about dawn, we sighted the maritime plain of Jeddah.

Shortly after leaving the city our party was joined by other travellers, and towards evening we found ourselves in force, the effect of an order that pilgrims must not proceed singly upon this road. Coffee-houses and places of refreshment abounding, we halted every five miles to refresh ourselves and the donkeys. At sunset we prayed near a Turkish guard-house, where one of the soldiers kindly supplied me with water for ablution.

Before nightfall I was accosted in Turkish, by a one-eyed old fellow, who,—

"With faded brow,
Entrenched with many a frown, and conic beard,"—

and habited in unclean garments, was bestriding a donkey faded as himself. When I shook my head, he addressed me in Persian. The same manœuvre made him try Arabic: still he obtained no answer. He then grumbled out good Hindostani. That also failing he tried successively Pushtu, Armenian, English, French, and Italian. At last I could "keep a stiff lip" no longer; at every change of dialect his emphasis beginning with "Then who the d—— are you?" became more emphatic. I turned upon him in Persian, and found that he had been a pilot, a courier, and a servant to eastern tourists, and that he had visited England, France, and Italy, the Cape, India, Central Asia, and China. We then chatted in English, which Haji Akif spoke well, but with all manner of courier's phrases; Haji Abdullah so badly, that he was counselled a course of study.

It was not a little curious to hear such phrases as "Come 'p, Neddy," and "*Cré nom d'un baudet*," almost within ear-shot of the tomb of Ishmael, the birthplace of Mohammed, and the Sanctuary of El Islam.

At about 8 P. M. we passed the Alamain, which define the Sanctuary in this direction. They stand about nine miles from Meccah. On the road, as night advanced, we met long strings of camels, some carrying litters, others huge beams, and others bales of coffee, grain, and merchandise. Sleep began to weigh heavy on my companions' eye-lids, and the boy Mohammed hung over the flank of his donkey in a most ludicrous position.

About midnight we reached a mass of huts, called El Haddah. At "the boundary," which is considered to be the half-way halting-place, pilgrims must assume the religious garb, and infidels travelling to Taif, are taken off the Meccan road into one leading northwards to Arafat. The settlement is a collection of huts and hovels, built with sticks and reeds, supporting brushwood and burned and blackened palm leaves. It is maintained for supplying pilgrims with coffee and water. Travellers speak with horror of its heat during the day; Ali Bey, who visited it twice, compares it to a furnace. Here the country slopes gradually towards the sea, the hills draw off, and every object denotes departure from the Meccan plateau. At El Haddah we dismounted for an hour's halt. A coffee-house supplied us with mats, water-pipes, and other necessaries; we then produced a basket of provisions, the parting gift of the kind Kabirah, and, this late supper concluded, we lay down to doze.

After half an hour's halt had expired, and the donkeys were saddled, I shook up with difficulty the boy Mohammed, and induced him to mount. He was, to use his own expression, dead of sleep; and we had scarcely advanced an hour when, arriving at another little coffee-house, he threw himself upon the ground, and declared it impossible to proceed. This act caused some confusion. The donkey-boy was a pert little Bedouin, offensively republican in manner. He had several times addressed me impudently, ordering me not to flog his animal or to hammer its sides with my heels. On these occasions he received a contemptuous snub, which had the effect of silencing him. But, now, thinking we were in his power, he swore that he would lead away the beasts, and leave us behind to be robbed and murdered. A pinch of the windpipe, and a spin over the ground, altered his plan at the outset of execution. He gnawed his hand with impotent rage, and went away, threatening us with the governor of Jeddah next morning. Then an Egyptian of the party took up the thread of remonstrance; and, aided by the old linguist, who said, in English, "By G——! you must budge, you'll catch it here!" he assumed a brisk and energetic style, exclaiming, "Yallah! rise and mount, thou art only losing our time; thou dost not intend to sleep in the Desert!" I replied, "Son of my uncle, do not exceed in talk!"* rolled over on the other side heavily, as doth Enceladus, and pretended to snore, whilst the cowed Egyptian urged the others to make us move. The question was thus settled by the boy Mohammed, who had been aroused by the dispute: "Do you know," he whispered, in awful accents, "what *that* person is?" and he pointed at me. "Why, no," replied the others. "Well," said the youth, "the other day the Utaybah showed us death in the Zaribah Pass, and what do you think he did?" "Wallah! what do we know!" exclaimed the Egyptian. "What *did* he do?" "He called

* "Fuzul" (excess) in Arabic is equivalent to telling a man in English not to be impertinent.

for his dinner," replied the youth, with a slow and sarcastic emphasis. That trait was enough. The others mounted and left us quietly to sleep.

I have been diffuse in relating this little adventure, which is characteristic, showing what bravado can do in Arabia. It also suggests a lesson, which every traveller in these regions should take well to heart. The people are always ready to terrify him with frightful stories, which are the merest phantoms of cowardice. The reason why the Egyptian displayed so much philanthropy was that had one of the party been lost, the survivors might have fallen into trouble. But in this place, we were, I believe,—despite the declarations of our companions that it was infested with Turpins and Gasperonis,—as safe as if in Meccah. Every night, during the pilgrimage season, a troop of about fifty horsemen patrols the roads; we were all armed to the teeth, and our party looked too formidable to be "cruelly beaten by a single footpad."

Our nap concluded, we remounted and resumed the weary way down a sandy valley, in which the poor donkeys sank fetlock-deep. At dawn we found our companions halted, and praying at another little coffee-house. Here an exchange of what is popularly called "chaff" took place. "Well," cried the Egyptian, "what have you gained by halting? We have been quiet here, praying and smoking for the last hour!" "Go, eat thy buried beans,"* we replied. "What does an Egyptian boor know of manliness?" The surly donkey-boy was worked up into a paroxysm of passion by such small jokes as telling him to convey our salaams to the Governor of Jeddah, and by calling the asses after the name of his tribe. He replied by "foul, unman-

* The favorite Egyptian "kitchen;" held to be contemptible food by the Arabs.

nered, scurril taunts," which only drew forth fresh derision, and the coffee-house keeper laughed consumedly, having probably seldom entertained such "funny gentlemen."

Shortly after leaving we found the last spur of the hills that sink into the Jeddah Plain. This view would for some time be my last of—

> "Infamous hills, and sandy, perilous wilds;"

and I contemplated it with the pleasure of one escaping from it. Before us lay the usual iron flat of these regions, whitish with salt, and tawny with stones and gravel; but relieved and beautified by the distant white walls, whose canopy was the lovely blue sea. Not a tree, not a patch of verdure was in sight, nothing distracted our attention from the sheet of turquoises in the distance. Merrily the little donkeys hobbled on, in spite of their fatigue. Soon we distinguished the features of the town, the minarets, the fortifications, and a small dome outside the walls.

The sun began to glow fiercely, and we were not sorry when, at about 8 A. M., after passing through the mass of hovels and coffee-houses, cemeteries and sand hills, which forms the eastern approach to Jeddah, we entered the fortified Bab Makkah. Allowing eleven hours for our actual march,—we halted about three,—those wonderful donkeys had accomplished between forty-four and forty-six miles, generally of deep sand, in one night. And they passed the archway of Jeddah almost as nimbly as when they left Meccah.

Shaykh Nur had been ordered to take rooms for me in a vast pile of madrepore, once the palace of Mohammed bin Aun, and now converted into a Wakalah. Instead of so doing, Indian-like, he had made a gipsy encampment in the square opening upon the harbor. After administering the requisite correction, I found a room that would suit me. In less than an hour it was swept, sprinkled with water, spread with mats, and made as comfortable as its capability admitted. At Jeddah I felt once more at home. The British flag was a restorative, and the sight of the sea acted as a tonic. The Maharattas were not far wrong when they kept their English captives out of reach of the ocean, declaring that we are an amphibious race, to whom the wave is a home.

After a day's repose at the caravanserai, the camel-man and the donkey-boy clamoring for money, and I not having more than tenpence of borrowed coin, it was necessary to cash at the British vice-consulate a draft given to me by the Royal Geographical Society. With some trouble I saw Mr. Cole, who, suffering from fever, was declared to be "not at home." His dragoman did by no means admire my looks; in fact, the general voice of the household was against me. After some fruitless messages, I sent up a scrawl to Mr. Cole, who decided upon admitting the importunate Afghan. An exclamation of astonishment and a hospitable welcome followed my self-introduction as an officer of the Indian army. Amongst other things, the vice-consul informed me that, in divers discussions with the Turks about the possibility of an Englishman finding his way *en cachette* to Meccah, he had asserted that his compatriots could do everything, even pilgrim to the Holy City. The Moslems politely assented to the first, but denied the second part of the proposition. Mr. Cole promised himself a laugh at the Turks' beards; but, since my departure, he wrote to me that the subject made the owners' faces look so serious, that he did not like recurring to it.

Truly gratifying to the pride of an Englishman was our high official position assumed and maintained at Jeddah. Mr. Cole had never lowered himself in the estimation of the proud race with which he has to deal, by private or mercantile transactions with the authorities. He has steadily withstood the wrath of the Meccan Sherif, and taught him to respect the British name.

Jeddah has often been described by modern pens. Burckhardt (in A. D. 1814) devoted 100 pages of his two volumes to the unhappy capital of the Tehamet el Hejaz, the lowlands of the mountain region. When I visited it, it was in a state of commotion, owing to the perpetual passage of pilgrims, and provisions were for the same reason scarce and dear. The two large Wakalah, of which the place boasts, were crowded with travellers, and many were reduced to encamping upon the squares. Another subject of confusion was the state of the soldiery. The Nizam, or Regulars, had not been paid for seven months, and the Arnauts could scarcely sum up what was owing to them. Easterns are wonderfully amenable to discipline; a European army, under the circumstances, would probably have helped itself. But the Pacha knew that there is a limit to man's endurance, and he was anxiously casting about for some contrivance that would replenish the empty pouches of his troops. The worried dignitary must have sighed for those *beaux jours* when privily firing the town and allowing the soldiers to plunder, was the oriental style of settling arrears of pay.

Jeddah displays all the license of a seaport and garrison town. Fair Corinthians establish themselves even within earshot of the Karakun, or guard-post; a symptom of excessive laxity in the authorities, for it is the duty of the watch to visit all such irregularities with a bastinado preparatory to confinement. My guardians and attendants at the Wakalah used to fetch araki in a clear glass bottle, without even the decency of a cloth, and the messenger twice returned from these errands decidedly drunk. More extraordinary still, the people seemed to take no notice of the scandal.

The little "Dwarka" had been sent by the Bombay Steam Navigation Company to convey pilgrims from El Hejaz to India. I was still hesitating about my next voyage, not wishing to coast the Red Sea in this season without a companion, when one morning Umar Effendi appeared at the door, weary, and dragging after him an ass more jaded than himself. We supplied him with a pipe and a cup of hot tea, and, as he was fearful of pursuit, we showed him a dark hole full of grass under which he might sleep concealed.

The student's fears were realised; his father appeared early the next morning, and having ascertained from the porter that the fugitive was in the house, politely called upon me. Whilst he plied all manner of questions, his black slave furtively stared at everything in and about the room. But we had found time to cover the runaway with grass, and the old gentleman departed, after a fruitless search. There was, however, a grim smile about his mouth, which boded no good.

That evening I went out to the Hammam, and, returning home, found the house in an uproar. The boy Mohammed, who had been miserably mauled, was furious with rage, and Shaykh Nur was equally unmanageable, by reason of his fear. In my absence the father had returned with a *posse comitatus* of friends and relatives. They questioned the youth, who delivered himself of many circumstantial and emphatic mis-statements. Then they proceeded to open the boxes; upon which the boy Mohammed cast himself sprawling, with a vow to die rather than to endure such a disgrace. This procured for him some scattered slaps, which presently became a storm of blows, when a prying little boy discovered Umar Effendi's leg in the hiding-place. The student was led away unresisting, but mildly swearing that he would allow no opportunity of escape to pass. I examined the boy Mohammed, and was pleased to find that he was not seriously hurt. To pacify his mind, I offered to sally out with him, and to rescue Umar Effendi by main force. This, which would only have brought us all into a brunt with quarter-staves, and similar servile weapons, was declined, as had been foreseen. But the youth recovered complacency, and a few well-merited encomiums upon his "pluck" restored him to high spirits.

The reader must not fancy such escapade to be a serious thing in Arabia. The father did not punish his son; he merely bargained with him to return home for a few days before starting to Egypt. This the young man did, and shortly afterwards I met him unexpectedly in the streets of Cairo.

Deprived of my companion, I resolved to waste no time in the Red Sea, but to return to Egypt with the utmost expedition. The boy Mohammed having laid in a large store of grain, purchased with my money, having secured all my disposable articles, and having hinted that, after my return to India, a present of twenty dollars would find him at Meccah, asked leave, and departed with a coolness for which I could not account. Some days afterwards Shaykh Nur explained the cause. I had taken the youth with me on board the steamer, where a bad suspicion crossed his mind. "Now, I understand," said the boy Mohammed to his fellow-servant, "your master is a Sahib from India, he hath laughed at our beards." He parted as coolly from Shaykh Nur. These worthy youths had been drinking together, when Mohammed, having learned at Stamboul the fashionable practice of "Bad-masti," or "liquor-vice," dug his "fives" into Nur's eye. Nur erroneously considering such exercise likely to induce blindness, complained to me; but my sympathy was all with the other side. I asked the Indian why he had not *riposté*, and the Meccan once more overwhelmed the "Miyan" with taunt and jibe.

It is not easy to pass the time at Jeddah. Whilst the boy Mohammed remained he used to pass the time in wrangling with some Indians, who were living next door to us, men, women, and children, in a promiscuous way. After his departure I used to spend my days at the vice-consulate; the proceeding was not perhaps of the safest, but the temptation of meeting a fellow-countryman, and of chatting "shop" about the service, was too great to be resisted. I met there the principal merchants of Jeddah.

I now proceed to the last of my visitations. Outside the town of Jeddah lies no less a personage than Sittna Hawwa, the Mother of mankind. The boy Mohammed and I, mounting asses one evening, issued through the Meccan gate, and turned towards the north-east over a sandy plain. After half an hour's ride, amongst dirty huts and tattered coffee-hovels, we reached the *enceinte*, and found the door closed. Presently a man came running with might from the town; he was followed by two others; and it struck me at the time that they applied the key with peculiar *empressement*, and made inordinately low congees as we entered the enclosure of whitewashed walls.

"The Mother" is supposed to lie, like a Muslimah, fronting the Kaabah, with her feet northwards, her head southwards, and her right cheek propped by her right hand. Whitewashed, and conspicuous to the voyager and traveller from afar, is a diminutive dome with an opening to the west; it is furnished as such places usually are in El Hejaz. Under it and in the centre is a square stone, planted upright and fancifully carved, to represent the omphalic region of the human frame. This, as well as the dome, is called

El Surrah, or the navel. The cicerone directed me to kiss this manner of hieroglyph, which I did, thinking the while that, under the circumstance, the salutation was quite uncalled for. Having prayed here, and at the head, where a few young trees grow, we walked along the side of the two parallel dwarf walls which define the outlines of the body: they are about six paces apart, and between them, upon Eve's neck, are two tombs, occupied, I was told, by Usman Pacha and his son, who repaired the Mother's sepulchre. I could not help remarking to the boy Mohammed, that if our first parent measured 120 paces from head to waist, and 80 from waist to heel, she must have presented much the appearance of a duck. To this the youth replied, flippantly, that he thanked his stars the Mother was under ground, otherwise that men would lose their senses with fright.

On leaving the graveyard I offered the guardian a dollar, which he received with a remonstrance that a man of my dignity should give so paltry a fee. Nor was he at all contented with the assurance that nothing more could be expected from an Afghan dervish, however pious. Next day the boy Mohammed explained the man's *empressement* and disappointment,—I had been mistaken for the Pacha of El Medinah.

* * * * *

For a time my peregrinations ended. Worn out with fatigue, and the fatal fiery heat, I embarked on board the "Dwarka," experienced the greatest kindness from the commander and chief officers (Messrs. Wolley and Taylor), and, wondering the while how the Turkish pilgrims who crowded the vessel did not take the trouble to throw me overboard, in due time arrived at Suez. And here, reader, we part. Bear with me while I conclude, in the words of a brother traveller, long gone, but not forgotten—

Fa-hian—this Personal Narrative of my Journey to El Hejaz: "I have been exposed to perils, and I have escaped from them; I have traversed the sea, and have not succumbed under the severest fatigues; and my heart is moved with emotions of gratitude, that I have been permitted to effect the objects I had in view."

THE END.